The COMPLETE ILLUSTRATED ENCYCLOPEDIA of

Dogs
& Puppies

Publisher and Creative Director: Nick Wells
Project Editor: Cat Emslie
Assistant Project Editor: Victoria Lyle
Picture Research: Victoria Lyle and Gemma Walters
Art Director: Mike Spender
Layout Design: Imagefile Ltd
Illustrator: Ann Biggs
Digital Design and Production: Chris Herbert
Copy Editor: Emily Anderson
Proofreader: Naomi Waters
Indexer: Sue Farr

Special thanks to: Sara Robson, Claire Walker, Ellie Bowden and Helen Tovey

13 15 17 16 14

1 3 5 7 9 10 8 6 4 2

This edition first published 2013 by
FLAME TREE PUBLISHING
Crabtree Hall, Crabtree Lane
Fulham, London SW6 6TY

www.flametreepublishing.com

ISBN 978-0-85775-879-8

A copy of the CIP data for this book is available from the British Library

Printed in China

The COMPLETE ILLUSTRATED
ENCYCLOPEDIA *of*
Dogs
& Puppies

Sean O'Meara

Michael Hayward (Contributor)

**FLAME TREE
PUBLISHING**

Contents

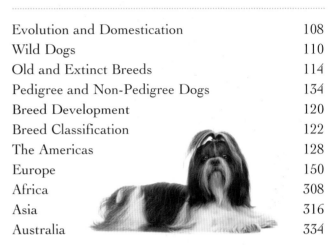

History, Culture & Anatomy   10

Care & Management   72

The Breeds   106

How to Use This Book

This book is divided into three main chapters, each designed to enhance an understanding of dogs, their practical care and enjoyment, and the various breeds that exist.

History, Culture & Anatomy

This is an introduction to dogs—their many roles throughout history and their involvement in human culture, such as art and literature, alongside their physical characteristics and behavior.

Care & Management

This chapter offers a practical guide to dogs, taking you all the way through from becoming a dog owner, to taking care of it, to even breeding dogs. If you are interested in showing off your beloved pet, you can learn about dog shows and how to enter.

The Breeds

This chapter begins with a closer look at the evolution and domestication of dogs. It discusses the extinct, old, and wild breeds of the world, then explains what a "breed" is and the way breeds are classified around the world. This is followed by a hefty section that details almost all known breeds of dog that exist today, divided into the main continents of the world, organized within those sections by geographical sub-area and size, from small to large. Breeds are placed according to where they are thought to have originated or where their "home" is considered to be.

Possible colurs

Coat care level

Diet—food consumption level

Official categorization by three main registries

Height range

Weight range

Names also known by

LABRADOR RETRIEVER

OFFICIAL CATEGORIZATION: UK: Gun Dog, AKC: Sporting, FCI: Group 8, Section 1

Color: Yellow, black, or chocolate

Coat Care: Moderate/high maintenance

HEIGHT: 21–24½ in. (55–58 cm)   WEIGHT: 55–80 lbs. (25–36 kg)

Diet: Moderate/high consumption

OTHER NAMES: Labrador, Lab

NEWFOUNDLAND

OFFICIAL CATEGORIZATION: UK: Working, AKC: Working, FCI: Group 2, Section 2

HEIGHT: 25–29 in. (65–72 cm)   WEIGHT: 110–152 lbs. (50–69 kg)

OTHER NAMES: Newfie

Color: Black or brown with white tip on chest

Coat Care: High/very high maintenance

Diet: Very high consumption

The Labrador Retriever is one of the most popular pet dog breeds in the world. This is no surprise to anyone who has ever owned or trained one of these friendly, intelligent, and obedient dogs. Labrador Retrievers are companionable and get along with people and other pets, including dogs and cats. They are still used as working retrievers in rural areas and, due to their kindly temperament and high intelligence levels, they are commonly used as assistance dogs—especially guide dogs.

An Intelligent Breed
The Labrador Retriever was bred originally in Canada, taking the first part of its name from the region of Canada where the breed originates and the second part from the role that it was bred to perform. The

Labrador Retriever still retains many of its working instincts, so a game of "fetch" is always welcome. The Labrador Retriever is descended from the Newfoundland and the now-extinct Saint John's Water Dog (see page 114–15).

Originally bred for retrieving game birds in water and long grass, its high level of intelligence and strong play drive made the Labrador Retriever a formidable working dog. These same qualities are what make it such a popular pet today. It is a relaxed and playful breed, easy to train and well-mannered.

Companionship and Obedience
Many people who are involved in obedience training believe that the Labrador Retriever represents the ideal pet dog breed. It is willing to be taught, obedient, and intelligent, which means that inexperienced trainers and owners can integrate

the Labrador Retriever into their life successfully without the need for overly firm handling.

Due to its relaxed and intelligent temperament, combined with a high intelligence, the Labrador Retriever makes a very effective assistance dog. Put to work as a guide dog and hearing dog the Labrador Retriever thrives in an environment of cooperation and companionship, because it loves to please its owner.

*LEFT
Labrador Retrievers are friendly, intelligent, tolerant, obedient, and fun-loving; no wonder they are the most popular breed globally.*

The Newfoundland is a large, water-going dog bred originally in Canada. It is one of the ancestors of the popular Labrador Retriever. The Newfoundland is a particularly large and heavy dog but the breed is very popular due to its gentle and calm nature. It is an excellent swimmer due to its water-resistant coat, great strength, and webbed feet, and is used as a water-rescue dog.

Due to its contribution to the Labrador Retriever bloodline, the Newfoundland is in the bloodline of many of the most popular breeds of pet dog that we know today, including the Golden Retriever and the Curly-Coated Retriever. It is not and has never been a gun-dog breed, but its

intelligence and character have been passed on to a whole new generation and type of working dog.

The Gentle Giant
The Newfoundland makes a great family pet in the right circumstances. The breed is friendly and placid, but does require a certain amount

of space to accommodate its size. As with many large breeds, any minor indiscretion, such as jumping up or pawing, can become a serious problem, as such an action can cause injury to people, especially children.

It is for this reason that a Newfoundland kept as a family pet must be properly trained for obedience and manners.

The Newfoundland is looked upon fondly by many people due to its devotion to man. Having worked as a lifesaver onboard ships and boats in ice-cold seas, the breed as a whole has done a lot to earn the respect of dog lovers all over the world. Even today, the Newfoundland as a pet displays remarkable dedication and loyalty to its human companions. It is typically well-behaved and affable, but if mistreated or provoked, it can prove to be a formidable adversary due to its size and strength.

Fascinating Facts

Residents of Swansea, in South Wales, are often nicknamed "Jacks." This is a reference to a Newfoundland called Swansea Jack that rescued many people during the 1930s.

130

131

Color

These icons give the various possible color and pattern combinations in which the dog can occur (or those "allowed" by the official bodies). They are only a guide and can cover a wide range of permutations, as clarified by the text.

 White

 Cream, Biscuit, or Off white

 Yellow, Lemon, Blonde, Light wheaten, Straw yellow, or Beige

 Gold, Sandy, Tawny, Straw, Wheaten, Fawn, Mustard, or Apricot

 Light brown or Fallow

 Tan, Yellowish red, Golden red, Red wheaten, Lion gold, Amber, or Golden rust

 Brown, Dark brown, Chocolate, Liver, Sable

 Red, Red-gold, Copper, Reddish brown, Chestnut, Ruby, Mahogany, Maroon, Stag red, Reddish fawn, Cinnamon, Orange, Isabella, Blenheim, or Rust

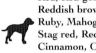 Light gray, Salt and pepper, Silver-fawn, Silver-gray, Greyish Isabella or Mouse gray

 Dark gray, Elephant gray, Steel gray, Wolf gray, Iron gray, Earthy gray, Yellow-gray, Gray-brown, Pewter silver, or Grizzle (gray-white mixture)

 Blue, Steel blue, Blue-gray

 Black

 Bicolor (any two-color combination)

 Tricolor (any three-color combination)

 Brindle (almost *striped*, mixture of black with brown, tan, gold, or silver)

 Marbled/dappled (such as merle, belton, speckled)

 Tipped/Ticked (such as sable, sesame)

 Spotted

 Patched (such as badger, a mixture of white, gray, brown, and black; pinto, black saddle and face on white body; and generic patched)

 Roan (a pattern of intermingled white and colored hairs)

 All colors (or too many to show)

Coat Care

This gives the approximate level of grooming and coat care necessary for the breed.

 Zero maintenance

 Minimal maintenance

 Low maintenance

 Low/moderate maintenance

 Moderate maintenance

 Moderate/high maintenance

High maintenance

Very high maintenance

Diet

This gives a general idea of the amount of food a breed goes through. Remember that there are other factors to keep in mind in regards to the *type* of food you must feed your dog.

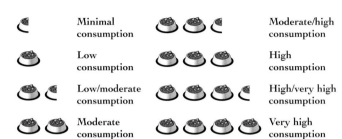

Minimal consumption

Low consumption

Low/moderate consumption

Moderate consumption

Moderate/high consumption

High consumption

High/very high consumption

Very high consumption

Official Categorization

This gives the category that the breed falls into according to three main registries: the UK Kennel Club (UK), the American Kennel Club (AKC), and the FCI (Fédération Cynologique Internationale). Sometimes a breed is yet to be recognized by some or all of theses registries.

Height

Gives the approximate height of the adult dog. This is a range from the shortest height for a bitch to the tallest height for a male dog.

Weight

Gives the approximate weight of the adult dog. This is a range from the lightest weight for a bitch to the heaviest weight for a male dog.

Other Names

Gives the various other names by which a breed is known, often more colloquial or in different languages.

This information is followed by a more in-depth discussion of the breed, including a look at its origins, history, development, and status today; its physical characteristics, temperament, and behavior, and its common uses (such as working dog as opposed to pet dog).

Reference Section

At the end of the encyclopedia is a list of useful addresses and contacts, from kennel clubs and registries to welfare organizations; there is also a list of titles suggested for further reading to expand on the subjects and breeds covered here. A glossary explains any terms that might be unfamiliar or sums up what you have already learned, and a thorough index will allow you to instantly locate a particular topic.

Introduction

Whether curled up in front of the fire or diving into the icy North Atlantic to rescue people lost at sea, dogs have made the role of man's companion their own. Man and dog have forged a partnership that is about 15,000 years old and has lasted through wars, revolutions, and even plagues. Dogs come in all shapes, sizes, and colors and every single breed has its own unique and compelling history. This encyclopedia explains how the evolution of dogs occurred, from the first wolves to domesticated pets, to the breeds that are so new that their names are yet to be confirmed.

A Comprehensive Selection

There are more than 300 breeds featured in *The Complete Encyclopedia of Dogs* and each one receives a detailed examination, revealing key historical facts, at-a-glance statistics, images, and details of the history, work, appearance, temperament, and behavior of each breed.

The detailed and comprehensive breeds section is organized geographically and then by size, so it could not be easier to locate the breed information you are looking for. Whether you want to know the height of an Alaskan Malamute or the coat color of an Australian Cattle Dog, this book puts the information at your fingertips. If you want to know what country the Great Dane, Italian Greyhound, or Australian Shepherd really come from, you will find out here. You will also discover how the gigantic Saint Bernard and the tiny Chihuahua evolved from the same animal!

International Relationships

Dog breeding is a truly global practice and each country around the world produces its own very distinct type of dogs—from the powerful and dedicated hunting hounds of North America to the watchful and alert spitz breeds of Northern Europe. Climate, terrain, culture, and politics all affect the process of breed development. For example, did you know that the Alsatian became known as the German Shepherd in the United States because of World War II? Or that the French Revolution influenced the length of the basset hound's legs? All the fascinating facts and intriguing insight of the history of dogs and their relationships with man are covered in this engaging and thought-provoking collection of canine research. The book takes a continent-by-continent look at the world's dogs, from small to big and ancient to modern.

What is most amazing about man's relationship with dogs is how the evolution of the dog as a species has been shaped and guided by man. Man has worked with the canine since before he could speak right up to the present day. From the deserts of Northern Africa, where the first hunting hounds became established, to the science laboratories and space shuttles of the modern day, dogs have been there playing a starring role.

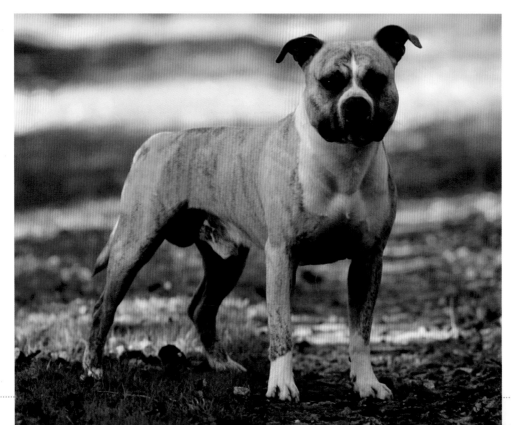

Getting to Know Your Dog

There are numerous governing bodies and authorities in the world of dogs and each one has its own set of rules and regulations regarding breeds. This book takes into account the standards set by the three main bodies—the UK Kennel Club, the American Kennel Club, and the Federation Cynologique Internationale (FCI)—to give you the most up-to-date and accurate information on your favorite dog breeds.

With practical information on dog showing, breeding, whelping, and raising a litter of puppies, *The Complete Encyclopedia of Dogs* is a great resource for people interested in taking their dog ownership to a new level, whether as a breeder, show competitor, or dog trainer. Ideal for experienced dog owners as well as those considering getting their first dog, the book contains useful information on how to prepare for the arrival of a new dog, how to provide the best nutrition, and what to do in a medical emergency. Every aspect of pet dog ownership is covered, from taking care of and training puppies to details on how to accommodate an older dog.

Detailed diagrams and in-depth descriptions of the anatomy, senses, and abilities of the dog will allow the reader to know their animal from head to paw, dewclaw to dewlap, inside and out. Canine instinct and behavior will be brought to life as the book guides you through the many, varying stages of species and breed evolution right up to the present. As well as detailed descriptions of the breeds, their history, and man's unique relationship with the working dog, *The Complete Encyclopedia of Dogs* uncovers some of the less well-known historical and cultural aspects of the life of dogs. From dogs that starred in their own movies to the artist that had a breed named after him, there are many strange and unusual dog stories, each one more fascinating than the last.

History,
Culture
&
Anatomy

A CREATURE OF MANY ROLES

Dogs are adaptable and willing to please and fulfill many functions in modern society, from assistance dogs to police dogs and pet dogs to therapy helpers. Different breeds have differing sets of skills—some were bred to be good swimmers, others good guardians and protectors. The ancient instincts that many dog breeds developed are still useful today; herding dogs make excellent watchdogs, while scent hounds and the gun-dog breeds make invaluable scent-detection dogs. The domestic canine truly has developed to become an animal with many varied talents.

Dogs at War

Throughout history dogs have laid down their lives for us, which is why without the help of man's best friend the history of warfare would be different. In fact, every war since the formation of the Persian Empire in 550 B.C. has featured dogs. From the Roman conquests to the modern and high-tech wars of today, dogs have played many important roles—carrying supplies, finding injured soldiers, and even going behind enemy lines.

Whether they were sniffing out weapons in Iraq, such as Buster the Springer Spaniel from England, or warning their masters of impending attack, as Bandit the German Shepherd did in Vietnam, dogs are invaluable to man during conflict. Attila the Hun, Frederick the Great, and Adolph Hitler all had dogs specially trained for war. Certain breeds only exist today because of their usefulness during conflict. With their diverse range of skills and their unrivaled courage, dogs are often the difference between victory and defeat when used in warfare.

How Dogs Conquered the Americas

When the Spanish conquistadors invaded the Americas in 1492 they did not realize what a battle they were about to face. The natives were prepared to fight to protect their land and the Spanish invaders were often outnumbered. One of the advantages the army of invaders had over those whom they were attempting to colonize was the help of their dogs.

The invaders brought with them an ancient breed of dog, similar to the Bloodhound of today. However, these were no pet dogs—they were four-legged warriors, trained to hunt down and catch escaping natives on command. The dogs were lean, strong, and primed for battle, and without them it is doubtful that the outnumbered and tired invaders would have succeeded in conquering the Americas.

ABOVE

Hitler playing with a young German Shepherd dog, 1940s. Famed for their loyalty, dogs have been trained by many military leaders.

LEFT

The keen sense of smell of Buster the Springer Spaniel helped the British uncover a huge cache of arms, Iraq, 2003.

Fascinating Facts

During World War I, the Red Cross used Airedale Terriers to help them find injured soldiers.

LEFT
Serving with the Red Cross in 1915, this disciplined dog tracks down a wounded German soldier.

Fascinating Facts

Many European dog breeds came close to extinction after World War II due to food rationing, which prevented people from breeding their dogs because there was insufficient food to feed them.

Fascinating Facts

During World War II, 25 Dobermans were killed in the Battle of Guam. There is now a statue commemorating the dogs at the location on the Pacific island where they lost their lives.

BELOW
A scraggy stray "guarding" a napping American Marine, Palau Islands, 1944. The bond between man and dog is deep and mutual.

From The Western Front to Hollywood

Rin Tin Tin is one of the most loved and remembered of canine film stars. "Rinty," as his fans knew him, had his own radio series, numerous movie roles, and a healthy income. But life could have been different for this plucky German Shepherd. During routine procedures on the Western Front in the final stages of World War I, an American serviceman named Lee Duncan found a shell-shocked and scared little pup in a bombed-out shelter in Northern France. The American took the dog back to the United States after the war, trained him to do some tricks, and the rest is history.

Specially Trained Dogs Defeat the Nazis

Many historians credit the harsh Russian winters for helping the Allies to defeat the Nazis in World War II. Hitler's armies could not penetrate the frozen terrain to reach the Russian forces. But if the weather was keeping the Nazis from reaching the Russians, how did the Russians reach the Nazis? The answer was that the Red Army had more than 50,000 dogs. These enabling soldiers who were lost or injured to be rescued and thereby ensuring that the hostile conditions did not radically deplete their numbers as they marched toward Germany.

A German Helping the Allies

During one battle near the town of Duminichi in Russia, a German Shepherd named Bob managed to find 16 men hiding in the trenches. Bob laid down beside the wounded men, offering warmth, while the soldiers used the medical supplies that he was carrying around his neck. During the course of the war, Russian sled dogs managed to carry more than 1,000 injured men to safety and transported more than 330 tons of ammunition.

Dogs in Sport

Dogs have played a big part in many sporting and leisure pursuits throughout their domestication. Some are proudly remembered and even continued today, while others were cruel and barbaric and every effort is made to keep those practices confined to history. The dog has many attributes that man has endeavored to improve on—scenting, hunting, running, and even guarding—and there is much competition in developing these canine skills. Whether performing alone or competing alongside us, sporting dogs represent a proud tradition.

Racing

Sight hounds, such as the Greyhound and the Whippet, are bred for speed and stamina. Their lean, lithe physiques made them inescapable pursuers on the plains of Africa, where they were initially bred to chase and catch big game, and in the now-banned sport of hare coursing in Britain. Nowadays racing is a very popular spectator sport;

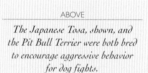

ABOVE
The Japanese Tosa, shown, and the Pit Bull Terrier were both bred to encourage aggressive behavior for dog fights.

Greyhound racing in particular attracts large crowds and is a popular sport on which to gamble. The dogs instinctively are driven to chase when they see fast movement, hence the name "sight hound." It is not necessary, therefore, to train a hound how to race, but professional racing-dog owners put a lot of effort and planning into diet and fitness programs. Unfortunately, there are concerns about the welfare of dogs used for racing. A dog's racing retirement age is around four or five years old; after that they are of no use to the trainer and, in some cases, they are neglected or killed.

Dog Fighting

Thankfully, dog fighting is mostly a thing of the past, although it still goes on in certain parts of the world. Many breeds of dog, such as the American Pit Bull Terrier and the Tosa Inu (or Japanese Tosa), were bred specifically for their tenacity and strength, and when these

ABOVE

Dogs were not only encouraged to fight one another; another vicious sport devised by man and involving dogs was badger baiting.

set upon the bears who, typically, were impeded in some way—often having their claws removed so that they could not injure the dogs. The bloody outcome was usually defeat for the bear, because when one dog became injured or tired more would be sent into the pit. Fortunately, bear baiting is extremely rare nowadays and rightly is considered barbaric.

The Pachon Navarro is a rare Spanish hunting dog. It has an unusual nose, which has a split down the center, that gives the impression of the dog having two noses.

Fascinating Facts

attributes were historically of use to us—for hunting and guarding, for example—it was common for dogs to be pitted against each other. The owner of the winning dog could expect to be rewarded with money, prestige, and fame. Dog fighting has been

outlawed in most parts of the world for a long time, and many of the breeds used for the pursuit have now become popular pets.

Baiting

In some cultures, badger and bear baiting were once popular "blood sports." In England during the nineteenth century, bear baiting attracted large and enthusiastic audiences. Large, strong dogs would be

Agility

When dogs compete in any sport they are displaying their natural abilities as a breed. Any natural ability that a dog possesses is of use to man, which is why there has been a tradition of people wishing to demonstrate the prowess of their dog. Today, canine agility is a popular sport where dogs compete against each other.

Assault courses containing jumps, seesaws, hoops, and other obstacles are the principal way to test a dog's agility. Herding breeds, such as the Border Collie and the German Shepherd, are naturally agile and thrive in the agility arena. Special training is required to equip the dog with the obedience and understanding required to compete at agility. Agility is a popular feature at The Westminster Dog Show, Crufts, and many other international canine events.

Dogs and Travel

Before mechanization and the Industrial Revolution, dogs did many of the jobs that are now performed by machine. Prior to the invention of motor cars, dogs were essential to many people for travel. With many dog breeds possessing great strength, they have proven themselves as invaluable travel companions over the years. Even today, certain cultures and communities rely on dogs to get them about. There are even specific breeds of dog that were developed to help man get from place to place.

Sled Dogs

Pound for pound, the Husky is one of the strongest animals on the earth, with an impressive amount of weight-shifting strength, enduring stamina, and sheer will to "mush." Without the Husky and other sled-dog breeds, life would be decidedly difficult for the Inuit people of Alaska and Canada.

All sled dogs have a high pack drive, which means they are self-governing. There is always an alpha that leads the pack and the other dogs then fall into line behind the lead dog. The Alaskan Malamute is a popular pet in Europe and North America, but it still possesses strong pack instincts. To look at and touch a sled dog breed is to appreciate their impressive pulling and running abilities.

Carriage Dogs

The distinguished Dalmatian was initially bred to be a carriage dog. The dog's role was to run alongside carriages and chariots occupied by noble men and women. With strong guarding instincts, the dalmatian was favored for its protectiveness over the occupants of the carriage. For this reason, Dalmatians are often associated with royalty and nobility, but in reality they are inextricably linked to ancient travelers, such as the Roma or Romany Gypsies.

Today, the Dalmatian is a popular pet, but the breed still retains many of the qualities that first made it popular. Many trainers claim that the dalmatian is a difficult dog to teach due to its independent and inquisitive streak, but the truth is that its intelligence and confidence when properly harnessed make it an excellent working or family dog.

Fascinating Facts

A Great Dane named Just Nuisance is the only dog ever to have been enlisted in the Royal Navy. He started life as a pet after following sailors to their ships when they docked in Cape Town, South Africa, but was given the rank of Able Seaman so that he would become entitled to rations.

Guardian Dogs

Many guardian breeds were developed to protect property and others were used to protect those who had to travel, such as traders. The Rottweiler, now popular for its confident and friendly temperament, was originally bred to accompany merchants in Germany. Before refrigeration, butchers had to get their meat to their customers quickly, but they also faced the threat of robbery from highwaymen. In the town of Rottweil in Germany, which was a trading center, a group of notable residents bred a strong, courageous dog to protect those delivering meat.

Another German breed, the Doberman, was bred by a tax collector named Louis Dobermann. Dobermann was often attacked due to his job, so he bred Manchester Terriers with German Shepherds and Rottweilers to produce a formidable traveling guard dog.

Seafaring Dogs

Many breeds became popular among sailors, fishermen, and pirates due to their swimming, retrieving, and compan- ionship attributes. The Portuguese Water Dog, with its thick, waterproof coat, was employed to bring in the nets when fishing boats went ashore. The Newfoundland, a large and strong breed with exceptional swimming abilities, would accompany sailors on their journeys as a canine lifeguard. If a man went overboard, the Newfoundland would be commanded to enter the ice-cold sea (kept warm by his thick coat) to bring the man back to the boat. The Coton De Tulear was popular among pirates and sea merchants as a lap dog. The breed is one of the best-traveled in history, having been established in many parts of the world for centuries.

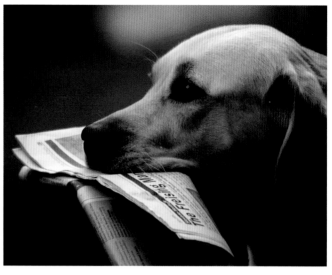

Dogs as Pets and Helpers

The concept of dogs as house pets is a relatively new one. Man domesticated the wolf 15,000 years ago to assist his own evolution; every dog had a job. Due to technological innovations many dog breeds are now redundant, but over the course of their relationship man and dog have forged strong bonds. The dog's loyalty and intelligence have made canine companionship a desirable commodity for the human race. And as our needs change we find new and complex jobs for dogs to do for us.

Pet Dogs

Labrador Retrievers, German Shepherds, and Boxers are among the most popular pet breeds in the world. The first people to keep dogs as companion animals instead of working dogs are thought to have been Chinese emperors. Small breeds, such as the Shih Tzu, were

Fascinating Facts

The first dog to be trained as a Seeing Eye dog in the United States was a female German Shepherd called Buddy.

favored for their size and personality, often displaying great devotion and loyalty to one person above all others.

Today, people choose pet dogs for many different reasons. Some people like their dogs to match their own personality, while other people choose dogs that will fit in well with their lifestyle or home environment. Many of the attributes that made certain breeds popular for working are now reasons for their popularity as pets. Conversely,

RIGHT

Chinese emperors, who favored the Shih Tzu, are often thought to be the first people to own dogs simply for their companionship.

some dogs have seen their original working attributes bred out to accommodate them as pets. Many present-day dog breeds are comparable to their working ancestors in only appearance.

Pet Dogs That Work

Some dogs that are kept as pets may still be used for a combination of work and companionship. Many retriever breeds, such as the Labrador Retriever and the Springer Spaniel, are popular

choices for pets but are used frequently for assistance in leisure pursuits, such as hunting and shooting. Often people who hunt or shoot find that keeping their working dog as a pet enables them to forge a closer and more co-operative relationship with their dog.

Herding dogs are often kept as pets, too, particularly dogs that work on farms. In many cases, a working dog may retire due to old age or ill

health and will simply make the transition from working companion to pet.

Assistance Dogs as Pets

Due to the domestic nature of their work, most assistance dogs are kept as pets. Guide dogs are required to assist their blind owners at all times and, therefore, need to be present throughout the day and night. To facilitate this, it is necessary that the dog fulfilf the role of pet and working dog simultaneously. This is normally the best arrangement, because the dog benefits from the company and interaction with the owner and becomes familiar with their needs and requirements in terms of assistance. Pastoral and retriever breeds are popular choices as assistance dogs due to their high intelligence and biddable nature.

Fascinating Facts

Dogs have the ability to detect the onset of an epileptic seizure in humans and have been trained as seizure-detection assistance dogs.

The Many Types of Assistance Dog

Dogs are bred and trained to help humans in many different situations. People with disabilities are often the beneficiaries of canine help. Dogs have been trained successfully to serve as guide dogs for blind people, hearing dogs for deaf people, and as epilepsy-seizure-alert dogs. Sometimes people requiring the assistance of a dog will receive a companion that is trained to suit their unique needs. People using wheelchairs and people with limited mobility are given specially trained assistance dogs that can perform roles as diverse as using cash machines, picking up items from store shelves, answering the door, and even, in the case of one Labrador Retriever from England, putting its owner into the recovery position.

ABOVE

Companion or colleague, several breeds of dog, such as the Labrador Retriever and Springer Spaniel, make both excellent pets and working dogs.

BELOW RIGHT

Dogs are used to assist people with many disabilities. Here a boy with cerebal palsy enjoys the company of his assistant.

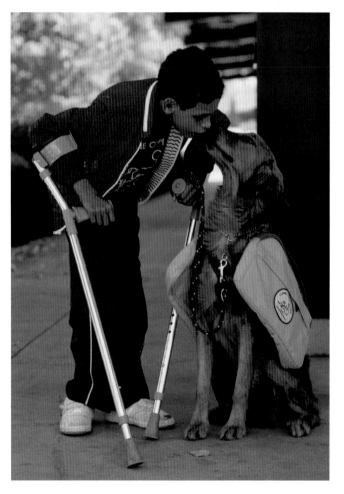

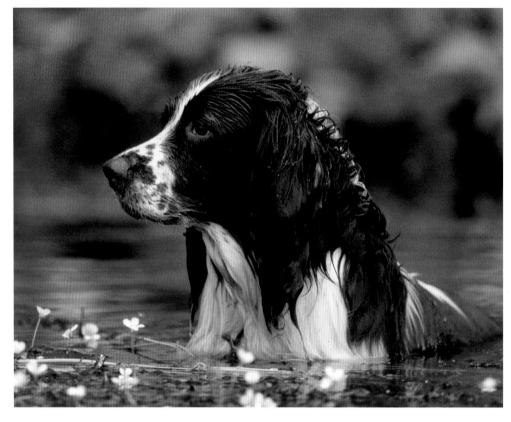

Search-and-Rescue Dogs

One of the few things that dogs can do better than any machine is detect scent. Some dogs can even track scent across running water. This is why dogs are still called upon to help in search-and-rescue situations. A combination of agility, scenting ability, and intelligence means that dogs remain the ultimate tool in finding missing or injured persons.

Dogs and Natural Disasters

Search and rescue in natural-disaster situations requires dogs that are calm

and intelligent. All dogs have a strong sense of smell so the most sophisticated canine nose is not always necessary—it is often more important for the dog to be agile and intelligent, so that it can be commanded to perform very specific functions. In earthquake situations, Springer Spaniels are often seen searching collapsed buildings to find people who are trapped. Dogs can differentiate between survivors and people who have died, which means, in extreme situations, their handlers can prioritize.

Hostile Environments

Cold countries are often home to excellent tracking dogs. This is due to the environmental factors that

were at play when breeds were being developed. The Saint Bernard is one of the most popular breeds used in mountain rescue. The dog needs to have a keen sense of smell as well as the ability to help a person to remain warm. This is achieved by training the dog to lie with a victim once they are located. There are many search-and-

rescue methods that involve dogs. Sometimes dogs are required simply to signal the location of a person in need of help; at other times it is necessary for them to pull the victim out.

Gun dogs and Sporting Dogs

Retriever breeds, such as the Springer Spaniel and

Fascinating Facts

Sight-hound breeds take longer than most other breeds to come around after being given an anesthetic.

LEFT

A German Shepherd in training for the fire service, to help firefighters search collapsed buildings and landslides for missing people.

Cocker Spaniel, are often used to locate people trapped and injured in natural disasters. These dogs are specially trained for the job, and they need to be intelligent, obedient, and calm-natured. Due to their instinct for finding and retrieving, these dogs are very effective at locating a scent. Large dogs are often unsuitable for this type of work, which often rules out scent hounds.

Scent Hounds

Bloodhounds, Beagles, and Basset Hounds are all popular search-and-rescue breeds and many people owe their lives to the highly sensitive noses of these dogs. The power of the canine sense of smell is often under-

---

RIGHT

Briards, as well as Border Collies and German Shepherds, are intelligent and tenacious, willing to keep searching for victims in need of rescue.

estimated, and scent hounds are the best of all types of dog at tracking a scent.

Originally bred to track prey using the sense of smell, all scent hounds are in possession of highly sophisticated and large scent receptors. Look at a scent hound and you will notice it has large ears and a wrinkly face. This is to enable the dog to perform better scent detection, because the large ears shield a scent source from the wind and the folds in the face trap scent near the nose. Scent hounds are important in cases where people are mobile—an escaped prisoner, for example. In these situations, the dog needs to be able to track a moving scent instead of a static one, so this work can only

be done by dogs with the strongest sense of smell.

Pastoral and Herding Breeds

Breeds used for herding, such as Border Collies, Briards, and German Shepherds, are effective in search-and-rescue situations due to their high intelligence and tenacity. Many police forces favor these breeds, and they are often the first dogs on the scene at any situation requiring search and rescue.

LEFT

Disciplined but formidable, many breeds, such as German Sherperds, are invaluable in police crowd control.

BELOW LEFT

Dogs are trained by the armed forces to detect explosives and to freeze immediately on discovering a device.

Police and Tracking Dogs

Dogs possess a phenomenal array of different skills, so from guarding to scent detection police forces around the world have found numerous uses for the dog. Certain breeds are more suited to police work than others, with herding and gun-dog breeds being particularly popular choices. Intelligence, obedience, agility, and natural instincts are the most important canine characteristics sought by the police.

Crowd Control and Public Order

The most common usage of dogs in police forces is in controlling the movement of large groups of people. Sporting events, protests, and public meetings often require a police presence and, to reinforce that presence, the police will commonly employ dogs. German Shepherds, Belgian Shepherds, and sometimes other breeds will be at the side of their handler—equipped and trained to restrain and hold any person that breaches the peace or poses a threat to public safety. The dogs have to be self-controlled and obedient but capable of neutralizing any threats posed by people or crowds. Often, the bark of a well-trained police dog is enough to deter a would-be criminal.

Contraband Detection

Drugs, illegal firearms, and counterfeit goods are unlikely to get past the well-trained and highly sensitive nose of a police contraband-detection dog. Springer Spaniels, Labradors, and Cocker Spaniels are commonly used by border-control and airport officers in order to stem the flow of such contraband. The dogs are trained from an early age to respond to the scent of an illegal item. The dogs will typically sit, or otherwise indicate to their handler that they have a scent. Some dogs have been trained to detect the ink used in counterfeit currency.

Explosives Detection

In order to ensure public safety, there is an elite group of specially trained explosives detection dogs patrolling the world's streets and corridors. Explosive detection dogs have to be specially trained to "freeze" when they

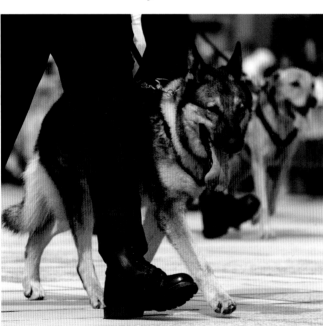

identify an explosive. An overexcited or curious dog could end up activating any explosive devices if it does not immediately hold its movement. This abrupt coming to a halt is a sure sign to the handler that the dog has a find. Dogs that are trained to find

explosives are able to identify the scent through a brick wall.

Personal Security

Due to the nature of police work, some officers require personal dogs for their own security. German Shepherds and Belgian Shepherds are ideal for this because of their agility, loyalty, and obedience. Many dogs have given up their own lives to protect their handlers.

Cadaver Detection

One of the more unpleasant aspects of police dog work is that of the cadaver-, or human-remains, detection dog. Many cases of murder and abduction have been brought to their grizzly conclusions by well-trained dogs. Popular breeds for this work include scent hounds, such as the Basset Hound and Bloodhound, as well as

gun-dog breeds, such as the Springer Spaniel and Cocker Spaniel. Although this work does not prevent crime, it does help bring prosecutions against criminals and enables families to know exactly what happened to a victim. The dogs are specially trained and highly skilled, enabling them to detect the chemicals that a body gives off during decomposition.

Escapee or Missing Person Detection

Bloodhounds and other scent-hound breeds are often used to find escaped criminals. Bloodhounds have exceptionally powerful noses and will find someone hiding miles away, over many different types of terrain. The dogs are trained not to harm any escapees they find, but to hold them. If the dog is tracking a missing person, they will be commanded to either signal the find or to assist the missing person if they are in need of help.

ABOVE

Bloodhounds scenting a trail; once they find a missing person, the Bloodhound will remain with him or her until human assistance arrives.

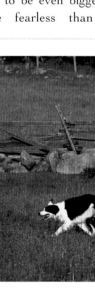

Herding Dogs

Humans and dogs have a strong history of cooperation. We have put dogs to work in many roles, developing and refining their instincts and abilities to enable us to evolve together. One of the most important jobs dogs have performed for us is herding. Before refrigeration, food had to be moved around for trading before it was killed; with livestock transportation came the need to protect and guard the valuable herds—help that dogs could provide.

Herding Breeds

As our habits and needs changed, so did the jobs of the livestock-herding dogs. Some were bred to protect, some were bred to herd in fields, and others were bred to help with travel. The most common type of job performed by herding or pastoral breeds was that of the sheepdog. sheepdogs have two main functions: to herd and to drove. Herding is done in a field under a shepherd's instruction, while droving is done in order to move flocks through towns and villages. Other functions of herding or pastoral breeds include flock watch dogs (bred for their alertness) and flock guard dogs (bred for strength and tenacity). Popular pet breeds that were originally bred for herding include the Anatolian Shepherd Dog, the Australian Cattle Dog, the Australian Shepherd, the Belgian Shepherd, and the Border Collie.

Herders

Many of the most intelligent and agile breeds today derive from herding stock. The German Shepherd, Border Collie, and Briard were all bred to assist a shepherd with his flock. The dogs were required to put the sheep back into their pens and move them around the fields and farms at the shepherd's command.

Drovers

In order for shepherds and farmers to trade their livestock, they needed to be able to move it as a group from place to place. This required the skill and determination of a specially bred droving dog, such as an Old English Sheepdog or Border Collie. The shepherd would have a set of commands that he would use to control the movement of the flock or herd through the actions of his dog. The dogs would instinctively be driven to nip at the heels of any livestock that was breaking away from the herd.

Protectors

The type of environment in which a dog worked determined the role it would need to play. Herding dogs based in places where predators were large, such as wolves and big cats, would need to be even bigger and more fearless than that

Both guarding and herding instincts were bred in the Anatolian Shepherd Dog, so they could protect their flocks from wolves and bears.

predator in order to keep the herd safe. The Anatolian Shepherd Dog was bred specifically to protect herds from wolves and bears. Guarding and herding instincts were bred into these dogs to ensure that they could fulfill both roles.

Modern Herding Breeds
Today, the need for herding dogs is small compared to the number of herding dogs that are in existence. Herding

Fascinating Facts
More than 30 percent of Americans have admitted to talking to their dogs; some even admitted to leaving answer-phone messages for their pet!

breeds make popular pets due to their intelligence and temperament. Border Collies, German Shepherds, and various breeds of sheepdog are now as popular as companion animals as they once were for their working abilities.

Competition
Despite fulfilling the role of pet, most herding or pastoral breeds retain strong herding instincts. This is why herding competition is so popular today. Sheepdog trials and agility contests are designed to judge and assess the abilities of the trainer as well as the latent instincts of the herding dogs.

Exploiting the Herding Instinct
Despite being bred originally for pastoral or

RIGHT
Intelligent and fiercely loyal, German Shepherd dogs make ideal assistance dogs in a wide variety of situations.

herding purposes, many of the skills and attributes of herding dogs have been applied to more modern requirements. German Shepherds make fantastic

guard and assistance dogs due to their instincts for protecting a pack. Their agility enables them to perform this function better than many breeds.

shooting, otherwise referred to as bird or gun dogs, have extremely strong instincts to retrieve, which is why they love to fetch a stick or ball. Some of the most popular and well-known gun-dog breeds are Labrador Retrievers, Golden Retrievers, Springer Spaniels, Cocker Spaniels, Pointers, and Weimaraners.

Gun Dogs and Hound Packs

Sometimes we forget that our pet dogs were once highly skilled working animals. Many of the most popular pet breeds in the world were once favored for their abilities to hunt and help us gather food. The dogs have

ABOVE

Many of the most intelligent, good-natured breeds are now simply owned as much-loved pets and companions.

not lost any of those instincts, but often they do not need to use them anymore. When we domesticated our dogs and started to keep them as pets, we relieved them of their

duties and encouraged them to settle into retirement. However, with Springer Spaniels able to detect cancer in humans and Bloodhounds able to find people trapped in collapsed buildings, who knows what the future holds.

Traditional Gun Dogs

Breeds associated with

There were many different jobs for a gun dog, from flushing the birds up into the

BELOW LEFT

Pointers were bred to point to the game and then, just as retrievers do, to retrieve it while on a shoot.

BELOW

Salukis are both lean and swift. They were originally bred to hunt gazelle in the deserts of Arabia.

air to retrieving game that had been shot. Each gun-dog breed was a specialist at a certain job, which is why some of the breeds have very specific names, such as the Nova Scotia Duck Tolling Retriever.

The skills that were developed and trained when dogs were required to work are now being put to use in the modern world. Intelligence, obedience, and an ability to follow instructions make bird dogs the ideal choice for assistance work. This is why many of the guide dogs that work today are Labrador Retrievers.

Modern Gun Dogs

Shooting is still a popular activity and dogs play a large part in making it enjoyable for the participants. Many people make a good living out of training and supplying the best gun gogs to shooting parties. Though not as popular or necessary today as it was in the past, shooting and hunting still provides work for many talented and intelligent dogs.

Hound Packs

Hounds come in three types: those that use their sight, those that use their sense of smell, and those that combine both. Sight hounds are fast, lean, and athletic, which would have enabled them to chase down their quarry across long distances to win food for their masters. Greyhounds and Salukis are good examples of this.

Scent hounds are bigger and stronger but traditionally relied on their tracking abilities to find prey, even if it was hiding. Today, there is still a call for the skills of a scent hound. Man has not managed to invent anything to rival the awesome power of the canine nose. Sight hounds are less in demand, but still bring pleasure and satisfaction to many through competing in races.

Hunting parties often use packs of hounds. Fox hunts traditionally incorporate packs of scent hounds, normally Beagles and Basset Hounds, that use a combination of sight and

scent to find and flush out foxes. This is a controversial pursuit and is not as popular as it once was, having been banned to various degrees in certain countries.

Modern Hounds

Members of the hound group were once used to chase and catch prey, which is why they love to run when we let them off the leash. Hounds make fantastic pets due to their innate loyalty and obedience.

Fascinating Facts

Every pack of dogs will have an alpha male. The alpha male is always the most dominant dog, even if it is not the largest.

They will retain strong instincts but in the hands of a confident trainer they adapt wonderfully to domestic life.

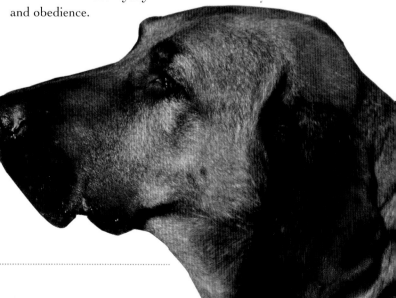

Performing Dogs

People are often amazed at the agility and level of training that some dogs can achieve. Heelwork, obedience, and Schutzhund (a sport that tests a dog's training and behavior) are just some of the ways in which dogs perform for our enjoyment. Because dogs often are not required to work anymore, it is through demonstrating, competing, and performing for our pleasure that they can display their instinctive talents. Many hours of training goes into preparing dogs for performance—it is a serious business.

Heel Work

Heel work is an activity that measures a dog's ability to perform certain routines on command. Herding breeds such as Border Collies and German Shepherds are good at this due to their keen intelligence and ability to learn. Trainers teach dogs specific commands for each move and put together an impressive sequence, which is then judged by a panel of experts.

Obedience

Competitive obedience sees highly trained and intelligent dogs responding to complex and demanding instructions. Basic obedience, such as teaching a dog to stay, is commonplace, but in competitive obedience dogs are required to perform tasks involving all types of skills. Finding hidden items, solving problems, and resisting instinct are all measures of a dog's obedience.

Instinct-Based Performance

Every dog has a set of core working instincts. Displaying those instincts in a competition is an ideal way for us to enjoy the abilities and talents of our dogs. Gun gogs compete in field trials, herding breeds compete in sheepdog trials, and Greyhounds compete in races. One of the most important aspects of this type of performance is the integrity with which a dog represents its skill. Certain breeds are equipped to perform varied roles, but in the context of instinct-based performance it is essential that the dogs perform in a traditional manner.

Schutzhund

Schutzhund was developed in Germany to test the abilities of German Shepherd Dogs. Up until then dogs were judged on only appearance. It combines elements of agility, obedience, and protection and is commonly used by police forces to test the abilities of prospective dogs. German Shepherds, Belgian Shepherds, and Border Collies frequently perform in Schutzhund competitions— a popular spectator sport.

Circus Dogs

Dog acts were traditionally a popular part of circus performances. Today, it is rare to see dogs in circus performances, but they have certainly made their mark on performing history. Poodles were popular as canine clown performers due to their combination of striking looks and agility. Jumping through hoops, balancing acts, and performing in magic tricks are all jobs that circus dogs have undertaken.

Dogs on the Stage

Many popular theater productions have included dogs. Specially trained dogs, often members of performers' unions, have been used in stage productions of *The Wizard of Oz*, *Little Orphan Annie*, and even Shakespeare plays.

Fascinating Facts

The term "Fido," which is a common nickname for dogs, comes from the Latin word for "faithful."

RIGHT

A popular breed in dog circuses, Poodles are nimble and biddable and are able to learn skills, such as skipping.

Private Entertainers

Throughout history, people have sought the company of dogs for entertainment. In medieval Europe, rich and important figures who had far to travel would often take a servant and a dog in order for a performance to be delivered to relieve the boredom of the journey. Noblemen and leaders have often called upon the services of dogs to provide them with fun and amusement. Centuries ago, rich Italians would dress up their pet Pugs in pantaloons to provide them with amusement.

Novelty Performances

Many pet dogs achieve fame with their unusual and quirky abilities. One notable example is Tyson the skateboarding Bulldog. Tyson's owner published footage on the Internet of him skating, which led to cult fame for the talented dog. He went on to appear on *The Oprah Winfrey Show*, where he performed in front of a massive American television audience.

Dogs and Royalty

From King Canute to the current Queen of England, dogs and royalty have always been inseparable. New breeds have been brought into existence on the whim of past kings, and other breeds reserved for ownership by only royal decree. Were it not for the Shang Dynasty and one emperor's desires, we would not have the Pug, while the Cavalier King Charles Spaniel owes its whole existence to the royal who named and created the breed.

King Canute (1016–35)

King Canute, the second Dane to rule England, invented the concept of toy dogs. He passed a law making it illegal for large dogs to be used in hunting, in order to make it fairer on the prey. Because of this, breeders went to great efforts to use only the smallest mating stock, until the breed known at the time as the Toy Spaniel was established. This breed went on to be a forefather of the Cavalier King Charles Spaniel.

King James I (1603–25)

King James I, who was ruling monarch of England, Scotland, and Ireland, loved dogs. He had many hunting hounds, but his particular favorite was a dog named Jewel. Sadly, she was found dead, killed by a single bullet. The King was outraged to find out that the killer was his wife, Queen Anne, who had accidentally shot Jewel while deer hunting.

King Charles II (1660–85)

King Charles II was known as Cavalier King Charles due to the way in which he dealt with his parliament. He was also known for his love of dogs. One dog in particular, a Toy Spaniel, was often prescribed to the sick by doctors (its warming presence on the lap was deemed to help fight a cold). The breed was later renamed the Cavalier King Charles Spaniel in honor of its most powerful admirer.

Prince William of Orange (1689–94)

This Dutch aristocrat, who later became King William III, was a big admirer of Pugs. He traveled with them from England to Holland, where he resided at the

LEFT

Queen Victoria's pet Pomeranian, named Turi, seen here in 1899, was at her bedside when she died in 1901.

Fascinating Facts

Two dogs survived the sinking of the *Titanic* by jumping into lifeboats—one was a Pomeranian and the other was a Pekingese.

House of Orange. When the Dutch repelled a Spanish invasion shortly before the Prince became King of England he believed the good fortune was due to the dog, which became the official symbol of the House of Orange.

Queen Victoria (1837–1901)

Queen Victoria played a large part in developing a popular modern breed. In the 1700s, Queen Charlotte, wife of George III, had already brought to England a white dog, from the area of eastern Germany once known as Pomerania. Victoria later owned similar dogs—perhaps descended from Charlotte's— and, upon the death of her husband Prince Albert in 1861, she focused her attention on tending to them. Concerned with their size, she bred them with smaller breeds to establish the dog known today as the Pomeranian.

King George V (1910–36)

King George V founded the House of Windsor and was Grandfather of the current Queen of England. He loved Sealyham Terriers and Cairn Terriers and many royally commissioned paintings picture him doting on his dogs.

Queen Elizabeth II (1952–present)

The reigning British monarch is possibly the most well-known royal dog lover. Currently, the Queen has ten dogs: Emma, Linnet, Holly, and Willow are the names of her Corgis; she also has three "Dorgis," a cross between a Dachshund and a Corgi.

Queen Elizabeth has owned more than 30 Corgis. The first was Susan, given to her on her eighteenth birthday by her father, King George VI. The Queen is a keen dog trainer and is well known for her admiration of working gun-dog breeds, such as Springer Spaniels.

BELOW

George, Duke of York, (the future King George V) c. 1895, encouraging his pet to beg for a tidbit.

BELOW

Queen Elizabeth II has owned many dogs over the years, favoring the Corgi, as seen here at Sandringham, Norfolk, 1970.

STATUS AND RELATIONSHIP WITH MAN

In many cultures, the dog is seen as man's faithful companion, but that has not always been the case. Dogs originally were bred to work and those that could not were a burden on their keeper. Only in more recent times has the value of dogs as pets become apparent. In Eastern cultures, dogs are considered to be impure; in the West, they are treated as one of the family. Throughout history dogs have been valued as helpers, cherished and sacred companions, and even as status symbols.

Dogs in Ancient Past

The domestication of dogs predates Christianity. There is evidence in the form of cave paintings and fossils that man and dog have been partners for up to about 15,000 years. The first dog breeds are thought to have been established in the Middle East and it is widely believed that the oldest breed is the Saluki. The Saluki is a sight hound, similar in some ways to a Greyhound. It is the only breed of dog in the world that is not considered unclean by the Bedouin, due to its historical connections to ancient tribes.

BELOW

The dog-man hunting partnership was developed in ancient times, as seen in this ancient European relief sculpture.

LEFT

Two Hounds by Hsuan-te, 1427. The Saluki is thought to be the oldest breed of dog.

Fascinating Facts

In ancient Egypt, it was traditional for families to shave off all their hair to signal that they were mourning the death of a dog.

BELOW

In this Libyan Neolithic cave painting depicting a hunting scene, note the dog, bottom left, a valued companion and fellow hunter.

Evidence of Companionship
A 7,000-year-old grave has been found in Sweden that suggests dogs were customarily buried with their owners. The dog's neck had been broken, indicating that the dog was killed as part of a ritual upon the death of its master. Although today this would be seen as a cruel and barbaric practice, cultural anthropologists maintain that this was one of the greatest signs of love and devotion that could be bestowed upon a companion.

Other fossilized remains go some way to proving that man was providing primitive

LEFT
The Canaan Dog has been used since earliest times by the Israelite to guard both their flocks and their towns.

Man Turns on His Dog

During Biblical times, the dog came to be viewed with suspicion, particularly in the East. Considered filthy and not worthy of respect as one of God's creatures, the dog was seen as synonymous with depravity and evil, a roaming emblem of lust and a scavenger with no place to call home. This development in man's relationship with dogs still has ramifications to this day. In Islam, the dog is considered unclean; if a dog enters a Muslim house, great offense can be taken by the occupiers. Dogs are mentioned many times in the Bible, but at no time is the dog cast in a good light.

veterinary care to dogs as long as 10,000 years ago. Remains of dogs have been found with evidence of broken bones that had been encouraged to heal, most likely through the use of a splint. Even euthanasia appears to have been carried out, with bones disfigured in such a way as to cause lameness being found on the same canine bodies as those with broken necks.

Early Devotion to Pets

Primitive rock carvings in the Sinai Desert dating back tens of thousands of years suggest that dogs were valued and admired long before they were fully domesticated. Cave drawings, canine remains,

and literary evidence suggest that man was protector of his dog in ancient times and relied on the dog for company and friendship.

Dogs and Early Civilization

Dogs and man made the journey to civilization together. Without the companionship and assistance of dogs, the civilization of the human race may have happened differently. In ancient Israel, dogs were kept to guard towns as they were built. Ancient Canaan Dogs were used to guard flocks and

settlements as the early Israelite settlers traveled. The same dogs have appeared throughout history alongside the Druz tribe on Mount Carmel—he possible site of the Garden of Eden.

RIGHT
Natural scavengers, dogs have long scrounged for food; even Jesus in the Bible refers to "dogs under the table."

All Kinds of Partnerships

Ever since the wolf began to evolve into what we now know as the domestic dog, canines have forged long-lasting partnerships with man, other dogs, and other animals. The dog is one of the most cooperative species in the world, having evolved to meet the needs of any species that can bring it protection, food, or company. On its long journey through the centuries, the dog has shrared with man various important experiences.

The whole relationship between canine and man is based on a partnership. Like the shark and the pilot fish, the relationship that man and dog share is symbiotic — we both benefit from each other. Over time we have rewarded the dog with shelter, food, and healthcare

and in return the dog has performed jobs that we simply could not do. Farming, travel, early settlements, cultural milestones, and even technological innovations, such as the invention of Velcro and space travel, have involved dogs in a big way.

Dogs and Women

Women and dogs have a special partnership.

Traditionally, the dog is "man's best friend," but history shows us that without the bond between

BELOW

Both men and women work in the veterinary field. Women have often fronted the campaign against animal testing, too.

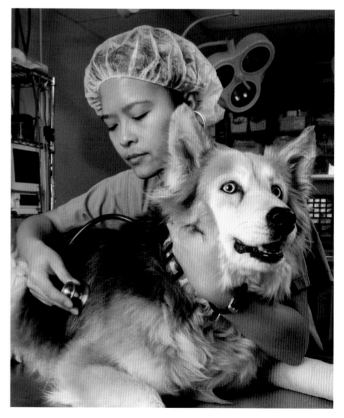

BELOW

"Man's" best friend was often fed and tended by women, particularly when sick or whelping. This little girl continues the tradition.

women and dogs this friendship could not have lasted. Despite being the subject of its male master, it was typically the woman that tended to the dog, especially if the animal was sick or a mother with pups. This has led to a very different but equally strong bond forming between women and dogs.

Traditionally, women have been at the forefront of the animal-welfare movement. During Edwardian times, groups of female academics objected to vivisection and animal testing. During female-led protests in London, a group of women trying to protect the rights of dogs around the world struck the first blow in the fight against animal cruelty. This march led to a political controversy called "The Brown Dog Affair." The women used the image and memory of one particular brown dog to prompt the

academic community to take unified action against vivesction and testing—it worked wonderfully and still has ramifications in many cultures today.

Dogs and Children
The evolutionary process has given dogs a natural protective instinct when it comes to children. In the same way that most people find little puppies adorable, dogs find themselves instinctively drawn to protect human infants. This

has been bred into them for thousands of years.

There are numerous examples of great partnerships between dogs and children, some portrayed on screen, others in literature, and many others in real life. There have even been documented accounts of feral children living and growing up with and becoming accepted by packs of wild dogs, especially in rural Romania and other parts of Eastern Europe, where child abandonment was relatively high.

Horse and Hound
Of all the members of the animal kingdom, the horse has the strongest links to the dog. Traditionally, horses and dogs have worked together well, on hunts particularly, but also in wars. While the horse provides a means of transport for the man, the dog provides him with protection and food. This has been the case throughout history and the relationship between horses and dogs still endures today.

ABOVE
Both domesticated for man's own ends and for companionship, the horse and dog can work together harmoniously.

Dogs and Other Creatures
Despite being portrayed as mortal enemies, dogs and cats have a history of cooperation. In pre-industrial dwellings, typically a dog would be kept and used to rid the home of rats, while the cat took care of the mice. Dogs have enjoyed long-lasting relations with other animals, too, such as farm animals and wild mammals. There are even cases of dogs adopting abandoned pigs and raising them as their own among their puppies.

Fascinating Facts

The only dog to be registered as a Japanese prisoner of war was an English Pointer called Judy that belonged to the Royal Navy.

Myths and Magic

The dog has been an essential and invaluable aid to the development of the human race. This is why the animal features so prominently in mythology and magic. In ancient times, man was aware of the dog's ability to do certain things, but he was unsure of how it was done. Dogs can often detect the invisible or the hidden, which was seen as a form of magic to early man.

Dogs in Different Cultures

Some cultures have stronger links with dogs than others. Dogs typically are more predominant in Western civilizations and are certainly more popular: Greek, Norse, Egyptian, Inuit, and Roman mythology and legend feature many dogs. Some cultures fear and respect the dog, other cultures worship it.

The Inuit, for example, have a long and close history with dogs. In fact, up until mechanization the dog was crucial to the survival of the

Inuit people, and Inuit mythology features various dogs with magical powers. Akhlut is a dangerous and evil lupine spirit. Inuit mythology claims that the Akhlut takes the form of wolf on land and whale in the sea—paw prints leading from land to water are said to be a sign of its presence. Amaguq is an Inuit wolf god that plays tricks on people, while Amorok is a giant dog or wolf that kills the lone hunter.

Greek Mythology

In Greek mythology, the dog is portrayed as a fearless protector and learned advisor—a mythical canine creature is said to have swum alongside the Greek God Xanthippus. Argus was another loyal and faithful dog, portrayed in Homer's epic poem *The Odyssey*. It was the only being to recognize Ulysses, the King of Ithaca, on his return from

the Trojan War. Ulysses returned disguised as a beggar, but Argus dropped his ears and wagged his tail when he saw his master. In Greek religion, it was thought that the lick of a dog could heal the sick.

Hell Hounds

Norse mythology features a lot of earthly creatures with supernatural and magical powers, and one such being was the dog Garm, which was portrayed as a fearsome and evil hound sent to kill Tyr, the god of single combat. Similarly, in Viking mythology, there are many mythical doglike creatures. Black Shuck was a demonic hell hound that terrorized clergymen in East Anglia, England, but the dog is also portrayed as a king in many Viking legends.

Perhaps the most famous mythical hell hound is Cerberus, the hound of

Legend has it that the dog was green in color, and when it barked the noise was so loud that it could be heard by boats at sea.

Wolves

The dog's cousin, the wolf, also features often in mythology and folklore. Usually it is portrayed as vicious and evil, or cunning, as in the well-known fable of the Wolf in Sheep's Clothing. One, more positive image of the wolf is known from the Roman legend of Romulus and Remus. The tale goes that the two newborn sons of the priestess Rhea Silvia, who had been sworn to

chastity and, therefore, had her babies taken away from her when she gave birth, were suckled by a she-wolf on the Palatine Hill.

BELOW

The Wild Hunt myth, of horsemen and dogs charging through the night sky, is known across Europe and Britain. Engraving by F. Blanch.

RIGHT

Closely related to dogs, wolves do not, however, enjoy a bond with man — except, perhaps, in the extraordinary tale of Romulus and Remus.

Hades. Cerberus was portrayed in many types of mythology, notably in Greek mythology, as a wild and evil guardian at the gates of Hell.

British Mythology

Pagan and Celtic mythology have been present in Britain for centuries. One example is the Wild Hunt, when the ghosts of men, hounds, and horses fly through the skies; thunderstorms were often attributed to the Wild Hunt.

Celtic mythology paints the dog as a powerful and fearless creature. Cu Sith was a legendary hound of giant proportions that hunted silently throughout the Scottish Highlands.

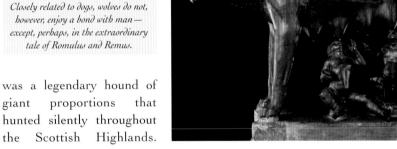

Dogs and the Church

Dogs, religion, and the Church are inextricably linked throughout history. In religious texts and iconography, the dog has been portrayed as everything from evil to sacred and from magical to lowly and pitiful. In some religions and religious cultures, dogs are valued and cherished; in other faiths, the dog is considered unholy and a cause of great offense. Every religion has its sacred animals and the domestic canine is gradually attaining near-sacred status among some modern Christian cultures.

Dogs and Christianity

The dog is mentioned in the Bible on many occasions, but in most instances these references portray the dog as a lowly, wandering creature and a harbinger of depravity. There are, however, a few references to the dog as valued companion, notably in the story of Lazarus who was nursed back to health from serious illness by having dogs lick at his sores. The Catholic Church recognizes a Patron Saint of Dogs, Saint Rocco, who is said to have been cured of the plague by his dogs.

Dogs and Judaism

Dogs have been held in high esteem in Judaism for centuries. The ancient Canaan Dog famously protected early Jewish settlements from wolves as well as invaders. Dogs are generally not popular in the East, but history prescribes that early Jews kept dogs for guarding and herding.

Dogs and Islam

Islam views dogs as unclean and unholy. It is considered to be against the will of Allah to keep a dog, except for the purpose of hunting. Muslims must wash their hands seven times before eating if they have been in contact with a dog.

Despite these negative views, Islam also advocates kindness toward animals and this includes dogs. Modern Islam is more tolerant toward dogs, but on the whole the animal is not conducive to good Islamic faith. In Iran, the dog is seen as a symbol of Western decadence and is banned in some areas.

Dogs and Hinduism

Dogs are worshipped by Hindus; it is believed that a

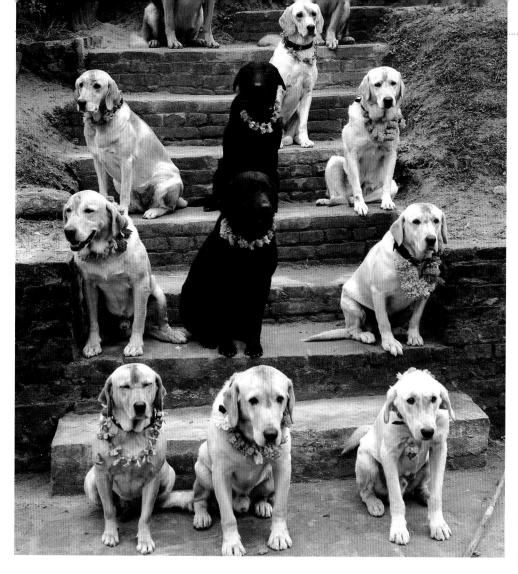

dogs into homes for scenting will cause great offense to the home owner.

The problem with stray dogs in Thailand is massive, but being a mainly Buddhist country it is forbidden for dogs to be killed. The common solution is for poisoned meat to be left out for stray dogs, thereby absolving any person of the duty of actually killing the dog. In reality, this turns out to be crueler than veterinary euthanasia, which is at least painless and controlled.

LEFT
Hindus revere dogs. These police dogs have been garlanded on the dog-worship day, part of the Deepawali festival.

BELOW
A dog sleeps on a Bangkok street; other dogs in Thailand are not so lucky, because strays are often intentionally poisoned.

dog guards the gates of Heaven. This is why many Hindu worshippers see the dog as sacred and keep the dog in the home as a guard. Dogs are seen as so important that they are celebrated every November on "Dog's Day." Incense is burned and special slogans are chanted in honor of the all-important canine.

However, in modern Hindu culture, dogs are often left to roam. The problem of stray dogs in India in particular is often exacerbated by the popularity of the animals. People want to own dogs due to their wide-reaching reverence, but subsequently are unable to care for them.

Dogs in Buddhism
Followers of Buddhism are sworn to treat all animals with compassion and kindness, but dogs are not regarded with any particular reverence above other species. The concept of rebirth allows that those who act like dogs shall be born among dogs. This suggests that dogs are considered to be relatively lowly.

Religion and Animal Welfare
Most mainstream religions advocate kindness toward animals, but in certain instances that message of kindness becomes warped. In Islamic countries, attitudes toward dogs can be affected by religious beliefs. Foreign armies bringing

Fascinating Facts

Two dogs named Belka and Strelka were the first animals to survive an orbital flight in space; they returned healthy and happy from their journey on the Russian shuttle Sputnik 5.

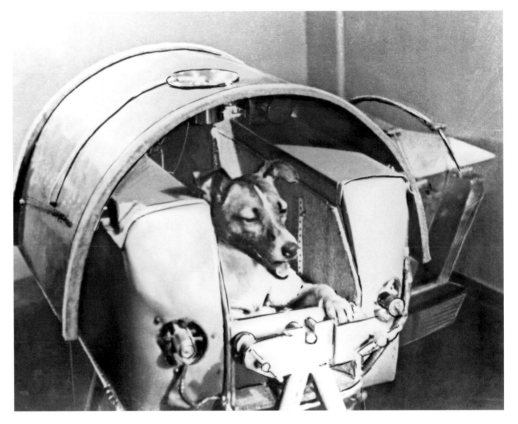

Canine Heroes

Dogs are by nature brave, loyal, and courageous. This is why the dog has performed heroically alongside man on many occasions. Dogs have helped man win wars, repel invasions, and advance civilizations. From ancient guarding dogs protecting settlers in the East, to modern pet dogs aiding scientific progress and rescue dogs saving lives, the combination of intelligence and devotion to man has enabled various dogs throughout history to perform heroic acts.

Laika

Laika was the first living creature to enter space. She was found as a stray dog in Moscow and put into a training regime for the Soviet-run Sputnik 2 space program. She made her heroic journey into space on November 3, 1957, but perished shortly after take off due to stress.

Laika's efforts proved that a living creature could enter space and survive, albeit very briefly in the case of this dog. Without the data and experience that the Soviet program gleaned from Laika's trip, the space race could have gone very differently.

Pickles

Many soccer fans will know who Pickles is. In 1966, the English soccer team made history when they won the World Cup for soccer for the first and, to date, only time. They defeated Germany in England and were awarded what was then known as the Jules Rimet Trophy.

Shortly after the victory parade, the trophy was stolen from its display at Westminster Hall. The news of the theft was huge and a mass search for the missing trophy began in earnest. The trophy was eventually found by a terrier called Pickles, who retrieved the 9-in. (23-cm) solid-gold statue after it was discarded by the thieves in a back garden.

Fascinating Facts

The World Trade Center Dogs

When the World Trade Center was attacked by terrorists on September 11, 2001, the whole world looked on in horror. Among the tragedy and panic were many feats of heroism, most notably at the time the firefighters who performed selflessly in rescuing those who had managed to escape the blaze.

After the initial shock of what had happened, there was an enormous effort to find survivors trapped in the wreckage of the two skyscrapers. There was only one way this task could be completed—with dogs. Springer Spaniels, scent hounds, and many other breeds all turned up to help, locating bodies and survivors. A Rat Terrier named Ricky was singled out for special praise after it was reported that he had wriggled through twisted and singed ironworks to reach two people trapped in the remains of the building.

Beautiful Joe

Fans of Canadian literature will recognize the name "Beautiful Joe"; the story of this heroically brave dog is so inspiring that it is an integral part of Canadian culture. *Beautiful Joe* is the tale of an abused dog that is rescued from the cruel owner who had cut off his ears and tail. It was written by a struggling novelist, Margaret Saunders, who used her middle name of Marshall as a male pseudonym. She crafted a book so powerful and moving that it retains literary classic status in Canada to this day.

Stubby the War Dog

Stubby, or Sergeant Stubby as he was known, is the most decorated dog to have served in World War I. He served in 102 Infantry in the French trenches and saved many lives. The dog, who is believed to have been a Boston Terrier mix, was nearly killed in a gas attack, leaving him hypersensitive to the smell of gas. He helped to avert many attacks due to his superior hearing and scenting abilities. Stubby was able to detect the sound made by the launch of shells before anybody else in the unit and always warned his men in good time.

Fascinating Facts

Bulldog judging at Crufts. The world's largest international annual dog show takes place at the National Exhibition Centre, Britain.

Dog Shows

Since the decline in available work for dogs man has found ever more interesting ways of measuring their value. In recent decades, the popularity of conformation shows has increased massively. Initially conformation shows, or dog shows, were used to display so-called typical specimens of a breed and to establish a universally accepted standard by which that breed could be measured. As the audiences at these various shows increased, the need to make them more entertaining became more pressing.

Crufts

Crufts is the largest dog show of its kind in the world, hosted in Birmingham, England, by the UK Kennel Club. It is first and foremost a formal conformation show, but it encompasses many other features, including agility competition, working trials, unusual breeds yet to be recognized by the Kennel Club, and exhibitions put on in accordance with the Kennel Club Good Citizen Scheme. It attracts visitors and exhibitors from all over the world and is televised in Britain and abroad.

It has a long history. Established by Charles Cruft in 1866 in London, it was originally billed as a conformation show for terriers. It has moved locations numerous times in order to accommodate the ever-growing audiences. Crufts holds many world records related to dogs and dog showing. In recent years, competition to become recognized by the notoriously strict Crufts judges has resulted in controversy. Cases of sabotage and cheating have marred the event's otherwise prestigious reputation.

Westminster Dog Show

The Westminster Dog Show, which is run and governed by the American Kennel Club, was established as a gun-dog show in 1877. It is the largest event of its kind in the United States, but it is much smaller in scale than Crufts. The show typically lasts two days and is hosted in New York City.

All dog conformation shows are based, either entirely or partly, on Crufts—the original dog conformation show. The Westminster Dog show is prestigious and to win any award there is a huge accolade for a breeder or trainer. The highest award is Best in Show, which identifies the dog that most closely represents the ideal standard for that breed.

Judging at Crufts: the "Best in Show" is awarded to the dog that most closely resembles the ideal for the breed.

Fascinating Facts

Fédération Cynologique Internationale

The Fédération Cynologique Internationale is an international governing and administrative body for purebred dogs. It covers many countries and puts its name to many smaller shows, including conformation shows and working trials. Most countries around the world hold dog-conformation events of some size.

The Drawbacks of Dog Shows

Typically, entry into a conformation show requires the dog to be a complete purebred. Dogs are judged on how closely they match the standard for that breed. This process is often criticized because it encourages breeders to use limited

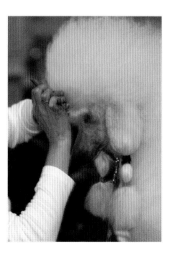

breeding stock in order to create offspring that match the standard. This damages the gene pool, and while the

ABOVE
Hound judging at the Westminster Dog Show, New York City. This dog show is the largest of its kind in the United States.

dogs may look like the ideal example of their breed they are likely to have less robust health than dogs from a wider gene pool.

Other Dog Shows

While the stereotypical image of a dog show involves Poodles being preened and physically examined, many dog shows are set up in order to judge dogs on temperament, ability, and obedience rather than simply on their appearance.

Working trials are held in order to raise the standard of work performed by certain

breeds. They also enable people to judge dogs on what they can do and as such encourage breeders to seek good health, good temperament, and robust genetics when breeding. Gun-dog trials, field trials, sheepdog trials, and agility contests are all extremely popular among the working-dog community.

LEFT
If you plan to enter your dog into competitions, it needs to learn to carry itself confidently, according to the breed standard.

BELOW
Dog shows are not just about beauty; sheepdog trials test the skills of working Border Collies.

EARLY DOG CARE

The dog is a valuable asset to man and has been for centuries. As such, the animal has been subject to special care and devotion. Certain concepts, such as boarding, veterinary care, and obedience training, are new, while the practices of grooming, selective breeding, and husbandry have their foundations further back in history. Necessity for more effective workers or stronger and healthier breeding stock was the main motivation for early dog care.

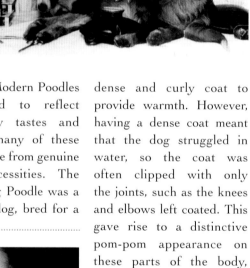

Veterinary Care

Fossilized remains suggest that early man was capable of treating injured or sick dogs. The concept of husbandry preceded the practice of veterinary medicine, which did not arise in Europe until as recently as the eighteenth century. Resting dogs with disease and treating injuries with splints and compression are early examples of husbandry. Good animal husbandry is still a very important element of modern dog care.

Grooming

Early grooming was not done for cosmetic reasons but for practical working reasons. A case in point is the Poodle. Modern Poodles are groomed to reflect contemporary tastes and styles, but many of these styles originate from genuine working necessities. The early working Poodle was a water-going dog, bred for a dense and curly coat to provide warmth. However, having a dense coat meant that the dog struggled in water, so the coat was often clipped with only the joints, such as the knees and elbows left coated. This gave rise to a distinctive pom-pom appearance on these parts of the body, which is still popular as a style today.

Specialized Feeding

Throughout the ages of primitive dog ownership, dogs ate what they killed. It was rare for early man ever to part with food and even rarer for him to willingly give food to his dog. As time went by and dogs were

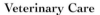

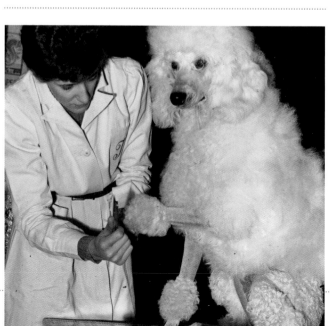

concepts such as conditioning (learning consequences through repetition) and advanced reinforcement (rewarding or discouraging actions by providing or removing a stimulus) were not considered useful until the dog became domesticated.

BELOW

In the wild, a dog would naturally eat a carnivorous diet with the pack, feeding on a carcass.

valued as more than just hunters, it was necessary for their owners to provide food so that the dog could work. Much of the time this was limited to leftover scraps and carcasses.

Dogs in the wild are omnivorous, but mainly eat meat. They get their vegetable intake from gorging on the decaying food in the stomachs of their prey. When this was recognized by humans, vegetation and cereal-based food was often included in the canine diet. Dogs are robust and can eat most things, so feeding has become specialized only very recently, when technology and lifestyle permitted it.

Selective Breeding

Selective breeding is the cornerstone of the canine's evolution—without it the domesticated dog of modern times would not exist. The concept of selective breeding

began in a very primitive fashion, with large specimens being matched with strong specimens. But as the needs of mankind evolved, we sought new and more complex ways of breeding dogs. Crossing terrier-type dogs with larger, heavier breeds gave rise to formidable hunting and guarding dogs. Only recently has the concept of breeding for appearance become relevant. In the past, any selective breeding was done to produce the healthiest, strongest, most intelligent, and capable dogs possible.

Training

Dogs are instinctive and man has had very little need to instruct the dog. Upon noticing strong instincts that would prove to be of value, man encouraged that dog to reproduce. Guiding a dog to perform a certain role is a very new phenomenon and

historically dogs that were of no working use were abandoned. Punishment for failure and reward for success—the two most common ways of training today—were used in early dog training. However,

DOGS IN THE ARTS

From royal commissions to ancient stone carvings, dogs have been a popular subject for many artistic disciplines over the centuries. Much of what we know about early dogs was gleaned from northern African cave paintings, and the history of many breeds has been traced back through works of art. Television, film, and even music have proven to be extremely compatible media for man to express and articulate his relationship with the canine. From Sir Edwin Landseer to the Rolling Stones, the range of art that features dogs is wide and varied.

Literature

Popular and classical literature is crammed with references to dogs and many classic novels and books about dogs are popular today. The dog has been used as a literary device to evoke loyalty, bravery, strength, and fun, and in some cases the dog becomes the focus and even title of a novel or series of stories. In classic and ancient literature, the dog is often a mythical creature, and through time the changing role of the domestic dog has been reflected in its portrayal within literature.

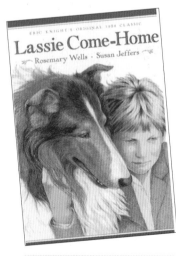

ABOVE

Lassie is perhaps the most famous dog in literary history, featuring in more than 50 well-loved books, as well as in movies.

RIGHT

Greyfriar's Bobby's monument, commemorating this brave Skye Terrier's 14-year vigil on his master's death, until his own in 1872.

Shakespeare

Many literary historians attest that despite his frequent reference to dogs in his works, William Shakespeare disliked the animal. Shakespeare often used the dog as a metaphorical device to portray disorder and deviousness. In his play *Macbeth*, Shakespeare describes an entire list of dogs and uses canine comparisons to insult certain characters. Even the perceived good qualities of dogs are presented as unpleasant in the works of Shakespeare; comparisons to a "fawning dog" are made very frequently with his less likeable characters.

Kipling

Rudyard Kipling was noted for his affection for dogs. His poetry was often used as a means of communicating his fondness for the animal, with many examples of entire poems being dedicated to dogs. *Red Dog* and *The Power of a Dog* are both powerful works that evoke the loyalty

of the animal and the lamentable shortness of the dog's life.

Lassie

Perhaps the most well-known literary dog, Lassie has featured in more than 50 books and numerous films. Author and creator of the Lassie character, Eric Knight, first introduced Lassie to the world in a newspaper column. Perhaps the most popular Lassie novel is *Lassie Come Home*.

Greyfriars Bobby

"Greyfriars Bobby" is possibly the most popular true dog story. Many people are familiar with the legend without knowing that it is based on true events that

Fascinating Facts

The first ever use of the phrase "watchdog" appeared in Shakespeare's *The Tempest*.

happened in Scotland in the nineteenth century. A tale of undying loyalty and devotion, the story of Bobby (who is immortalized in a statue located in Edinburgh, Scotland) has been parodied and reworked many times.

White Fang and *Call of The Wild*

Jack London is a noted novelist and dog lover, having written two very popular novels about dogs.

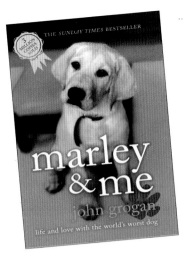

White Fang is a tale of love, devotion, and morality that has achieved classic status, and *Call of the Wild* deals with the sometimes unnatural effects of domestication.

Spot

Spot is a character in a series of children's books created by Eric Hill. These books are often a child's first experience of a dog (or rather, a puppy) and, starting with *Where's Spot?*, first published in 1980, they have become one of the most successful and widely read series of children's books ever published. They have also been made into an animated television series.

Marley and Me

John Grogan's *Marley and Me* is a biographical account dealing with some of the modern issues surrounding dog ownership. Published in 2005, it is now one of the best-selling books ever to appear on the retail Web site Amazon.

Grogan's work is sincere, honest, and touching, reflecting the feeling of loss encountered by dog owners the world over. The approach that Grogan takes in depicting Marley as "the world's worst dog" resonates with many dog owners who see through their own dog's indiscretions.

The Legend of Mick the Miller

Another true story that has achieved enormous popularity is Michael Tanner's tale of the Greyhound, Mick the Miller. The story deals with the heroism, bravery, and inevitably sad demise of a dog that the reader cannot help but feel close to by the end.

BELOW
Mick the Miller, the enthusiastic Greyhound who broke many racing records, and helped to popularize the sport during his racing career 1929–31.

Dogs in Art

Art, notably painting and sculpture, has been a popular and engaging medium for man to communicate his love and admiration for the dog. From primitive stone carvings and cave paintings, through to classical oil paintings and even contemporary art, the dog is and always has been a favored subject. Quite often dogs have been used as a status symbol and, works of art featuring dogs in sporting, pastoral, or working scenes have always been sought after.

Popular Canine Art

Much of the world's most famous dog art has resulted from private commissions. Wealthy landowners would regularly commission a painting of their hounds at work, not just for the love of dogs, but for the love of the art.

Canine art tends to be divided into two types. It is usually either a work that depicts a specific dog, perhaps a family pet or loyal working dog, or work that represents a breed. In the case of the latter, dogs in traditional scenes related to that particular breed were favored. There are many magnificent images of hunt hounds in stunning countryside that were commissioned as a record of their activity and existence as much as they were for art's sake.

Famous Works

One of the most famous images of a dog is contained in a painting of a Fox Terrier called Nipper. The piece is entitled *His Master's Voice* and depicts a scene of an inquisitive dog peering into the horn of a gramophone, apparently responding to a recording of his deceased master speaking. The painting, by the artist Francis Barraud, became very famous in Europe when it was used as the corporate logo for the music retailer HMV. The retailer's name was taken from the title of the painting.

The artist, Sir Edwin Landseer, who was acclaimed for *The Monarch of the Glen* and the lion sculptures at the foot of Nelson's Column in London, England, painted some moving pictures of dogs, revealing the strong bond between man and his 'best friend'. Examples include *The Old Shepherd's Chief Mourner* and a piece entitled *Saved*. The latter depicts an image of a Newfoundland and a young

BELOW
The Old Shepherd's Chief Mourner *by Edwin Landseer c. 1825–73; his faithful and devoted dog waits alone by his coffin.*

Famed for his dog paintings, Edwin Landseer features a Newfoundland and a Border Collie in Burns' Twa Dogs, 1858.

girl in a boat, the dog having rescued the child. So revered was Landseer for his portrayal of the breed that the depicted coloring of black and white, which is rare for a Newfoundland, was named Landseer in his honor.

Notable Dog Artists

Sir Edwin Landseer is known as a master of capturing nature on his canvas. He worked with other subjects as well as dogs, but some of his most notable work was of dogs. Another British artist, Nigel Hemming, is popular for his portraits of dogs in domestic and pastoral settings. He claims that his approach is to paint pictures about dogs rather than of dogs.

Before photography was as accessible as it is today, the only way to record the standard of a breed was by painting. Maud Earl, a celebrated British artist popular in Victorian times, was known for her canine works, which are still relevant today. Earl, who died in 1943, was said to be Queen Victoria's favorite artist.

For an artist to focus solely on one subject is rare in any genre, but occasionally artists become synonymous with certain themes. Today, much commercial art is done to personal specification. When the art is concerning dogs the commissioner normally wants an image that represents the personality of their dog. Which is why there are not a lot of canine artworks in circulation, as most of the people that ordered the work have chosen to keep it as a treasured memory rather than sell it on as an investment.

Maud Earl was thought to be Queen Victoria's favorite painter, both women sharing a love of dogs. The Red Cushion.

Fascinating Facts

The Labrador, Newfoundland, Akita, and Chihuahua are all named after the provinces of the countries in which they originated.

Dogs in Film and Television

From Lassie to Rin Tin Tin and Old Yeller to Toto, there are legions of canine characters that make some of our favorite movies even more memorable. Quite often dogs feature as the main character in a movie, with the plot dedicated to documenting their

experiences. Some dogs portray typical canine roles, while other dog characters are portrayed in unusual roles for dramatic effect. In older films, dogs tend to have been used metaphorically, often representing themes, such as loyalty and family.

Rin Tin Tin

Rin Tin Tin is a famous movie dog, with more than 14 feature films to his name. Rin Tin Tin was a real dog, but was portrayed in film by canine actors. What is somewhat confusing, however,

is the fact that although Rin Tin Tin was played by other dogs, the original Rin Tin Tin also portrayed other dogs in film—he even played a wolf. The 1923 film *Where the North Begins*, which starred Claire Adams and Rin Tin Tin, is credited as being the movie that saved Warner Bros. Studios from bankruptcy.

The Wizard of Oz

The *Wizard of Oz* is one of the most popular feature movies of all time, with Toto the dog companion to the principal character, Dorothy. The character of Toto is of unspecified breed, but the dog that played him in the 1939 version of the movie was a Cairn Terrier. Toto is used as a metaphor for the life that Dorothy used to lead and he is involved in a crucial scene where the wizard is revealed to be a fraud. The character of Toto has been played by more than one breed over the years.

Lassie Come Home

Possibly the most famous canine film character is Lassie, the loyal and faithful Rough Collie. Based on a series of novels, there were many movies adaptations of the Lassie story and there were many different canine actors that portrayed the famous dog, including

some male dogs. Lassie's films, including the 1943 classic *Lassie Come Home*, typically involved the plucky and extremely intelligent dog overcoming great odds, or somehow saving the day. She had the uncanny ability to communicate with humans, which has given rise to the popular catchphrase "What is it Lassie?"

Old Yeller

This 1957 Walt Disney production directed by Robert Stevenson was a very popular feature movie in the

United States. Based on the story of one boy and his dog, it dealt with some important issues, such as morality. The main part of the plot revolves around the relationship between Old Yeller and Arliss, the young boy who takes him in. The ending is well known for being something of a tearjerker.

The *Back to the Future* Trilogy

The *Back to the Future* movies, which achieved widespread popularity in the 1980s, feature a canine character named Einstein. In this science-fiction comedy, the dog is possessed with what can be described as extremely advanced canine senses. In one of the movie plots, the dog is portrayed using scenting ability to find

a girl who has been kidnapped, and at other times he displays the ability to survive plutonium explosions and to travel through time to thwart a terrorist attack.

Turner & Hooch

Turner & Hooch is a well-loved moview made in 1989, starring Tom Hanks as Scott Turner, a police detective who acquires Hooch after the murder of the previous owner of the dog. Laughter and adventure abound as Hooch turns the reluctant detective's life upside down

and eventually helps Turner to uncover and solve a money-smuggling and laundering operation. Hooch is one of many lovable canine characters of the big screen, despite his sloppy drooling problem.

Beethoven

Another comedy featuring a dog is 1992's *Beethoven*, directed by Brian Levant. Even if you have not seen

the movie, most people know that it features a Saint Bernard named Beethoven—his droopy face on the

RIGHT

Shadow, a wise old Golden Retriever, co-starred in Homeward Bound: The Incredible Journey *with a cat and an American Bulldog pup.*

LEFT

The adorable Hooch of Turner and Hooch *is a Dogue de Bordeaux, a breed originally kept for pit fighting and pulling carts.*

posters sticks in the mind! Beethoven is adopted as a puppy by the Newton family, and the movie follows the inevitable scrapes and adventures that ensue as he grows larger and larger.

Homeward Bound

Homeward Bound: The Incredible Journey is a 1993 remake of the 1963 movie *The Incredible Journey* based on the best-selling novel of the same name by Sheila Burnford. It features two dogs named Shadow and Chance, and a cat named Sassy, who, when their owner leaves them on a friend's farm, set out on the long journey home. Grossing over 40 million dollars at the box office, the movie is yet another example of the power of our canine (and feline!) companions to intrigue and endear themselves to us.

ANATOMY, PHYSIOLOGY, AND APPEARANCE

By studying the physical makeup of a dog, it is possible to observe the way in which nature equipped this animal to survive and evolve. Eyes designed for seeing danger at a distance, a keen sense of smell in order to seek out prey, and teeth shaped for tearing open a carcass are just three of the reasons that the canine has been an evolutionary success. Man has influenced the appearance of the dog through selective breeding, but it took nature thousands of years to create the animal that man has found so valuable.

Skeleton and Physique

The dog comes in many shapes and sizes but its skeletal anatomy typically is uniform from breed to breed. All dogs have around 319 bones, with length being the only distinguishing factor between breeds—particularly in the leg bones. The front and hind legs' form and function are different from each other, with the hind legs being stronger but less flexible. Discernible differences in anatomy between breeds are due normally to the size of certain bones and the muscle mass in certain parts of the body.

Fascinating Facts

Due to their short legs and relatively heavy bodies, Basset Hounds are unable to swim.

The Skeleton

Skull The shape and size of the canine skull varies from breed to breed, but it is typically long to the muzzle and dome-shaped at the top.

EXTERNAL POINTS OF THE DOG

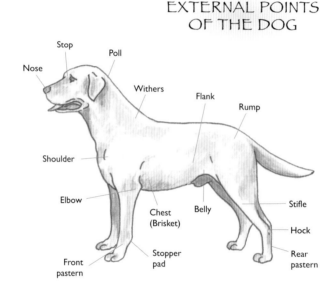

Stop, Poll, Nose, Withers, Flank, Rump, Shoulder, Elbow, Chest (Brisket), Belly, Stifle, Hock, Rear pastern, Front pastern, Stopper pad

SKELETON OF THE DOG

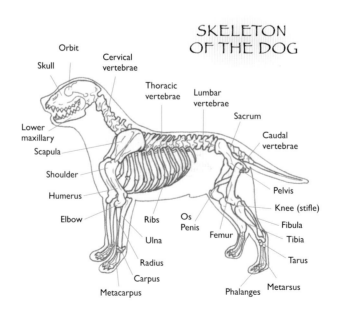

Orbit, Skull, Cervical vertebrae, Thoracic vertebrae, Lumbar vertebrae, Sacrum, Caudal vertebrae, Lower maxillary, Scapula, Shoulder, Humerus, Elbow, Ribs, Os Penis, Ulna, Radius, Carpus, Metacarpus, Femur, Phalanges, Metarsus, Pelvis, Knee (stifle), Fibula, Tibia, Tarus

Cervical vertebrae These are the bones in a dog's neck; some breeds display longer necks than others.

Thoracic vertebrae These are the spinal bones that run from the bottom of the neck to the middle of the back, covering the same area as the chest.

Lumbar vertebrae These are the spinal bones that run from the middle of the back to the base of the tail.

Sacrum This is the set of bones located in the rump.

Caudal vertebrae These are the bones that form the tail; they do not run to the tip of the tail.

Pelvis This enables mobility; it is located above the hind legs.

Femur This is the bone that forms the top part of the hind leg, going up from the knee to the pelvis.

Fibula This is one of the two bones that form the lower part of the hind leg.

Tibia This is the other bone that forms the lower part of the hind leg.

Tarsus This is the heel bone that leads from the paw to the lower part of the hind leg.

Metatarsus The metatarsal

bones form the basis of the rear paw.

Phalange This is the bone that occurs in the canine digits, of which there are three on each paw.

Metacarpus The metacarpal bones form the front paw; its movement is more flexible than that of the hind paw.

Carpus This is the wrist bone of the front leg; the carpus enables greater flexibility of the metacarpus.

Ulna This is one of the two bones of the lower part of the front leg.

Radius This is the other bone in the lower front leg.

Humerus This large bone forms the uppermost part of the front leg.

Rib This is part of the rib cage; the dog has 13 ribs.

Scapula This is the shoulder bone, located at the top of the front legs.

Lower maxillary This bone forms the lower part of the jaw, independent of the skull.

MUSCULAR SYSTEM OF THE DOG

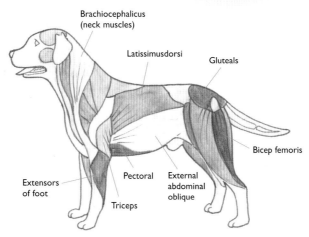

Brachiocephalicus (neck muscles)
Latissimusdorsi
Gluteals
Bicep femoris
Extensors of foot
Pectoral
External abdominal oblique
Triceps

Orbit This is the eye cavity; these cavities are shaped differently from breed to breed.

Physique

Physical differences between dog breeds are created by differences in length and in the mass of muscles. All dogs possess the same skeletal form—the differences in physique, shape, and build relate to the formation and size of certain muscle groups compared to others.

Herding breeds are typically lean, with well-proportioned but not bulky thigh muscles. Molosser breeds, such as the Rottweiler, tend to have dense muscles throughout the body, but particularly in the chest and hind legs.

ABOVE
Molosser breeds, such as Rottweilers, are heavily built, thick chested, and have sturdy haunches.

LEFT
Sight hounds, such as Whippets, tend to be lean and long-legged, enabling them to pursue their prey at high speed.

Sight hound breeds typically have leaner muscles that are longer in order to increase propulsion when running. Dogs that are bred for strength tend to have shorter leg bones in relation to the rest of the body in order to lower their centre of gravity.

CARDIOVASCULAR SYSTEM OF THE DOG

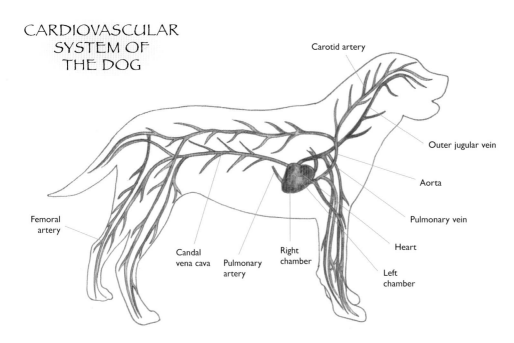

Carotid artery

Outer jugular vein

Aorta

Pulmonary vein

Heart

Left chamber

Right chamber

Pulmonary artery

Candal vena cava

Femoral artery

Internal Makeup

The internal makeup of a dog is typical of most omnivorous land mammals of its size. Through evolution the dog has developed a group of internal systems that perform functions essential to growth and survival. Deficiencies in these systems lead to illness and, in extreme cases, death if veterinary care is not delivered. Some conditions relating to the cardiovascular and digestive systems are the result of modern breeding methods, others are more widespread through the animal kingdom and are not a result of human actions.

Cardiovascular System

The cardiovascular system includes the heart and blood vessels. It is responsible for pumping blood through the body, enabling the rest of the body's organs and extremities to function. The heart is located in between the tops of the front legs. The resting heart rate for a healthy dog is 70–120 beats per minute. Inherited heart problems are common in certain breeds—notably the Bulldog, which has a lower life expectancy today than it used to.

Digestive System

The digestive system performs the functions of ingesting, digesting, and eliminating food products from the body. Externally, the digestive system comprises the mouth, teeth, and tongue. Internally, the digestive system is made up of, from mouth to tail, the esophagus, stomach, small intestine, large intestine, pancreas, colon, liver, and gallbladder. The canine digestive system is robust and can handle food that would make humans very sick. The stomach of a canine is long and relatively narrow, which means that it is prone to gastric torsion—a condition that can lead to severe illness and death if not treated. This is more common in large-breed dogs, such as the Rottweiler.

Integumentary System

This is the organ system that governs the skin and fur. It is a very important part of the canine body because it controls insulation; it is also the largest organ in the body. Dogs do not sweat through the skin, only through the paw pads and nose. They also lose water through the tongue when panting.

Respiratory System

The respiratory system governs the intake of oxygen and breathing. It is also the system responsible for expelling waste gas and

DIGESTIVE SYSTEM OF THE DOG

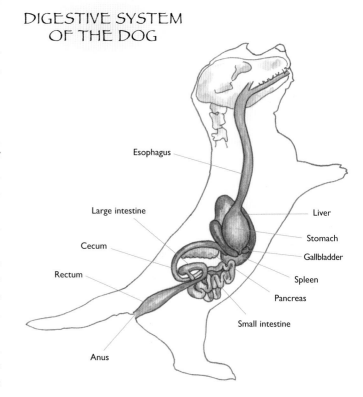

Esophagus

Large intestine

Cecum

Rectum

Anus

Liver

Stomach

Gallbladder

Spleen

Pancreas

Small intestine

RESPIRATORY SYSTEM OF THE DOG

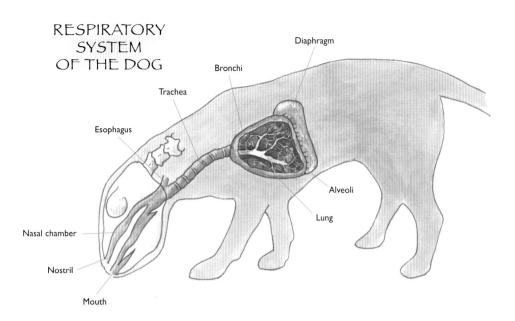

- Diaphragm
- Bronchi
- Trachea
- Esophagus
- Alveoli
- Lung
- Nasal chamber
- Nostril
- Mouth

Fascinating Facts

Dogs do not sweat by panting; dogs sweat through the pads of their feet and regulate body temperature through panting.

distribution of hormones. It is made up of thyroid glands, adrenal glands, and parathyroid glands.

Differences between Breeds

There are few fundamental differences between the inner workings of different dog breeds but breeding and evolution has influenced certain parts of the body to function to a higher level than others in different breeds. For example, some breeds, such as the Bloodhound, have more nerve endings in their noses, which enables them to have a more sensitive sense of smell. Other breeds, such as German Shepherds, may have higher tolerance to cold or pain, which enables them to function better in their working role.

regulating body temperature. The body temperature for a healthy dog is 100.5–102.5 degrees Fahrenheit (38–39.2 degrees Celsius). The internal elements of the respiratory system are the trachea and lungs, and externally the mouth and nose.

Urogenital System

This system includes the sex organs and the urinary excretion organs—the kidneys, bladder, urethra, and genitalia. Its function is two-fold: to facilitate reproduction and to remove waste from the blood.

Nervous System

The nervous system controls the rest of the body. It governs movement, instinct, impulse, and reflex. It enables the nerves inside the body to function and the organs to operate and is made up of the brain, spinal chord, and nerves. The canine's nervous system has evolved to enable it to react quickly to impulses and instincts.

Endocrine System

The endocrine system governs the function of the organs through the

UROGENITAL SYSTEM OF THE MALE DOG

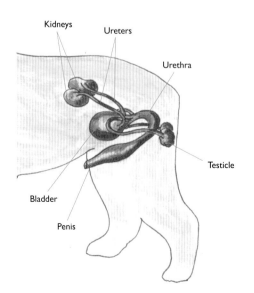

- Kidneys
- Ureters
- Urethra
- Testicle
- Bladder
- Penis

NERVOUS SYSTEM OF THE DOG

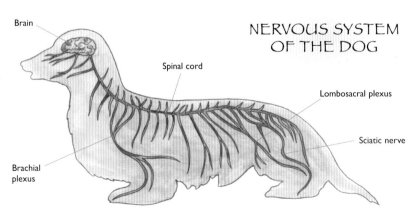

- Brain
- Spinal cord
- Lombosacral plexus
- Sciatic nerve
- Brachial plexus

Skull, Teeth, and Nails

The canine skull is one of the most distinguishing factors between breeds. The shape of the skull has influence on the senses of sight, hearing, and smell. It also influences a breed's ability to deliver a bite and has ramifications in terms of how well a breed can defend itself against attack. The teeth are essential for feeding and defending—poor teeth would lead to death in the wild. Good oral health in dogs is essential to prevent wider health problems throughout the body.

The Skull

Evolution has primarily influenced skull shape, with inherited skull shapes and sizes coming from the original wolves that were used to breed the first domesticated dogs. Human intervention, such as breeding dogs with pronounced skull shapes to produce dogs with larger skulls, has led to a wide diversification in shape.

Different Skull Shapes

There are two main shapes of the canine skull: one is long and narrow with a long muzzle; the other is rounder, with a heavier jaw and a more pronounced dome at the top. However, there are many different variants in between these two extremes. Face shape is also widely diverse between breeds—this is affected to an extent by skull shape but is also influenced by weight, fur type, and breeding.

The shape of the canine skull and, to a lesser extent, the size of the skull play a large part in determining the general appearance of a breed. Combined with face shape, fur type, and weight, these factors create distinguishing features that enable us to differentiate between breeds.

Teeth

Dogs are predatory, and meat constitutes a large part of their diet. The shape and formation of their teeth reflect this as dogs have the sharp teeth needed for killing prey and chewing tough meat. Dogs have 42 permanent teeth and 28 deciduous teeth. There are four sets of teeth in the canine mouth:

Incisors The incisor teeth are located at the front of the mouth and are used for tearing and shearing food.

SELECTION OF SKULL TYPES

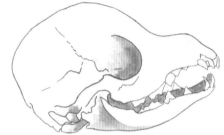

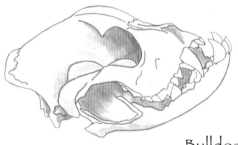

Terrier skull

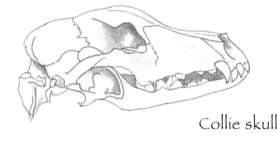

Bulldog skull

Collie skull

BELOW LEFT
The skull shape, size, and proportion are key to defining a breed and to determining how a dog can feed and defend itself.

Fascinating Facts

Breeds with heavy jaws, such as the Rottweiler, are less able to communicate with other dogs due to their inability to move their facial muscles.

A DOGS TEETH

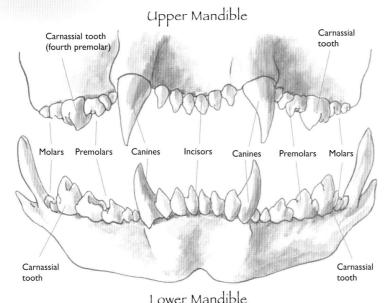

Upper Mandible

Carnassial tooth
(fourth premolar)

Carnassial tooth

Molars Premolars Canines Incisors Canines Premolars Molars

Carnassial tooth

Carnassial tooth

Lower Mandible

Canines The canine teeth are used for holding food while it is being sheared and are located to the rear of the incisors.

Premolars The premolar teeth are located behind the canines and are used for crushing and grinding. Premolars are considered transitional teeth over which food passes during chewing.

Molars The molar teeth are located at the back of the mouth and are used for crushing food, but to a lesser extent than the premolars.

Dental Health

The overall health of a dog is dependent on the health of its teeth. In the wild, a dog with broken or unhealthy teeth would soon die from either starvation or an inability to defend itself, whichever came first.

The modern, domesticated dog tends not to get enough of the food items that promote good oral health. In the wild, dogs would eat almost all of any animal they killed—each part of the carcass would bring its own benefit. Now that most dogs are fed soft, processed pet food the friction needed to clean the teeth is missing. Infected teeth and gums can quickly lead to toxins being spread through the digestive system. It is essential that dogs have healthy teeth.

Nails

In an evolutionary context, nails, or claws, were essential for hunting, feeding, and burying—three things that come to the dog instinctively. Because dogs use their claws far less in the domestic world, it is important that they are clipped before they become too long. In the wild, the nails would wear down naturally, but overlong nails can lead to limited mobility and be painful.

THE PAW AND NAILS

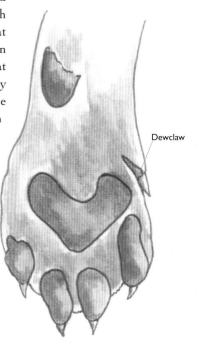

Dewclaw

The Senses

Nature has given the dog a set of senses that has equipped it to thrive in the wild, principally sight, hearing, and smell. The dog has proven to be a valuable ally to man due to the sophistication of some of its senses. Dogs have been bred for their sight and their scenting ability and all dogs have exceptional hearing. The development of the canine senses has been shaped by nature and evolution, as well as by man.

Any environment that limits a sense tends to promote the development of the other senses. Dogs that evolved in open areas, such as desert, tend to have strong eyesight to enable them to locate prey from a distance. Dogs that evolved in areas where food prey and predators were able to hide will typically have extremely advanced scenting capabilities. Dogs

with strong hearing tend to have evolved in areas where the ability to use sight or scent for protection was limited.

Sight

Almost every breed of dog has really good eyesight. Some have exceptional eyesight, having evolved over time to accommodate the sharpest vision possible. Natural selection dictates that dogs with weak eyesight would not survive as well as dogs that are able to see food sources and predators.

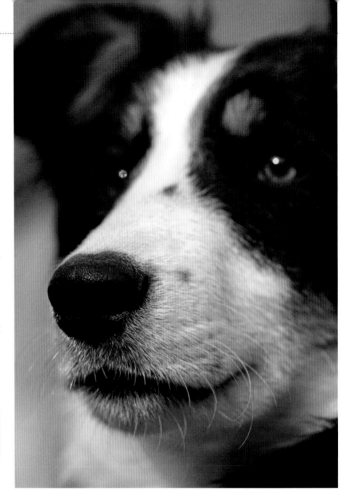

RIGHT

The nose, like the paw pads, contains sweat glands. Humans cannot begin to mimic a dog's sense of smell with technology.

The extent to which a breed's sight is developed depends on its role. The shape of a dog's skull also strongly influences its visual ability. Dogs with long, slender heads tend to have better peripheral vision, while dogs with round heads have sharper front-on and long-distance vision.

Scent

One of the most valuable skills a dog has in the working environment is scenting, simply because it is something that humans cannot do for themselves. Comparing the scenting ability of a human and a

LEFT

The Afghan Hound is a sight hound, with good peripheral vision, as required by his hunting and living in the mountains of Afghanistan.

dog, it is easy to see just how advanced the canine is. If a human can identify a smell as sausages, a dog will be able to identify every ingredient, the chemicals contained therein, and the effects that refrigeration and cooking have had on those ingredients.

Fascinating Facts

Dogs are not color blind; they have a limited capability to see color, but can discern between bright and dark shades.

It stands to reason that dogs with large noses have better scenting capabilities, but other physical factors influence this sense as well. A dog with large ears and loose skin around the muzzle will generally be able to retain scent particles near the nose for longer than a dog with short ears and fur. This is why many scent hounds have thick folds of skin on the face and large, drooping ears.

Hearing

The hearing capabilities of the dog are generally more advanced than our own;

Fascinating Facts

Dogs have over 200 million scent receptors in their nose; humans have 5 million.

A Siberian Husky gazes attentively, his ears pricked, making the most of his excellent hearing.

however, a dog's hearing deteriorates earlier in life and more rapidly than that of a human. Evolution has influenced the hearing of many dog breeds, particularly those that originally inhabited wooded or grassed areas where vision would have been limited. Dogs have the ability to move their outer ears to pick up on sounds and they can also hear extremely high-frequency noises that are not detected by human ears.

Senses Used to Our Advantage

These three vital senses possessed by the canine are all of use to man, hence why we have put the dog to

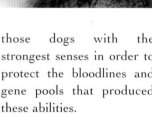

work in so many different environments. A guard dog needs to have excellent hearing in order to alert its master to an intruder; hunting dogs rely on either sight or scent, or in some cases both.

In order for us to exploit the canine senses, it has been necessary for us to breed those dogs with the strongest senses in order to protect the bloodlines and gene pools that produced these abilities.

Air-scenting is one of the tools used by the German Shorthaired Pointer to track wounded prey when working as a gun gog.

Skin and Coat

The general appearance of a dog is influenced largely by its coat. Coloration, length, and type of hair are often the only distinguishing features between two otherwise identical breeds. Nature has played its part in developing many varying types of coat and some breeds are noted particularly for the type of coat that they have. The skin of a dog tends to be the same from breed to breed, but there are certain variations and subtle differences that are the result of selective breeding and evolution.

Coat

The coat is the overall combination of fur or hair and the condition and appearance thereof. The health of a dog can be judged by the condition of the coat: a shiny, glossy coat indicates excellent health and good diet; a dull, patchy coat that is lacking luster points to ill health and a poor diet. The coat of a dog is determined by nature (for example, climate) and sometimes by selective breeding and the working role of the animal.

Fur

Almost all of the world's dogs are covered in fur, with the exception of certain

hairless breeds. The fur or hair serves the main purposes of protecting the skin from the elements and keeping the dog warm. There are two types of fur found on the coat of a dog: soft undercoat hair, which is commonly found in dogs that evolved in cold countries, such as the Siberian Husky; and guard hair, typically stiffer and coarser and there to protect the skin and undercoat from the cold.

Types of coat
Some dogs are double-coated, meaning that they have an abundance of undercoat and guard hair, while other breeds have only short, coarse guard hair. Certain breeds exist in long-coated and short-coated varieties, but this is due more to selective breeding than to evolution. The most common type of coat is short, as most dogs evolved in countries where short hair was necessary. Dogs that were regularly in water tend to have denser, often very curly hair that would have helped to keep them warm when swimming.

Shedding
Shedding is the process by which excess hair is expelled from the coat; this normally happens during the warmer months. Not all dogs shed their hair and Poodles are popular for this reason. Shedding is normally due to a dog evolving in a location that has extreme climates, such as central Europe. Dogs that evolved in the far north of Europe, such as the Spitz breeds, tend not to shed as much hair because they require a thick coat all-year round. Similarly, dogs that evolved in permanently hot countries tend not to shed as much.

Skin
The skin of the dog is rarely seen as it is almost always covered in fur. Some dogs have looser skin, which gives them a wrinkly appearance, while other dogs have noticeably tighter skin, often a result of

selective breeding because of the role that dog was intended to play. The skin of a dog is normally pinkish or white in complexion and should be free of dryness and irritation.

When observing skin types it becomes apparent just how much man has influenced the physical appearance of the dog. The Shar Pei has exceptionally loose skin, which can cause it severe health problems. This has happened because of man's desire for the breed, which was used for fighting, to be able to tolerate being bitten and to be able to move while another dog has a grip.

BELOW
Dogs from temperate climates tend to shed their fur most to deal with extremes of temperature. Chow Chows shed little.

Colors and Markings

The complex genetics associated with the canine species have created a whole host of interesting and attractive colorings. Many of the colors are referred to in their specificity to dogs, while others are merely standard colors. For every color, from the jet black of the Russian Black Terrier to the snow white of the Samoyed, there are a multitude of combinations and mixtures. Different colors and patterns are associated with different breeds and many dog types are often defined by the appearance of their coat.

Common Canine Colors
The most common colors found in modern dog breeds are black, white, brown, tan, and combinations of these. Some dogs exhibit lighter or darker shades of these colors, depending on breeding and genetics.
The coloration of many dogs is due to the presence of other breeds in the bloodline—for example, the Doberman inherited its distinctive black and tan coloration from the Rottweiler. Sometimes cross breeding two purebred dogs can result in new, or at least rare, colorations and patterns. Interestingly, a small number of dogs retain all of the physical attributes of one parent with the exception of coloration, which they inherit from the other. In these cases, the dog may look like a purebred breed in the "wrong" color, but it is in fact a crossbreed. It is rare for this to happen, but some new colors have been developed this way.

Unusual Canine Colors
Shades, such as apricot, lemon, chocolate, and merle, are more rare than the standard blacks and browns, but some dogs are associated strongly with these colorations. Spaniels, for example, come in a variety of colors, patterns, and color combinations. Some colorations are more unusual than others and occasionally breeders will be wary of dogs exhibiting rare colorations because it indicates a deviation from the typical standard.

Canine Patterns and Markings
Aside from color, dogs can be identified by their markings. The Dalmatian is well known for its spotted coat, which occurs in black and white and, less frequently, liver and white. Some types of Great Dane, notably the Harlequin Great Dane, also exhibit spotted coats.

Brindle, which appears as blended striping of two similar shades, is associated

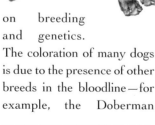

coats, as do many hunting hounds.

Patterns, such as merle, sable, and ticked, are often very striking—mixing lighter and darker shades of the same color or even contrasting colors ,such as black and white. It is often considered a departure from a breed standard for a dog not to display certain patterns.

What Do Colors Mean?

Nature often uses color in order for animals to understand the world and environment around them. While this does not hold true to the same extent in the canine world as it does with, for example, poisonous animals, it still has an effect.

The color of a dog is caused in the most part by genetics—environment and working role have much less to do with it. However, in certain instances color is

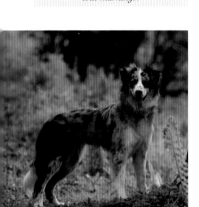

with certain breeds and is a very eye-catching pattern. Staffordshire Bull Terriers often exhibit wonderful brindle

associated directly with behavior and health. Dogs that are a solid white color are more prone to skin cancer than other dogs. The color white is also associated with deafness in many breeds, especially in Boxers. In cases where white is rare for a certain breed, differences in standard behavior

Fascinating Facts

Dog breeds that are white are more susceptible to cancer and other serious diseases than breeds that are not white.

may be present. For example, German Shepherd dogs are typically a mixture of brown, black, or gray, but occasionally all-white German Shepherds are born. The gene that gives the dog this coat of solid white is associated with instances of difficult behavior and extreme temperament.

Canine Terminology

There are many terms and phrases that are specific to dogs. In order for the dog to be referenced accurately in terms of form, shap,e and appearance, it is important to understand the specific names that are used.

Head and Skull Terminology

When discussing the physiology of the canine

head, certain terms are used to ensure that descriptions are accurate. Dog heads come in many different shapes and sizes and it is essential, for the purposes of breeding and conformation, that there are sufficiently accurate and descriptive terms.

Brachycephalic The type of skull that is broad with a short muzzle and flat face; Pugs are a good example of this.

Dolichocephalic A skull that is long and narrow; Greyhounds and Dobermans have this type of shape.

Flews The flews are the top lips, but this term is used more commonly to describe upper lips that happen to be pendulous and large, as seen on breeds from the Molosser family of dogs.

Mesatacephalic A medium-sized head, both in width and in length.

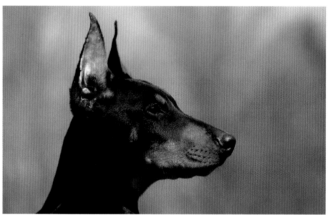

Bite The way a dog's jaw sits when the mouth is closed; a dog can have a level bite, an undershot bite, or an over-shot bite.

Occiput The highest point at the back of the skull, where the head and neck meet.

Stop A typically depressed area of the face above the muzzle.

Drop ears A description used for large, low-hanging ears, such as those of the Bloodhound or Bassett Hound.

Ear carriage This phrase is used in two contexts: first, it describes the way the ears of any given breed naturally sit on the head; and second, it refers to the movement of the dog's ears as it uses them to communicate mood.

Ears set on Dogs' ears are set either on high, on low, or on wide.

Ear feather The specific growth of thick fur on the outer ears, as seen in some breeds, such as Springer and Cocker Spaniels.

Prick ears Prick ears stand erect and are set on high;

examples include Spitz-type dogs and the German Shepherd dog.

Body Terminology

When talking about the body of a dog, people often refer to body parts and areas in human terms. Although this is applicable in some contexts, the shape of a dog's body and the fact that it is not upright or bipedal means that there are parts that don't exist in the human form, and there are specific terms that refer to these parts.

Similarly, there are terms that are used to differentiate context. When talking about dogs in general it may be acceptable to refer to chest or shoulders. But when talking about the physiology of the canine, it is much more appropriate to use the correct terminology, such as brisket and withers.

Brisket The chest, specifically when mentioning the appearance and shape of the outer chest.

Hock A joint found on the hind leg roughly where the knee would be, although it is more comparable to the heel in function.

Topline The line of the spine as it runs from the neck to the tail.

referred to as nails or toenails. The term claw is more common when referring to the nails when used all together, in the same way that the human hand is referred to as a fist when all fingers are in use.

Quick Canine toenails contain a blood vessel called the quick; when grooming it is essential not to cut the quick but to trim the nail just below it.

Tail Terminology

Tails can be short, long, well coated, and come in many different shapes. There are a handful of terms that are used when referring to the tail of a dog.

Tapered A tail that gets thinner toward the end.

Docked A tail that has had part or most of it removed by a cosmetic or veterinary process.

Screw tail A short, curly tail.

Bob tail A short stumpy tail, as found on the Pembroke Welsh Corgi.

Dewlap The fold of skin that hangs below the lower jaw; it is more prominent in heavier breeds with looser skin, such as the Bull Mastiff.

Withers The highest point of the dog aside from the head, where the shoulders would be on a human. This is the point to which dogs are typically measured.

Shoulders The shoulders on a dog are located at the front, where the top of the foreleg meets the brisket.

Loin The area around the lower ribs and pelvis, where the genitals are located.

Forequarters Terminology

Due to the fact that the fore- and hind legs look and work differently, it is very important to be able to differentiate between the different parts of the limbs. The front legs bend backward at the pastern, while the hind legs should not bend.

Foreleg The anatomical term for the front leg, which is formed and functions differently from the hind leg.

Pastern The part of the foreleg where the limb bends above the paw.

Paw The base of the dog's foot.

Paw pad The leathery parts of the sole of the paw.

Toes Dogs typically have three toes on each foot but sometimes there are four, depending on breeding.

Dewclaw This is considered to be an additional toe, located above the foot, which occurs in some breeds.

Hare foot A foot that has two elongated middle toes; breeds with this feature include the Greyhound and the Borzoi.

Webbed Some dogs, notably those bred for water work, such as the Field Spaniel and the Newfoundland, have webbed feet, which enable greater propulsion through the water.

Nails Claws sometimes are

Coat Terminology

There is a multitude of coats found among the various dog breeds. In most cases, simple descriptions are inadequate and it is necessary to use the correct terms when describing a dog's coat.

Corded A coat that grows in such a way that it becomes intertwined; this type of coat is found on the Komondor—a very distinctive-looking herding dog.

Single coat Any coat that lacks an undercoat is single coated.

Jacket Dogs with a short coat, such as the Staffordshire Bull Terrier, are described as having a jacket.

Mane This describes the growth of hair around the back of the neck when it is out of proportion with the hair growth on other parts of the body; the Leonberger is a breed with a mane.

Plume A heavily feathered tail that is carried over the back is described as a plume; the Bichon Frise has a plumed tail.

Stand-off coat This describes the type of coat in which the hairs stick out, almost as if they have been blow-dried.

Topknot The topknot is a tuft of hair on the top of the head, as found on the Afghan Hound.

Double coat Found on dogs from cold climates, a double coat features both underhairs and guard hairs.

Feathered Feathering of a coat occurs at the ears, tail and various other parts of some breeds, such as a Saluki.

Flag This describes long tufts of hair on the tail.

BEHAVIOR

Throughout man's long relationship with the dog, an understanding of their emotional, physical, and environmental needs has developed. The dog is no longer a wild hunter, but a tame and adaptable companion. Through domestication, dogs have become more sensitive to the human environment and, in turn, man has taken a closer interest in the way dogs function and behave. An understanding of the behavioral patterns of these animals is essential for any dog owner, and is particularly useful when deciding which breed to buy.

Intelligence and Psychology

Cognition is a scientifically accepted concept used for measuring the relative intelligence of animals, and the dog has been proved to be one of the most intelligent animals on the earth. Dogs display certain behaviors, such as problem solving and decision making, which mark them out as being particularly intelligent. While intelligence is a broad concept to apply, it is true to say that the dog as a species has a high level of intelligence. The Border Collie is believed to be the most intelligent breed of all.

ABOVE
It is the ability to remember instructions that make even young puppies trainable in a variety of skills.

Learning

To learn and develop new skills, animals must possess the ability to process information. The dog has the requisite mental capacity for developing and remembering new skills. For example, a dog can be trained to perform any number of functions in response to a given stimulus. In order to do this, a process called operant conditioning comes into force, by which patterns of association are made between actions and consequences.

Cognition

A dog will associate actions, functions, and operants with stimuli and consequences. For example, if a dog puts its paw on a hot surface, it will remember that putting its paw in that place results in physical pain and will, therefore, if it is wise, not do the same thing again. While

Fascinating Facts

The Russian psychologist Ivan Pavlov (1849–1936) used his dogs to develop the concept of classical conditioning, a process that now forms the basis of modern dog training.

it will not understand the concept of either heat or pain, it will make a connection between the action and the consequence. However, if the dog puts its paw on a hot surface while somebody blows a whistle, the dog is just as likely to associate the sound of the whistle with the consequence of pain as it is to associate it with the act of putting its paw on the hot surface. This concept enables us to manipulate the dog's actions through various stimuli.

Instincts

Through the process of evolution, nature has equipped the canine with a set of instincts that have enabled it to survive as a species. Almost all of the instincts we witness in domestic pet dogs are retained from previous generations of wild dogs. While certain instincts may relate to territory, reproduction, food, or dominance, each instinct is inextricably linked back to the survival of the species. Protection of the weak, such

Fascinating Facts

Every dog's behavior is governed by its latent instinct for survival; undesirable actions, such as digging and howling, derive from the behavior of dogs in the wild.

as puppies, dominance over inferiors, and howling are all instinctive behaviors.

Food
Dogs see all food as their food; this is because

nature has taught them to eat whatever they can. Sometimes this instinct will overpower all other stimuli, such as training and distraction. Each dog is governed more strongly by certain instincts, but all instincts relate to survival. Aggression around food is instinctive for some dogs but this may be overridden by the instinct to avoid conflict, which is why some dogs give in if challenged for food.

Reproduction
To enable a species to thrive and survive, the strongest must breed. The female is instinctively driven to mate with the strongest and healthiest male she can find, typically the alpha male in the pack. All males are driven to mate with whichever female they can in order to continue their bloodline. Nature gave every dog the need to reproduce so that the competition among

them would ensure the strongest thrived.

Protection
Instincts, such as turning around before lying down, sleeping in a curled up position, or puffing out the chest when frightened, are all related to the dog's need to protect itself. By turning around before settling, a dog is subconsciously ensuring that nothing dangerous is about before it rests. The habit of sleeping in a curled up position is done in order to protect vital organs when vulnerable.

Fascinating Facts

If a dog sleeps on its back, it is a sign that the dog feels safe and secure. In the wild, dogs curl up to protect their vital organs in the event of an attack.

Communication

Dogs communicate in a sophisticated and clear manner. The majority of canine communication is done via body language: eye movement, body shape, ear position, and even tail height are all very clear signs that other dogs will easily understand. Barking, growling, and howling are used far less frequently as a means of communication than body language. Much of the dog's language is derived from instinct—even puppies will display communicative body language within the litter, and this often helps establish pack order.

ABOVE

Dogs' tails are vital in communicating with other dogs; a tail sticking straight out indicates aggression. A dog may also attempt to out-stare another dog to establish dominance.

Aggression

Signs of aggression are more subtle than people realize. Before a dog resorts to growling or biting, it will have given many warning signs. Holding its gaze, licking its lips, and holding its tail high outward are all signs that a dog is feeling threatened. The main instinct when feeling threatened is to avoid

violence; this is done by communicating an intention to act if and when called for.

Fear

If a dog is scared, it may display this in a number of possible ways. Some dogs will become submissive, exposing their stomach and, therefore, their vital organs in an act that shows that they are not a threat. Other dogs will become defensive and may bark, growl, or bare their teeth. Barking is a language in and of itself— each type of bark has its own meaning: loud, constantly

repeated barks signal the intention to make an aggressive move; high-pitched, intermittent barking is a sign of fear but with less intention of acting in defense.

Dominance

Dogs need to know who is the more dominant. A submissive dog will never attempt to dominate a more superior dog. Dominance is communicated through posture, head position, body language, and general actions. A dominant dog may indicate its superiority by pushing past an inferior dog or may do so by holding the gaze of another dog until the inferior animal looks away.

Breed Differences and Personality Types

Personality differs from dog to dog, but it differs even more so from breed to breed. Certain breeds are associated with certain types

Fascinating Facts

Dogs with docked tails are more likely to become involved in confrontations with other dogs. This is due to their limited ability to use their tail to communicate.

of behavior and personality, and these attributes can be traced back to the working roles of that particular breed. In some cases, dogs demonstrate atypical personality attributes for their breed. All dogs share some very important personality traits, such as a drive to eat, reproduce, and protect, but other attributes are more specific a breed.

Intelligence

Intelligence is associated with working pastoral and herding breeds, such as the Border Collie and German Shepherd. Due to the breeding stock that was initially used and the type of work the dogs are used to doing, any dog that has a history of droving or herding will be of above-average intelligence.

BELOW
Border Collies are famed for their intelligence.

Aggression

Aggression is present in all breeds, because it is linked to the survival instinct, but some dogs are more prone to becoming aggressive more easily. These tend to be breeds that were bred originally for guarding or for fighting because their ancestors were selected especially because of their propensity for aggression.

Loyalty

Almost every breed is inherently loyal, with the possible exception of a few breeds that are used for lone hunting. Hound breeds are likely to be more loyal than most dogs, often to the exclusion of other family members. The Greyhound is known for its devotion; this is because of the natural inclination the dog

Fascinating Facts

Wearing sunglasses around a dog increases a person's chances of being bitten. To a dog, it appears that the person wearing sunglasses is staring directly at them, and in the canine world this is threatening.

has to form a partnership with a master due to its working origins.

Tenacity

Tenacity, manifested either in play or work, is most prevalent in terrier breeds. Terriers were required to be hard, energetic workers, so only the ones with the right skills were used for breeding, meaning that the terriers of today typically display a great deal of tenacity and vigor.

Care
&
Management

BECOMING A DOG OWNER

Dog ownership is a big commitment. There are hundreds of thousands of dogs in rescue shelters around the world because people did not do their research before acquiring a dog. Owning a dog is not just about picking a cute pup and taking it home; a responsible dog owner will consider a whole host of factors before making the decision to buy. The size of your home, the people in your family (whether you have children, for example), the amount of free time you have, and even the nature of your work can have a large influence on your suitability as a dog owner.

Points to Consider

Sharing your life with a dog is fulfilling, rewarding, and fun. But good dog ownership starts even before you choose a breed. A good dog owner will research what type of dog he or she is best equipped to look after. Dogs have differing requirements and personalities—some dogs require a lot of exercise, food, and space, while others are more laid back and prefer a quiet life. Knowing what you can realistically offer a dog in terms of care is the first step in finding the right dog for you. A good dog owner will also be confident that they can afford the veterinary bills, food, and

grooming costs associated with dog ownership over the animal's entire lifetime.

Puppy or Adult?

The joy of bringing home a new puppy is hard to match. But getting an older dog has many advantages, too. In most cases, older dogs are already housebroken and have a history that enables new dog owners to make more informed choices regarding suitability. With so many older dogs in rescue homes, there is a wide choice of breeds and ages for prospective dog owners to choose from, and the cost is

often much lower than that of buying a puppy. In some cases, dogs at a rescue center are "free to a good home."

BECOMING A DOG OWNER

often breed-specific—rescue homes usually take a profile of prospective owners, and then match a specific dog to you to avoid "returns" as much as possible.

From a Friend

You may choose to take a puppy from a dog with which you are already familiar. The advantage of this is that you will know the parent dogs and can make a better judgement of how the puppy is likely to turn out.

ABOVE

Do proper research into which breed will suit you before visiting an adorable litter that will be hard to resist.

Finding Your Dog

There are numerous ways a potential dog owner can go about finding the right dog for him or her, but you have to be sure that you are properly equipped in terms of time, space, lifestyle, and funds before beginning the search. It is easier to decide that you are not quite ready for dog ownership prior to seeing a lot of adorable pups. Once the decision is made to get a dog, it is important to find out what breed, sex, age, and type will suit you.

Breeder

Although you can purchase a puppy from a pet store, buying directly from a breeder can have many benefits. A breeder is often enthusiastic about the breed

he or she specializes in and will be prepared to give plenty of advice. If you buy a dog from a breeder, he or she should be able to show you the puppies with their mother. This will allow you to see how each litter member interacts, thus enabling you to pick the one with the personality that best complements your situation. Breeders typically breed for the love of the dog, rather than for money, so do not be surprised if the breeder you visit bases his or her operations at home. The breeder may also ask for your references, and some insist on visiting potential homes. Make sure you ask a lot of questions, and do not select a dog until you are absolutely sure.

Rescue Center or Shelter

Some people prefer to get their dog from a shelter or rescue center. These places are home to many types of dogs, of varying breeds, ages, and backgrounds.

Some may have been abandoned or mistreated, so seek advice from the staff on which dogs may be more challenging. There will also be a good number of older dogs looking for a home; these will be housebroken and less active than pups.

Before handing over a dog, all good shelters will require a visit to your home to ensure that your setup is suitable. Also, the better—

BELOW

An older dog from a rescue group can be great choice, but ask about any potential behaviorial problems.

ACCOMMODATING YOUR DOG

There are a handful of important things to do before you are ready to receive your dog. These issues relate to health, safety, and good animal husbandry and care. Speaking to the breeder and other experienced dog owners is a good first step. It is essential to decide before receiving a dog into your home where your dog will sleep, what access it will have to other parts of the house, and how it will be transported.

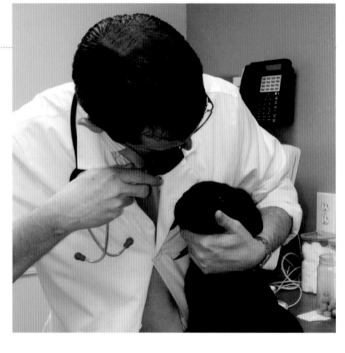

dog; speak to others and be prepared to respond to your pet's individual needs.

Health

When choosing a dog, especially a purebred, you should endeavor to get as much information relating to health as possible. Hip scores (points-based scores indicating the risk or levels of hip dysplasia, achieved by assessing radiographs of the dog's hips) and other health information should be readily available from the breeder. Also be aware of breed-specific problems, such as heart complaints in Bulldogs and skin problems in Bull Mastiffs.

It is essential to research the veterinarians in your area—knowing where the nearest

one is will be useful but ensure that you research all of your options. Veterinary prices and services vary greatly, so ensure that you find a vet with whom you are comfortable. You will need a vet to give vaccinations if you are bringing home a puppy.

Safety

Before you bring home your dog, you should be aware of the likely behavior of the breed. Being equipped with this information will enable you to make judgments pertaining to safety. Removing any potential hazards from the immediate vicinity is essential. Be aware of which items and areas the new dog is showing an interest in. Many dogs like to investigate fireplaces because of the smells— obviously this is a bad habit for the dog to get into.

ABOVE

Many purebred dogs have tendencies to a health weakness of some sort or other; Bulldogs are prone to heart disease.

First Things First

There are a number of things to consider before bringing a dog into your life. Research and planning are essential to providing good care for your

LEFT

Dogs often enjoy the warmth of a fire, choosing prime position. A fire guard is essential with a curious pup.

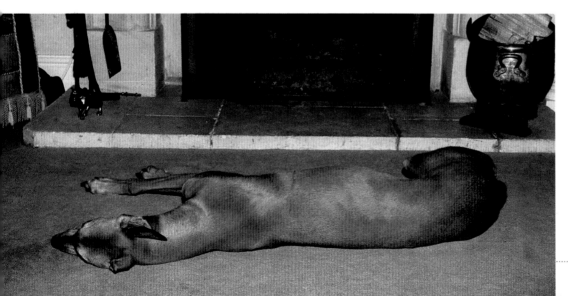

Your Dog's Environment

Prior to bringing your new dog home it is essential to ensure that your house or apartment is dog- or puppy-friendly. This means that it must be safe, comfortable, and conducive to good mental health. Common sense dictates many of the necessary steps in preparing your home, but also seek advice from other dog owners. It is not essential that all dogs have access to a large yard, but it must be possible for dogs to be given fresh air, exercise, and stimulation regularly. Dogs need to relieve themselves several times a day. Thus, for example, if you go out to work all day, you must take your dog out in the morning before you leave, as soon as you return home, and again before bedtime. During the day, it should be let out by someone, or perhaps have access to outdoors via a dog-flap. But, ideally a dog is never left alone all day.

Bed or Sleeping Area

For it to be happy, the dog must have an area of the home that it can call its own. This is typically a dog bed or basket located in a quiet part of the house. The area must be clean, preferably near to an outside door to aid house-breaking and free from hazardous objects, such as potentially poisonous plants. Your dog must feel safe and secure in this area.

Out-of-Bounds Areas

Deciding before its arrival in the home where the dog is allowed to go and making sure that this can be enforced is essential. Some people prefer to give their dog a free reign, but it is wise to limit a dog's access to certain areas, such as the garage, stairs, workshops, sheds, and any area used to store tools. A child safety gate is a good method of restricting access to certain parts of the home.

Any area where the dog could feasibly escape should be classed as out-of-bounds. Broken fences, low walls, and open driveways should be rendered inaccessible for a dog. Use discouragement training methods to ensure that the dog is not tempted to wander out of the yard.

RIGHT

The boundaries of your yard should be dogproof to prevent your dog from straying or getting injured by traffic. These dogs could easily squeeze or dig under this gate if they really wanted. It should have some strong plastic-coated mesh attached to the bottom.

The Feeding Area

The area where the dog is fed must be clean and free from distractions. Many dogs are territorial and protective when eating, so any area that is busy, such as the kitchen, is not necessarily suitable as a dog-feeding area.

Nature has taught dogs to keep their immediate environment, known as the den, clean and tidy. It is essential when house-breaking a dog that it is not forced or encouraged to go to the toilet in or near the area where it sleeps and eats. This is counterinstinctive and will cause distress to a dog, especially a brood bitch.

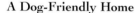

A Dog-Friendly Home

A dog's home needs to be secure, clean, and safe. Sharp corners and slippery surfaces are potentially hazardous for a dog. Large breeds often struggle to keep their footing across polished or smooth surfaces; however, many dog owners prefer smooth surfaces, such as wood or tiles, for ease of cleaning. Putting down a rug on a slippery floor is a good way of getting around this problem. The corners of low work units are difficult to avoid, but discouraging your dog from encountering

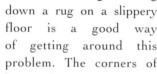

such hazards can be achieved by placing his bed away from such areas.

A Dog-Friendly Yard

Ponds and pools must be made safe. Dogs may have no difficulty jumping into the water, but getting out if the sides are steep is difficult.

Never leave a dog unsupervised in or near water and use training to discourage your dog from exploring water features.

A yard should be free from other hazards, such as poisonous vegetation and gravel, particularly loosely packed gravel that can become stuck in between a dog's paw pads, leading to infection and discomfort. Ensure that your yard takes into account a dog's inquisitive nature.

Traveling and Boarding

Dog ownership, being the large commitment that it is, requires the owner to make many major lifestyle choices (such as vacation destination and even the type of car he or she drives) with the needs of the pet in mind. Many people choose to vacation domestically so that they can bring their dog along; others choose to board their dog while they are away. There are numerous

factors to consider that affect both choices and sufficient research and planning is essential.

Traveling

Traveling with a dog can be easy, but it is necessary to provide a safe, secure place in the car so that the dog is restrained. Crates, canine car seats, or improvised rear-storage spaces, provided they are safe, are all popular means of transporting a dog. Large breeds offer more problems when traveling, because often they do not fit comfortably into crates.

It is a good idea to introduce your dog to the car prior to making that first journey. This ensures that the dog is familiar with the environment before undergoing the new and highly stimulating experience of car travel. Taking some treats along is also advisable, as is taking some familiar bedding that will smell like their 'territory'.

Boarding

Sometimes it is necessary to put a dog into boarding accommodation. Many dog

owners try to avoid this scenario, but in reality a boarding kennel is often preferable to leaving a dog with an inexperienced friend or relative.

Ensure that you speak to, meet, and inspect the premises of any boarding-kennel owner or manager before committing your dog to their care. Following one's instincts with regards to boarding kennels is a good idea; if a place does not feel right then find somewhere

else. It is absolutely essential that the boarding staff are aware of any medical and feeding requirements your dog may have.

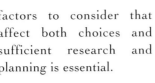

Dogs that are left in places without ventilation, such as cars, are not able to regulate their own body temperature and are at risk of death.

ESSENTIAL EQUIPMENT

Becoming a dog owner brings with it an obligation to invest in essential items to provide good animal care. Toys, grooming tools, feeding paraphernalia, and other items—as well as the dog food itself—do not come cheap, so it is a good idea to budget for these items before committing to bringing a dog into your home. Depending on the breed of your dog, certain speciality items may be necessary, such as sophisticated grooming items or a special harness; researching which items will be needed is essential.

RIGHT

Metal food bowls are hygienic and unbreakable. But if you have a medium or large-size dog, it is liable to tip over such lightweight bowls.

Grooming

Some dogs require far less grooming than others, but it is important for all dogs to be groomed, even if it is just a quick comb through of the coat to remove dead skin, dirt, and excess hairs. Depending on the level of grooming, the equipment can be relatively cheap or fairly expensive.

Coat The coat may be groomed with a slicker brush or a stiff metal comb, depending on coat type.

Cleanliness It is important to bathe dogs, but not too regularly. Special shampoos and conditioners are available.

Claws Trimming the claws can be done at home or by a vet or groomer. Normally a pair of standard dog nail clippers is sufficient. It is essential you know what you are doing, and do not cut into the quick of the dog's claws.

Feeding Equipment

The environment in which a dog feeds must be clean and free from hazards. It is always best to invest in good-quality items that your dog will come to associate with feeding time.

Metal food and water bowl A metal food bowl is easy to clean, durable, and

lightweight. There must be a separate bowl for water and this must be kept filled up with fresh, clean water throughout the day.

Ceramic food bowl Ceramic bowls are heavier and, therefore, stay in place when the dog is eating from them. Larger dogs need heavier bowls, otherwise they can tip food all over the floor and create a hazard. Ceramic food bowls are more difficult to clean than metal. Due to a dog's extremely sensitive nose, any food residue that is decaying on a ceramic bowl can cause a dog to be put of its food, so you must double-check that you have cleaned it thoroughly.

Food dispenser Keeping a dog's food fresh and free from bugs and insects is essential. Vermin are often attracted to pet food if it is left in a bag in the garage. A plastic, closable food dispenser keeps the food fresh and untainted.

Other Essential Equipment

Apart from grooming and feeding equipment, there are other items that will be vital for your dog's safety and happiness.

Collar and leash These come in many styles and designs. Large and strong breeds may be better suited to a harness, which enables more control. A retractable

Fascinating
Facts

The average cost of owning
a dog in the United States
is more than $25,300 per
dog over its lifetime. This
includes veterinary bills,
food, and toys.

Dogs require a number of toys that stimulate them in different ways to prevent boredom. Investing in good-quality, durable toys is more economical over time.

Toys that are designed to reward the dog, such as those that contain food, are good for keeping the dog entertained. A ball is a popular toy, but some dogs will simply chew it rather than fetch it.

favor having a microchip implanted into the dog's skin. This contains all of the information required should a dog be found, which is read by a scanner and traced back to the owner. The benefit of this is that it cannot fall off.

leash is good for giving a run to a dog that cannot be trusted off the leash. Seek advice from a trusted seller or vet, because some collars are not suitable for some breeds and can be dangerous.

Identity All dogs should carry some form of identification in case they get lost. A simple name tag attached to the collar is useful, provided that the details are up-to-date. Alternatively, many people

Toys Money spent on toys and training equipment should be budgeted for.

ABOVE
Dog toys and chews are vital to prevent your dog from getting bored and while teething as a puppy.

RIGHT
An identity tag on a collar is very useful should your dog become lost. Check it often, however, because the tags can come off.

PUPPY CARE

Caring for a newborn puppy is not something that an untrained and inexperienced person should attempt to do. Puppies should never be separated from their mother before eight weeks after birth. The mother is the best source of food, protection, and nurturing that the puppy can have. It is counterproductive to remove the puppy from the mother unless due to illness or the mother otherwise being unable to care for the litter, in which case hand rearing may be necessary.

Feeding

For the first weeks of their life, puppies suckle at the mother's teat. This is their only source of food at this time and they get all of the nutrients they need from the mother's milk. Newborn and very young puppies do not have teeth. This is because their bodies are not able to tolerate solid food and also because it would cause pain to the nursing bitch.

It is important that a puppy is not weaned from its mother too soon—that is, before six weeks. In order to wean the puppy, it is essential to allow it to come off the teat in its own time. Allowing it access to, but not forcing it to eat its mother's solid meals, is a suitable method of encouraging the pup to

wean. Dogs may also take small amounts of water, as well as mother's milk during the weaning process.

Hand Rearing

When caring for a young pup in a domestic situation, it is essential that the owner fulfills the role of hunter-gatherer. Providing suitable puppy food and formula is essential. Puppies grow extremely quickly and

their nutritional needs change rapidly.

The best way to judge the success of hand rearing a puppy is to observe the young dog's condition, behavior, and energy levels. If it attempts to suckle

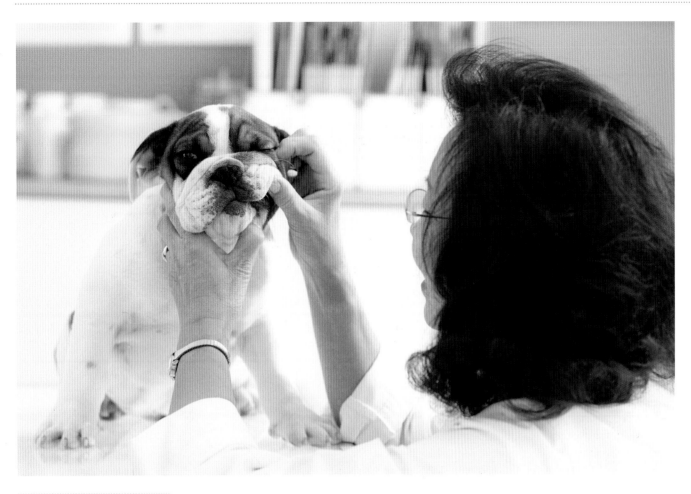

continually, this can be a sign that it is not getting sufficient sustenance from its mother and, therefore, will need supplementing with other food.

Vets

Vets are a valuable source of information, advice, and guidance for owners of young puppies. They are on hand, if required, to monitor the growth and progress of the pup. Weighing the puppy and checking its responses to certain stimuli will give a good indication of general health and well-being.

The vet will also administer vaccinations for the puppy that protect against harmful diseases, such as parvovirus, distemper, and leptospirosis. He or she will also treat the puppy for worms and other parasites. Be sure to keep an up-to-date record of the vaccinations that your puppy has received, and do not let the dog out to mix with other dogs until all vaccinations are completed.

Setting Up Home

When puppies are removed from the litter and the mother they can become distressed and disorientated. It is essential that the pup's progress is monitored during this stage. One way of making the transition from being in a litter to being in a new and unfamiliar home is to ensure that your own home provides adequate warmth, security, peace, and privacy for the puppy to become accustomed to its new environment.

In the wild, puppies are raised in a den. Mimicking a den environment will, to a certain extent, help the puppies accept their new surroundings. Some puppies will make the transition seamlessly and will investigate the new smells and sights of your home with interest. Other puppies will be a little more timid. Whichever way it happens, all puppies will need a clean, warm, and comfortable area to call their own in which they can sleep.

TRAINING AND EXERCISE

F or a dog to be happy in the domestic environment, it needs to be secure of the boundaries and rules that limit behavior. This is why obedience- and housebreaking are essential. Training can begin in earnest when the puppy is brought home, but this should involve encouraging the puppy to do the right thing, rather than attempting to teach it to obey commands. The best way to aid training is to begin as you mean to go on—consistency is the key.

Early Learning and Exercise

Probably the first thing that owners will be keen to teach their puppy is knowing where and when to go. Patience, a good routine, and a balance of discipline and reward should make this and any other learning process reasonably straightforward. Letting your dog exercise through play and by taking it for regular walks will also aid training and obedience.

Housebreaking

Due to their young age and limited capacity for self-control, puppies will have accidents and relieve themselves in the wrong place. The key is not to make a fuss. Putting down newspaper (ensuring it is not close to where the puppy eats or sleeps) should encourage the dog to go in the same place.

It will be necessary on the first few occasions to place the pup on the paper when it is exhibiting the signs of needing to relieve itself. These signs may include sniffing at a door, turning in circles, whining, or sniffing

ABOVE
When housebreaking your puppy it is vital to be calm and consistent and to reward him for going in the correct place.

BELOW
Puppies are naturally inquisitive and full of play—they will happily scamper about exercising themselves. Parson Russell Terrier puppies.

the ground. If you suspect the pup needs to go, gently and without excitement guide it to the newspaper. When the puppy relieves itself appropriately reward it. Never rub a dog's nose in the mess if it accidentally goes in the wrong place. This is cruel and does nothing to encourage housebreaking.

Routine
Establishing a solid routine is essential to help the puppy adapt to domestic life. Planning for the dog to relieve itself after waking up and after eating is important, as it increases the chances of it going in the right place.

Letting the dog outside after eating is important, but this

Fascinating Facts

Using a rolled-up newspaper to discipline a dog is pointless. The only result will be that the dog is scared of the newspaper.

should wait until the dog is ready to go outside. Encouraging the dog to exercise may not be needed at first, because puppies tend to be full of energy for short periods of time, during which they will romp and play until exhaustion.

Rewards

Rewarding a dog's good behavior is far more effective than punishing bad behavior. It the dog does misbehave, putting it in its basket or removing a toy tends to be enough. Praise, food, and play are all rewarding to dogs, and

theses all can be used as encouragement during basic training.

Discipline

It is very simple to discipline a dog. Provided that the discipline is even-handed, fair, and consistent, the dog will learn quickly. By judging what motivates a particular dog, it is possible to find the most effective method of discipline. Some dogs respond more to noise, others to sensation, such as being pulled gently, for example if they are pulling on the leash. If the dog does something wrong, issue the

correction, whether it is in the form of a verbal command, such as "No," a gentle smack on the rump, or an aural stimulus, such as whistle or clicker, in a timely and clear fashion. Punishing a dog too long after the deed is ineffective and confusing.

Walking and Play

Puppies will play instinctively—it is how they interact with other puppies in the litter. Walking on a leash, however, is counter-instinctive and, therefore, requires training and encouragement. Start the process by letting the dog become familiar with the leash; then, on a loose leash, allow the dog to wander around. Gently guide it back if it wanders too far, while issuing the "heel" command. As the puppy becomes used to the leash, gradually shorten it until you have complete control over the dog. Combine walking on the leash with general obedience training.

ABOVE

Puppies are very responsive to your displeasure; be consistent and calm when admonishing them.

Obedience and Further Training

Obedience is the cornerstone of the dog's history of cooperation with man. Without obedience, dogs would not have performed any of the valuable functions we needed them to.

Dogs are driven by instinct and environment; some of the things we ask them to do are counterinstinctive, such as sitting, which is why we need to train them to do so. Establishing the favor and cooperation of a dog takes time and patience, but is very rewarding.

The "Sit" Command

The "sit" command is probably the first command a dog can master. It is easily achieved through a combination of positive reinforcement and encouragement.

Teaching a dog to sit should be done in a calm and distraction-free environment.

Capturing the dog's attention is the most important thing to do. Follow this by repeating the "sit" command while encouraging the dog to sit. This can be done by standing in a position where it is more comfortable for the dog to sit in order to see, perhaps by leaning over the dog, or by gently pushing the rump to the ground. Once the dog hits the sit position, issue praise and reward to the dog so that it associates its action with the positive consequence. Also ensure that it associates your command with the action.

The "Down" Command

Once you have mastered the "sit" command, you can move on to the "down" command. A clever way of achieving this command is by placing a treat in a place where the dog needs to lay down to get it, perhaps under your legs if you are sitting on the ground. The dog will be focused on the treat, but as it attempts to get the treat issue the "down" command. As soon as it hits the floor, let it have the treat.

Fascinating Facts

Dogs can be taught commands in more than one language. This enables them to work in different countries under different handlers.

Controlling Bad Behavior

Many of the canine's natural instincts are not suited to the domestic environment. Digging and howling, for example, may have served the dog well in the wild but are problematic for dogs living alongside humans. Much bad behavior associated with domestic dogs is not instinctive but rather the result of the dog pushing its luck to see how far it can go before being corrected. It is often linked to food and access to mates.

Bad Habits

Bad canine habits, such as climbing on furniture or scratching at the door, can easily be controlled. Simply ensure that the dog understands that each time it performs such an action there will be a

negative consequence. For practical reasons, it is always preferable that the negative consequence is your voice issuing the "No" command.

Inappropriate Behavior

Certain actions, such as jumping up at people, incessant barking, and digging are inappropriate and can lead to wider problems if left uncorrected. Discouragement and prevention are preferable to punishment. Manufacturing a situation in which a dog is not tempted to misbehave is a good way of rewarding positive behavior rather than punishing bad behavioor. Consistency is the key to disrupting bad behavior patterns. If something is

unacceptable, it should be unacceptable at all times. Dogs will become confused if they get away with an action in one situation but are punished for it in another situation. To do so is cruel and counterproductive.

Aggression

All dogs are capable of acting aggressively, which is why it is essential to correct and discourage such behavior. The dog should understand its place in the pack or family

and, therefore, should not feel the need to act aggressively. It is essential that you respond to aggression confidently, but not aggressively, because this can exacerbate the situation.

FEEDING

The dog has evolved into a fairly adaptable eater. In the wild, dogs would hunt and kill their prey, but, in the domestic environment, their food is often bought at the supermarket. Despite this, the nutritional needs of the canine have not changed. The main part of the diet is meat, with cereals, vegetation, fish, some dairy, and roughage also required. The food may be all natural or commercial, served in one portion or throughout the day.

Nutritional Needs

It is essential for a dog owner to provide a balanced and nutritional diet for their pet. There are a number of components that should always be present, as well as a few that should be avoided at all costs.

Protein Dogs receive protein through foods, such as chicken and meat.

Fat Fat is an essential part of the canine diet, especially for puppies. Meat and fish are good sources of fat.

Calcium Eggs and milk are a good source of calcium.

Fiber Brown rice and oats contain fiber.

Vitamins Parsley and seaweed are good sources of vitamins A, C, and E.

Harmful food Grapes, raisins, and chocolate are all harmful to dogs.

Feeding Techniques

There are various methods by which an owner can deliver the right nutrients to a dog. The technique with which a dog is fed often depends on the breed, and the role and the age of the dog. Other considerations related to feeding technique include the type of diet that the dog is on, any specific health requirements, and its personality.

Regular Meals

Most owners prefer to feed their dogs at regular intervals. This enables the owner to control more closely the exact intake of nutrients throughout the day, as well as ensuring that the dog has something to look forward to.

One Meal

Some dogs receive just one meal a day, typically in the evening. This is usually quite a large portion, depending on the breed, and contains all of the daily recommended vitamins and nutrients. The practice of feeding one meal per day is suitable for dogs with high energy levels and for dogs that work.

Comfort

If you have a large or tall dog, such as a Great Dane, or any of the larger hounds, it will be more comfortable for them—and will ease digestion—if their food bowl is placed on a small shelf or stool, so that they do not have to stoop.

More than One Dog

Dogs are instinctively competitive over food. So if you have more than one dog, it is important to give each dog the same, and always separate, feeding spot. Separate dogs with a child gate, or by placing them in different rooms if necessary.

Free Feeding

Working dogs are often given a carcass or lump of meat to gorge on. This is analogous to the way dogs feed in the wild.

Food Types

Depending on breed, activity level, age, and owner preference, there are many types of food a dog can eat. Some dogs have special dietary requirements that limit which types of food they can have, but most dogs are adaptable and will eat whatever is put down for them. Some owners prefer to stick to a natural diet, which tends to involve more preparation and expense, while others prefer to give a commercial diet that is cheaper and more convenient.

Complete Food
A commercially available complete food is designed to deliver all of the required nutrients; there is no need for supplements, such as biscuits or kibble. These products are normally marketed as meals. Complete food is typically packaged in a can or a sachet and is moist, although dry food with meat in it is also classed as "complete."

Dry Food
Dry food is designed to be complementary to other food types, such as meat. It is normally in the form of a biscuit and is good for friction, which helps to clean the teeth of the dog. Feeding a meat and mixer diet, such as organ meats and dry food, is now less common, because people find complete food more convenient.

Fresh Food
Some dog owners prefer to feed their dogs entirely on fresh produce. Meat and vegetables mixed with some dry food is a popular meal for domestic dogs. This is typically a more messy and expensive method of feeding, but in general is more appealing to the dog.

Raw Food
Because traditionally dogs ate raw food in the wild, some people prefer to feed a raw diet. Raw meat, while being messy and inconvenient, is very appealing to a dog and, because it is uncooked, it contains many enzymes that are valuable to aid digestion in dogs. Raw dog meat often comes in the form of butchers' scraps.

ABOVE
These domesticated working dogs are gorging on hunks of fresh meat, more akin to their diet in the wild.

ABOVE RIGHT
While, as dog owners, we may not find it as cheap or convenient, dogs really enjoy raw meat and it suits their digestive system.

BELOW
Complete processed meals for dogs can be bought moist in sachets or cans, or dry as kibble.

Fascinating Facts

British dog owners spend an average of £3,360 ($6,500) on food during the lifetime of their dog.

FEEDING

89

GROOMING

Grooming is essential to your dog's overall health and well-being. Parasitic infestations and tangled fur are extremely distressing and unpleasant for dogs; this scenario is easily avoided with regular and thorough grooming. Longhaired breeds obviously require more grooming than shorthaired breeds, but a basic level of grooming, with good-quality, suitable tools, is required by all dogs. Grooming is also a good way for a dog owner to bond with their pet.

Grooming Kit

There are some items that are essential equipment for grooming and others that are optional, depending on the type of dog or preference of the owner.

Slicker brush Used for brushing out dirt and tangles from a dog's fur. Not

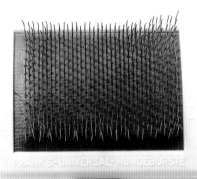

necessary for use on short-haired dogs.

Rubber brush
A rubber-bristled brush for use on shorthaired coats, to loosen dead hair and surface dirt.

Clippers Used for trimming the nails. If a dog owner is unsure of how to clip the nails, they can take the dog to a vet or a professional groomer.

Metal comb Used for removing dirt and loose hair from the coat; it is especially useful for shorthaired breeds.

Shedder Used to remove loose and dead hair from a dog that is shedding its coat; it can be used throughout the year.
Shampoos

Specially formulated shampoos are available for dogs; these are mild and do not sting the eyes but are sufficiently strong to clean the fur.

Sprays Some people like to use specially formulated dog grooming spray, which can leave a dog's coat looking shiny and smelling nice.

Grooming glove It enables the owner to remove stray hair and dirt simply by stroking the dog.

Scissors Some dog breeds will require their coat to be trimmed regularly to avoid matting and tangling.

Massage tools Some dog owners like to massage their dog's body during grooming; this enables the dog to relax and also improves circulation. Massage tools come in many different forms, ranging from a massage brush, which

also removes dead hair, to electrically powered massage tools that vibrate.

ABOVE
Combs tend to be more useful for breeds with shorter coats.

FAR LEFT
The slicker brush is useful for removing tangles, particularly from tails and from breeds with longer, finer coats.

Grooming Process

The grooming process can be long and drawn out or short and sweet, depending on the breed and the style desired by the owner. Most dog owners prefer to groom their pets in a manner that is traditional, but some people are keen to add a little style to their dog's appearance by using accessories, such as bows and ribbons. Grooming encompasses everything from clipping nails to trimming hair, bathing, and cleaning out the ears.

The Coat
All dogs require their coat to be combed clean and made free of tangles and knots.

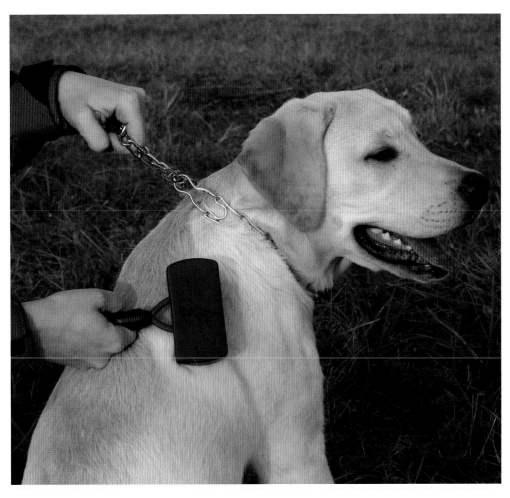

length. And with many medium-coated dogs, such as all the spaniels, sheepdogs, and Tibetan Terriers, you need to groom at least weekly. If your dog has been out in grass or fields, you need to check or groom every time to remove burrs or furzes.

Bathing

Dogs should not be bathed too frequently, because this can deplete essential oils in their coat. It is good practice to bathe the dog three or four times a year, depending on the breed and how dirty it gets. After bathing a dog, it makes sense to also towel-dry the coat and trim it, if needed, in that order. Never attempt to trim a dirty coat.

Nails

If a dog's nails are left to grow too long, they can cause the dog severe discomfort, affect its gait, and lead to painful scratches for the owner. If you are unsure of your ability to clip the nails properly, get a professional groomer or vet to do it. In some cases, dogs need to be sedated in order for them to allow their nails to be clipped.

Start with a rubber brush on shorthaired dogs. On longer-haired dogs, starting with a slicker brush, you should run the tool gently across the

BELOW
You can learn to clip your dog's nails yourself, or ask the vet or a professional groomer.

dog's coat, being careful not to tug at any knots or matted areas. If you find any tangles, which are common on the belly and at the back of the hind legs in some longhaired breeds, gently tease them out. Getting the dog used to being groomed and touched often is

essential to making regular grooming quick and painless.

It is important to remember that longhaired dogs, such as Afghans and Pekinese, require virtually daily grooming—or at least regular clipping to keep to keep the coat at a more manegeable

HEALTH

It is inevitable that dogs are not going to be in good health all of the time. However, a balanced diet, plenty of exercise, a clean living environment, and regular health checks will go a long way toward keeping a dog healthy. Certain breeds, due to selective breeding, are more prone to specific health problems. It is important to be able to judge a dog's health and to spot potential problems before they become very serious, especially when the dog is older and more prone to ailments.

A Healthy Dog

Dogs are incapable of expressing directly that they feel unwell. An owner may notice their dog being a little off-color, but by the time a dog allows illness to prevent it from acting normally it can be too late. However, there are ways of assessing the overall health of a dog that will enable an owner to become aware of any slight changes.

Appearance

The way a dog looks is a good indicator of health. The coat should be full and glossy, not dull and patchy. The eyes should be bright, never discolored. The general behavior of a dog may change

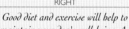
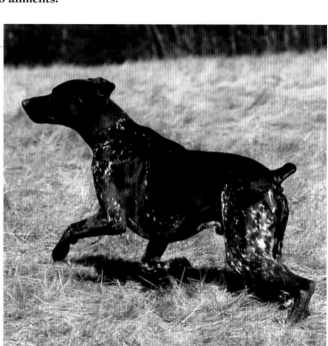

RIGHT
Good diet and exercise will help to maintain your dog's well-being. As ever, prevention is better than cure. German Shorthaired Pointer.

BELOW
Routine vaccinations, worming, and health checks will help to keep your dog in good health and catch serious ailments early on.

due to illness—lower energy levels or a loss of appetite are telltale signs that there is something wrong. Inspecting a dog's stool if you are worried about illness is another good way to clarify

your suspicions; anything out of the ordinary should be referred to a vet.

Routine Health Care

It is good practice to visit the vet for a regular check-up (annual or six-monthly checkups are the norm for healthy dogs), so that he or she can assess whether the dog is showing any signs of

Fascinating Facts

Approximately 2.7 million days a year are taken off work by the British population to care for a sick pet.

illness. Performing a health check at home, perhaps while grooming, enables you to act quickly in the case of illness. Check the coat condition, teeth and gums, inside their ears, and do a thorough hand-pass over the dog, checking for lumps or tenderness. Strange-smelling breath, loss of weight or appetite, loss of energy, a dry nose, or aggression are all potential signs of illness or disease.

Canine Ailments

Dogs are susceptible to certain viruses and diseases. Many diseases, such as cancer, are common across all breeds, but other conditions are peculiar to a breed or size of dog. Due to the process of selective breeding, the gene pool used for dog breeding is relatively small. This is because breeders want to magnify and improve on desirable elements of appearance. Unfortunately, this process does not give the species an adequate chance to rid itself of genetic disorders.

Acquired Conditions

As with humans, there are some illnesses and viruses that dogs can catch, either from other dogs or from the atmosphere. There are many vaccinations that prevent against the more common viruses, but if vaccinations are not kept up to date, these viruses can spread quickly among dogs, particularly those that live in close proximity to one another.

Parvovirus This is an extremely contagious and serious virus that will affect either the heart and cardiovascular system or the intestines, depending on the strain. The symptoms include vomiting, diarrhea, fever, and lethargy. It is not curable but it can be treated. Victims typically have dehydration, which can lead to other complications. Puppies are particularly prone to the virus but are usually vaccinated against it. Black-and-tan breeds, such as Rottweilers and Dobermans, are prone to parvovirus.

Cancer Any dog breed is prone to cancer, but some breeds are more susceptible to certain types of cancer than others. Dogs with solid white coloring are particularly prone, especially to skin cancer. Because dogs are unable to tell us if they discover a lump or unusual growth, it is essential that owners perform regular health checks (as described earlier) to ensure that any causes for concern can be picked up on immediately. Diet can contribute to cancer risk in dogs; those with poor diet and dogs that are overweight may be more prone to developing various cancers.

Distemper This is a virus that affects puppies and, to a lesser extent, mature dogs. The virus cannot be cured

Fascinating Facts

Golden Retrievers, Labradors, and Basset Hounds are highly susceptible to obesity and require regular exercise.

but the symptoms can be treated with swift veterinary attention; symptoms include dull eye color, weight loss, fever, and vomiting.

Leptospirosis Transmitted through contact with infected urine, this disease is

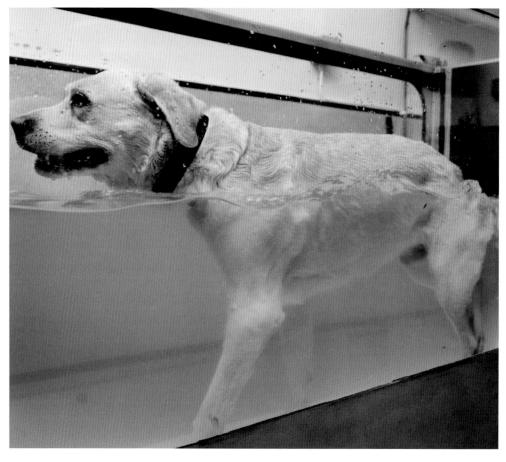

zoonotic—meaning it can be passed between species. It affects the liver and kidneys and can be very serious if left untreated; treatment does not always work due to its complexity. Some of the strains can be vaccinated against, but there are many strains that cannot.

Epilepsy Any breed can develop epilepsy, which causes seizures and neural disruption. Once the condition is diagnosed, vets may prescribe medication. Owners should be careful to be prepared to deal with their dog and prevent it from injuring itself during a seizure. Quite often the dog will recover by itself from a seizure, but it is essential to ensure that it does not bang its head or swallow its tongue when having an episode. It is possible that environmental stimuli or stress can trigger a seizure, so owners are often advised to monitor any common factors related to seizures in order to eliminate them.

Diabetes This manifests itself in canines in the same way it does in humans. A dog with this condition will require a specialized diet and regular checkups to monitor the condition. Dachshunds are prone to diabetes but it can occur in any breed, particularly older dogs.

Arthritis Most older dogs will have arthritis to a certain extent. Active and, conversely, heavy breeds are particularly prone to the condition, which can be painful and will seriously affect mobility in chronic cases. Feeding oily fish and flax oil can sometimes prevent the onset of arthritis, while physio-

therapy, hydrotherapy, and magnotherapy can all help reduce pain.

Bloat This is a potentially fatal condition that effects large-breed dogs, particularly those with deep chests, such as the Rhodesian Ridgeback. Bloat is brought on by a concentration of gases that forces the stomach to rotate, causing it to twist. Bloat can be caused by dogs being active too soon after eating, or eating too large an amount of food too quickly.

Hip dysplasia An abnormal positioning of the hip joint, this is commonly associated with poor breeding, and if a parent develops it, then it is likely that the offspring will have it, too. Dogs that have hip dysplasia can be observed walking with a stilted gait and may often become lame. The condition can worsen if the dog walks frequently on a smooth, polished surface.

Elbow dysplasia Like hip dysplasia, elbow dysplasia is associated with poor breeding. It is less common than hip dysplasia but can cause equally severe pain and limitation of mobility. Large dogs are more prone to both types of dysplasia.

Cataracts These are relatively common in all breeds of dog when they reach old age but Poodles are particularly prone. They are treatable through surgery but will lead to blindness if left untreated. Looking for signs of clouding in the eye or evidence of limited sight, such as the dog acting clumsily, can help an owner identify cataracts early on.

Deafness Some breeds are prone to deafness, such as Bull Terriers and Boxers and dogs that have solid-white coats, but it can occur in any breed. Dogs can cope with deafness relatively easily but any training will require the use of exclusively visual stimuli.

Fascinating Facts

On average, one in three Dalmatians will have a hearing disability.

Rabies Vacinations are required to prevent a dog from being infected with this disease. Rabies can be passed between species—for example, from raccon to dog—and humans can catch this normally fatal disease. The symptoms include hyperactivity, aggression, excitability, and paralysis. It is rare that a rabid dog will survive.

ABOVE

Hip dysplasia is most common among the larger breeds, such as Great Danes. It can be a genetic condition.

Breed-specific inherited conditions There are certain conditions and diseases that are more prevalent in certain breeds. Attempts to breed out such inherited diseases

are being made, but the limited breeding stock that has been used in many modern breeds means that it is essential for breeders themselves to avoid using dogs with certain diseases.

General Health Problems

Dogs are prone to developing diet- and environment-related conditions—allergies, skin problems, and parasites are relatively common among most breeds of dog. Good husbandry, grooming, and diet are the best way to prevent a dog from suffering unnecessarily from such problems.

Vets can advise on treatments and preventions for the various conditions that are common in dogs. Flea infestations and other parasitic infestations can be prevented with medication and good grooming. If left untreated, worms and other parasites can cause complications that will eventually lead to death if ignored. Loss of hair and rapid weight loss are signs

ABOVE

While you are grooming your dog, this is an ideal time to check for lumps or parasites.

RIGHT

Dogs, such as Spaniels, that enjoy swimming in rivers can be prone to eye and ear infections.

that a dog may be carrying a parasite. Health problems can be treated by various traditional or alternative methods. Vets may prescribe a course of treatment that combines both approaches. On some occasions a vet

may prescribe a special diet for a dog to get over the symptoms of an infection or illness. Certain foods, such as seaweed and flaxseeds, are very good at ensuring dogs remain in good and robust health.

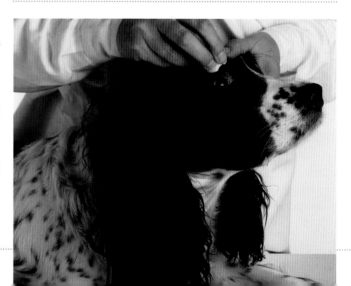

Accidents and First Aid

Being inquisitive and active animals, it is likely that every dog will have an accident at least once in its life. Prevention is always better than cure when it comes to accidents, and limiting the exposure to risk that a dog encounters in and around the home is part of responsible dog ownership.

Road Accidents

In the majority of cases, dogs sustain serious trauma if hit by a motor vehicle. Head injuries and broken bones are common; crushing is also a serious risk when a dog is involved in a collision with a car. If a dog is hit by a car, the most important thing to do is seek emergency

veterinary assistance. Any bleeding should be stemmed by applying pressure to the wound. If it is necessary to move the dog, make sure that the head and neck are kept stable at all times.

Falls

Dogs that have fallen, either from a great height or down a flight of stairs, may sustain a variety of injuries. Head trauma, broken bones, and shock are common. If a dog goes into shock, it is important to help the dog remain calm. Keep it warm and ensure that it takes water. Stabilize any damaged limbs and seek veterinary help immediately.

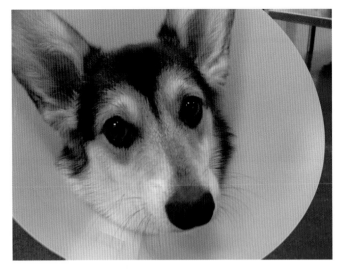

Preventing dogs from having access to areas where they could fall is universally more preferable than dealing with the consequences.

Burns

Burns are typically incurred on the paw pads, nose, tail, and mouth. When dealing with a burn, clean the affected area and apply cold water or a damp cloth. Always see the vet in the case of a burn so that the wound can be dressed correctly. Severe burns can cause a dog to go into shock; try to ensure that the dog does not become excited and attempt to regulate body temperature using a blanket.

Poisoning

There are some substances that are harmful to dogs but which are commonly kept within a dog's reach. Education and prevention is

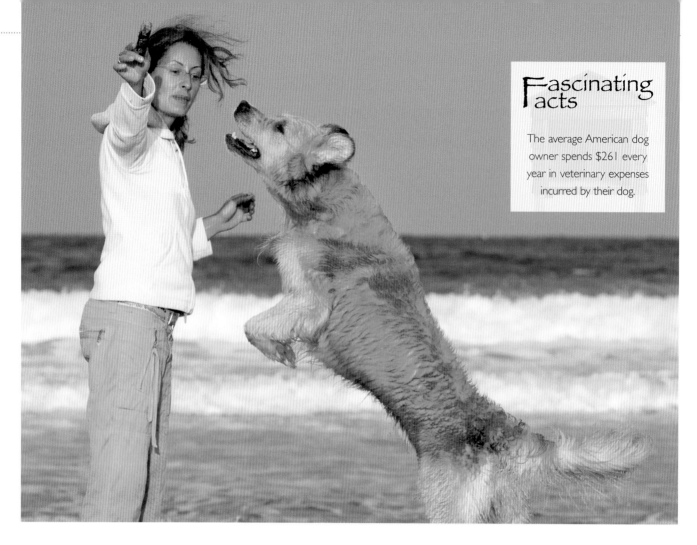

Many breeds of dog adore retrieving sticks, but be aware that they pose a choking hazard.

essential to limit the chances of dogs ingesting harmful substances. If a dog ingests a toxin, such as antifreeze, it may not be evident until the dog begins to become ill. If you suspect the dog has been poisoned, seek veterinary assistance immediately. It is a good idea to take a sample of the poison to the vet if possible. Terriers are often poisoned if they catch a rat or mouse that has already ingested poison. Induce vomiting with salt water only on the advice of a veterinary professional.

Choking

Choking, either on food or brittle substances, such as bones or twigs, is a risk that most dogs face. Ensuring that bones are not likely to splinter and that any sticks thrown for the dog are dry and solid is a necessity. If the dog begins to choke, attempt to remove the offending item from the airway. If this is not possible, remain calm and get the dog to the vet. In some cases, a vet may advise you to attempt to pump the chest if time is limited; do this by holding the dog's head below its body and squeezing the rib cage, ensuring not to break the ribs.

Drowning

Cases of dogs drowning in ponds and pools are more common than many people realize. Depending on the

If your dog has breathed in water after getting into difficulties, it may be advisable to pump the chest. Ask your vet for details.

amount of water taken in, it may be necessary to pump the chest. Do so until the dog begins to expel the water, then always seek subsequent veterinary assistance to reduce the possibility of complications, such as pneumonia or shock.

Caring For an Elderly Dog

As sad as it is, the health of a dog will inevitably decline with old age. This may cause limited vision, hearing, and mobility. In more serious cases, dogs can become lame

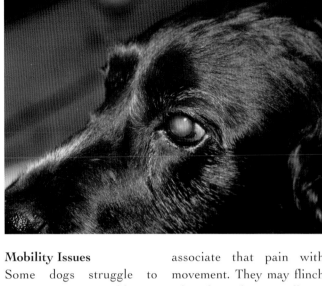

extent due to old age, but some dogs lose their hearing completely. This can cause certain problems but there are ways to cope with it. Making changes to the layout of your home, where possible, so that the dog is able to rely more on sight will help the dog adjust.

Blindness

As with deafness, loss of sight is common, but complete blindness in old age is a

and crippled through arthritis. Taking steps to ensure that the dog is comfortable and that its quality of life is not diminished unnecessarily is essential. Simple, practical changes often make a large difference; sometimes more drastic steps are required.

Deafness

Most dogs experience hearing loss to a certain

possibility, too. Ensuring that there are no hazards in the home, such as sharp objects or open fires, is a good way of limiting the risk of injury to a blind dog. Dogs will adapt remarkably well to loss of sight, but their owners can help by not creating unnecessary challenges, such as rearranging furniture, because dogs will often rely on their memory to move about the home.

Mobility Issues

Some dogs struggle to remain active in old age. Keeping the dog's toys in an easy-to-reach place ensures that the dog does not injure itself. Dogs, despite being in pain due to old age, do not

associate that pain with movement. They may flinch when hurt, but it will not stop them from attempting to act like a young dog. Ensure that the dog does not injure itself by running or jumping unnecessarily.

BREEDING

All dogs have a natural urge to reproduce, but because there are many dogs now in need of a home the canine population requires monitoring. Breeding should only be carried out with the intention of advancing the breed or continuing a strong and healthy bloodline. Matings should be conducted responsibly, with the welfare and health of the dogs being paramount. Special care should be taken to ensure the health of pregnant and brooding bitches, as well as the resulting litter.

Why Breed?

Breeding dogs is a huge responsibility for anyone. Only people with a sound knowledge of and passion for a particular breed should attempt it. Nothing other than dogs free from health problems and of good temperament should be used for breeding. Commercial breeding has a negative effect on dogs because it creates an incentive for over-breeding. The aim of breeding is to magnify and continue desirable traits in a breed.

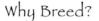

LEFT

Despite the ever-cute lure of adorable puppies, do not forget that breeding a litter is a large responsibility.

ABOVE RIGHT

During the proestrus phase of their heat cycle, female dogs may need sanitary wear.

Mating

Bringing two dogs together to mate should be done with care and consideration. Bitches come into season only approximately twice a year, while dogs are able to reproduce at any time. The process

Fascinating Facts

It is illegal to spay or neuter a dog in Sweden unless it is for medical reasons. The Swedish Kennel Club believes it is the responsibility of the owner to prevent unwanted litters.

of reproduction can be aggressive in certain cases, with bitches likely to feel discomfort when being mated. It is essential for breeders to be on hand to supervise a mating in case anything goes wrong. Typically, natural urges will be enough for the bitch and the dog to mate successfully.

Fascinating Facts

When a male dog becomes a father it is called a "sire" and when a female dog becomes a mother it is called a "dam."

Reproduction

Male dogs have typical mammalian reproductive organs: a penis and testicles are located at the loins. The erect penis will deliver semen from the testes into the bitch. Bitches also have typical mammalian reproductive organs.

Around twice a year a bitch will come into heat. The first phase of this cycle is called proestrous, lasting from 4 to 15 days, where there may be discharge from thevagina that may be bloody. After this is estrous, when she is ready to be fertilized, and will give off a scent that is irresistible to male dogs. She will become sexually interested in most male dogs that she encounters. In many cases, a bitch will become moody when in heat, while dogs typically become restless, distracted, and aroused if they can detect the hormones that indicate a bitch's availability. Howling, whining, and heavy panting are signs that a male dog has picked up a scent froma female that is available for mating.

The Mating Process

In the wild, the male will approach the female. He will signal his intent to mate in many ways, including folding his ears back and mimicking the mating movements. He may not signal any intent and simply attempt a clumsy negotiation of the bitch, to which she may react aggressively. If amenable, the bitch will typically display herself to the dog, enabling him to mount her. In some cases, however, despite being in season, a bitch will not want to mate with a particular dog. If a dog attempts to mate a bitch in this scenario, she may become aggressive toward him. The mating process is often forceful and can result in bites and nips being delivered from both participants.

In a successful mating, the dog will mount the bitch from behind and penetrate her almost instantly. The intercourse can last from a few minutes to almost an hour or more, depending on the dogs. Once the male has mated the female the two dogs will tie. This is caused by the

female clasping the male while his penis is still penetrated. This is a natural instinct to prevent other dogs attempting to mate the female while she is vulnerable. Tying often causes the dogs to become distressed and aggressive, often with the dog attempting to remove himself from the bitch, which can cause pain to both dogs.

ABOVE

There's no "wining or dining," so either of the dogs can become distressed during mating. Here, an owner comforts her bitch.

BELOW

This pair of dogs have "tied"—after mating the male dog dismounts and turns around, but remains inside the female for a while.

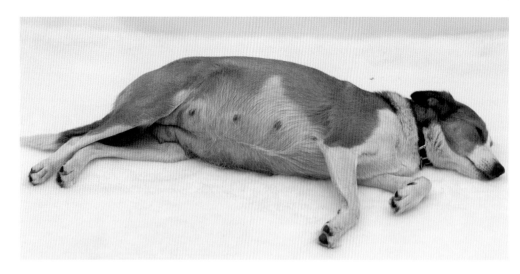

During the Pregnancy

A pregnant bitch will need some extra care. Typically, she will be governed by her instincts to remain safe, but the owner should take responsibility for ensuring that she has the right diet to optimize the chances of a good pregnancy. It is also important for the owner to provide a calm and safe environment for her. The bitch will experience bodily changes during pregnancy, such as weight gain, stomach enlargement, and pronounced teats.

Gestation

In order to establish whether a bitch has become pregnant, the owner will take her for two pregnancy tests. The first will determine the likelihood of pregnancy and the second will confirm this. The instances of miscarriage and phantom pregnancy in dogs are very high. It is also possible that a bitch may be traumatized during the pregnancy, which may cause her to lose the puppies. Evolution has determined that bitches unable to provide adequate care for their litter are more likely to lose the pups before they develop past the embryonic stage.

Gestation lasts from between 60 to 64 days. During the pregnancy, the bitch may become withdrawn and moody—this is a protective instinct. It is essential that the bitch is monitored throughout the pregnancy to ensure her health and the health of the pups.

Behavior

Behavior during pregnancy varies from bitch to bitch. Some may remain completely normal throughout the pregnancy, showing no signs of broodiness or discomfort, while others may be overcome by maternal instincts and act in a very protective nature. It is not uncommon for pregnant bitches to practice maternal behavior by nesting with toys. Hormonal changes within the body can lead to certain noticeable changes in temperament.

The Birth and Aftercare

Before the delivery, a bitch will begin to prepare herself by denning, that is, making a den out of her bed. She will need peace, quiet, and privacy in preparation. The owner or breeder should be on hand to ensure everything goes to plan and to act in case of complications, but nature usually takes its course. Some breeders prepare a whelping box for the delivery and aftercare, but the bitch may prefer to find her own space—typically a secluded spot away from noise.

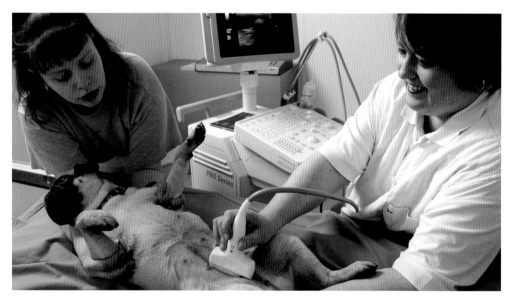

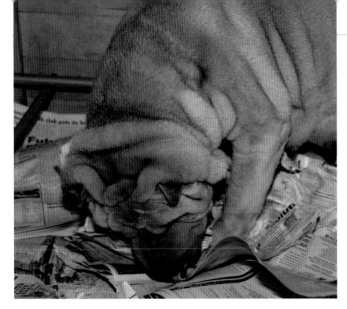

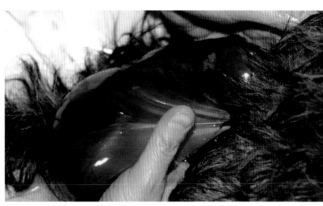

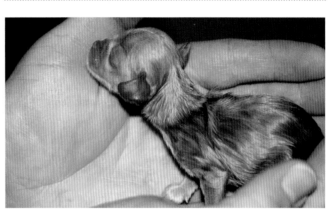

Fascinating Facts

Larger breeds typically produce bigger litters, while toy breeds may only produce one single puppy or a maximum of four puppies.

Litters range in size but typically are around six in number. Stillborn pups are common and it is also not rare for pups to die shortly after birth. In less common cases, the mother may kill certain pups. There are varying opinions on why this is, but it is thought to be linked to the bitch attempting to preserve her resources for the healthier puppies.

TOP LEFT

This bitch is denning—making a secure place in which to have her litter.

TOP RIGHT

If you are breeding, you may need to call out a vet while the bitch whelps.

TOP CENTER RIGHT

A one-day-old Cocker Spaniel puppy. It will be another two weeks before it can see or hear.

Delivery

During the delivery, the bitch may experience pain or distress. This is normal and the bitch will prefer to be left to her own devices. Her temperature will increase just prior to delivery, which may cause her to pant heavily. The delivery will last anywhere from 6 to 12 hours, and possibly longer for larger breeds.

Once the pups are born the bitch may become very protective over them, or she may appear harassed by their presence; both behaviors are normal. In some cases, the pups may need special attention, so it is necessary for the breeder or owner to pay attention to any puppies that are moving less than their siblings. It is likely that the mother will need to relieve herself after giving birth and she will be keen not to soil the den.

As mentioned in the "Puppy Care" section of the book (see pp. 82–83), thorough aftercare is required once delivery is complete.

DOG SHOWS

Dog shows are a popular competitive pursuit for many breed enthusiasts. They are an opportunity for breeders, owners, and dog lovers to meet and see many purebred dogs of differing breeds. It is also an important part of breed culture, with standards being examined and good examples of breeds being displayed for the public. Dog shows for conformation are typically open only to purebred or pedigree dogs, but there are conformation competitions for crossbreeds and mixed breeds, too.

Entering Your Dog

A dog owner may want to enter a conformation contest in order to see how well their dog measures up to the accepted standard for its breed. Breeders that do well in conformation shows will receive acclaim and respect from their peers. The fees paid to breeders for their pups or the use of their stud dogs and brood bitches often increase if their animals have performed well in a conformation show.

Some people enter their dogs for fun, while others enter due to their passion for advancing and improving the breed. Competition is

often heated, but in general most competitors are there for their love of the dogs.

How to Enter
In order to enter a dog into a conformation show, it must be a purebred or pedigree. A pedigree is issued and accredited by the kennel club or equivalent of the country in which the dog was born. It lists the

ancestors of the dog and any of their relevant awards and titles. A pedigree dog will have an official pedigree name, typically containing the affix of the kennel where it was bred.

Each dog show is different, so it is necessary for people to consult the guidelines of their national kennel club for information on how to enter, but typically entry involves preliminary qualification at

---

ABOVE
If you are planning on breeding, winning placements in dog shows can help demonstrate the purity of your dog's pedigree.

RIGHT
Dog conformation shows judge dogs on their closeness to the standard. Lady Sally Guise with her Best of Breed-winning Scottish Deerhound.

Preparing and Showing Your Dog

When showing a dog the most important thing to demonstrate is how good an example of the breed the individual dog is. Some breed standards are more specific than others, but they all will offer a comprehensive guide as to the size, weight, color, and general appearance of the dog. Breed standards purport to govern temper-ament, but it is difficult for a judge to assess temperament during a short encounter in the show ring.

Preshow Grooming

It is important for the dog to look in good health. A glossy, well-groomed coat is all-important. Feeding speciality food prior to the show to improve the appearance of the coat is common. The dog should be clean and free from blemishes and marks. The teeth should be healthy and brushed and the coat should be presented traditionally.

Preparation

The dog should be used to being handled and demonstrated. Practicing the moves that will be performed on the day is essential, as is good socialization. The dog will have to perform alongside a lot of other dogs during the show, so it should not be affected by their presence.

A show judge will want to see that the dog carries itself in accordance with the breed standard and will require a competitor to walk with their dog. If the dog gets excited or distracted, it may be disqualified or marked down.

Judging

To the inexperienced observer, the judging process can appear to be arbitrary. In reality, the judges are looking for conformation to type. In the instance of two dogs being too close to call physically, their gait and general demeanor in accordance to the breed standard will be taken into account. The judge will also base his or her decision on the apparent health and condition of the dog.

local and regional levels before competition at national or international level.

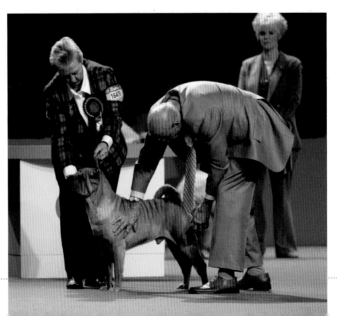

The Breeds

EVOLUTION AND DOMESTICATION

It is a misconception that man domesticated the dog. Man in fact domesticated the wolf, and the offspring of the domesticated wolf evolved into the dogs of today. Under man's guidance, dogs have been bred, interbred, and crossbred to create new bloodlines and to improve on old ones. Breeds have come and gone, disappearing into extinction as their value diminished; other breeds have remained wild, unable to find a role alongside man. Even today new breeds are becoming established to fulfill our need for companionship.

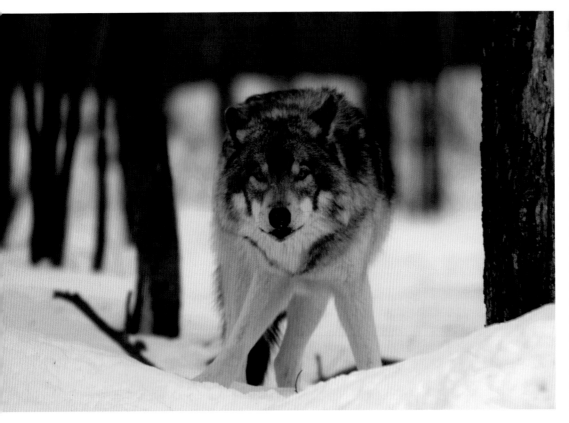

Fascinating Facts

Winston Churchill used to talk to his pet Poodle and would cover the dog's eyes when watching scary movies.

ABOVE

The Timber Wolf. Gradually, through many generations of selective breeding, an ideal hunting partner was bred—the dog.

LEFT

Nature played its part in the evolution of the dog, equipping Huskies, for example, with thick coats for freezing conditions.

The Start of Selective Breeding

More than 15,000 years ago different tribes came into contact with wolves as they migrated over landmasses. One of the first things man noticed about the wolf was its ability as a hunter. As man evolved, he realized that alongside the wolf he could improve his own chances of survival and evolution. However, it was not to happen quickly—it took generations of wolves and men coming into contact before the latter could impose any influence. As man noticed characteristics in the wolf that were of value to him, he attempted to make these more prominent through a process known as selective breeding.

Two strong wolves bred together would create even stronger offspring, while an intelligent wolf and a fast wolf would, in theory, create fast and intelligent descendants. Things did not always go to plan and sometimes the intended

ABOVE

Having a strong desire to help defend the pack, dogs make ideal lookout sentries and guards.

offspring would turn out weak, sickly, and of no use to humans. In other cases, results would occur that man did not plan but that benefited him nonetheless.

The First Dogs

As the wolf species diversified, the generations of new wolves began to look more and more different from the wolves with which man had first come into contact. As these new animals evolved, man's ability to select desirable

mating partnerships improved. Nature played its part, too, equipping wolves living in cold climates with thick coats. It was a long process, but man was able to control it to a certain extent. Eventually, the animals were sufficiently different from the original wolves to serve man's changing needs; these animals were the original domesticated dogs.

The Evolution of the Canine

As the needs of the human race changed, man was able to produce and train dogs capable of helping and serving.

Man was able to control livestock with a dog, so only dogs that displayed the ability to do this were used for breeding. If the offspring did not match the

LEFT

It is amazing that the tiny Yorkshire Terrier's ancestral line reaches back to the wolf.

BELOW

There are approximately nine breeds of wolf, of which the Gray Wolf (shown) is one.

desires of man, they would be abandoned. Gradually, humans became able to produce dogs that catered for very specific needs. Swimming ability was valued as man realized the importance of water in early farming and travel. When man began to establish modern dwellings he required dogs of courage and strength to protect them.

The Modern Canine

Every breed of dog was bred for a purpose and

these purposes or jobs are used to define the breed groups we know today. Herding, hunting, protecting, retrieving and transporting were all skills for which man needed a dog. Although we may no longer require all these services, the dog still proves to be of value by combining skills from the past and applying them to modern needs. The most valuable asset a

dog offers today's society is companionship. Some dogs were bred specifically for companionship, while others have adapted to provide company as their original duties ceased to exist. It is amazing to consider that from the wolf came both the tiny Yorkshire Terrier and the giant Saint Bernard.

LEFT

While large, like the wolf, the Saint Bernard is renowned for its biddable nature and ability to undertake complicated mountain-rescue operations.

WILD DOGS

The domestic canine has many wild cousins. Certain types of dog have remained untouched by domestication, thriving on their own without man for millennia. Other types have gone through the process of domestication and then reverted to a wild state due to mass abandonment or overbreeding; these dogs are known as pariah or feral dogs. Some wild canine ancestors have lived on the fringes of domestication, only coming into contact with humanity intermittently. Each wild dog varies in its similarity to the domesticated canine.

Defining a Wild Dog

There is much debate among the scientific community about the definition of both "wild" and "dog." Certain arguments propose, for example, that the fox is not a true dog species and is in fact a subspecies of the wolf, while others maintain that the fox and the wolf are both descendents of the same, now extinct, animal. Others contend the use of the term "wild," claiming that some species are not truly wild but are semidomestic, such as the Dingo. To be defined as a dog, it is typical for the animal to belong to the *Canidae* family.

Wolves

Wolves are larger and stronger than most breeds of dog. There are approximately nine wolf types, including the Timber Wolf, Arctic Wolf, and European Wolf. All are skillful predators and live in packs. When studying the behavior of domestic canines, many behaviorologists look to the wolf for answers. The wolf can be found in a range of habitats, from isolated forests to semi-urban areas. They exist in desert, tundra, forest, and mountain and are present in Europe, North America, Asia, and Africa.

Foxes

Depending on how they are classified, there are approximately 27 different types of fox, including the

Red Fox and the Gray Fox. Most foxes are smaller than the average dog breed,

although the Red Fox, commonly seen in and around cities in Britain, is slightly

larger—similar in size to a small Border Collie. Foxes have many varying habitats, ranging from deserts to the Arctic. Typically, the fox is a scavenger and opportunistic hunter—it eats what it can when it can.

Jackals
Jackals are typically of a similar size to foxes but are less widely distributed geographically, inhabiting only Africa and Asia. The jackal is a scavenger and a hunter; it will hunt small prey and scavenge at the site of another animals kill. There are three types of jackal—the Golden Jackal, the Black-Backed Jackal, and the Side-Striped Jackal.

Coyotes
The Coyote lives exlusively in North America, in various

ABOVE
The Black-Backed Jackal is one of three types of jackal; similar in size and lifestyle to the fox, but found only in Africa and Asia.

environments ranging from rural to urban. There are 19 types of coyote, all of which are predatory but typically evasive of humans. Due to urban sprawl, where human settlements encroach on wild habitats, the instances of coyotes and people coming into contact are rising.

African Hunting Dogs
The African Hunting Dog, or African Wild Dog, is a large, vividly multicolored dog native to Africa that hunts large mammals, such as antelope. It is also known as the Painted Wolf due to its strikingly patterned coat. The species hunts in packs and is known to communicate through vocalization with other pack members when hunting.

Fascinating Facts

The New Guinea Singing Dog is so called due to its unique howl. Rather than emitting a typical howl, the New Guinea Singing Dog modulates the pitch of the sound, which creates an almost melodic effect.

RIGHT
The African Hunting Dog, also known as the African Wild Dog, is now becoming endangered in the wild.

RIGHT
A strong swimmer, the Dhole likes to chase its prey into water, where it can overcome it more easily.

Dholes

The Dhole is a species of wild dog native to India. It lives predominantly in dry forest where it feeds on large mammals, in some cases, mammals that are substantially larger than the Dhole itself. The Dhole hunts both in packs and alone, depending on the prey. A common hunting technique is for the Dhole to chase its quarry into water, where the strong-swimming dog can exercise its advantage.

hunter, with short legs and longish tan fur. Little is known about the species.

Racoon Dogs

The Racoon Dog has a weaker genetic relationship to the domestic dog than most species in the *Canidae* family. It bears a resemblance to the racoon and exhibits little behavior

LEFT
Extremely rare and found in Central and South America only, the Bush Dog is a nocturnal hunter, making it harder to come across.

typical of dogs. It will not fight, preferring to hide or escape, and mating pairs normally remain monogamous. The Racoon Dog is also distinct from every other canine in that it enters a state of torpor (a short period of inactivity similar to hibernation) during winter.

Pariah and Feral Dogs

For various reasons, certain formerly domesticated dogs revert to wild or feral states. This is often due to man vacating an environment formerly shared with a dog, or by simple overabundance of a type of dog. The Canaan

Dog, which is considered by many to be a standard dog breed, is typical of a pariah dog in that it exists in the wild as well as domestically. There are many varieties of pariah dog around the world and, due to their semi-wild status, there is limited human influence on breeding, resulting in typically stronger and healthier animals.

BELOW
The Racoon Dog is unlike a dog in many ways, forming a monogamous mating relationship and hibernating through the winter.

Bush Dogs

The Bush Dog is an extremely rare animal that is native to Central and South America. It is so rare that its fossils were found before the breed had been discovered alive. It is a nocturnal pack

The Bush Dog's habitat is typically wetlands and forest.

Feral dogs and pariah dogs differ in that the pariah is a recognized type of dog descended from Indian Pariah Dogs, whereas "feral" is the name given to the state of domestication or wildness that a dog exhibits. It is possible for any breed of dog to revert to a feral state, where it becomes reliant on its survival instincts. A feral dog can, in theory, be born into a purebred litter and then be left to fend for itself. It will come to rely on its instincts and will either die or reach a feral state.

In Australia, the Dingo is considered to be a feral dog, having been subject to domestication by the Aboriginal people before the arrival of European settlers drove them out. This is disputed by some, who claim the dog is wild as opposed to feral. In Asia, the Canaan Dog is a well-known feral;

although it was domesticated centuries ago, large numbers of the breed now live in packs free from human influence. The same is true of the Carolina Dog, which, when first discovered, was believed to be a stray domestic dog. However, after DNA testing, it was revealed that the dog was primitive and its genetics were not distributed through the rest of the North American dog population.

Dingoes
Dingoes look similar to certain species of domestic dog, particularly the Australian Cattle Dog— strongly believed to be a Dingo descendent. Debate over the status of the Dingo as wild or feral still occurs. The Dingo typically has a short, reddish coat and large erect ears. In terms of evolution, the Dingo represents a point somewhere between the

wolf and the domestic dog. Taxonomists believe that the Dingo has remained the same for the majority of its existence. Although they are strongly associated with Australasia, they also exist in Southeast Asia, which is where the species originated. The two main

differences between the Dingo and the domesticated dog are that the Dingo breeds only once a year and it does not bark.

OLD AND EXTINCT BREEDS

There are many dog breeds that have become extinct. Because man is in control of breeding, it is most often man that causes a breed to become extinct. Certain factors, such as changing requirements for work, new and "better" breeds evolving, and even war have caused various breed bloodlines to disappear. Conversely, there are some ancient and primitive breeds of dog that have not only managed to survive, but have done so without changing at all. Whatever the fate of the breed, the outcome is nearly always man-made.

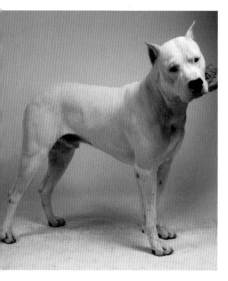

Extinct Breeds

There are a number of breeds that are now extinct, for certain reasons, such as a decline in work or evolution into a new breed.

Cordoba Fighting Dog

The Argentine bred Cordoba Fighting Dog was a huge, powerful descendent of the Molosser. Unlike the

LEFT

Argentine Dogo is descended from the Cordoba Fighting Dog, a breed that died out when dog fighting became unpopular.

Bulldog or certain Mastiff breeds, it was not given the chance to evolve after dog fighting became a socially unacceptable practice. Due to its fighting instincts and abilities, the Cordoba Fighting Dog played a part in its own demise—pitching two of these dogs against each other in a fight would normally result in death for at least one of them. Of cours,e without man, there would have been no organized dog fights, but the breed was a victim of its own success. When fighting declined in

popularity the Cordoba Fighting Dog had no function to perform and the breed was left to die out. Certain of the last Cordoba Fighting Dog offspring went on to become established as a new, more docile breed known as the Argentine Dogo.

Saint John's Water Dog

The Saint John's Water Dog was a large, powerful breed that was popular in Canada, where it was originally bred. It was used as an all-purpose working dog up until the nineteenth century, at which time the Canadian authorities put a tax on dog ownership in order to stem the decline of the sheep population. This meant that many people could not afford to keep the dog, so breeding was slowed down.

Export of the breed was also restricted due to a rabies outbreak, so fewer dogs became established overseas. Of the few

ABOVE

The Newfoundland breed was created by breeding from remaining stock of Saint John's Water Dogs.

remaining Saint John's Water Dogs that made it out of Canada, only the smaller ones were used for breeding. Eventually, the breed as it was once known disappeared, to be replaced with a smaller and lighter-boned breed that went on to become the Labrador Retriever. Back in Canada, the breed had also disappeared and remaining stock had been used to create the Newfoundland breed.

RIGHT

Thought to have descended from the Molossus war dog of Greco-Roman times, Molosser breeds of several varieties exist today.

Molossus

The Molossus is an ancient Greek dog. It was kept by ancient Greeks and later by ancient Romans and was used as a war dog and hunting dog. The breed gives its name to the modern Molosser type of today; the Molosser is not a breed itself, but is the name given to a certain type of dog with a common ancestry. The Rottweiler, Saint Bernard, Mastiff, and Bernese Mountain Dog are all classified as Molosser breeds. The typical characteristics of a Molosser breed include a heavy jaw, heavy dewlap, large strong body, and broad skull. The breed that was known as the Molossus was not left to become extinct in the way that other breeds were—it simply disappeared in its pure form due to extensive crossbreeding caused by travel and migration.

English White Terrier

The English White Terrier was an exceptional working dog—tenacious, intelligent, and highly driven to control vermin. But as times changed and conformation showing became increasingly popular, the English White Terrier was used only as breeding stock for new, better-looking breeds. It is a direct ancestor of many breeds, including the Parson Jack Russell Terrier, Fox Terrier, Rat Terrier, and Boston Terrier, but as a breed in its own right the bloodline was not upheld and the dog ceased to exist.

Talbot

The Talbot was a French breed of hunting dog that was imported to Britain by William the Conqueror. It was popular due to its size and strength, which enabled it to hunt game the size of

stag. But as the stag population in Britain declined so did the need for

the Talbot, which was used instead to contribute to a new, smaller breed with a better sense of smell—what we now know as the Beagle.

Other Extinct Breeds

There are many other breeds of dog that became extinct due to their evolution into new breeds. The Scottish breed that was known as the Blue Paul Terrier was used in the development of the Staffordshire Bull Terrier. Other breeds were discontinued because another breed could out-

Fascinating Facts

In the United States, August 26 is National Dog Day.

perform them at work. The English Water Spaniel line was discontinued altogether due to people's preference for the Irish Water Spaniel.

Extinct Types

The difference between an extinct breed and an extinct type is simple. The bloodline of an extinct breed no longer exists in its pure form—it will have been mixed with blood from other breeds. The bloodline of an extinct type does exist, but the dogs have evolved so drastically that the type to which they once conformed no longer exists.

Old English Bull Dog
The Old English Bull Dog is not the name of an extinct breed, but the name given to

LEFT
The Staffordshire Bull Terrier is descended from the Paul Blue Terrier, thought to have arrived in Scotland with a sailor c. 1770.

ABOVE RIGHT
Bulldogs, c. 1880. Congenital problems can occur with extreme selected breeding, and the Bulldog is one such sufferer.

the type of Bulldog that used to exist. Conformation showing has influenced how the Bulldog has developed, with breed fans preferring the smaller, large-headed type over the formerly stronger and taller type.

The diversification of the breed can be traced back to a Bulldog show in 1891. Two very different examples of the breed were competing for a conformation prize. One dog

BELOW
Note the very flat muzzle of the modern English Bulldog, which is associated with breathing difficulties.

Pug

The Pug has experienced a similar decline in health and appearance. It was once a lean and athletic breed, but standards have dictated that the squashed face and condensed proportions are preferable, causing the breed to be unrecognizable in comparison to old paintings depicting the traditional Pug.

Oldest Breeds

The oldest breeds of dog still in existence are thought to be sight hounds. The existence of the Saluki, the Greyhound, and the Azawakh can all be dated back many thousands of years. Spitz breeds, such as the Siberian Husky and the Samoyed, are also ancient; they are thought to be the oldest living direct descendents of the wolf. Ancient breeds tend to be healthier than newer breeds because the gene pool is more diverse.

called Dockleaf, who was smaller, with the typical squashed face of today's Bulldog, was put up against a dog named Orry—a lean and strong example of the old type. The decision for the award went to a vote and was unanimous. Dockleaf was designated there and then as the "ideal" Bulldog and all subsequent Bulldogs were to be judged by her standard. As the breed has evolved, more extreme versions of the Bulldog have come to pass, taking the breed to a point now where the head of a puppy is typically wider than the pelvis of an adult female, making Bulldog births particularly dangerous. Most Bulldog puppies are delivered by caesarean section.

Custodians of the breed are attempting to revive and reestablish the old type of Bulldog by outcrossing with

ABOVE

The athletic Pug, as seen c. 1880, has been bred to encourage condensed proportions and, unfortunately, congenital problems have arisen.

Staffordshire Bull Terriers and American Bull Dogs. This will, they hope, stem the tide of congenital health problems that have caused the average life expectancy of the Bulldog to drop to around seven years.

PEDIGREE AND NON-PEDIGREE DOGS

A pedigree is a document that confirms the ancestry and heritage of a purebred dog. Any dog that has a pedigree is classified as a pedigree dog or purebred. Having a pedigree enables a person to see the lineage and parentage of a dog and the value of a dog is affected by the strength of that pedigree. If the dog descends from notable specimens, such as champions or conformation winners, its value may increase. Pedigrees, typically, are administered by the national kennel club of the country in which the dog was born.

RIGHT
The Lhasa Apso is generally a very healthy breed, but the most common complaint is kidney disease.

Pedigree and Purebred

Any dog that conforms to a set type of a breed tends to be named by that breed. In the true sense, for a dog to be a purebred or pedigree it must have a lineage of only members of its breed. It is up to the governing body in the relevant country to issue pedigrees and the criteria used vary from organization to organization.

Naturally, if a dog is descended from only members of its own type, there is a significantly higher incidence of inbreeding. Inbreeding is caused when closely related dogs mate and the offspring may exhibit signs of weak genetics. The more inbreeding that occurs, the more likely a breed is to develop health problems.

Pedigree dogs conform to a physical and characteristic type. They will be about the same size throughout the breed and have the same set of working instincts. This is one of the reasons people favor pedigree dogs over non-pedigree dogs.

Fascinating Facts

The Lowchen, Havanese, and Portuguese Water Dog are considered to be the rarest purebred dog breeds in the world.

Non-Pedigree Dogs

Dogs that are not issued with a pedigree certificate are non-pedigree dogs. Non-pedigree dogs include crossbreeds, mixed breeds, or mongrels and mutts. Typically, non-pedigree dogs have a more diverse gene pool, which commonly means they are of more robust health and live longer. Although there is little or no uniformity among non-pedigree dogs in terms of appearance, many people favor their more rugged look.

BELOW
An adorable scruffy mutt. Crossbreeds can live healthier lives than pedigrees, avoiding the weaknesses inherent in inbreeding.

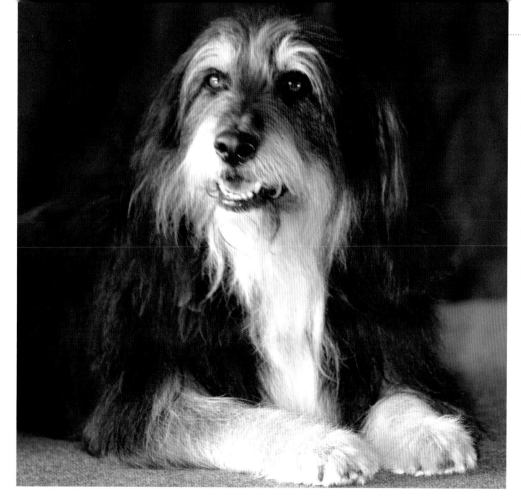

Fascinating Facts

If a dog has two different sight-hound breeds as parents, it is referred to as a "longdog."

BELOW
A Puggle—a Pug and Beagle crossbreed. New designer crossbreeds will help expand the gene pool.

ABOVE
A crossbreed showing the long fur on the muzzle typical of the Bearded Collie and the darker coloring of the Border Collie.

Crossbreeds

A crossbreed is the name given to the offspring of two purebred dogs of different breeds. For example, if a Labrador Retriever and German Shepherd mate, the offspring will not be purely one breed, even if they inherit their appearance from only one parent. Normally, the offspring will inherit physical and mental attributes from both parents. Many true breeds came about from crossbreeding, only to be established as a breed in its own right when the offspring displayed uniformity with sufficient regularity. It is often desired for two different breeds to mate for working purposes, so that the offspring inherit appealing qualities of both parents. Some crosses are deliberately carried out to create so-called "designer" dog breeds. Popular crosses of this nature include the Labradoodle (Labrador and Poodle) and Puggle (Pug and Beagle).

Mixed Breeds

Mixed breeds are dogs that are of unknown or undeterminable heritage. A mixed-breed dog will have visible signs of heritage from more than two breeds. This can mean that the dog's parents were crossbreeds or mixed breeds. In some cases, it is possible to identify certain aspects of a dog's heritage through factors, such as color, size, coat, or head shape. Mixed-breed dogs are less uniform than crossbreeds and pedigree dogs, but are generally healthier.

Mixed breeds are also known as "mongrels," "mutts," or "curs." Most dogs that are of such mixed parentage are more or less individual. Some inherit more characteristics from one parent than the other, while other mixed breeds inherit equal amounts of physical characteristics from both parents. In some instances, mixed breeds go on to become established breeds in their own right. For example, in some countries, the Jack Russell Terrier used to be known as the Parson Russell Terrier, or a cross of that breed.

BREED DEVELOPMENT

It is amazing to look at the huge Great Dane and the tiny Chihuahua and consider that they evolved from the same animal. There are few animal species on the earth that display such a degree of physical diversity as the domestic dog. This is mainly due to man having controlled dog breeding since ancient times. The development of individual breeds is a long process that goes through many stages. There are environmental, social, natural, and even political factors that influence the development of dog breeds.

Selective Breeding

The next step is when man breeds certain dogs with other dogs to generate a set of desired characteristics. This happened when man domesticated the wolf and it happened when Louis Dobermann wanted an agile, strong and fearless guard dog for protection. It takes generations for the desired characteristics to present themselves consistently, but when they do the dogs with the strongest likeness to

Fascinating Facts

Shar Pei Fever is a disease that causes the hocks to swell; it is particular only to the Shar Pei.

man's original plan are used for breeding. The dogs are tried and tested in the role that they were bred for, with the most suitable being used to continue the bloodline.

Necessity

The first stage of the development of a dog breed is when man identifies a need or desire for a certain type of dog. Whether it is a herding dog that can work in the cold or a companion dog that is small and alert, every dog breed has come into existence because man identified a need for it. It may be that a dog existed that only partly fulfilled a need and was then used to develop a new, more suitable breed. Some entirely new breed groups have come into existence due to man's need for a certain type of dog.

LEFT

Each breed of dog has been bred to meet a need in man; whether to help herd sheep or simply for companionship.

Breeding True

"Breeding true" is a term that is applied to the stage of development where the majority of dogs are of a predictable and

yet to be recognized by foreign organizations or even their own kennel club or equivalent body. This can be due to social or political reasons or simply because the dog is not present in high enough numbers in that particular part of the world.

Retriever and German Shepherd, for example, have achieved worldwide popularity as both pets and working dogs. They exist in almost all parts of the world and are instantly recognizable as being of their type. Other breeds are less well known,

controlled appearance and temperament. This is where the breed begins to exhibit uniform characteristics, such as coat color, size, temperament, and intelligence level, that will become typical of that breed.

RIGHT

These Irish Soft-Coated Wheaten Terrier pups are identical, showing that that pedigree line is "breeding true."

in existence for centuries before it reaches the stage of standardization.

Standardization

A breed becomes standardized when an agreed set of criteria is written that governs how the dog should look and act. It is often done in the form of an official breed standard administered by one of the many national kennel clubs. A dog can be

Acceptance

When a breed is accepted by an official governing body, such as the American Kennel Club or the Fédération Cynologique Internationale, it becomes an officially recognized breed. Even today there are old and established breeds that are

Popularity

Each dog breed will attain a different level of mainstream popularity. The Labrador

offering a more specific or niche appeal to owners. The popularity of breeds declines and increases under the influence of our own lifestyles. Fighting breeds are less popular because dog fighting itself is now regarded as socially unacceptable.

Herding breeds tend to be constantly popular due to their versatility and intelligence, which enables them to function in many different and varied roles.

LEFT

Labrador Retrievers are globally popular, with appeal and characteristics that make them suitable as both domestic pets and working dogs.

BREED CLASSIFICATION

Pedigree breeds are classed in many ways, for example, by size, ancestry, type, or function. The most common way dog-breed administrators classify the breeds is by function; this relates to the role for which the dog was originally bred. However, the classification process is not simple and is subject to widespread debate. Certain breeds are classified differently by different organizations, which can lead to confusion. Non-pedigree breeds are not subjected to such formal classifications and are ineligible for registration with most authorities.

Fascinating Facts

Sigmund Freud's Chow Chow, which was named Jo Fi, used to sit in with him on therapy sessions.

Governance

There are many authorities that administer and register pedigree dog breeds. In many cases, the standards and classifications that are used vary from organization to organization, which can cause disagreement and confusion regarding what is considered typical for a breed. Commonly, these variations are linked to matters of environment and taste. For example, certain breeds are considered to be larger in the United States than they are elsewhere and this is reflected in the American Kennel Club breed standards. For the statistics given for each individual breed, this encyclopedia uses a combination of the information that is provided by the UK Kennel Club, the American Kennel Club, and the Fédération Cynologique Internationale (FCI) in order to reflect the wide range of data that is available.

It is also common for certain kennel clubs or authorities not to recognize a breed. This does not mean the breed is any less legitimate or valid, but is most likely due to the rarity or new status of a breed in a particular country. Some countries have breeds that were established to meet the needs of only that country and, therefore, are a long way from being established elsewhere.

In order for a dog to receive a pedigree certificate, it must be registered with the relevant authority or kennel club. The owner or breeder is required to provide documents detailing the ancestry of the dog or litter in question, which is typically in the form of a pedigree detailing the parents' heritage. Most authorities register a dog based on trust that the owner is supplying accurate, honest, and complete information.

ABOVE

The terrier category includes the Staffordshire Bull Terrier, which was bred to find quarry underground.

Dogs in the Kennel Club "utility" category have been used for a variety of jobs. Akitas were used in Japan for bear hunting.

The UK Kennel Club

The UK Kennel Club, or simply the Kennel Club as it is known in Britain, is the oldest official all-breed registry of purebred dogs. It was set up in 1873 and administers British pedigrees. The UK Kennel Club classifies dog breeds by function and uses seven categories.

Hound

This group contains almost all hound breeds. The definition of a hound is loosely applied in most instances; it typically refers to a dog that was bred to hunt either in packs or alone, using sight, scent or a combination of both. Certain breeds that are houndlike are not classed as such— for example the Italian Greyhound, which is not classed as a hound in Britain but as a toy breed. Hound breeds are among some of the oldest in the world. The Greyhound, Beagle, and Rhodesian Ridgeback are some of the most popular hound breeds.

Gun Dog

Gun-dog breeds include retrievers, spaniels, pointers, setters, and water dogs. The term is linked to the fact that most of the breeds in the group were bred to work on hunts and subsequently around guns. One of the most important aspects of a gun dog is its ability to remain calm around gunfire. The Labrador Retriever, Irish Setter, and Cocker Spaniel are just three of the Kennel Club's well-known gun-dog breeds.

Terrier

The term "terrier" is believed to be derived from the Latin word *terra*, which means "earth." Terriers were bred to "go to ground," which is a possible explanation for the link. Certain terrier breeds, such as the Yorkshire Terrier, although derived from terrier stock are not true terriers according to the UK Kennel Club and are classed as toy breeds instead. Terriers range in size from very small to large and have fulfilled roles as hunters, vermin catchers, guards, and even retrievers on occasion. The Staffordshire Bull Terrier and the Border Terrier are the two most popular terrier breeds in Britain.

Utility

The utility group contains the widest variation of dogs in terms of size, type, and function. Many dogs that have unique functions, such as the Dalmatian as a carriage dog, are contained within this group, as are many of the newest dog breeds. The Bulldog, Chow Chow, and Akita are all members of this group.

Working

The working group contains dogs that were bred for guarding, protecting, rescue, and, less commonly, hunting. Some of the largest breeds recognized by the UK Kennel Club are in this group, including the Great Dane, Saint Bernard, Rottweiler, Siberian Husky, and Mastiff.

The working-category dogs were bred for guarding and protecting, and the breeds are consequently very large, such as the Great Dane.

Pastoral

The pastoral group is where the traditional herding breeds are classified and includes some of the most intelligent and agile dog breeds. Typically, pastoral breeds originate in temperate climates, such as Europe, parts of Asia, and North America. There are few pastoral breeds from Africa because there is limited habitat for grazing animals and, therefore, little need for pastoral dogs. Many of the pastoral breeds have evolved to fulfill other working roles, such as police dogs and search-and-rescue dogs.

The German Shepherd, Border Collie, and Briard are popular pastoral breeds.

Toy

Toy breeds are typically those that were bred exlusively for companionship or those that have evolved to fulfill this need after the work for which they were intended diminished. Often they are small breeds, with varying degrees of activity and energy. The Yorkshire Terrier, Cavalier King Charles Spaniel, and Bichon Frise are all included in this group.

The American Kennel Club

The American Kennel Club is very similar in function and administration to the UK Kennel Club. It has categories for dogs that are of undetermined origin, such as dogs that were born to unregistered parents, and it also has a foundation stock service (FSS), which allows owners to register breeds that are not yet fully recognized by the authority. There are nine categorizations used by the American Kennel Club.

Sporting

The sporting group is analogous with the UK Kennel Club's gun-dog group. The American club also refers to gun breeds as bird dogs and includes setters, pointers, retrievers, and spaniels. The American Water Spaniel, Wirehaired Pointing Griffon, and Irish Setter are all in this group.

Hound

The hound group classifies breeds in the same way that the UK Kennel Club does, although it includes the Plott

and the Black-and-Tan Coonhound, neither of which are recognized by the UK Kennel Club.

Working

The American Kennel Club working group functions in the same way as the UK Kennel Club's. There are 25 breeds in this group, bred to guard, protect, and pull. However, the group does not contain certain breeds that are among the 26 working breeds of the UK Kennel Club, including the Beauceron and the Bouvier des Flandres.

ABOVE
Known as Griffon Bruxellois in Europe, the Brussels Griffon falls into the toy category in the United States.

LEFT
Dalmatians fall into the American nonsporting category.

Terrier

This group is much the same as that of the UK Kennel Club. It classifies dogs that were bred to control vermin and dig out pests from burrows. In this country, a terrier is sometimes referred to as a "feist."

Toy

The toy group functions in the same way as most toy groups, featuring smaller breeds that were established as companion animals. The group includes the Brussels Griffon, which is an American spelling of the Griffon Bruexellois.

Nonsporting

The nonsporting group is similar to the utility group of the UK Kennel Club, but certain members of the nonsporting group are considered to be "large toy breeds." It includes the Dalmatian, Shar Pei, and French Bulldog.

Herding

The herding breed group is the same in function as the pastoral group of the UK Kennel Club and includes most breeds that were established to herd, drove, and, less commonly, to protect flocks. The American Kennel Club classes the Belgian Shepherd varieties as separate breeds and refers to them as the Belgian Sheepdog, known as the Belgian Shepherd (Groenendael), Belgian Tervuren, known as the Belgian Shepherd (Tervuren), and the Belgian Malinois, known as the Belgian Shepherd (Malinois). It does not recognize the Belgian Shepherd (Laekenois).

Miscellaneous

The miscellaneous group does not have a comparable group within the UK Kennel Club. Breeds that are advanced from the foundation stock service stage but are not established enough to enter one of the actual breed groups are classified as miscellaneous.

Foundation stock service (FSS)

The foundation stock service group is used to classify breeds that are not established in the United States. This includes rare and new breeds that are not sufficiently numerous to constitute being a breed in their own right.

Fédération Cynologique Internationale (FCI)

The FCI is an organization that governs and administers 80 smaller kennel-club organizations. It is based in Belgium, but its members include South American, European, and Asian national kennel clubs. The

ABOVE
Part of the American herding category, the Groenendael is the most popular of the Belgian Shepherd varieties.

FCI recognizes 335 breeds; while the standards are authored by the individual national kennel clubs they are updated and translated by the FCI. It classifies breeds in a different way to the UK Kennel Club and the American Kennel Club. There are 11 groups, of which 10 are specific to breed types and one is for breeds that are provisionally accepted. A breed is classified firstly by group, which refers to its type, then by subgroup, which refers to its form and function.

Group 1

This group categorizes sheepdog and cattle-dog breeds, with the exception of the Swiss Cattle Dog.

Group 2

Group 2 categorizes Pinscher and Schnauzer breeds, Molosser breeds and Swiss Mountain and cattle breeds.

Group 3

Terriers are the only type of breed in this classification, distinguished thereafter by type, such as "bull" and "toy" terriers.

Group 4

This group recognizes only Dachshunds and categorizes the different varieties as separate breeds.

Group 5

This group categorizes Spitz-type and primitive-type breeds. Along with the Spitz-type breeds this group includes the Basenji, Thai Ridgeback, and Canaan Dog.

Group 6

Scent hounds and related breeds make up the sixth group. Breeds that are considered to be related to scent hounds include the Dalmatian and the Swedish Dachsbracke.

Group 7

Pointing dogs, such as the Irish Red Setter and Gordon Setter, that would otherwise be classed as gun or sporting dogs are attributed to their own cynological group.

Group 8

Retrievers, spaniels, and water dogs are classed together in Group 8. Unusually, the Labrador Retriever is listed as English by the FCI, which contrasts with the typical Canadian ancestry for which the breed is normally credited.

Group 9

Companion and toy breeds are categorized in this group, except for toy terrier breeds, which are distinct due to their terrier ancestry. There are 11 subcategories in Group 9, which distinguish between type and ancestry.

Group 10

Sight hounds are the only breeds in this group. The Italian Greyhound is classified as a true hound by the FCI, but not by the UK Kennel Club.

Group 11 (breeds provisionally accepted)

The eleventh group contains a handful of rare breeds that are not sufficiently well-established to be classed by form and ancestry, so are classed together by virtue of their rarity.

RIGHT
According to the Federation's classification, pointers and setters, such as the Gordon Setter, form the seventh group, distinct from other gun dogs.

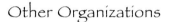
BELOW LEFT
Retrievers, spaniels, and water dogs, such as the Spanish Water Dog, form group 8 of the Federation's categories.

Other Organizations

There exist many other authorities that register and administer pedigrees. These may be groups set up for specific types of working dogs, or national groups that are separate from the FCI and other more mainstream bodies. Others include The United Kennel Club (an American club that deals with working or performance dogs independently of the American Kennel Club), Canadian Kennel Club, Australian National Kennel Council, and the Kennel Union of Southern Africa.

Fascinating Facts

The Blue Lacy, a newly established American hound breed, is known for its high resistance to snake bites.

BELOW
The Italian Greyhound, with the other sight hounds, forms group 10 of the Federation's categories.

The Americas

The Americas are home to a wide range of popular dog breeds: from the frozen Northern reaches of Alaska and its sledding dogs to Canada and its retriever and water breeds; through the United States and its many varieties of dog breeds, all the way down to South and Central America, home to the impressive Argentine Mastiff and the tiny Chihuahua. *The Complete Encyclopedia of Dogs* will guide you from north to south, taking in the largest and smallest breeds found in the Americas.

Native and Foreign Breeds

There are dogs of many different types, with varying roles and personalities, to be found in the Americas. Some of the breeds are descended from European dogs, while others are entirely native. Canada is home to the world's most popular breed, the Labrador Retriever, which is named after the province on Canada's east coast. All four corners of the United States are home to well-known dog breeds, from the Boston Terrier in the northeast to the Treeing Tennessee Brindle in the south.

Central and South America

Some of the world's largest and smallest breeds were developed in Central and South America—the

Mexican Chihuahua is the smallest breed on the earth. Mexico is also home to the Mexican Hairless, one of only a handful of hairless dogs in the world.

Cuba and Peru have their own dog breeds, too, which are now popular throughout the world. Brazil and Argentina are famous for their large and powerful breeds, such as the Argentine Dogo and the Brasil Mastiff, but small and feisty terriers are also native to that part of the world.

Some of the breeds that are native to the Americas have never become established outside of their home countries, such as the fast and powerful hound breeds that were bred in the Southern American states, while others are popular throughout the world.

NOVA SCOTIA DUCK TOLLING RETRIEVER

OFFICIAL CATEGORIZATION: UK: Gun Dog, AKC: Sporting, FCI: Group 8, Section 1

HEIGHT: 17–21 in. (55–58 cm)   WEIGHT: 55–80 lb. (25–36 kg)

OTHER NAMES: Toller, Little River Duck Dog, Yarmouth Toller

Color: Yellow, black, or chocolate

Coat Care: Moderate/high maintenance

Diet: Moderate/high consumption

As the name suggests, the Nova Scotia Duck Tolling Retriever is a Canadian retrieving breed. In fact, not only does the breed have a particularly self-explanatory name, it is one of the longest dog breed names in the United States.

It was originally bred for hunting waterfowl in rural Canada, where it would assist on shoots located near to water. The breed is intelligent and lively, making it a suitable family pet. The Nova Scotia Duck Tolling Retriever is rare due to the unique appeal of its working abilities. As a pet breed, particularly in Europe, it is uncommon. This is not due to the temperament of the breed but mainly to issues of demand. Even during its peak in popularity there was limited need for such a specific breed. As a pet, the Nova Scotia Duck Tolling Retriever displays many of the qualities and attributes that make related breeds, such as the Labrador Retriever and Golden Retriever, so popular.

LEFT
The Nova Scotia Duck Tolling Retriever originated in Canada in the early nineteenth century.

CANADIAN ESKIMO DOG

OFFICIAL CATEGORIZATION: UK: Working, AKC: Not recognized, FCI: Not recognized

HEIGHT: 19–28 in. (50–70 cm)   WEIGHT: 40–88 lb. (18–40 kg)

OTHER NAMES: Qimmik, Canadian Inuit Dog

Color: White or black and white

Coat Care: Moderate/high maintenance

Diet: Moderate/high consumption

The Canadian Eskimo Dog is typical of many Spitz-type breeds. It has a thick coat, large upwardly pointing ears, and a sturdy physique. Originally bred to work in snow pulling sleds, it is more suited to pulling large weights for shorter distances rather than lighter weights at a fast pace.

The breed is athletic and strong with a well-proportioned body partially concealed by the thickness of the coat. As with many sled-dog breeds, the Canadian Eskimo Dog is very pack-orientated and has a strong pack instinct. It is hardy and alert and its character reflects the work for which it was originally bred. The Canadian Eskimo Dog displays a confidence that can contribute to it being a fantastic pet or a troublesome pet, depending on which way this confidence is harnessed by the owner. To make a good pet, it requires a similarly confident owner.

LABRADOR RETRIEVER

Color: Yellow, black, or chocolate

Coat Care: Moderate/high maintenance

Diet: Moderate/high consumption

OFFICIAL CATEGORIZATION: UK: Gun Dog, AKC: Sporting, FCI: Group 8, Section 1

HEIGHT: 21–24½ in. (55–58 cm)   WEIGHT: 55–80 lb. (25–36 kg)

OTHER NAMES: Labrador, Lab

The Labrador Retriever is one of the most popular pet dog breeds in the world. This is no surprise to anyone who has ever owned or trained one of these friendly, intelligent, and obedient dogs. Labrador Retrievers are companionable and get along with people and other pets, including dogs and cats. They are still used as working retrievers in rural areas and, due to their kindly temperament and high intelligence levels, they are commonly used as assistance dogs—especially guide dogs.

An Intelligent Breed

The Labrador Retriever was bred originally in Canada, taking the first part of its name from the region of Canada where the breed originates and the second part from the role that it was bred to perform. The Labrador Retriever still retains many of its working instincts, so a game of "fetch" is always welcome. The Labrador Retriever is descended from the Newfoundland and the now-extinct Saint John's Water Dog (see page 114–15).

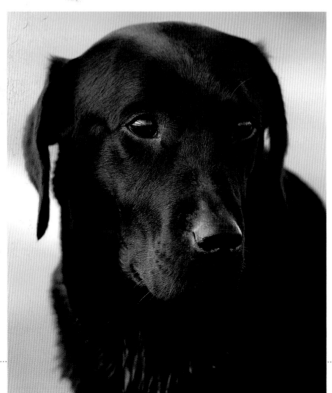

Originally bred for retrieving game birds in water and long grass, its high level of intelligence and strong play drive made the Labrador Retriever a formidable working dog. These same qualities are what make it such a popular pet today. It is a relaxed and playful breed, easy to train and well-mannered.

Companionship and Obedience

Many people who are involved in obedience training believe that the Labrador Retriever represents the ideal pet dog breed. It is willing to be taught, obedient, and intelligent, which means that inexperienced trainers and owners can integrate the Labrador Retriever into their life successfully without the need for overly firm handling.

Due to its relaxed and intelligent temperament, combined with a high intelligence, the Labrador Retriever makes a very effective assistance dog. Put to work as a guide dog and hearing dog the Labrador Retriever thrives in an environment of cooperation and companionship, because it loves to please its owner.

LEFT
Labrador Retrievers are friendly, intelligent, tolerant, obedient, and fun-loving; no wonder they are the most popular breed globally.

NEWFOUNDLAND

OFFICIAL CATEGORIZATION: UK: Working, AKC: Working, FCI: Group 2, Section 2

HEIGHT: 25–29 in. (65–72 cm)   WEIGHT: 110–152 lb. (50–69 kg)

OTHER NAMES: Newfie

Color: Black or brown with white tip on chest

Coat Care: High/very high maintenance

Diet: Very high consumption

The Newfoundland is a large, water-going dog bred originally in Canada. It is one of the ancestors of the popular Labrador Retriever. The Newfoundland is a particularly large and heavy dog but the breed is very popular due to its gentle and calm nature. It is an excellent swimmer due to its water-resistant coat, great strength, and webbed feet, and is used as a water-rescue dog.

Due to its contribution to the Labrador Retriever bloodline, the Newfoundland is in the bloodline of many of the most popular breeds of pet dog that we know today, including the Golden Retriever and the Curly-Coated Retriever. It is not and has never been a gun-dog breed, but its intelligence and character have been passed on to a whole new generation and type of working dog.

The Gentle Giant
The Newfoundland makes a great family pet in the right circumstances. The breed is friendly and placid, but does require a certain amount of space to accommodate its size. As with many large breeds, any minor indiscretion, such as jumping up or pawing, can become a serious problem, as such an action can cause injury to people, especially children.

It is for this reason that a Newfoundland kept as a family pet must be properly trained for obedience and manners.

The Newfoundland is looked upon fondly by many people due to its devotion to man. Having worked as a lifesaver onboard ships and boats in ice-cold seas, the breed as a whole has done a lot to earn the respect of dog lovers all over the world. Even today, the Newfoundland as a pet displays remarkable dedication and loyalty to its human companions. It is typically well-behaved and affable, but if mistreated or provoked, it can prove to be a formidable adversary due to its size and strength.

Fascinating **F**acts

Residents of Swansea, in South Wales, are often nicknamed "Jacks." This is a reference to a Newfoundland called Swansea Jack that rescued many people during the 1930s.

TOY FOX TERRIER

Color: Combination of black, white, and tan

Coat Care: Low maintenance

Diet: Low consumption

OFFICIAL CATEGORIZATION: UK: Not recognized, AKC: Toy, FCI: Not recognized

HEIGHT: 8–11 in. (21–29 cm)   WEIGHT: 3.5–8 lb. (1–3 kg.)

OTHER NAMES: None

The geographical origins of the Toy Fox Terrier are disputed, but many people claim that it was bred originally in Britain and subsequently became more established in North America. Ancestors of the breed include the Chihuahua and the Manchester Terrier, which is why the Toy Fox Terrier exhibits a unique combination of feistiness and calmness, depending on its environment.

RIGHT

The American Kennel Club-recognized Toy Fox Terrier has, as its name suggests, both toy and terrier characteristics.

The Toy Fox Terrier has, typically, a mixture of toy and terrier attributes, making it an interesting specimen. The hardiness and playfulness of a terrier is present in many Toy Fox Terriers, but this is sometimes tempered with a more relaxed personality. The breed is noted for its robust health and suitability for apartment living, making it an ideal choice as a pet for city dwellers.

Due to its ancestry, the Toy Fox Terrier has a noticeably outgoing personality. This is not to every person's taste, but it certainly ensures that the breed does not go unnoticed.

AMERICAN ESKIMO DOG

Color: White

Coat Care: High maintenance

Diet: Moderate consumption

OFFICIAL CATEGORIZATION: UK: Not recognized, AKC: Nonsporting, FCI: Not recognized

HEIGHT: 9–19 in. (23–48 cm) (3 sizes)   WEIGHT: No standard

OTHER NAMES: None

Despite what the name may suggest, this breed originated in Europe. It is a member of the Spitz family of dogs and was bred as a companion and to work in snow. It has a thick coat for warmth and pricked upright ears for heat conservation. It comes in three sizes: toy, miniature, and standard.

The temperament of the American Eskimo Dog reflects its working attributes: it is strong-willed yet playful and friendly. The American Eskimo Dog is favored for its loyalty and dedication to the pack, which is typical of most Spitz-family dogs.

Like many sled breeds, the American Eskimo Dog is driven by strong pack urges and instincts. This characteristic was valuable to those who put the dog to work, but in the domestic environment it can prove to be a challenge when attempting training, especially when other dogs are around.

BOSTON TERRIER

OFFICIAL CATEGORIZATION: UK: Utility,
AKC: Nonsporting, FCI: Group 9, Section 11

HEIGHT: 15–17 in. (45–51 cm)   WEIGHT: 15–25 lb. (7–11 kg)

OTHER NAMES: None

Color: Brindle with white markings

Coat Care: Low maintenance

Diet: Low/moderate consumption

The breed is admired for its characteristically expressive face; this is due to the fact that it used to be a lot bigger than it is today. With ancestors from the Molosser group of dogs, the Boston Terrier has inherited a heavy jaw and prominent jowls, the latter being a feature that is traditionally associated with larger, heavier dogs.

LEFT
The Boston Terrier is distinctive by having an 'all-American' lineage, and also for having up-standing ears, despite its Mastiff ancestry.

The Boston Terrier was originally bred for fighting in the United States. However, as this sport diminished in popularity, the dogs were bred to be smaller and the modern Boston Terrier is notably more diminuitive than the original. Today, the dog is a friendly and fun companion animal with an interesting appearance due to its ancestry of Bulldog and Mastiff.

All-American

The ears are one of the most distinguishing features of this breed, sitting perfectly upright and framing an already unique face. It is rare for dogs descending from Mastiffs to have upright ears. It has a compact, sturdy little frame and its head is described by admirers as "endearingly boxy." One of the main reasons for the popularity of the Boston Terrier breed in the United States is that it

represents one of a handful of "all-American" dogs with a strong lineage of traditional breeds.

Challenging but Rewarding

Although it no longer retains its fighting instincts, the Boston Terrier is very lively, good-natured, and occasionally naughty. The breed is friendly but often proves to be too much to handle for inexperienced or ill-prepared owners, because it is energetic and is often considered boisterous and challenging. However, with firm and confident training it can and will make a rewarding and fulfilling pet.

There is no typical personality found in Boston Terriers—most members of the breed are independent, which means that their temperament is influenced far more by their environment than by inherited habits and characteristics.

Fascinating Facts

John F. Kennedy was allergic to dogs but he owned two German Shepherds, one named Charlie and one named Clipper.

RAT TERRIER

Color: Various

Coat Care: Low maintenance

Diet: Low consumption

OFFICIAL CATEGORIZATION: UK: Not recognized, AKC: Terrier, FCI: Not recognized

HEIGHT: 13–18 in. (4.5–6 cm)   WEIGHT: 10–25 lb. (5–12.5 kg)

OTHER NAMES: American Rat Terrier, Ratting Terrier

The Rat Terrier is an American breed with an unclear history. There are many varieties of dog that have been referred to as Rat Terriers throughout the development and establishment of breeds. In fact, many terriers initially were bred for rat catching so it is a very common reference to make. However, the dog that is widely acknowledged as **the Rat Terrier is a feisty, tenacious breed that was bred in farming communities.**

The role for which the Rat Terrier was bred means that the working stock that still exists exhibit very strong hunting instincts and are easily stimulated by movement. As pets, Rat Terriers are suitable in most environments and, due to their lively and active personas, are very much suited to families with high activity levels. The Rat Terrier is an intelligent and adaptable breed that is quite happy to conform to the environment in which it is living.

RIGHT
The Rat Terrier is not recognized by the UK Kennel Club or the FCI, and there is no standard for its height, weight, or color.

BOYKIN SPANIEL

Color: No standard color; typically comparable to other spaniels

Coat Care: Moderate/high maintenance

Diet: Moderate/high consumption

OFFICIAL CATEGORIZATION: UK: Not recognized, AKC: Not recognized, FCI: Not recognized

HEIGHT: No standard   WEIGHT: No standard

OTHER NAMES: None

This breed is an American variant on other spaniel breeds. It performs a very similar role to other spaniels around the world, namely **to flush and retrieve game, but it was bred to do so in a specific environment of grassy riverbanks. It is not suited to working in cold water due to the relative lightness of its coat.**

There are two very good reasons why the Boykin Spaniel is a popular working dog. First, it exhibits great stamina in hot weather. Second, and more importantly, due to its compact size, it does not take up much room in a fishing boat.

The Boykin Spaniel exhibits many of the same personality traits as other spaniels—it is friendly, energetic, and intelligent. Adapting well to the domestic environment, the Boykin Spaniel will play happily with family members and thrives when its retrieving instincts are stimulated.

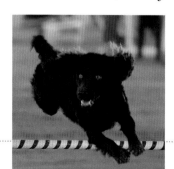

LEFT
Height, weight, and color are not standardized for the Boykin Spaniel.

AMERICAN WATER SPANIEL

OFFICIAL CATEGORIZATION: UK: Not recognized,
AKC: Sporting, FCI: Group 8, Section 3

HEIGHT: 15–18 in. (30–46 cm)   WEIGHT: 25–40 lb. (11–20 kg)

OTHER NAMES: None

Color: No standard; typically liver and white

Coat Care: High maintenance

Diet: Moderate/high consumption

This breed is best known in the United States, but mostly unknown elsewhere. It performs a typical retriever role and is adept at bringing back fowl from water. It is most likely that this breed is the ancestor of the following breeds: Curly-Coated Retriever, Tweed Water Spaniel, **Irish Water Spaniel, and Chesapeake Bay Retriever.**

The American Water Spaniel was bred for a very specific environment of grassy riverbanks. The breed retains many of its working instincts but makes a versatile and adaptable pet with a keen fondness for play. The American Water Spaniel does not require constant attention or stimulation—it has a very admirable independent streak that enables certain dogs of the breed to entertain themselves.

Like most spaniel breeds the American Water Spaniel is intelligent and determined. It lends itself well to training, and in many cases advanced obedience and agility can be achieved with this breed.

TREEING TENNESSEE BRINDLE

OFFICIAL CATEGORIZATION: UK: Not recognized,
AKC: Not recognized, FCI: Not recognized

HEIGHT: No standard   WEIGHT: No standard

OTHER NAMES: Tennessee Brindle

Color: Brindle

Coat Care: Moderate maintenance

Diet: High consumption

The Treeing Tennessee Brindle is particularly rare outside of the United States. It was bred here and has not become established outside of it. It is a large and powerful hunting dog that is popular among rural communities, particularly in the South, due to its athletic build and powerful scenting abilities. As the name suggests, its origins are in the state of Tennessee.

The breed is affectionate, intelligent, companionable, and brave, which makes it a very popular choice as a pet. Many people rely on the distinctive loud and deep baying of the Treeing Tennessee Brindle because it serves as guard dog on rural properties. Although its instinct is to hunt, the dog is calm and affable in the domestic environment. Despite its size and occasional volume, it makes a good pet and can adapt easily to domestic life.

LEFT
Tending to be large and heavily built, with a brindle coat, the Treeing Tennessee Brindle remains officially an unrecognized breed.

AMERICAN STAFFORDSHIRE TERRIER

Color: Various, including brindle, brown, white, black, or liver

Coat Care: Low maintenance

Diet: High consumption

OFFICIAL CATEGORIZATION: UK: Not recognized, AKC: Terrier, FCI: Group 3, Section 3

HEIGHT: (17–19 in. (42.5–50 cm)   WEIGHT: 57–67 lb. (26–30 kg)

OTHER NAMES: Am Staff

The American Staffordshire Terrier is more closely related to the American Pit Bull Terrier than it is to the Staffordshire Bull Terrier. It is a powerfully built and impressive-looking breed that was intended to function as the domestic version of the working American Pit Bull Terrier. Sadly, the American Staffordshire Bull Terrier has been involved in organized dog fighting in the past.

Despite being associated with fighting and having a heavy jaw, the American Staffordshire Terrier is friendly and loyal. Although brave and eager to defend its pack, the breed is not overtly aggressive. One thing that many people do not realize about dogs of this kind is that nature dictates that they do not like to fight. Certainly some breeds are better equipped physically to fight, but they only fight for survival. In order to get two dogs to fight for entertainment, it is necessary to provoke the dog and manufacture a situation where it feels in danger—hence the widespread condemnation of the "sport."

AMERICAN PIT BULL TERRIER

Color: Any

Coat Care: Low maintenance

Diet: High consumption

OFFICIAL CATEGORIZATION: UK: Banned under the Dangerous Dogs Act 1991, AKC: Not recognized, FCI: Not recognized

HEIGHT: No standard   WEIGHT: No standard

Other Names: Pit Bull

The American Pit Bull Terrier is a strong, powerful breed with the tenacity of smaller terriers and the power that is more often associated with Mastiff breeds. It is inextricably linked with organized dog fighting and is subject to breed-specific legislation in many countries.

The American Pit Bull Terrier possesses a well-muscled and powerful physique that lends itself well to fighting other dogs. The body is taut and strong and the legs are lean but not thin. The jaw is very wide and deep, enabling the dog to deliver a powerful bite. Despite its reputation, the American Pit Bull Terrier is not an inherently dangerous dog. It is a skilled and powerful fighter but it does not fight unless trained to do so. The breed is banned in Britain due to its association with illegal fighting. However, it is a popular pet in the United States thanks to its loyalty, confidence, and relaxed nature.

LEFT
Large and muscular, the American Pit Bull Terrier remains a popular pet in this country.

AUSTRALIAN SHEPHERD

OFFICIAL CATEGORIZATION: UK: Pastoral,
AKC: Herding , FCI: Group II

HEIGHT: 19–23 in. (43–58 cm)   WEIGHT: 35–75 lb. (16–34 kg)

OTHER NAMES: None

Color: Various, including blue merle and black merle

Coat Care: High/very high maintenance

Diet: Moderate consumption

LEFT
Actually an American breed developed over the past century, the Australian Shepherd won Best in Show at Crufts, 2006.

Despite its name, this is an American breed. The Australian Shepherd is a popular herding dog in the United States and is a relatively new breed, established only within the past 100 years. One of the reasons that the breed is referred to as Australian is due to its ancestry: it counts the Australian Cattle Dog and the Kelpie as contributors to its bloodline.

The Australian Shepherd is a lively and inquisitive breed, making it an excellent choice for herding work. Like nearly all herding breeds, however, it does require mental stimulation and plenty of exercise to cater for its strong working instincts.

The Australian Shepherd has developed significantly as a domesticated pet and in the show ring it is beginning to achieve success. In recent years, conformation shows have acknowledged the careful breeding that has gone into the breed, and the Australian Shepherd even won Best in Show at Crufts in 2006.

PLOTT HOUND

OFFICIAL CATEGORIZATION: UK: Not recognized,
AKC: Hound, FCI: Not recognized

HEIGHT: 20–25 in. (50–64 cm)   WEIGHT: 40–60 lb. (18–27 kg)

OTHER NAMES: None

Color: Any shade of brindle

Coat Care: Moderate maintenance

Diet: High/very high consumption

The Plott Hound has German and American ancestry. Two Germans named Plott brought dogs to North Carolina and bred them to produce a boar-hunting scent hound. The Plott Hound of today is a large and imposing dog with a startling bark. The breed has excellent scenting skills and has the power to bring down big game. However, the Plott Hound is used less for hunting now and is favored more as a semidomestic pet, typically living on farmland. The dog has latent aggression but is not overtly confrontational with people or dogs; it is more accurately described as loyal, brave, and fearless.

Due to the combination of its hunting background and impressive physical dimensions, the Plott Hound is seen by many as an unsuitable pet. This is not true. In the right hands, and given the right amount of space and freedom, the Plott Hound makes a fantastic, happy and devoted family pet.

CATAHOULA LEOPARD DOG

Color: Various

Coat Care: High/very high maintenance

Diet: High/very high consumption

OFFICIAL CATEGORIZATION: UK: Not recognized, AKC: Not recognized, FCI: Not recognized

HEIGHT: 19–25 in. (50–65 cm) WEIGHT: 45–95 lb. (21–45 kg)

OTHER NAMES: Catahoula Hog Dog, Catahoula Cur

The Catahoula Leopard Dog is one of the longest-established American breeds. Originally bred as a war dog in Louisiana, the Catahoula Leopard Dog is now more popular as a rural working dog used to track and hunt small game and vermin. The breed has proven to be a versatile companion, adapting its role to suit the needs of man.

Like many tracking breeds, the Catahoula Leopard dog is relatively relaxed when not in a working scenario. The change in temperament when the hunting instincts are stimulated is quite drastic. The breed, like many large and powerful breeds, exudes an air of quiet confidence that is very appealing to some people, especially in rural areas. The Catahoula Leopard Dog is very protective of its territory, meaning that in the right circumstances and with the right training it can perform as a very effective guard or watchdog.

LEFT
The Catahoula Leopard Dog is a sturdy, confident tracking dog and a reassuring guard dog in rural areas, originating in Louisiana.

TREEING WALKER COONHOUND

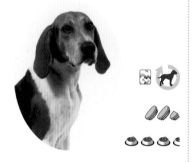

Color: Various; typically tan and white

Coat Care: Moderate/high maintenance

Diet: High/very high consumption

OFFICIAL CATEGORIZATION: UK: Not recognized, AKC: Not recognized, FCI: Not recognized

HEIGHT: No standard WEIGHT: No standard

OTHER NAMES: None

The Treeing Walker Coonhound is a descendent of the English Fox Hound. It is a popular hunting hound in rural areas of the United States and functions as part of a hunting pack. The Treeing Walker Coonhound is fast, agile, and intelligent. It was first recognized as a breed in its own right during the middle of the last century.

Treeing is a method of hunting where the hounds chase quarry that would normally hide in a tree. The method involves the hound baying and barking at the quarry until it leaves the tree. Because of this instinct, Coonhounds are often difficult to control once stimulated into treeing. Typically for a scent hound, in the domestic environment the Treeing Walker Coonhound is very affectionate and loving.

The breed is suited to inclusion in families with children, but it does prefer an outdoor life that stimulates its retained instincts and urges.

AMERICAN FOXHOUND

OFFICIAL CATEGORIZATION: UK: Not recognized,
AKC: Hound, FCI: Group 3, Section 4

HEIGHT: 21–25 in. (53–63 cm)   WEIGHT: 65–75 lb. (25–34 kg)

OTHER NAMES: None

Color: Tricolor; any

Coat Care: Moderate/high maintenance

Diet: Moderate consumption

The American Foxhound is a close relative of the English Foxhound. It is a typical hunting dog, using scent to track quarry—particularly foxes. Physically, it resembles its English cousin, standing at a similar height and displaying the distinctive tricolor markings. Many people describe the American Fox Hound as resembling a Beagle, only much larger. This is true in relation to coloration and the shape of the head, but seen in motion the distinction between the two breeds should be very easy to make.

The American Foxhound is intelligent and alert. It requires socialization and stimulating training in order to keep it from getting bored. Unlike many breeds, the American Foxhound is still governed strongly by its scenting and tracking instincts and can often wander off following a scent. This is just one reason why the breed is best-suited to confident and experienced dog owners.

CHINOOK

OFFICIAL CATEGORIZATION: UK: Not recognized,
AKC: Not recognized, FCI: Not recognized

HEIGHT: 21–27 in. (53–60 cm)   WEIGHT: 59–90 lb. (23–40 kg)

OTHER NAMES: None

Color: Sandy

Coat Care: Moderate maintenance

Diet: Moderate consumption

The Chinook is a very rare and unusual breed. It was bred in the northeast of the United States by crossing a Husky-type breed with a Mastiff-type breed, which is why the dog has a heavy-set face on an otherwise lean body. Intended for sled work, the Chinook demonstrates many typical sled-dog characteristics, but it also lacks many of the more traditional sled dog characteristics, such as bushy tail, white coat, and pricked ears.

Described as friendly and calm, this rare breed makes a desirable pet. It still retains working instincts despite general domestication, but with good training and firm handling these can be managed. Like other sled-dog breeds, the Chinook is likely to display strong pack-orientated behavior. This has both benefits and drawbacks in domestic life but provided that the dog is secure of its own place within the pack it should thrive in a family home.

CHESAPEAKE BAY RETRIEVER

OFFICIAL CATEGORIZATION: UK: Gun Dog, AKC: Sporting, FCI: Group 8, Section 3

Color: Red-gold, brown, or straw

Coat Care: Very high maintenance

Diet: Moderate/high consumption

HEIGHT: 23–26 in. (58–66 cm)   WEIGHT: 55–80 lb. (18.5–26 kg)

OTHER NAMES: Chessie

Like many retriever breeds, the Chesapeake Bay Retriever is named in honor of the region from which it originates. Many of the world's most established retriever breeds hail from the northern United States and Canada, including the Chesapeake Bay Retriever. The breed is a descendant of the Newfoundland; it retains many qualities inherited from its ancestors, including intelligence and energy.

A Loyal Friend

The Chesapeake Bay Retriever is a graceful yet highly energetic dog. It has a waterproof coat, which requires a fair amount of grooming, that sits on a well-formed and lean frame. The head is similar in shape to that of many retriever breeds, with a well-defined nose and jaw. The breed combines loyalty and friendliness with a territorial and protective streak. The loyalty of a Chesapeake Bay Retriever typically extends to only one person, usually the one perceived to be the most dominant member of the pack. It is certainly more rowdy than most retrievers, fond of extended and energetic play sessions. The breed makes a rewarding yet often challenging pet due to its passion for activity.

One of the most interesting things to note about the personality of the Chesapeake Bay Retriever is the way that it sometimes curls its lip when happy. To the untrained eye this can look like a sign of aggression, but some dogs perform this action when they are contented or excited.

Youthful Exuberance

Typically, the Chesapeake Bay Retriever is slow to mature, with dogs acting like puppies for a longer than average time. This can present its own challenges when it comes to training, but owners are encouraged to be patient and to remember that while the dog is physically maturing it is still mentally immature. Quite often this slow maturation can be perceived as disobedience or bad behavior, so it is important that owners of Chesapeake Bay Retrievers put extra effort into their training.

LEFT

A descendant of the Newfoundland, the Chesapeake Bay Retriever is a thoroughly North American dog, even named after an East Coast bay.

REDBONE COONHOUND

OFFICIAL CATEGORIZATION: UK: Not recognized,
AKC: Not recognized, FCI: Not recognized

HEIGHT: 19–23 in. (53–68 cm)   WEIGHT: 45–70 lb. (20–32 kg)

Color: Red

Coat Care: Moderate/high maintenance

OTHER NAMES: None   Diet: Moderate/high consumption

The Redbone Coonhound is a versatile and adaptable hunting hound that was bred to control racoon populations in rural

Georgia. It is a strong swimmer and exhibits high levels of intelligence and prey drive. Its ancestors are various strains of Foxhounds and Bloodhounds, and the Redbone Coonhound exhibits the most desirable traits of each.

Modern Redbone Coonhounds retain their hunting instincts and thrive on play and interaction that

appeals to these urges. The breed is large but graceful and combines a muscular physique with a gentle demeanor. When excited it can become boisterous and requires a confident, firm owner with previous training experience.

Today, many Redbone Coonhounds live an enviable life. Due to the breed's popularity in the rural parts of the South,

LEFT

The Redbone Coonhound originates from rural Georgia, and is often seen enjoying life on a ranch.

it is normal to see a Redbone Coonhound having the run of a large ranch. Many are still required to work, but the Redbone Coonhound's friendly nature and guarding abilities makes it a valuable pet.

BLACK-AND-TAN COONHOUND

OFFICIAL CATEGORIZATION:
UK: Not recognized, AKC: Hound, FCI: Group 6, Section 4

HEIGHT: 23–27 in. (58–68 cm)   WEIGHT: 64–125 lb. (29–45 kg)

OTHER NAMES: None

Color: Black and tan

Coat Care: Moderate maintenance

Diet: High/very high consumption

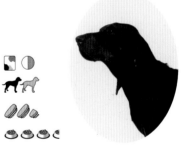

The Black-and-Tan Coonhound was bred in the United States to hunt racoon and larger game, including bears. It is a large, powerful breed with extremely sophisticated tracking and scenting abilities. The Black-and-Tan Coonhound represents a combination of strength, agility and determination.

In modern times, the need for the breed to work has decreased, but the Black-and-Tan Coonhound is still well represented in the southern states, particularly in rural areas.

The breed is strong of character but obedient.

It is considered to be gentle but is very well-built. Training can be disrupted by its instinct to track. The Black-and-Tan Coonhound has a very loud, baying bark that can make it appear rather fearsome, but in reality the breed is relaxed and calm — exuding an air of confident charisma.

AMERICAN ENGLISH COONHOUND

OFFICIAL CATEGORIZATION: UK: Not recognized, AKC: FSS, FCI: Not recognized

HEIGHT: No standard   WEIGHT: No standard

OTHER NAMES: None

Color: Red and white

Coat Care: Low maintenance

Diet: High/very high consumption

The American English Coonhound is a working hound bred in the United States. It is descended from the English Foxhound but was adapted here to cope with American climates and American game, notably racoons and small bears. It is noticeably similar in size and appearance to other Coonhounds. The breed is well-muscled and appears to be built for speed and endurance. It has a dignified appearance, with large ears and a noble face. The coat is coarse, harsh, and short.

Primarily a working hound, the American English Coonhound is not particularly well-established as a pet breed. Its ability to work either as part of a pack or alone suggests it has a versatility that would serve it well as a pet. As a working hound it is obedient, loyal, and intelligent. Coonhounds in general are brave and strong, making them popular pets in and around the regions in which they were bred for work.

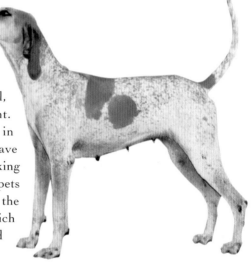

ALASKAN MALAMUTE

OFFICIAL CATEGORIZATION: UK: Working, AKC: Working, FCI: Group 5, Section 1

HEIGHT: 23–25 in. (58–63 cm)   WEIGHT: 75–85 lb. (33–38 kg)

OTHER NAMES: None

Color: Light gray, black, or red

Coat Care: High/very high maintenance

Diet: High/very high consumption

The Alaskan Malamute is a strong and energetic sledding breed, originally bred by the Mahlemut tribe in Alaska. It is one of the oldest dog breeds on the earth and is a very close descendent of the Gray Wolf. Due to its breeding, the Alaskan Malamute is strong, powerful, and pack orientated. It makes a good pet, but only in experienced and confident hands.

The Alaskan Malamute is often mistaken for a Siberian Husky. It possesses a striking coloration and has an impressively athletic physique. It is considered to be one of the wildest domesticated dogs ever bred and as such can sometimes prove to be a training challenge.

Due to its wild bloodline, the Malamute sometimes struggles to accept smaller animals in the domestic environment. Amiable and obedient around humans, the breed will need a firm hand during training. It makes a good companion for children, when properly trained.

BLUETICK COONHOUND

OFFICIAL CATEGORIZATION: UK: Not recognized,
AKC: Not recognized, FCI: Not recognized

HEIGHT: 21–27 in. (49–64 cm)   WEIGHT: 40–80 lb. (18–37 kg)

OTHER NAMES: None

Color: Black, white, or gray with blue or black ticks

Coat Care: High maintenance

Diet: High consumption

L ike most Coonhounds the Bluetick Coonhound originates from the southern states. It is a more distinct-looking hound when compared to the Redbone Coonhound or the Black-and-Tan Coonhound due to its striking blue-ticked colorations. The breed is descended from the English Foxhound but the modern Bluetick Coonhound is diversifying as a breed even today.

The breed is very intelligent and is often overcome with the urge to act on a scent that it has picked up. Scenting is very important to the interaction of the Bluetick Coonhound and it will not hesitate to sniff a person thoroughly on first meeting. Like other Coonhounds the Bluetick Coonhound can appear intimidating due to its large physique and baying bark, which can be heard over long distances. However, owners of the breed will attest that this is a misconception and that the Bluetick Coonhound is a friendly, confident, and happy dog.

MEXICAN HAIRLESS

OFFICIAL CATEGORIZATION: UK: Utility,
AKC: Nonsporting, FCI: Not recognized

HEIGHT: 9–23 in. (25–60 cm)   WEIGHT: 10–50 lb. (4–20 kg)

OTHER NAMES: Xolo

Color: Black, dark gray, brown, liver, or blonde

Coat Care: Zero maintenance

Diet: Low consumption

T he Mexican Hairless is a unique and very unusual-looking dog breed. As the name suggests, it has no body hair except for a very fine, short down in some cases. It is unclear how the dog evolved to become hairless, but it is likely that it is due to the heat of the country of origin. The breed has large ears, which is another characteristic shared with other dogs bred in hot countries.

The Mexican Hairless is a sensitive and affectionate breed, often noted for its extremely devoted attitude toward family members. The dog does not crave attention but does love to interact with people and other pets. The popularity of the Mexican Hairless as a pet is increasing, due in part to its unusual appearance but mainly to its compatibility with modern family life. It is adaptable to new situations and is very intelligent, meaning that a neglected dog will become unhappy quite quickly.

BELOW
The large, batlike ears and minimal coat of the Mexican Hairless dog are both the results of the hot climate in which it was bred.

CHIHUAHUA

Color: White, spotted, brindle, piebald, tan, sable, or combinations thereof

Coat Care: Moderate maintenance

Diet: Minimal consumption

OFFICIAL CATEGORIZATION: UK: Toy, AKC: Toy, FCI: Group 9, Section 6

HEIGHT: 6–10 in. (15–25 cm)   WEIGHT: 4–7 lb. (1.5–3 kg)

OTHER NAMES: None

The Chihuahua is named after the region of Mexico where it was discovered. This is the smallest breed of dog in the world, but what it lacks in stature it makes up for in personality. It is a mysterious breed with little known about its genetic background. Some members of the scientific community believe that the Chihuahua is descended from the Fennec Fox as opposed to the Wolf, rendering it not a "true" dog. This has not been proven but is a firmly held belief for some researchers.

A Distinctive Appearance

Physically, the Chihuahua is very unusual. It has large, bulbous eyes in relation to the shape and size of its head. The ears are oversized, which accentuates the unusual dimensions of the eyes. In many cases, the coat is a mixture of many colors and patterns and the tail varies from strain to strain in shape, length, and coat coverage.

ABOVE

Named after an area in Mexico, the Chihuahua is a loyal and dainty dog, which some people actually think descends from a fox.

Small Yet Feisty

The Chihuahua is feisty, lively, and energetic. Devoted to its owner and loyal to pack members it makes a great family pet. One of the most notable things about the temperament of the Chihuahua is the disregard it gives to its own stature. Chihuahuas, despite being small and comparatively weak, are happy to play with other dogs, even when the going gets rough.

A Chihuahua will display dissatisfaction when the person to whom it is loyal receives attention from other people or other dogs. It also has a tendency to nip or bite when scared, which differs from most dogs that prefer to growl as a warning first. This presents certain logistical problems for people with children who want to own a Chihuahua. It is advisable that both the children and the dog go through a process of training and socialization to ensure that there is harmony in the family dynamic. A Chihuahua can be aloof toward people with whom it is not familiar.

Fascinating Facts

The Chihuahua is the only breed that is born with a soft spot on its head, which is called a moleras. The softness is the result of the skull being incompletely developed at birth, although it does disappear as the skull forms.

HAVANESE

OFFICIAL CATEGORIZATION: UK: Toy, AKC: Toy,
FCI: Not recognized

HEIGHT: 8–12 in. (21–30 cm)

WEIGHT: No standard

OTHER NAMES: None

Color: Any, although most commonly white

Coat Care: High/very high maintenance

Diet: Low/moderate consumption

The diminutive Havanese is a member of the Bichon family. It originates from Cuba, being descended from matings between other Bichon-type dogs that were introduced to each other on sailboats. Although there is no standard color and any color is permissible, most examples are white. The breed is small with a rounded face and a dainty gait. Very rare and sought after, it can command a large fee as a purebred puppy.

The Havanese is a toy breed and as such exhibits traditional companionship qualities. It is friendly, easy-going, and calm around children and other animals. Its temperament is comparable to other members of the Bichon family of dogs. Despite its diminutive proportions, the Havanese is not afraid of getting involved in play, especially when there are children or other dogs around.

RIGHT

Descended from Bichon-type dogs owned by sailors on the Cuban coast, the Havanese is often, although not necessarily, white.

BRAZILIAN TERRIER

OFFICIAL CATEGORIZATION: UK: Not recognized,
AKC: Not recognized, FCI: Group 3, Section 1

HEIGHT: 14–16 in. (35–40 cm)

WEIGHT: 14–20 lb. (6–9 kg)

OTHER NAMES: None

Color: White, black, tan, brown, or blue

Coat Care: Moderate maintenance

Diet: Moderate consumption

The Brazilian is a medium-small terrier originating from Brazil. It is a descendent of the Fox Terrier, as well as other unknown terrier breeds. It has an alert composure that has made it a popular ratting breed in Brazil and other parts of South America.

The Brazilian Terrier is one of the most active and feisty terrier breeds. It has a high prey drive and a keen instinct to hunt. Typically used for hunting in packs, it is relatively pack orientated, with strong tendencies to instigate play around other dogs. Due to its active temperament and high intelligence, it can become destructive and disruptive when bored, so leaving the dog alone and unstimulated for long periods of time is not recommended.

Leaving the Brazilian Terrier alone with a small animal, such as a pet rabbit, is also not advisable because of its strong hunting instincts.

Fascinating Facts

Dogs are able to hear sounds of a far higher frequency than humans, but they also suffer a higher percentage of hearing loss in old age.

BRAZILIAN MASTIFF

OFFICIAL CATEGORIZATION: UK: Banned under the Dangerous Dogs Act 1991, AKC: Discovery Group, FCI: Group 2, section 2

Color: Solid yellow, reddish tan, black, or brindle

Coat Care: Minimal maintenance

Diet: High/very high consumption

HEIGHT: 27–29½ in. (65–75 cm)   WEIGHT: 86–90½ lb. (39–41 kg)

OTHER NAMES: Fila Brasileiro

The Brazilian Mastiff, or Fila Brasileiro, is an exceptionally powerful and large breed. Originally, it was bred for guarding and herding, but latterly it has been associated with organized dog fighting. It is one of four dogs that are banned in Great Britain under the Dangerous Dogs Act 1991. It does not have a typical fighting dog appearance but displays drop ears and loose jowls. It counts the Bulldog and the Bloodhound among its ancestors.

Despite its negative associations with organized dog fighting in Great Britain, it is a popular pet elsewhere. Naturally averse to strangers yet affectionate and friendly in its own territory, the Brazilian Mastiff makes a fantastic guard dog and a good family pet. It has a striking confidence about it that can sometimes be mistaken for arrogance, but on the whole this breed is loving, loyal, and playful. Despite its size and strength it makes a good house pet.

PERUVIAN INCA ORCHID

OFFICIAL CATEGORIZATION: UK: Not recognized, AKC: Hound, FCI: Group 5, Section 6

Color: Chocolate brown, elephant gray, copper, or mottled

Coat Care: Zero maintenance

Diet: Moderate consumption

HEIGHT: 20–26 in. (50–65 cm)   WEIGHT: 26–50 lb. (12–23 kg)

OTHER NAMES: Inca Hairless Dog, Viringo

The Peruvian Inca Orchid is an ancient and very unusual breed. Like the Mexican Hairless, the Peruvian Inca Orchid has the unusual appearance of being completely bald, with the exception of very fine down on some specimens. It is one of the oldest breeds of dog in the world and is believed to have been developed by the Inca tribe, although some canine historians claim that the Peruvian Inca Orchid dog predates the Inca tribe and that the name is a misnomer.

Due to its lack of fur, or hair, the Peruvian Inca Orchid has evolved as

RIGHT

The Peruvian Inca Orchid Dog is thought by some people to have been bred by the Incas, but others say that it predates even them.

a nocturnal dog with an intolerance of sunshine. Although it is adaptable and easy-going, the breed is happiest being active in the cool of the night, but the Peruvian Inca Orchid is likely to fit into any lifestyle. The breed is sharp, intelligent, and fun.

ARGENTINE DOGO

OFFICIAL CATEGORIZATION: UK: Banned under the Dangerous Dogs Act 1991, AKC: FSS, FCI: Group 2, Section 2

HEIGHT: 24⅓–27 in. (62–68.5 cm)   WEIGHT: 80–100 lb. (36–45 kg)

OTHER NAMES: Argentinian Mastiff, Dogo Argentino

Color: White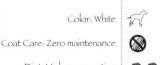

Coat Care: Zero maintenance

Diet: High consumption

Fascinating Facts

Dogs are able to move their ears independently of one another, enabling them to tune in to sounds coming from various directions.

The Argentine Dogo , or Argentinian Mastiff, is a large and powerful breed from the Molosser family **that was originally bred for fighting. Due to its history, the breed has a negative reputation in some cultures but, like the American Pit Bull Terrier, the Argentine Dogo makes a fine pet dog in the right hands. It is loyal, brave, friendly, and intelligent.**

The Argentine Dogo is a striking breed but it does not have the typical look of a fighting dog. Its appearance reflects its personality: strong and powerful but calm, confident, and friendly. Certainly the fighting instincts and abilities are present, but only appear when the dog itself is fearful. The breed is playful and active, especially as it is growing up, and its athletic physique lends itself well to extended play sessions. It requires a good level of training.

BELOW
In the Argentine Dogo , the ears may be cropped (as here), or hang naturally, close to the skull.

GREENLAND DOG

OFFICIAL CATEGORIZATION: UK: Working, AKC: Not recognized, FCI: Group 5, Section 1

HEIGHT: 23–27 in. (58–68 cm)   WEIGHT: 75–105 lb. (34–47.5 kg)

OTHER NAMES: Esquimaux Dog

Color: All known dog colors, or combinations thereof

Coat Care: Moderate/high maintenance

Diet: High consumption

The Greenland Dog is a striking and highly sought after working sled dog. Similar in appearance to other sled dogs and members of the Spitz family, the Greenland Dog displays many of the traditional attributes and physical characteristics associated with dedicated sledding breeds. It was bred **in Greenland as a sledding dog and is particularly strong. The Greenland Dog is still a popular working sled dog today.**

Because it is bred for strength, endurance, and stamina, less attention is paid to temperament. Although not an inherently aggressive or unsuitable pet, the Greenland Dog requires a strong and confident owner. Like many dogs in its family, the Greenland Dog's work is reflected in its personality— it is tough, direct, and determined. The Greenland Dog prefers pack life to games, and thrives in the company of other dogs when given the chance to follow its instincts for work.

BELOW
The Greenland Dog, also called the Esquimaux Dog, is a much-prized sled dog that really enjoys its pack work.

OTHER AMERICAN BREEDS

In most parts of the world, there are dog breeds that are not recognized officially by the relevant authorities. This may be because they are yet to become established, are rare, or simply have not fulfilled all of the criteria that apply to breed recognition. This does not mean that they are not valid breeds, and they may some day become recognized officially. Many of the lesser-known American breeds are newly established and are still in development.

breed of otherwise typical Rat Terriers was born hairless. This dog was used with the inclusion of other Rat Terriers to begin a breeding program to establish the American Hairless Terrier as a new breed. The dog is smoothly muscled, small, and predominantly hairless.

English Shepherd

The English Shepherd, or Farm Shepherd as it is also known, is a working herding dog that was established using English and Scottish Collie breeds. British settlers in the United States tried creating a versatile and hard-working breed. It was not bred for conformation and is a notably healthy breed as a result. It has worked as a herder of cattle, sheep, and pigs and is also used to protect and guard livestock. It is medium-sized, with a variety of colors and coat types.

King Shepherd

The King Shepherd is a working breed that is descended from German

ABOVE AND RIGHT

Still a very new breed, being developed from the 1970s, the American Hairless Terrier is just one of many new American breeds.

American Hairless Terrier

The first descendent of the American Hairless Terrier was born in the United States in 1972. The breed is a direct descendent of the Rat Terrier and came about when one female puppy in a

BELOW LEFT AND RIGHT

The English Shepherd was bred and developed by British sheep farmers in the United States, using their Scottish and English Collies.

Alapaha Blueblood Bulldog

In this country, many dogs are bred in rural areas to fulfill certain roles that are not performed anywhere

Bulldogs. It was established to perform as a guard and watchdog on the plantations in the Alapaha River region of Georgia. It makes a good guard dog and pet.

Shiloh Shepherd

The Shiloh Shepherd breed was established by a German immigrant living in New York who wanted to preserve a line of dogs that represented what she remembered of the original German Shepherd breed. The Shiloh Shepherd is larger and stronger than both the European and American types of German Shepherd. The breed displays many coat colors and varieties and is popular as a working herder. It is supremely intelligent, agile, and obedient. The Shiloh Shepherd is considered to make an excellent pet due to its confident, affectionate nature and general willingness to adapt to family life.

ABOVE

Bred as a guard dog in the Alapaha River region of Georgia, the Alapaha Blueblood Bulldog remains rare elsewhere.

Shepherds and Alaskan Malamutes. It is bred for intelligence, agility, and curiosity and is judged by its willingness to perform. The breed is typically heavy and muscular, with a protective and obedient nature. The King Shepherd, despite being bred for work, makes a good pet due to its friendly and affectionate nature, high level of intelligence, and its fondness for socializing with family and visitors.

Alaskan Klee Kai

The Alaskan Klee Kai was bred to fulfill a requirement for companion-sized versions of Alaskan sledding breeds. Typically sledding

breeds are large and powerful, but otherwise present themselves as particularly desirable companions. The breeder used small specimens of the breed to establish a bloodline, which produced smaller dogs uniformly.

The breed has been developed very carefully in order to ensure no health or temperament problems become endemic and for this reason the breed is still very rare.

else in the nation. This is true of the Alapaha Blueblood Bulldog, which is descended from the old variety of Bulldog and demonstrates certain physical characteristics, such as its height and athletic build, that are now lost in modern

BELOW

In memory of the German Shepherd breed back home, a German immigrant in New York State bred the Shiloh Shepherd.

Europe

Europe is home to more breeds of dog than anywhere else in the world. This section includes a wide variety of large, small, fast, and intelligent breeds. Because Europe is such a diverse continent, there are many types of dog present there. It is a place where grass grows abundantly so there are plenty of herding breeds, and in the northern countries of Scandinavia the breeds are covered in thick fur. Moving south through Spain and across to France and Italy the variety of breeds is even larger.

A Varied Picture

Going from north to south and then west to east, there is a staggering variety of dogs on display. The Icelandic Sheepdog, Norwegian, Swedish, and Finnish hounds, and even Danish bird-dog breeds all display an array of coats, colors, and personalities. Traveling south from Scandinavia and on to Britain, Scottish-bred terrier breeds meet English-bred herders, drover,s and gun dogs; then moving across to Ireland there is an array of water dogs, terriers, and the world's tallest dog, the Irish Wolfhound.

Famous European Breeds

Mainland Europe is a place where dogs were bred to guard, hunt, and retrieve, among other duties.

Belgium, France, Holland, Germany, Switzerland, Spain, and Portugal have all produced world-famous dog breeds, from the German Shepherd to the Saint Bernard and the Bloodhound to the Poodle. Heading east though the homelands of the Dalmatian, the Polish Lowland Sheepdog, and the striking and unique Komondor as far as the Asian border, there are yet more breeds of hugely differing types.

Moving from the eastern nations of Turkey and Hungary and northeast toward Siberia, the dog breeds become larger and stronger, able to work in snow and ice, pulling carts, driving sheep, and protecting flocks. Moving further east through Siberia, we approach the ancestral home of the ancient Borzoi sight hound.

ICELANDIC SHEEPDOG

OFFICIAL CATEGORIZATION: UK: Not recognized, AKC: FSS,
FCI: Group 5, Section 3

HEIGHT: 12–17 in. (30–45 cm)

WEIGHT: 20–30 lb. (9–14 kg)

OTHER NAMES: Icelandic Spitz

COLOR: All color varieties
and markings

COAT CARE: High maintenance

DIET: Moderate/high consumption

The Icelandic Sheepdog is a very unusual specimen because of its links with two very different types of dog. While it displays many of the physical attributes of a sledding breed and is even a member of the Spitz family, as the name suggests this is a herding breed. Its looks are due to the fact that it was bred and established in Iceland, where most other breeding stock would have been Spitz and sledding breeds, but the Icelandic Sheepdog has fulfilled a pastoral role since its development.

The Icelandic Sheepdog is not a typical herding breed; it has attributes associated with sledding work as well as characteristics associated with herding. It is one of the more serious breeds of dog,

most happy when put to work herding or droving. In the past, the dog's strength and inherited courage have made it a valuable guard and watchdog.

NORWEGIAN LUNDEHUND

OFFICIAL CATEGORIZATION: UK: Not recognized, AKC: FSS,
FCI: Group 5, Section 2

HEIGHT: 12–15½ in. (31–39 cm)

WEIGHT: 13–20 lb. (6–9 kg)

OTHER NAMES: Norsk Lundehund

COLOR: Reddish brown with white
or dark markings

COAT CARE: Low/moderate
maintenance

DIET: Moderate consumption

The Norwegian Lundehund is a peculiar breed of dog. Not only does it combine the looks of a sledding breed

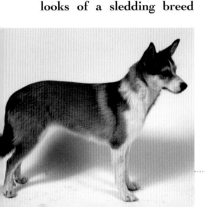

with the working attributes and personality of a hunting dog, it has the strange yet useful ability to bend its neck almost all of the way back, allowing it to look backward and upward at the same time. It can also close its ears, which it has evolved to do in order to protect the inner ear from snow during blizzards. The Norwegian Lundehund has extremely flexible joints. It is descended from Spitz breeds, but has been put to work as a hunter, typically hunting puffins.

This is a true working breed and is at its happiest in the outdoors. The Norwegian Lundehund can make a good pet, with high levels of intelligence and curiosity, but owners are always encouraged to ensure that the dog's working instincts are stimulated through training and play in order to avoid boredom. The breed is not overtly aggressive, but has always been bred for its working ability.

NORWEGIAN BUHUND

COLOR: Wheaten—any shade

COAT CARE: Moderate/high maintenance

DIET: Moderate/high consumption

OFFICIAL CATEGORIZATION: UK: Not recognized, AKC: Miscellaneous, FCI: Group 5, Section 3

HEIGHT: 17–18 in. (43–47 cm)   WEIGHT: 31–40 lb. (14–18 kg)

OTHER NAMES: Norsk Buhund, Norwegian Sheepdog

The Norwegian Buhund is a member of the Spitz family, closely related to the Icelandic Sheepdog. Although of sledding-breed descent, the Norwegian Buhund is less of a serious working dog and possesses many more attributes suitable to domestic life. It is relatively rare outside of Northern Europe. It has a thick coat, typically in white with gray patches.

Since the Norwegian Buhund has been bred for companionship as well as for work, it has attributes that make it more suitable for family life than its close relatives. Care has been taken in breeding to ensure that the Norwegian Buhund's working instincts are not bred out, but the modern Norwegian Buhund is adaptable, friendly, and intelligent.

The breed is alert, active, and agile, with a lot of energy. It is a popular participant in canine sports competitions due to its inherited sledding-dog physique and agility.

LEFT

Bred for companionship and sledding, the Norwegian Buhund adapts much more easily to family life than other sledding breeds.

NORWEGIAN HOUND

COLOR: Black or blue marbled saddle with pale fawn-and-white markings

COAT CARE: Moderate maintenance

DIET: Moderate/high consumption

OFFICIAL CATEGORIZATION: UK: Not recognized, AKC: Not recognized, FCI: Group 6, Section 1

HEIGHT: 18½–22½ in. (47–57 cm)   WEIGHT: 35–49 lb. (16–22 kg)

OTHER NAMES: Dunker

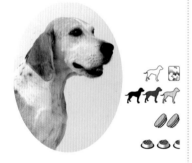

The Norwegian Hound, or Dunker as it is more commonly known, is a Scandinavian scent hound. Smaller than American scent hounds and with a much thicker coat, this breed does not conform to the traditional attributes of an established scent hound. However, its scenting abilities are strong, even though it possesses relatively small ears, as opposed to large and pendulous ears seen on other scent hounds. Its main quarry is rabbit and hare, which is why the Dunker has not been bred any larger.

The Norwegian Hound is not a popular breed outside of Norway. This is not because of poor scenting ability or any unsuitability as a pet, but because the dog has never been needed outside of Norway in a working environment and has, therefore, never been given the chance to become established. It is a friendly and intelligent breed, happiest when outside and at work.

ABOVE

The Norwegian Hound was bred as a scent hound to track rabbit and hare, but is not often found outside Norway.

HYGEN HOUND

OFFICIAL CATEGORIZATION: UK: Not recognized,
AKC: Not recognized, FCI: Group 6, Section 1

HEIGHT: 18½–21¾ in. (47–55 cm)   WEIGHT: 44–55 lb. (20–25 kg)

OTHER NAMES: Unknown

COLOR: Brown or
yellowish red, with or without
black shading, or black and tan

COAT CARE: Low/moderate
maintenance

DIET: High/very high consumption

ABOVE
The Norwegian Hygen Hound is a popular scent hound, but is not popular as a pet, despite being biddable and intelligent.

The **Norwegian-bred Hygen Hound is a rare but very adept hunting dog. It descends from a wide mixture of scent hounds, and the leaner and smaller Norwegian hunting dogs, such as the Norwegian Hound, have contributed substantially to the bloodline. The dog bears a resemblance to scent hounds more commonly associated with warmer climates, such as the Beagle.**

The Hygen Hound is unusual in that it is a scent hound but is a fast runner with impressive agility. Speed and stamina are more commonly associated with sight hounds to the exclusion of scenting hounds, but the Hygen Hound is able to track effectively while quickly chasing prey. This is one of the reasons that the breed is very popular as a hunting dog. Its popularity and availability as a pet is limited, despite its agreeable personality and high level of obedience and intelligence.

Fascinating Facts

Male dogs cock their legs in order to urinate as high up as possible. This is to give the impression of greater size when another dog finds the scent marking.

NORWEGIAN ELKHOUND

OFFICIAL CATEGORIZATION: UK: Hound Group,
AKC: Hound Group, FCI: Group 5, Section 2

HEIGHT: 19–22 in. (48–56 cm)   WEIGHT: 51–55 lb. (23–27 kg)

OTHER NAMES: Norwegian Moose Dog

COLOR: Gray of various shades,
with black tips to outer coat;
lighter on underside

COAT CARE: High maintenance

DIET: High/very high consumption

The **Norwegian Elkhound is one of the most popular Norwegian breeds outside of its home country. It is an ancient member of the Spitz family of dogs and has performed a wide range of working duties throughout its development, notably as a hunting dog. It bears the typical appearance of a Northern Spitz breed, with a very bushy, brushlike tail and lupine facial characteristics.**

This is a hardy breed with a diverse range of skills and instincts. The Norwegian Elkhound has been bred to survive in climates that regularly plummet below freezing and this is reflected in its serious nature. It is a valuable worker, but requires the right type of owner to cater to its specific needs. It has a high prey drive and can often become agitated if restricted, but it is well-known for forming strong bonds with its master.

HALDEN HOUND

COLOR: White with black spots or brown shading on the head and legs

COAT CARE: High/very high maintenance

DIET: High consumption

OFFICIAL CATEGORIZATION: UK: Not recognized, AKC: Not recognized, FCI: Group 6, Section 1

HEIGHT: 18½–21½ in. (47–55 cm)   WEIGHT: 42–46 lb. (19–21 kg)

OTHER NAMES: Haldenstovare

The Halden Hound is a scent hound named after the town in Norway from which it originates. It is a relatively unusual breed given its origins. It does not possess the typical thick coat of most dogs bred in Norway. It is a descendant of a variety of breeds, mainly hounds from Germany and England, and reflects this ancestry in its relatively large, pendulous ears and athletic physique.

The Halden Hound is a hardy and fast hunter, bred to work alone in unforgiving and harsh climates, and yet it also makes a good family pet. It is a loyal and affectionate breed with high energy levels and a fondness for play. As with many Northern European breeds, the Halden Hound has a thick coat that requires regular grooming to keep it in good condition.

BELOW
Named after the town in Norway from which it originates, the Halden Hound is used to working in harsh conditions.

SWEDISH DACHSBRACKE

COLOR: Fawn, black, or black and tan

COAT CARE: Low/moderate maintenance

DIET: Moderate consumption

OFFICIAL CATEGORIZATION: UK: Not recognized, AKC: Not recognized, FCI: Group 6, Section 5

HEIGHT: 11–16 in. (28–40 cm)   WEIGHT: 31–35 lb. (14–16 kg)

OTHER NAMES: Drever

The Swedish Dachsbracke, or Drever as it is also known, is a short-legged hunting hound. Its origins are in Sweden, but it counts the German Dachsbracke as an ancestor. It has much shorter legs than a typical hunting hound but a relatively normal-sized body, giving it a squat look.

The Swedish Dachsbracke was used for hunting small quarry, including hare and small deer. It is renowned for its stamina and tracking ability.

The breed is rare, and even rarer is the Swedish Dachsbracke that is kept as a pet. Nearly all the dogs of this breed are put to work in large packs during hunts. Despite its apparent lack of popularity as a pet, the breed is well-known for its even temper, affable nature, and obedience. The reason it has not established itself as a companion animal is simply because there are not enough of them around.

LEFT
A good working dog, with a friendly nature, the Swedish Dachsbracke, a descendant of the German Dachsbracke, hunts in packs.

SWEDISH VALLHUND

OFFICIAL CATEGORIZATION: UK: Pastoral, AKC: Herding,
FCI: Group 5, Section 3

HEIGHT: 12–14 in. (30–38 cm)   WEIGHT: 25–35 lb. (11–15 kg)

OTHER NAMES: Swedish Cattle Dog, Swedish Shepherd

COLOR: Sable pattern seen in colors of gray through to red

COAT CARE: Moderate maintenance

DIET: Moderate consumption

The Swedish Vallhund is an ancient herding breed associated with the Vikings. It is relatively small, but has a large character. It is a versatile breed, having been used for herding cattle, catching vermin, and guarding property, mainly as a watchdog. It is a forebear to the Welsh Corgi, to which it bears a passing resemblance.

The Swedish Vallhund is a popular pet, particularly in Europe. It displays a combination of working intelligence and companionable adaptability. The Swedish Vallhund, despite its relatively small size, makes an effective and very willing guard dog. It is a very territorial breed and can be wary of strangers, particularly in and around the home. As a puppy, the dog can be possessive of its owner; this behavior can become problematic in adult life if not corrected early. Generally, the Swedish Vallhund is a lively and fun-loving companion breed.

NORRBOTTENSPETS

OFFICIAL CATEGORIZATION: UK: Not recognized,
AKC: Not recognized, FCI: Group 5, Section 2

HEIGHT: 16½–18 in. (42–46 cm)   WEIGHT: 24–33 lb. (11–15 kg)

OTHER NAMES: Norrbottenspitz, Nordic Spitz, Pohjanpystykorva

COLOR: White with orange, brown, or tan markings

COAT CARE: Moderate maintenance

DIET: Moderate consumption

The Norrbottenspets is an ancient hunting breed of undetermined geographical origin. It is a small, compact, but quite sturdy breed that was used to work as a farm hunting dog. It is rare outside of northern European countries, but is relatively popular as a pet in Scandinavia. It is descended from old Spitz-family breeds but is smaller than the typical Spitz. It bears a passing resemblance to the Swedish Vallhund and it probably has similar ancestry.

The Norrbottenspets has a lively and energetic personality. Its square, robust look belies its gentle temperament, although it is known for displaying strong and often inconvenient hunting instincts. Like many Spitz-breed ancestors, it is used to harsh and challenging conditions. Generally of an even temperament, it can be prone to a low tolerance for being bothered by children or other animals.

BELOW
Norrbottenspets are very popular pets in Sweden, but are rarely found outside Northern Europe.

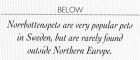

SMALAND HOUND

COLOR: Black with tan markings

COAT CARE: Low/moderate maintenance

DIET: Moderate consumption

OFFICIAL CATEGORIZATION: UK: Not recognized, AKC: Not recognized, FCI: Group 6, Section 1

HEIGHT: 17–20 in. (43–51 cm)   WEIGHT: 33–40 lb. (15–18 kg)

OTHER NAMES: Smalandstövare, Smålandsstövare

The Smaland Hound, or Smalandstövare, is Sweden's oldest scent hound. It is a hardy and robust breed with a long history of hunting. Hares and foxes were the main quarry but the versatile and adaptable Smaland Hound has been known to take care of vermin in rural areas. The Smaland Hound has an appearance that one would associate only loosely with the Spitz family of dogs. It bears similarities in its head shape and coat thickness but its colorations are black and tan, distributed in a fashion that would be associated normally with a Rottweiler or Doberman.

The Smaland Hound is not particularly well-known as a companion animal, although this is gradually changing, with more people becoming aware of its appealing qualities. It is generally a friendly dog, with loyalty, companionship and a tolerance of inhospitable conditions making it a breed growing in status among residents of its home country of Sweden.

RIGHT
Slightly resembling Spitz breeds, the Smaland Hound is becoming popular in Sweden where it can withstand the cold.

SCHILLER HOUND

COLOR: Black and tan

COAT CARE: Low/moderate maintenance

DIET: High/very high consumption

OFFICIAL CATEGORIZATION: UK: Not recognized, AKC: Not recognized, FCI: Group 6, Section 1

HEIGHT: 19½–23½ in. (50–60 cm)   WEIGHT: 39½–55 lb. (18–25 kg)

OTHER NAMES: Schillerstövare

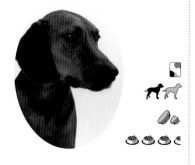

ABOVE
Despite looking like the Weimaraner (of German origin), the Schiller Hound originates from Sweden.

The Schiller Hound is a remarkable-looking dog. Despite being classified in Sweden as a hound, it looks very like a Weimaraner in terms of body and head shape. The coloration of the Schiller Hound is particularly interesting, with tan or brown colorings on the head, back, legs, and forequarters, contrasting with black or dark brown colorings on the back and stomach. The ears are fairly large, which suggests hound ancestry, but the Schiller Hound is unusually retriever-like.

The Schiller Hound was bred for hunting alone in the snow, the quarry being hare and small foxes. It is recognized as Sweden's fastest hunting dog with great hunting prowess. Its temperament reflects its original working role and the Schiller Hound often thrives best in a working environment. It is kept as a pet but typically this involves work-based training.

HAMILTON HOUND

OFFICIAL CATEGORIZATION: UK: Hound, AKC: Hound, FCI: Group 6, Section 1

HEIGHT: 21–24 in. (53–61 cm)

WEIGHT: 50–60 lb. (23–27 kg)

OTHER NAMES: Hamiltonstövare

COLOR: Black and brown with white markings

COAT CARE: Low/moderate maintenance

DIET: High consumption

The Hamilton Hound is a popular breed of hunting dog in Sweden, and increasingly in other parts of Europe. It is a descendent of various German and English hunting hounds and is well known for its tireless and energetic hunting efforts. The Hamilton Hound was used to hunt alone for large game, including deer and even bear.

The breed is very work orientated and this is reflected in its temperament. Relatively few are bred for companion dog stock, so many of the Hamilton Hounds that are kept as pets are not far removed from working animals, and may be distracted if exposed to stimuli that appeal to their strong hunting instincts. Although bred to be happy in very cold weather and to thrive in solitude, the Hamilton Hound makes an exceptionally good companion.

SWEDISH ELKHOUND

OFFICIAL CATEGORIZATION: UK: Not recognized, AKC: Not recognized, FCI: Group 5, Section 2

HEIGHT: 23–25 in. (58.5–63.5 cm)

WEIGHT: 64–68 lb. (29–31 kg)

OTHER NAMES: Jamthund

COLOR: Dark gray/black with cream undercoat

COAT CARE: High maintenance

DIET: High/very high consumption

The Swedish Elkhound, used for hunting and sledding, displays an impressive combination of working abilities. Descended from Spitz-family breeds, the Swedish Elkhound has an appearance more commonly associated with sledding breeds originating from North America and Canada.

It is strong and athletic, with a large bushy tail, thick coat, and upright ears. Like many Spitz breeds it is happy to work and is equipped to deal with harsh and unpleasant conditions.

Descended from hard-working sled dogs, and still used today as a working hunter and sledding breed, the Swedish Elkhound is a relatively new breed of pet dog in an historical context. Nevertheless, the breed makes an excellent pet, with bravery, loyalty, and strength of character just some of its more appealing characteristics. The breed is known for seeking dominance and special care around children is advised due to its robust personality.

BELOW
Large and powerful, the Swedish Elkhound was used to hunt bear, lynx, and elks, and closely resembles the North American sled dogs.

FINNISH SPITZ

COLOR: Varying shades of golden red

COAT CARE: Moderate/high maintenance

DIET: Moderate/high consumption

OFFICIAL CATEGORIZATION: UK: Hound, AKC: nonsporting, FCI: Group 5, Section 2

HEIGHT: 17½–20 in. (43–50 cm)

WEIGHT: 31–35 lb. (14–16 kg)

OTHER NAMES: Finsk Spets

A sophisticated and ancient hunting breed, the Finnish Spitz is one of the earliest types of Spitz-breed dog. Displaying the typical appearance of a Spitz breed, the Finnish Spitz is a striking and impressive-looking dog. Despite the breed evolving in snowy climates, it can display a red coat similar to that of the Arctic Fox's summer colors. The Finnish Spitz is a hardy and tough breed but displays a gentle demeanor when adapted to the domestic environment.

known to engage in a hunt and is capable of taking small prey, such as hares. Outside of its home country, the Finnish Spitz is a popular pet, displaying affection to children but occasionally roughness with other dogs.

In Finland, the Finnish Spitz is predominantly a working dog—typically used as a bark-pointer on hunts, where it identifies prey and signals to the huntsman. Despite this, it has also been

RIGHT
Unlike the wild animals of this climate, the Finnish Spitz stands out for its red coat. Puppies are born dark gray, black, brown, or fawn.

FINNISH LAPPHUND

COLOR: All colors are allowed, but in each case one color must dominate

COAT CARE: High/very high maintenance

DIET: High consumption

OFFICIAL CATEGORIZATION: UK: Pastoral, AKC: FSS, FCI: Group 5, Section 3

HEIGHT: 17½–21 in. (46–52 cm)

WEIGHT: 37–39 lb. (17–19 kg)

OTHER NAMES: Lapinkoira

The Finnish Lapphund is predominantly a herding dog, despite being closely related to many hunting breeds, such as the Finnish Spitz. Its appearance is unusual, with some aspects similar to Spitz-breed dogs to which it is related and other aspects decidedly uncommon. The Finnish Lapphund is

relatively small but displays prowess in herding larger animals, such as deer. Despite being a very popular breed in its home country of Finland, the Finnish Lapphund is rare as a pet in other countries.

The Finnish Lapphund makes a good pet, but it is

important for owners to pay heed to the breed's herding and working instincts. It is affectionate and lively, with a fondness for any type of play that can challenge it mentally. As with many dog breeds that have been used to work in a pastoral environment, the Finnish Lapphund is both physically and mentally agile.

KARELIAN BEAR DOG

OFFICIAL CATEGORIZATION: UK: Not recognized,
AKC: Not recognized, FCI: Group 5, Section 2

HEIGHT: 22–24 in. (54–60 cm)   WEIGHT: 44–50 lb. (20–23 kg)

OTHER NAMES: Karjalankarhukoira

COLOR: Black with white markings

COAT CARE: High maintenance

DIET: High consumption

This remarkable Finnish breed displays impressive hunting abilities that make it a national treasure in its home country; its status in Finland is comparable to that of the Bulldog in England or the

Fascinating Facts

Many dogs lick their lips as a warning to people and other dogs that they may become aggressive. This is a telltale signal that is often overlooked.

Boston Terrier in this country. The Karelian Bear Dog is a hardy and determined breed that was used originally to hunt and kill bears and other large game. It is large and strong and typically displays a thick black-and-white coat.

Despite being popular in Finland, the Karelian Bear Dog does not make a suitable pet for everyone. Due to the aggressive nature of some of the game that the Karelian Bear Dog was bred to hunt, the breed has inherited and developed some of its own aggressive tendencies. The Karelian Bear Dog tends to prefer solitude and can be slightly aloof. Its intelligence combined with its strong instincts make it a challenging breed to train.

OLD DANISH POINTER

OFFICIAL CATEGORIZATION: UK: Not recognized,
AKC: Not recognized, FCI: Group 7, Section 1

HEIGHT: 19½–23½ in. (50–60 cm)   WEIGHT: 57–77 lb. (26–35 kg)

OTHER NAMES: Unknown

Color: White with brown markings

Coat Care: Low/moderate maintenance

Diet: Moderate/high consumption

The Old Danish Pointer is a large, courageous, and versatile, multifaceted hunting dog. It is of Spanish and German descent—its ancestors include old Spanish and German pointing breeds and Danish hunting dogs. The breed bears a slight resemblance to members of the scent hound group, and the Old Danish Pointer does possess scenting abilities that suggest an ancestral link to some scenting hounds.

Popular as a pet in Denmark, the Old Danish Pointer is far less common outside of its home country. It makes a good pet, with many desirable attributes, such as obedience and intelligence. The breed is very work driven and originally was bred to be tenacious, bold, and courageous. The Old Danish Pointer is happy in the domestic environment but thrives when at work.

BROHOLMER

COLOR: Yellow, golden red, tan, or black with black mask

COAT CARE: Low/moderate maintenance

DIET: High/very high consumption

OFFICIAL CATEGORIZATION: UK: Not recognized, AKC: Not recognized, FCI: Group 2, Section 2

HEIGHT: 22–30 in. (70–75 cm)   WEIGHT: 87–176 lb. (40–80 kg)

OTHER NAMES: Danish Broholmer

The Broholmer is a large yet well-balanced Danish breed of the Molosser family. Its heavy jaw and sturdy build suggest that its early uses included hunting and guarding. The dog is notably well-built and displays either a tan or black coat with a black muzzle. It has an air of grace and sophistication and carries itself with calm confidence.

As with most members of the Molosser family, the Broholmer makes a friendly and loving pet with the added benefit of having relatively high intelligence. Its appearance suggests that it has the potential to be aggressive, which is true, but this is easily remedied with confident and thorough training. The Broholmer is not a well-distributed breed and is most popular in its home country. The breed is

often kept to combine the roles of companion dog and guard dog, in which case solid training is required to temper any aggression.

ABOVE
Very popular in Denmark, particularly as a guard dog and companion, it is unusual to find a Broholmer in other countries.

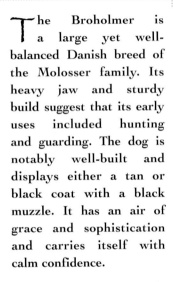

DANDIE DINMONT TERRIER

COLOR: Pepper or mustard

COAT CARE: Moderate/high maintenance

DIET: Low/moderate consumption

OFFICIAL CATEGORIZATION: UK: Terrier, AKC: Terrier, FCI: Group 3, Section 2

HEIGHT: 8–11 in. (20–28 cm)   WEIGHT: 18–24 lb. (8–11 kg)

OTHER NAMES: Dandie, Hindlee Terrier

The Dandie Dinmont Terrier is a rare Scottish breed. It is the only purebred dog breed in the world that is named after a fictional character—namely a farmer featured in Sir Walter Scott's novel *Guy Mannering*. It is a short-legged terrier descending from French breeding stock and was used initially as a

badger terrier, although today it is bred for companionship. It is one of the most rare breeds of dog in the world and is close to extinction.

The Dandie Dinmont Terrier makes a good pet breed but is not suitable for every type of dog owner. It

is notably difficult to train and has an exuberant and boisterous character. Despite this, when given considered and consistent obedience training, the Dandie Dinmont Terrier makes a very rewarding and lovable pet. The breed is good with children—affectionate and friendly—but can be mischievous.

YORKSHIRE TERRIER

OFFICIAL CATEGORIZATION: UK: Toy , AKC: Toy,
FCI: Group 3, Section 4

HEIGHT: 6–7 in. (15–17 cm)

WEIGHT: 5–9 lb. (2.2–4.2 kg)

OTHER NAMES: Yorkie

COLOR: Gray, dark steel blue,
or black and tan

COAT CARE: Moderate maintenance

DIET: Low/moderate consumption

T he Yorkshire Terrier is one of the most popular pet breeds in the world, loved for its dainty carriage and lively, engaging personality. It was bred originally as a working terrier but in many countries has been reclassified as a toy breed due to its popularity as a companion animal.

Small Frame, Big Character
One of the most notable aspects of this breed is its

bold personality, which is contained in one of the smallest dog physiques.

The Yorkshire Terrier is normally gray in color but does also display a black coat in some instances. It is commonly associated with the conformation show circuit—groomed and preened ready to be judged. As with many purebred breeds of high popularity, the Yorkshire Terrier is prone to various hereditary disorders, including luxating patella and Cushing's Disease.

A Lively Companion
Despite being bred almost exclusively for companionship in modern times, the Yorkshire Terrier still retains many of the terrier characteristics once associated with its work. Tenacious, lively, energetic, and intelligent, the breed is a happy and friendly companion. It is suitable for most domestic environments, ranging from rural to urban, and is happy in a small apartment.

The breed is unusual in that it can crave attention one minute and be aloof and independent the next.

Due to its high intelligence, the Yorkshire Terrier has many different moods and seemingly can switch readily from one to another.

Although a popular pet in the United States and much of Europe, the Yorkshire Terrier is not suited to everyone's taste. Its high intelligence and activity levels cause it to be criticized for being demanding. When training, the Yorkshire Terrier is generally responsive to

stimuli and instruction and will pick up on new commands with great vigour and enthusiasm.

Fascinating Facts

The Chihuahua is the smallest breed on average, but the smallest ever dog was a Yorkshire Terrier that weighed just 4 oz. (113.5 g) by the time it was two years old.

NORWICH TERRIER AND NORFOLK TERRIER

COLOR: All shades of red, wheaten, black and tan, or grizzle

COAT CARE: Low/moderate maintenance

DIET: Moderate consumption

OFFICIAL CATEGORIZATION: UK: Terrier, AKC: Terrier, FCI: Group 3, Section 2

HEIGHT: 9–10 in. (23–25 cm)   WEIGHT: 10–12 lb. (4–5 kg)

OTHER NAMES: Cantab Terrier

There is much debate about whether the Norwich and Norfolk Terriers should be given separate class-ifications. Up until relatively recently, the two breeds were classified as one, but in 1960 the UK Kennel Club designated that Norwich Terriers with folded ears should be named Norfolk Terriers.

A Question of Breed

Generally, therefore, they are recognized as separate breeds, although the definition of "breed" is often called into question in this respect. Looking at the two side by side, it is difficult to tell them apart, but given that some purebred breeds display large physical discrepancies from dog to dog, it has been proposed that the two should be reclassified separately.

Prior to the separation, the dog was bred to hunt vermin. It was one of the smallest purebred terriers but possessed excellent hunting and catching skills, assisted by its tenacious and fearless persona.

Adaptable Characters

In terms of temperament, there is nothing to separate the breeds. One of the reasons Norwich Terriers and Norfolk Terriers are so popular is because they

are readily adapt to the environment around them. Although lively and energetic, a slow pace of life will suit these dogs just as much as a high-energy atmosphere. Norwich Terriers and Norfolk Terriers are friendly, relaxed, and confident.

While still in possession of strong ratting and hunting instincts, the dogs are now almost always bred for form and temperament. The ongoing debate surrounding the class-

ification of the breeds does not change the fact that the dogs are inherently intelligent and obedient. Bred to hunt in packs, Norwich Terriers and Norfolk Terriers are generally friendly and sociable with other dogs. Their courage and bold spirit make canine interaction an interesting experience, because these little dogs show no fear.

ENGLISH TOY TERRIER (Black-and-Tan)

OFFICIAL CATEGORIZATION: UK: Toy, AKC: Not recognized, FCI: Group 3, Section 4

HEIGHT: 10–12 in. (25–30 cm)

WEIGHT: 6–8 lb. (2.6–3.5 kg)

OTHER NAMES: None

COLOR: Black and tan

COAT CARE: Low maintenance

DIET: Low consumption

The English Toy Terrier (Black-and-Tan) is a rare breed of dog that is considered to be vulnerable by the UK Kennel Club. Because of this statu,s the breed is subject to specialized breeding programs with the Manchester Terrier, which are designed to diversify the bloodline and protect the breed.

The English Toy Terrier is a small, slender breed that resembles the Manchester Terrier. It has a distinct black-and-tan coloration, very short, coarse coat, narrow skull, and upright ears.

The English Toy Terrier has a mixed ancestry, with terrier and toy breeds both contributing to the bloodline. It has a working history of ratting but in more recent times has been bred for companionship. It has a confident, bold, and brave temperament, with a cheerful and friendly disposition.

LEFT

English Toy Terriers have distinctive "candle flame" ears.

SKYE TERRIER

OFFICIAL CATEGORIZATION: UK: Terrier, AKC: Terrier, FCI: Group 3, Section 2

HEIGHT: 10 in. (25–26 cm)

WEIGHT: 35–40 lb. (16–18 kg)

OTHER NAMES: Terrier of the Western Isles

COLOR: Black, dark or light gray, fawn, or cream, all with black points

COAT CARE: Moderate/high maintenance

DIET: Low/moderate consumption

This lively and striking-looking terrier has wide-reaching and fascinating origins. Counting the Maltese, the Swedish Vallhund, and various now-extinct terriers among its ancestors, this truly is a breed with an interesting story. As with certain other breeds, the Skye Terrier's existence came about only because of sailors docking in foreign parts and allowing their dogs to breed with local dogs. The exact history of which dogs and in which order they contributed to the bloodline of the Skye Terrier is not known, causing much debate among fanciers of the breed.

As a pet, this rare breed is extremely loyal and affectionate. The famous Grayfriars Bobby (*see* page 146), now a canine metaphor for loyalty, was a Skye Terrier. Grooming care is required because of the length of the coat, although it is resistant to tangling. The Skye Terrier is very friendly but is considered by many owners as a "one-man dog."

BELOW

From Malta to Sweden, the origins of the Skye Terrier are bound up with the journeys made by sailors and their dogs.

ENGLISH TOY SPANIEL

OFFICIAL CATEGORIZATION: UK: Toy, AKC: Toy,
FCI: Group 9, Section 7

COLOR: Black and tan

COAT CARE: Moderate maintenance

DIET: Moderate consumption

HEIGHT: 12–13 in. (30–33 cm)   WEIGHT: 8–14 lb. (3.6–6.3 kg)

OTHER NAMES: King Charles Spaniel

The English Toy Spaniel, also known as the King Charles Spaniel, is not closely related to the Cavalier King Charles Spaniel. The two are separate breeds but are often confused. The English Toy is more closely related to the Pug and is less associated with the gun-dog breeding stock of the Cavalier. It was bred as a companion dog and has other companion dogs in its bloodline, including the Pug and the Japanese Chin. In the past, it did more closely resemble the Cavalier King Charles Spaniel, but the two breeds have moved apart in terms of appearance.

The English Toy Spaniel is typical of many companion breeds. It is extremely affectionate and loyal and does not retain any particular working instincts that may pose a challenge in training. The breed has a relatively high life expectancy, but poor breeding in the past has led to inherited health problems.

LEFT
The English Toy Spaniel is very similar to a Cavalier King Charles Spaniel, but the former has a very short, Puglike muzzle.

BORDER TERRIER

COLOR: Red, grizzle and tan, blue and tan, or wheaten

COAT CARE: Low maintenance

DIET: Low/moderate consumption

OFFICIAL CATEGORIZATION: UK: Terrier, AKC: Terrier,
FCI: Group 3, Section 1

HEIGHT: 13–16 in. (33–41 cm)   WEIGHT: 13–15½ lb. (6–7 kg)

OTHER NAMES: Coquetdale Terrier

The Border Terrier is one of the most popular pet dog breeds in the world, particularly in Britain. It is a hardy and likeable breed with strong ratting instincts. Its appearance is often described as rugged or scruffy, adding to its charm. The dog is well-known for being one of the healthiest purebred dogs, with an average life expectancy of up to 14 years and minimal breed-associated health problems. It originates from the Borders area of Scotland.

This breed makes an exceptional pet. It is fun-loving, tough, energetic, friendly, and adaptable. The dog gets along well in many different environments, from rural living where it will often thrive, acting on its strong terrier instincts, to urban living, where its size and personality makes it a very suitable breed for being kept in an apartment. The Border Terrier is friendly with other dogs and has high levels of intelligence.

LANCASHIRE HEELER

OFFICIAL CATEGORIZATION: UK: Pastoral, AKC: FSS,
FCI: Not recognized

HEIGHT: 10½–13½ in. (26.5–34.5 cm)   WEIGHT: 6–13 lb. (3–6 kg)

OTHER NAMES: Ormskirk Heeler

COLOR: Black or liver with
rich tan marking on muzzle

COAT CARE: Moderate/high
maintenance

DIET: Moderate consumption

The Lancashire Heeler is one of the smallest members of the herding and pastoral dog family. Despite its size, it was bred to be a phenomenally skilled droving and herding dog, displaying a tenacity that made it a very popular breed as a worker. It counts the Manchester Terrier and an unknown type of Welsh Corgi among its ancestors.

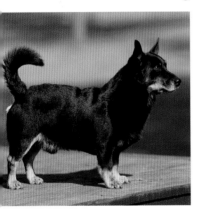

Despite its stature, the Lancashire Heeler is a surprisingly strong dog. It is a lively, determined, and energetic breed with strong terrier and herding instincts. It is particularly well-suited to rural life, where it can still be used as a working dog to deal with vermin, droving livestock, or simply providing company. Although it has experienced high popularity as a working dog, the Lancashire Heeler is considered an endangered breed by the UK Kennel Club. For this reason, there exist numerous special breeding progamsin operation to preserve the Lancashire Heeler's bloodline.

LEFT

The Lancashire Heeler is a farmyard dog, whose ancestors include the Welsh Corgi and the Manchester Terrier.

LUCAS TERRIER

OFFICIAL CATEGORIZATION: UK: Not recognized,
AKC: Not recognized, FCI: Not recognized

HEIGHT: 9–12 in. (23–30.5 cm)   WEIGHT: 11–20 lb. (5–9 kg)

OTHER NAMES: None

COLOR: Tan (all shades) with
white markings

COAT CARE: Low/moderate
maintenance

DIET: Low/moderate consumption

The Lucas Terrier is a relatively new breed, although the breeding stock used consisted of established breeds. It was bred in Britain by Jocelyn Lucas and Enid Plummer at their kennels in the south of England. The Lucas Terrier was the result of a breeding program that included the Norfolk Terrier and the Sealyham Terrier. The Lucas Terrier displays physical and temperamental attributes of both breeds. It is yet to become a particularly established breed.

The Lucas Terrier is one of the most rare breeds in the world, not due to a decline in ownership or popularity but simply because its numbers have never grown sufficiently. There are believed to be less than 100 Lucas Terriers in the United States. The breed is considered a friendly and intelligent dog, with some natural terrier instincts that it would have inherited from the breeding stock used.

JACK RUSSELL TERRIER AND PARSON RUSSELL TERRIER

COLOR: White with black or tan markings, or a combination—tricolor

COAT CARE: Low/moderate maintenance

DIET: Moderate/high consumption

OFFICIAL CATEGORIZATION: UK: Terrier (Parson), AKC: Terrier (Parson), FCI: Group 3, Section 1 (Jack and Parson)

HEIGHT: 13–14 in. (33–36 cm)

WEIGHT: 13–17 lb. (6–8 kg)

OTHER NAMES: Unknown

ABOVE
Jack Russell Terriers are often working dogs, while the similar Parson Russell Terriers are often show dogs.

These two breeds are very similar, with the only difference being which breeding stock is thought to have been used. They were bred by Parson John (Jack) Russell, but it is believed that his sister was also selling similar dogs. The Parson Russell Terrier is thought to represent the true standard and is used in shows, while the Jack Russell Terrier is mainly a working dog—hence the two different breed names. Although it is considered that they are two breeds that have descended from the same breeding stock, many people still confuse them as one and the same.

Descended from Fox Terriers, the terriers bred by Jack Russell to this day display strong working instincts. They are energetic and friendly with a balanced temperament that makes them suitable as pets, especially in large families with other dogs. Because of their strong hunting instincts, they are not suited to living with smaller pets, such as mice or rabbits.

ABOVE
Parson Russell Terriers' most noticeable difference from Jack Russells is that the former are longer in the leg.

SCOTTISH TERRIER

COLOR: Black, wheaten, or brindle of any color

COAT CARE: Moderate maintenance

DIET: Moderate consumption

OFFICIAL CATEGORIZATION: UK: Terrier, AKC: Terrier, FCI: Group 3, Section 2

HEIGHT: 10–11 in. (25–28 cm)

WEIGHT: 19–23 lb. (8.5–10.5 kg)

OTHER NAMES: Scottie

Scottish Terriers are small, compact dogs with a very resilient nature. Bred in the Highlands of Scotland, they are considered to be national treasures by the Scottish and are often used in iconography to denote bravery, tenacity, and hardiness. The original working Scottish Terrier was bred for ratting and controlling other quarry. The dog is muscular and strong, despite its small size.

The Scottish Terrier, or Scottie, of today is a popular pet in the United States and throughout the world. It is friendly and loyal with a quintessential terrier-

like personality. Some Scottish Terriers retain strong working instincts, while others are more likely to exhibit companion-animal qualities. Despite being a very popular pet, it is advised by breeders that special care and effort is taken when socializing Scottish Terriers with other dogs. If not properly socialized, Scottish Terriers can become aggressive toward other dogs.

PEMBROKE WELSH CORGI

OFFICIAL CATEGORIZATION: UK: Pastoral, AKC: Herding,
FCI: Group 1, Section 8

HEIGHT: 10–12 in. (25–30 cm)

WEIGHT: 22–26 lb. (10–12 kg)

OTHER NAMES: Corgi

COLOR: Red, sable, fawn,
or black and tan, with or
without white markings

COAT CARE: Moderate maintenance

DIET: Moderate consumption

A royal favorite, the Pembroke Welsh Corgi, a dog closely associated with Queen Elizabeth II of England, is one of the smallest members of the pastoral and herding family of dogs. It is descended from the Swedish Vallhund and exhibits certain physical similarities to its Northern European ancestors, such as the foxlike head shape and distinct, erect ears. The Pembroke Welsh Corgi is a compact and well-balanced breed, with a medium-thick coat that is exhibited in a range of colorations, including red, sable, fawn, and black, tan, and white tricolor.

Multitalented

The breed is a popular pet, but the Pembroke Welsh Corgi is also robust and hardy, tolerant of cold, and able to work tirelessly for long periods of time. The breed's original purpose was to herd sheep and cattle and, despite being small, its tenacity and energy made it very adept at this function. The Pembroke Welsh Corgi is a versatile worker, with scenting abilities as well as traditional herding skills. It is adaptable and smart, with a keen desire to excel at whatever task it is performing. As with a lot of herding breeds, the Pembroke Welsh Corgi has a protective instinct, but the degree to which this is manifested differs from dog to dog. In general, the breed is alert and sensitive to even the most subtle of sounds.

A Loyal Pet

The Pembroke Welsh Corgi is a popular pet because of its high levels of intelligence, which is typical of most pastoral breeds. It is an active dog with a strong sense of purpose, often on the lookout for things to herd, and sometimes this can lead it to nip at people's heels. However, this does not detract from its genuinely affectionate nature and, provided that firm training is given, the Pembroke Welsh Corgi is likely to remain one of the most iconic British dog breeds.

LEFT

Descended from several Northern European breeds, the Pembroke Welsh Corgi is hard-working and tolerant of cold conditions.

MINIATURE BULL TERRIER

COLOR: For white, pure white coat; for colored, any color can predominate

COAT CARE: Minimal maintenance

DIET: Moderate consumption

OFFICIAL CATEGORIZATION: UK: Terrier, AKC: Terrier, FCI: Group 3, Section 3

HEIGHT: 10–14 in. (25–35 cm)   WEIGHT: 24–33 lb. (11–15 kg) lean

OTHER NAMES: None

The Miniature Bull Terrier is a very distinctive breed of dog, derived from a breeding program that sought to miniaturize the larger Bull Terrier breed. Displaying the characteristic "egg-shaped head" that is so synonymous with both the traditional and miniature versions of the breed, the Miniature Bull Terrier is certainly eye-catching.

RIGHT

The Miniature Bull Terrier is very similar to the Bull Terrier from which it has been bred and retains the egg-shaped head.

Like its larger relative, the Miniature Bull Terrier is a hardy yet affectionate and friendly dog. Some specimens can be stubborn, but this is often overcome with proper and firm training. The breed is well-known for its intelligence and general love of company, but due to its terrier instincts the Miniature Bull Terrier requires a competent trainer. Miniature Bull Terriers do not always get along well with other dogs and generally will not back down if confronted.

PATTERDALE TERRIER

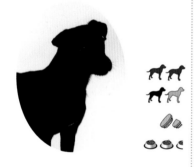

COLOR: Red, brown, black and tan, or black

COAT CARE: Low/moderate maintenance

DIET: Moderate/high consumption

OFFICIAL CATEGORIZATION:
UK: Terrier, AKC: Terrier, FCI: Not recognized

HEIGHT: 12–17 in. (30.5–40 cm)   WEIGHT: 10–17 lb. (4.5–7.5 kg)

OTHER NAMES: None

The Patterdale Terrier is a breed of working terrier that takes its name from the region of Cumbria, England, where it was bred. It is noted for its toughness, which sets it apart from many companion or pet terrier breeds. The Patterdale Terrier is relatively small, but extremely tenacious and high spirited. It has the traditional look of a working terrier, with a large head in proportion to the body and a lean, squat physique.

Traditionally, the Patterdale Terrier is not considered a pet breed. It has been bred predominantly for working and, as such, still retains a high prey drive. This prey drive is excellent for working terriers but is not always conducive to domestic living. People usually like to keep Patterdale Terriers in order to combine the role of working terrier and pet, but it is advisable that all Patterdale Terrier pets are worked to a degree to prevent boredom.

WEST HIGHLAND WHITE TERRIER

OFFICIAL CATEGORIZATION: UK: Terrier, AKC: Terrier, FCI: Group 3, Section 2

HEIGHT: 10–11 in. (25–27.5 cm)   WEIGHT: 15–20 lb. (7.5–10 kg)

OTHER NAMES: Westie (or Westy)

COLOR: White

COAT CARE: High maintenance

DIET: Moderate consumption

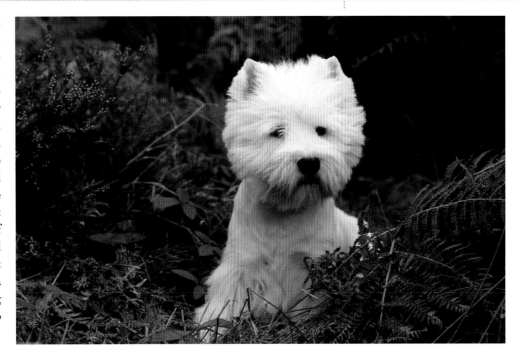

The West Highland White Terrier is an extremely popular and well-loved breed of dog. Originally bred in the Highlands of Scotland for ratting and hunting small quarry, it is now an established pet breed. The white coat was produced deliberately so that the little terrier would stand out against the heather of its original natural environment. The West Highland White Terrier is a short, stocky, and strong breed, closely related to the Scottish Terrier.

The West Highland White Terrier is one of the most popular terrier breeds in the world, and is the second most popular terrier breed in Britain after the Staffordshire Bull Terrier. Its adaptability and friendliness sets it apart from certain other terrier breeds as a suitable pet dog. While the West Highland White Terrier still retains working instincts and can be valuable in rural environments, it has proven to be extremely affectionate, good-natured, and friendly as a pet.

Independent But Affectionate

The West Highland White Terrier is a relatively independent breed and, if necessary, can withstand periods of isolation, which is another reason why the dog is so compatible with modern pet owners. It is tolerant of young children and displaysa remarkable affection to people with whom it is familiar. Occasionally, it can become aggressive toward other animals, such as rabbits or mice, due to its long history of hunting small quarry.

ABOVE
The West Highland Terrier's white coat was vital for when out shooting to avoid being mistaken for a fox.

Despite its small size, the West Highland White Terrier has a lot of energy and requires a good amount of space in which to exercise.

It is not uncommon for this breed to enjoy an energetic play session and to then spend the rest of the day sleeping. The West Highland White Terrier considers itself to be a good guard dog and it readily protects its territory. It does not bark frequently, but will do so if alarmed.

CAIRN TERRIER

COLOR: Any color except white

COAT CARE: Moderate maintenance

DIET: Moderate/high consumption

OFFICIAL CATEGORIZATION: UK: Terrier, AKC: Terrier, FCI: Group 3, Section 2

HEIGHT: 11–12 in. (28–31 cm)   WEIGHT: 14–16 lb. (6–7.5 kg)

OTHER NAMES: Unknown

The Cairn Terrier is one of the oldest terrier breeds. It was bred originally in the Scottish Highlands and is typical of terriers originating from that region. The working terrier was bred to hunt burrowing prey and still exhibits these instincts. It is a small, stocky dog with a distinctive harsh outer coat, which served it well when working in the cold Highlands. It is frequently much smaller today than it used to be, although larger examples are becoming more common due to selective breeding.

Like the majority of working terriers, the Cairn Terrier has high spirits, with a good degree of tenacity and energy. It makes a suitable pet in certain situations but is often guilty of giving in to its instincts and digging for prey. It may also be prone to obeying its hunting instincts. However, with proper training this friendly dog will make a great pet.

> **LEFT**
> *Cairn Terriers are very independent dogs and do not make good "lap dogs." The image of Toto from* The Wizard of Oz *is slightly misleading.*

PLUMMER TERRIER

COLOR: A bright, fiery red-tan with white

COAT CARE: Low/moderate maintenance

DIET: High/very high consumption

OFFICIAL CATEGORIZATION: UK: Not recognized, AKC: Not recognized, FCI: Not recognized

HEIGHT: No standard—medium   WEIGHT: No standard—lean

OTHER NAMES: None

A rare new breed, the Plummer Terrier is yet to become an established pet dog but is a popular and very skilled working terrier. Bred in the 1970s, the Plummer Terrier is descended from many breeds, including the Beagle, Bull Terrier, and working Jack Russell Terriers. It is a short, smooth-coated breed with an expressive face and athletic body. It has yet to be recognized by any major authority because of its status as a new breed; this is because there have not been sufficient generations for a standard to become established.

The Plummer Terrier is predominantly a working terrier, with strong hunting instincts and a powerful bite. Despite this, it can be kept as a pet, but typically after its working life has come to an end. The breed is tenacious and lively, with a strong prey drive and excellent ratting abilities.

CARDIGAN WELSH CORGI

OFFICIAL CATEGORIZATION: UK: Pastoral, AKC: Herding,
FCI: Group 1, Section 1

HEIGHT: 10½–12½ in. (26.5–31.5 cm) WEIGHT: 30–35 lb. (13.5–15.5 kg)

OTHER NAMES: Cardigan

COLOR: Any color, with
or without white markings

COAT CARE: Moderate maintenance

DIET: Moderate consumption

The Cardigan Welsh Corgi is one of two dog breeds referred to as Welsh Corgi, the other being the Pembroke Welsh Corgi. Despite their similarity in name, the two breeds are not related, although they do share common ancestors. The Cardigan Welsh Corgi, a traditional cattle dog, is one of the smallest herding breeds and has a distinctive long-bodied appearance with short legs. It was bred to be short so that it would be safely beneath the range of any kicks from the cattle that it herded.

The Cardigan Welsh Corgi is a popular pet breed because of its friendly personality and intelligence. It is thought that the breed has existed in its native Wales for more than 3,000 years. The dog is excitable but adaptable to domestic living. It is very loyal and affectionate, often forming a strong bond with one or two people within the family. Cardigan Welsh Corgis and children get along well together.

RIGHT

Bred with deliberately short legs to keep it safe from cattle kicks, the Cardigan Welsh Corgi is one of the smallest herding breeds.

SEALYHAM TERRIER

OFFICIAL CATEGORIZATION: UK: Terrier, AKC: Terrier,
FCI: Group 3, Section 2

HEIGHT: 10½–13½ in. (26.5–34.5 cm)   WEIGHT: 23–24 lb. (10–11 kg)

OTHER NAMES: None

COLOR: All white, or with lemon, tan, or badger markings on head and ears

COAT CARE: Moderate maintenance

DIET: Moderate consumption

The Sealyham Terrier is a very unusual-looking terrier originating from Wales. Particularly when groomed for conformation showing, the breed displays an unusual coat that covers a large portion of the head and face, giving the impression of an elongated and unusually shaped skull. The breed descends from Bull Terriers, West Highland White Terriers, Fox Terriers, and Bassett Hounds. The ancestry of Bull Terriers is denoted by the unusual shape of the breed's head.

The Sealyham Terrier is considered a "typical" terrier, with stubbornness being one of its less attractive qualities. Despite this, it makes a suitable pet and exhibits a friendly and affable personality. It is energetic and requires solid, comprehensive training. The breed is considered to be very intelligent, with a strong independent streak that can sometimes be mistaken for aloofness. Throughout the breed, different dogs display different combinations of the various Sealyham Terrier attributes.

CAVALIER KING CHARLES SPANIEL

OFFICIAL CATEGORIZATION: UK: Toy, AKC: Toy, FCI: Group 9, Section 7

COLOR: Blenheim (chestnut on white), tricolor, ruby, or black and tan

COAT CARE: Moderate/high maintenance

DIET: Moderate consumption

HEIGHT: 12–13 in. (30.5–33 cm)

WEIGHT: 13–18 lb. (6–8 kg)

OTHER NAMES: Cavalier

prominence of Asian toy breeds, including the Pug and the Japanese Chin, in the bloodline.

A Family Pet

The Cavalier King Charles Spaniel of today has very little in common with working and other pet spaniel breeds, aside from a shared ancestry with old working spaniels. Despite its long history of being a companion animal, remarkably it still retains some of the hunting instincts that were passed down from early breeding stock. These instincts are not strong but occasionally they will be stimulated by the low flight of a bird or presence of a small animal.

The breed is small in stature but has a large personality. It is a dedicated and affectionate companion animal, with a gentle demeanor that makes it very desirable as a pet all over the world. The Cavalier King Charles Spaniel is known as a very trusting dog, with seemingly limitless patience and tolerance, which makes it a good choice of pet for families with small children.

The Cavalier King Charles Spaniel is one of the most well-known and popular toy breeds of modern times and has a history reaching back to the eleventh century. The breed is related to spaniels, but in most cases is considered to be a toy breed. Its origins are fascinating: King Charles II, after whom the breed is named, is strongly associated with the dog as a very similar type of spaniel was kept as a pet for his children.

ABOVE

In King Charles II's day, it was fashionable for men to wear long-haired wigs resembling the ears of this spaniel.

Later on, when King Charles II decreed that the breed was never to be denied access into a public building, the spaniel became universally popular and began to feature in a lot of regal artwork. The breed is descended from working spaniels, but the small size and compact face of the Cavalier King Charles Spaniel are due to the

BULLDOG

OFFICIAL CATEGORIZATION: UK: Utility, AKC: nonsporting, FCI: Group 2, Section 2

HEIGHT: 12–16 in. (31–40 cm)

OTHER NAMES: British Bulldog

COLOR: Red, fawn, brindle, pale yellow, or white/with white

COAT CARE: Low/moderate maintenance

DIET: Moderate/high consumption

The Bulldog is considered the quintessential British breed, synonymous with former wartime Prime Minister Winston Churchill. Today's Bulldog is strikingly different to the original Bulldog that was bred for work. Still considered as a utility breed by the UK Kennel Club, the modern Bulldog is smaller and more compact than the originals, which were strong, lean, and athletic. The breed was used originally for bull baiting in the seventeenth century—the characteristically flat face was useful for enabling the dog to grip onto a bull without getting blood in its eyes.

Health Problems

When bull baiting was outlawed in Britain in 1835, there was no use for the lean, strong Bulldogs. Fans of the Bulldog continued to breed them in order to maintain the bloodline, but they were increasingly bred for looks rather than health. In more modern times, the Bulldog has been subject to careless breeding practices performed by people attempting to perfect their own interpretation of the breed. This has led to the Bulldog being a considerably unhealthy breed with a life span of around eight years and prone to heart problems and skin disorders. Attempts are being made to reestablish the original Bulldog, including breeding programs that incorporate American Bulldog and Staffordshire Bull Terrier stock.

Loyal and Docile

The Bulldog as a pet is a friendly and fiercely loyal animal, popular for its charming and affectionate nature and its extremely appealing idiosyncrasies. Many high-profile people have owned Bulldogs, which is partly why the breed is still popular despite its poor health. The Bulldog is known for its protective nature and dedication to all family members. It is an extremely loving dog with a fondness for play. Despite its history, the Bulldog is characteristically docile and peaceful, very content to accompany its owner quietly around the house or garden with little desire for exercise.

BELOW

Fascinating Facts

The Bulldog is extremely susceptible to heat stroke. Because of its flat face and folded skin, it can have difficulty breathing in hot weather.

LAKELAND TERRIER

COLOR: Black and tan, blue and tan, red, wheaten, red grizzle, liver, blue, or black

COAT CARE: Moderate/high maintenance

DIET: High consumption

OFFICIAL CATEGORIZATION: UK: Terrier, AKC: Terrier, FCI: Group 3, Section 1

HEIGHT: 13–16 in. (33–40.5 cm)

WEIGHT: 15.5–20 lb. (7–9 kg)

OTHER NAMES: None

The Lakeland Terrier is one of the oldest British terrier breeds. Bred for protecting sheep and lambs from foxes, the Lakeland Terrier was expected to kill any predators rather than simply scaring them away. It originates from the Lake District area of Britain and counts the Border Terrier and the Bedlington Terrier among its working ancestors. It has a noticeably wiry and harsh coat, characteristic of predominantly working dog breeds.

The Lakeland Terrier is similar in temperament to the Border Terrier. It has great stamina and a strong instinct for aggression toward perceived predators. Despite this, it is kept as a pet and makes a friendly and intelligent companion. Care must be taken to ensure the Lakeland Terrier is properly trained and socialized to prevent its terrier instincts from taking over. As with most working terrier breeds, it is hardy and very independent.

> LEFT
> *Lakeland Terriers were bred to be guard dogs with a difference; they were to kill potential predators of the flock, not just deter them.*

COCKER SPANIEL

COLOR: Black variety or any solid color other than black, with tan points

COAT CARE: High maintenance

DIET: High consumption

OFFICIAL CATEGORIZATION: UK: Gun Dog, AKC: Sporting, FCI: Group 8, Section 2

HEIGHT: 14½–15½ in. (37–39 cm)

WEIGHT: 15–30 lb. (7–14 kg)

OTHER NAMES: American Cocker Spaniel

Although widely known in this country as the Cocker Spaniel, in Britain, where the dog was originally bred, it is known as the American Cocker Spaniel. In Britain, it is recognized as a member of the Gun Dog group, but is distinct from the English Cocker Spaniel. It is descended from the English Cocker Spaniel and is now considered to be the American version that was adapted to meet American needs. Like the English Cocker Spaniel, it was bred to flush out birds at shoots.

The Cocker Spaniel is a popular pet, which shouldn't be surprising because many of the spaniel family of dogs are popular. The Cocker Spaniel is the smallest of the gun-dog spaniels, but exhibits many of the qualities that have made working spaniel breeds popular as pets. The breed is highly intelligent, with a friendly and adaptable persona that is appealing to a wide variety of pet owners.

BEAGLE

OFFICIAL CATEGORIZATION: UK: Hound, AKC: Hound, FCI: Group 6, Section 1

HEIGHT: 13–16 in. (33–40 cm)

WEIGHT: 22–25 lb. (10–11 kg)

OTHER NAMES: None

COLOR: Any recognized hound color other than liver; tip of stern white

COAT CARE: Low/moderate maintenance

DIET: High consumption

The Beagle is a popular pet breed, known for its striking looks and even temperament. It was established in Britain in the nineteenth century and is closely associated with hunting and, therefore, the aristocracy. The Beagle is a scent hound, although relatively small in comparison to other scent hounds, such as the Bloodhound. It was used originally for tracking rabbits, hare, and other small game.

Beagles are popular around the world as pets and as working hounds. The character of "Snoopy" that featured in the *Peanuts* comic strip was a Beagle. The breed usually displays a tricolor coloring of white, black, and brown and has an upright tail when working. Because of its lack of inherited health problems, the Beagle is often used in animal testing, much to the horror of many animal-welfare campaigners.

A Gentle Companion

The Beagle is known for its gentle and kindly disposition, which is one of the reasons the breed makes such a popular pet. It retains its working instincts and has what is thought to be the second-strongest sense of smell of any dog breed, bettered only by the Bloodhound.

The breed generally is intelligent and adaptable, with a strong pack drive that makes it a very loyal pet. Because of this driv,e the Beagle does not like being left alone and can sometimes be prone to displaying separation anxiety. It is inherently non-aggressive and does not serve well as a guard dog, but it will bark if startled or intimidated. Thanks to its loud bay, which is typical of many hounds, this is often enough to make it a useful watchdog.

Because of its largely relaxed and friendly temperament, the Beagle has been used as breeding stock in various crossbreedings in order to transfer its appealing personality traits.

BELOW
Because of its healthy robust physique, Beagles have often been used in animal testing.

SHETLAND SHEEPDOG

COLOR: Black, blue merle, and sable (ranging from golden through to mahogany); marked with varying amounts of white and/or tan

COAT CARE: High maintenance

DIET: Moderate/high consumption

OFFICIAL CATEGORIZATION: UK: Pastoral, AKC: Herding, FCI: Group 1, Section 1

HEIGHT: 13–16 in. (33–40.5 cm)   WEIGHT: 14–27 lb. (6–12 kg)

OTHER NAMES: Shetland Collie, Miniature Collie, Sheltie

The Shetland Sheepdog is a herding breed originating from the Scottish Shetland Isles. Although the Shetland Sheepdog appears to resemble a small version of the Rough Collie, it is not a strict miniaturization of one breed but the result of many crossbreedings involving various herding breeds. The breed's small size was desirable to shepherds working on the rough and uneven terrain of the Shetland Isles.

The Shetland Sheepdog is an unusually intelligent breed, due partly to its ancestry of other highly intelligent pastoral breeds. In general, it makes a fantastic family pet, displaying a particular affinity with children. Occasionally, Shetland Sheepdogs can display shyness with strangers and in extreme cases can become fearful of, and aggressive toward, new people. On the whole, the breed is easy to train, friendly, and gentle. Herding instincts are present in many Shetland Sheepdogs, but the breed's intelligence enables it to be highly trained.

Shelties can have eye problems. There is also risk of hypothyroidism, epilepsy, hip dysplasia, or skin allergies.

WELSH TERRIER

OFFICIAL CATEGORIZATION: UK: Terrier, AKC: Terrier, FCI: Group 3, Section 1

COLOR: Black and tan for preference, or black grizzle and tan

COAT CARE: Moderate maintenance

DIET: High consumption

HEIGHT: 14–17 in. (35.5–43 cm)   WEIGHT: 17½–22 lb. (8–10 kg) lean

OTHER NAMES: Welshie

The Welsh Terrier is a traditional terrier breed that exhibits an attractive, tightly curled coat that has evolved to repel dirt. It is popular as a working dog and pet. Bred originally for hunting birds and small game, the Welsh Terrier's physical appearance generally reflects its working origins; it is square shaped and muscular to the touch.

The Welsh Terrier is considered to display typical terrier attributes—namely a desire to chase anything that moves, a confidence that belies its relatively small size, and particularly high levels of energetic activity. It is a friendly breed of dog but noted for its lack of patience in the hands of inexperienced or timid owners. It needs confident training and relatively regular stimulation and exercise if it is to remain free from the boredom that can lead to destructive behavior.

> RIGHT
> *The Welsh Terrier has a tightly curled coat, bred this way to repel dirt from its work underground.*

STAFFORDSHIRE BULL TERRIER

OFFICIAL CATEGORIZATION: UK: Terrier, AKC: Terrier,
FCI: Group 3, Section 3

HEIGHT: 14–16 in. (36–41 cm)   WEIGHT: 28–38 lb. (13–17 kg)

OTHER NAMES: Staff, Staffy

COLOR: Red, fawn, white, black, or blue, or any of these colors with white

COAT CARE: Low maintenance

DIET: Moderate/high consumption

The Staffordshire Bull Terrier is an extremely popular breed of dog. Originating from the county of Staffordshire in England, where it was bred initially for ratting and bull baiting, this sturdy and compact breed is considered to be the ultimate pet terrier breed. Typically of robust health and even temper, the Staffordshire Bull Terrier is the most popular terrier breed in Britain.

Despite a history linked with dog fighting, the modern Staffordshire Bull Terrier is an exemplary pet dog breed. Loyal, brave, confident, and friendly, with minimal associated behavior problems or inherited illnesses, the Staffordshire Bull Terrier is considered by many to be a misunderstood breed. Although it has strong jaws and a powerful, yet relatively compact physique, the breed is rarely aggressive unless provoked. The Staffordshire Bull Terrier is famously affectionate to children and displays a loyalty and boldness that is rarely seen in other breeds.

LEFT
The Staffordshire Bull Terrier is the most popular breed of terrier in Britain, despite sometimes being wrongly thought an aggressive breed.

WIRE FOX TERRIER

OFFICIAL CATEGORIZATION: UK: Terrier, AKC: Terrier,
FCI: Group 3, Section 1

HEIGHT: 14–17 in. (35.5–43 cm)   WEIGHT: 15½–20 lb. (7–9 kg)

OTHER NAMES: None

COLOR: Predominantly white, with black, black and tan, or tan markings

COAT CARE: Moderate/high maintenance

DIET: High consumption

Originating from England, where it was bred to hunt foxes, the Wire Fox Terrier is an instantly recognizable breed. With its harsh, wiry coat and characteristic profile, the Wire Fox Terrier is one of the more individual-looking members of the terrier family of dogs.

The Wire Fox Terrier has experienced varying degrees of popularity throughout history as both a working and companion breed.

As a pet, the Wire Fox Terrier's strong working instincts make the breed unsuitable for certain situations. It is prone to digging, chasing, and barking but can be trained to a high level with a strong, comprehensive obedience program. The breed is known more for its instinctive behavior rather than its intelligence, although it is by no means considered an unintelligent dog. It is more suited to an owner who understands the needs and desires of dogs with strong working terrier instincts.

ENGLISH COCKER SPANIEL

OFFICIAL CATEGORIZATION: UK: Gun Dog, AKC: Sporting, FCI: Group 8, Section 2

COLOR: Various; no white allowed except on chest

COAT CARE: High maintenance

DIET: Moderate/high consumption

HEIGHT: 15½–16 in. (39–41 cm)   **WEIGHT:** 28–34 lb. (13–16 kg)

OTHER NAMES: Cocker Spaniel

As a modern pet breed the English Cocker Spaniel is universally popular. Originally, Cocker Spaniels and Springer Spaniels were considered to be the same breed, until they were made into two breeds separated by weight. The heavier dogs became Springer Spaniels and the lighter dogs became classed as Cocking Spaniels, later shortened to Cocker Spaniels. The English Cocker Spaniel was bred originally for flushing out birds from trees for hunters, but went on to become a skilled retriever. It is still useful as a working dog but is now better known as a pet breed.

The English Cocker Spaniel has been in existence in many different forms for more than 500 years. There are different varieties of Cocker Spaniel that are considered to be the standard, but the English Cocker Spaniel is the original, with the Cocker Spaniel (known as the American Cocker Spaniel in Britain) an ancestor of the English version. The differences in appearance between a working English Cocker Spaniel and one bred for conformation are considerable. A working Cocker has a noticeably shorter coat and ears, while a show-bred Cocker is meticulously groomed, which accentuates its longer coat and more pendulous ears.

Fascinating Facts

The English Cocker Spaniel has won the Best in Show title at Crufts more than any other breed.

LEFT

The English Cocker Spaniel can be used as a working dog, a show dog, or simply as a pet.

A Popular Pet

Most spaniel breeds are well-known for their intelligence and independence, which is often complemented by an affectionate and cheerful disposition. The English Cocker Spaniel is known for its lack of aggression. One of the main reasons it has become so popular is due to the ease with which it can be trained. Because of the breed's working origins the vast majority of English Cocker Spaniels are eager to learn, and display high levels of obedience and a will to please. This fact, coupled with the dog's attractive looks and ever-wagging tail, has established the English Cocker Spaniel as one of the world's favorite breeds.

SUSSEX SPANIEL

OFFICIAL CATEGORIZATION: UK: Gun Dog, AKC: Sporting, FCI: Group 8, Section 2

HEIGHT: 13–15 in. (35–38 cm)

WEIGHT: 35–45 lb. (16–20 kg)

OTHER NAMES: None

COLOR: Rich golden liver

COAT CARE: Moderate/high maintenance

DIET: Moderate/high consumption

The Sussex Spaniel was bred for a very specific working purpose. Existing spaniel breeds struggled to work effectively in deep undergrowth, so a breeding program was established to produce a smaller dog with shorter legs that could maneuver through the dense bushes in order to find quarry for hunters. The Sussex Spaniel is named after the English county in which it originated during the eighteenth century.

The Sussex Spaniel is considered to be a much calmer type of spaniel than the English Cocker or Springer, both of which were bred to be excitable in order to startle the birds that they were flushing out. The Sussex is known as an intelligent working dog with a kind and friendly disposition, but the call for it as a worker has decreased, resulting in fewer Sussex Spaniels being bred. For this reason, the breed has never been widely established as a pet in Britain.

MANCHESTER TERRIER

OFFICIAL CATEGORIZATION: UK: Terrier, AKC: Terrier, FCI: Group 3, Section 1

HEIGHT: 16 in. (41 cm)

WEIGHT: 15½–20 lb. (7–9 kg)

OTHER NAMES: None

COLOR: Jet black and rich mahogany tan

COAT CARE: Minimal maintenance

DIET: Moderate/high consumption

The Manchester Terrier was established to control the frequent and alarming rat infestations of nineteenth-century England. Large towns, such as Manchester, were over-run with rats, and people desperately needed ratting dogs to reduce the numbers. The Manchester Terrier was bred using Whippets and crossbreed black-and-tan-colored terriers to produce a dog with the looks and tenacity of the black-and-tan crossbreeds, but with the speed of the Whippet.

For those who are fond of terriers, the Manchester Terrier will make an excellent pet, provided it is raised and trained correctly. Because of its tenacious nature and high energy, the Manchester Terrier requires dedicated training to ensure it does not let its instincts overpower it. An obedient and well-socialized Manchester Terrier is an excellent pet. Loyalty, bravery, and typical terrier confidence are reasons why terrier lovers admire the Manchester Terrier.

LEFT
Bred specifically to help with rat control in nineteenth-century towns, the Manchester Terrier is remarkably swift.

SMOOTH FOX TERRIER

OFFICIAL CATEGORIZATION: UK: Terrier, AKC: Terrier, FCI: Group 3, Section 1

HEIGHT: 14–17 in. (35.5–43 cm) WEIGHT: 16–18 lb. (7.5–8 kg)

OTHER NAMES: None

COLOR: White, or white with tan, black and tan, or black markings

COAT CARE: Low maintenance

DIET: High consumption

Considered by many to be the father of the Fox Terrier-type dog, the Smooth Fox Terrier has a long-reaching history and impressive genealogical legacy. It is a sturdy, well-balanced breed, typical of the Fox Terrier, but differs from similarly proportioned breeds, such as the Wire Fox Terrier, due to its smooth, short coat. It has a tapering muzzle and distinctive folded ears. It is an ancestor of the majority of Fox Terrier breeds.

The Smooth Fox Terrier's temperament is indicative of its long working history. It is alert, bold, and has impressive stamina. The breed is noted for its characteristically expressive face. With a combination of high energy and impulsive behavior, the Smooth Fox Terrier can be a challenge for inexperienced dog owners, but its typically friendly and cheerful nature will come to the fore if the dog is given firm training.

RIGHT
The Smooth Fox Terrier's key role through history was to work with a pack of hounds, driving a fox from its hole if it went to ground.

BEDLINGTON TERRIER

OFFICIAL CATEGORIZATION: UK: Terrier, AKC: Terrier, FCI: Group 3, Section 1

HEIGHT: 14.5–17½ in. (37–44.5 cm) WEIGHT: 17–23 lb. (7–10 kg)

OTHER NAMES: Rothbury Terrier, Rodbery Terrier

COLOR: Blue, sandy, liver, blue and tan, sandy and tan, or liver and tan

COAT CARE: Moderate maintenance

DIET: High consumption

Bred in the northeast of England as a versatile, multipurpose dog, the Bedlington Terrier exhibits a wide range of instinctive habits. It also has a striking and unique appearance due to its woolly coat and tapered muzzle. The breed is strong, tenacious, and very agile, with a keen ability to defend itself. Its dainty gait and unusual looks belie its genuine toughness.

The Bedlington Terrier is a versatile worker with a love of water. As a pet, it is best suited to an active owner who can stimulate its working instincts; in the home, the Bedlington Terrier is friendly, bold, and confident. The breed is noted for its bravery and habit of not backing down, which can pose a problem for a weak or inexperienced trainer, as well as other dogs. Attempting to discipline the hardy Bedlington Terrier is often a fruitless act that yields little success.

WHIPPET

OFFICIAL CATEGORIZATION: UK: Hound, AKC: Hound,
FCI: Group 10, Section 3

HEIGHT: 19–22 in. (47–51 cm)   WEIGHT: 25–45 lb. (11–21 kg)

OTHER NAMES: None

COLOR: Any color or mixture of colors

COAT CARE: Minimal maintenance

DIET: Moderate/high consumption

The Whippet is an ancient sight-hound breed. Sight hounds resembling the Whippet have been recorded in artifacts dating back to Roman times, but the first recorded usage of the name did not occur until the seventeenth century. The Whippet has the appearance of a Greyhound in miniature, but in fact it has developed independently of that breed. It is lithe and extremely fast, with a sleek frame and narrow head. It exhibits a very wide variety of colorations, ranging from solid white to brindle and everything in between.

The breed is particularly popular as a pet in the north of England, and in British culture is often used as a metaphor for stereotypical northern values. As with almost all sight hounds, the Whippet's ancestry can be traced back to northern Africa.

ABOVE
Whippets are sight hounds and great runners, often referred to as the "poor man's racehorse."

An Adaptable Personality
The Whippet, as with many other sight-hound breeds, is extremely gentle and placid.

It is not prone to aggression, defensiveness, or boldness, but prefers to remain calm. The breed is extremely affectionate and loyal and takes to children very well. One of the most appealing aspects of the Whippet's personality is its apparent happiness to adapt to any situation.

Despite its extremely athletic physique and history of hunting, the Whippet's exercise requirements are no greater than that of other dogs of its size, although it relishes the chance to run and exercise. The perceived need for the Whippet to receive a lot of exercise is one of the reasons that some people choose not to get one. In reality, it is a quiet dog, well-suited to living in apartments because of its cleanliness and ease of grooming. Because the Whippet is a sight hound, it may be stimulated by sudden fast movement, so special care is needed when walking the dog in and around traffic.

BORDER COLLIE

OFFICIAL CATEGORIZATION: UK: Pastoral, AKC: Herding, FCI: Group 1, Section 1

COLOR: All colors or combinations of colors and/or markings

COAT CARE: Moderate maintenance

DIET: High/very high consumption

HEIGHT: 19–22 in. (48–55 cm)   WEIGHT: 30–45 lb. (14–20 kg)

OTHER NAMES: None

The Border Collie is a herding breed that originates from the border region of England and Scotland and is widely acknowledged as being the most intelligent breed of dog. In scientific studies conducted by the animal psychologist Juliane Kaminski, designed to measure the amount of commands that dogs could learn and the ease with which they perform them, the Border Collie consistently scored higher than any other breed.

The Border Collie typically is black and white in color, but examples of blue merle and red tricolor are not uncommon. It is a medium-sized dog with a coat that is typical of northern European breeds.

An Energetic Companion

Due to its extremely high levels of intelligence, combined with a strong herding instinct, the Border Collie requires a high level of stimulation. If left to make its own entertainment a typical Border Collie will become bored and destructive. The instinct of the breed is to control movement by lowering its head and herding whatever is moving, whether it be

people or other pets. A responsible and dedicated owner of a Border Collie will provide play and training that gives the dog an outlet for this natural instinct.

Despite the challenges faced with Border Collie ownership, the breed does make a good pet. When properly trained it is happy and contented. The dog is friendly, obedient, and active, which is a rewarding

combination for many dog owners. An alert Border Collie at the command of its owner is an impressive sight. The breed is attentive and energetic, which makes for a good response to well-

structured training. It is not known for being particularly affectionate and is more focused on pleasing its owner than being petted, but this does not mean that it is aloof or antisocial.

RIGHT
Widely agreed to be the most intelligent dog, the Border Collie can understand a large vocabulary of verbal and whistled commands.

FIELD SPANIEL

OFFICIAL CATEGORIZATION: UK: Gun Dog, AKC: Sporting,
FCI: Group 8, Section 2

HEIGHT: 16½–19½ in. (42–49.5 cm)   WEIGHT: 40–55 lb. (18–25 kg)

OTHER NAMES: None

COLOR: Black, liver or roan, or any one of these with tan markings

COAT CARE: Moderate/high maintenance

DIET: Moderate/high consumption

The Field Spaniel has its history in conformation breeding rather than work. It has a longer body than is typical of spaniel breeds and is prone to certain health problems associated with show breeding. It does have working abilities but is more closely associated with the show ring than the field. Its coat is more luxurious than that of other spaniels and is presented in a range of colors. It counts the Irish Water Spaniel and the English Cocker Spaniel among its ancestors.

The Field Spaniel has a lower prevalence of working instinct than the English Cocker Spaniel or Springer Spaniel and is a particularly adaptable domestic pet breed. It is a gentle and friendly dog with a minimal tendency for aggression; it is responsive to noise and can serve as a watchdog but typically will not confront or tackle an intruder. The Field Spaniel is a sociable breed that is interested in people.

WELSH SPRINGER SPANIEL

OFFICIAL CATEGORIZATION: UK: Gun Dog, AKC: Sporting,
FCI: Group 8, Section 2

HEIGHT: 18–19 in. (46–48 cm)   WEIGHT: 35–45 lb. (16–20 kg)

OTHER NAMES: None

COLOR: Rich red and white

COAT CARE: Moderate maintenance

DIET: High consumption

The Welsh Springer Spaniel is a traditional working gun-dog breed that has become a relatively popular pet dog breed as well. The Welsh Springer Spaniel is very similar to other working spaniel breeds in its appearance; the main difference between it and the English Springer Spaniel is that it has a more square body shape and is slightly smaller in size.

Although similar in terms of natural instinct to the more common English Springer Spaniel, the Welsh Springer Spaniel is typically hardier and more independent. The breed is considered to be more reserved around new people in particular, but with correct socialization is not normally suspicious of strangers. The Welsh Springer Spaniel is an adaptable breed with a happy and cheerful demeanor; some dogs are naturally playful while others tend to prefer peace and quiet. There is great degree of variation between members of the breed in terms of personality.

HARRIER

COLOR: Any color

COAT CARE: Minimal maintenance

DIET: High consumption

OFFICIAL CATEGORIZATION: UK: Not recognized, AKC: Hound, FCI: Group 6, Section 1

HEIGHT: 19–21 in. (48–53 cm)   WEIGHT: 45–60 lb. (19–27 kg)

OTHER NAMES: None

The Harrier is an English hunting scent hound, very similar in appearance to the English Fox Hound but slightly smaller. It is longer than it is tall, giving a relatively squat appearance. The Harrier has an excellent sense of smell and is a good worker, but despite this it is a very rare breed that is considered to be vulnerable by the UK Kennel Club.

The Harrier is a very pack-orientated breed with strong instincts for hunting. It is more playful than the typical pack hound but has a strong sense of working purpose, which leads many Harrier dogs to attempt to go exploring at any given opportunity. Despite its rarity, it is considered to be a great family pet, provided adequate exercise and space are provided. The Harrier likes to bay and is also stimulated by movement as well as scent, so the breed should be properly trained.

LEFT
Harriers are very s[i] maller and with comparatively longer bodies.

CLUMBER SPANIEL

COLOR: White with orange or lemon markings

COAT CARE: Moderate maintenance

DIET: Moderate consumption

OFFICIAL CATEGORIZATION: UK: Gun Dog, AKC: Sporting, FCI: Group 8, Section 2

HEIGHT: 18–20 in. (45–50 cm)   WEIGHT: 70–80 lb. (31–36 kg)

OTHER NAMES: None

This is arguably the stockiest of all spaniel breeds. The Clumber Spaniel is believed to have hunting hounds, such as the Bassett Hound, in its bloodline, which explains the characteristically houndlike facial features of the breed. The Clumber Spaniel has a working history but is an adaptable pet, too. Because of its heavy face and loose skin, the breed is prone to developing eye and skin problems.

The Clumber Spaniel has a gentle and affectionate disposition with a fondness for people. Unlike many spaniel breeds, it combines flushing instincts with retrieving instincts and can often be found carrying household items around in its mouth, so solid training is required. It has a particularly strong sense of smell, which can lead it astray if left unattended. The breed is typically obedient and eager to please with a high level of intelligence. It is also known for being very food driven.

ENGLISH SPRINGER SPANIEL

OFFICIAL CATEGORIZATION: UK: Gun Dog, AKC: Sporting, FCI: Group 8, Section 2

HEIGHT: 18½–21½ in. (47–54.5 cm) WEIGHT: 47½–52 lb. (21.5–23.5 kg)

OTHER NAMES: Springer, Springer Spaniel

COLOR: Liver and white, black and white, or either of these with tan markings

COAT CARE: Moderate/high maintenance

DIET: Moderate/high consumption

The English Springer Spaniel is a traditional working spaniel with a high degree of popularity among hunting parties for its excellent working abilities. The breed is an ancestor of many other spaniel breeds; physically, it is slightly larger and heavier than the closely related English Cocker Spaniel.

It was bred to work in a number of hunting situations, including locating game that had been shot, flushing out game, hunting water fowl, and, less frequently, marking game. The breed is noted for its exceptionally strong sense of smell, comparable in strength to certain scent-hound breeds. It is able to track scent in wet or dry conditions

and has been bred to be soft-mouthed in order to preserve any game that is retrieved.

Intelligent and Friendly

The English Springer Spaniel is a well-established breed and is popular as both a working companion and a pet—it is often used in a combination of the two roles. It is highly intelligent with a strong play drive, meaning

that it provides an active, fun companion for those wanting to keep the breed as a pet.

It is well-known for its impressive memory, which is often demonstrated by its digging up an old toy that was buried weeks or even months ago. It is also a very resourceful breed and, despite being active and intelligent, will find entertainment in any household object left within reach.

The typical English Springer Spaniel is very friendly and affectionate with most

Fascinating Facts

The Springer Spaniel and the English Cocker Spaniel used to be one and the same breed.

people, whether family members, occasional visitors, or complete strangers. It is relatively relaxed and pleasant in situations that are familiar to it but requires socialization to enable it to adapt to a wide range of other social situations, such as walking in towns.

BEARDED COLLIE

COLOR: Gray, black, blue, brown, or fawn, with or without white markings

COAT CARE: High maintenance

DIET: Moderate/high consumption

OFFICIAL CATEGORIZATION: UK: Pastoral, AKC: Herding, FCI: Group 1, Section 1

HEIGHT: 21–22 in. (53–56 cm)   WEIGHT: 40–60 lb. (18–27 kg)

OTHER NAMES: Highland Collie, Mountain Collie

The Bearded Collie is an old Scottish breed of herding dog. Debate still continues over the exact origins of this striking-looking breed, but it is generally agreed that the Polish Lowland Sheepdog contributed to the bloodline of the original Bearded Collie. It has a long shaggy coat that creates a fringed appearance. It has proven to be a valuable pastoral breed, with strong cattle- and sheepherding abilities. The coat of the Bearded Collie is typically gray and white, but this color changes throughout the life of the dog.

The Bearded Collie is a lively and active breed and, due to its herding instinct, is a relatively intelligent and driven type of dog. In more recent times, the breed has

Fascinating Facts

Because of their long hair, some Bearded Collies are given a "puppy cut" when they are young, so that there is less need to groom the dog.

become well-known on the conformation show circuit; it is often witnessed displaying its impressively long and glossy coat in the show ring.

A Willing Pupil

As a pe,t the Bearded Collie is more popular in Britain than elsewhere, although it is reasonably well-established outside of Europe. It is friendly and active—typically associated with a bouncy gait that sets it apart from various other herding breeds. Unlike the Border Collie, the Bearded Collie is less demanding of its owner, but still requires a good level of training and stimulation. The breed is also famous for

its constantly wagging tail, which exemplifies its cheerful and happy nature. The difference in temperament between males and females is very pronounced, with males typically being bolder and more confident, while females tend to be more reserved and cautious. Certain Bearded Collies may be considered to

be a little stubborn, but on the whole the breed is very trainable and eager to please its owner. The Bearded Collie is a rewarding, intelligent breed of dog to train.

BELOW
Favored by owners wanting to show, the Bearded Collie has an impressively luxuriant coat when groomed.

GOLDEN RETRIEVER

OFFICIAL CATEGORIZATION: UK: Gun Dog, AKC: Sporting, FCI: Group 8, Section 1

COLOR: Any shade of gold or cream

HEIGHT: 22–24 in. (56–61 cm)

WEIGHT: 65–75 lb. (29–33 kg)

COAT CARE: Moderate/high maintenance

OTHER NAMES: Yellow Retriever

DIET: High consumption

The Golden Retriever is instantly recognizable and is one of the most popular pet dog breeds in the world. It displays a luxurious and characteristic golden coat, although the shades found in modern Golden Retrievers vary from light yellow to a rich golden shade. Historically, it was a working retriever breed with a similar ancestry to the Labrador Retriever. Put to work bringing back game that had been shot or otherwise hunted, the breed has developed a very personable and obedient nature.

It is medium in size, with a good level of agility and reasonable strength, although this is rarely demonstrated to the full. Its ancestry can be traced back to the Newfoundland, although the modern breed as we know it today became established in Scotland. The breed's working abilities have now adapted to man's changing requirements: it can often be seen assisting blind people, helping the police with narcotics detection, and even being used as a therapy dog for people with mental and physical disabilities.

A Wonderful Family Pet
There are many reasons that the Golden Retriever is one

ABOVE
Affectionate and intelligent, the Golden Retriever makes an ideal pet with a playful streak.

Fascinating **F**acts

Golden Retrievers are crepuscular, which means that they are more active in the morning than at any other time of day.

Golden Retriever is easy to please and is very happy relaxing in the home for the majority of the time, provided it is well-trained and exercised on a daily basis. Play will appeal to the Golden Retriever's instincts, but this simply involves throwing a ball or stick for the dog until it is worn out.

Highly intelligent and loyal, the Golden Retriever's personality fits in well with modern family life. It enjoys the company of children and has a kind and very affectionate nature.

of the most popular breeds in the world. It exhibits an appealing look—medium in size with a sturdy build. But the main reason is the breed's extremely gentle and friendly disposition. The

ROUGH COLLIE

COLOR: Sable and white, tricolor or blue merle and white

COAT CARE: Very high maintenance

DIET: High consumption

OFFICIAL CATEGORIZATION: UK: Pastoral, AKC: Herding, FCI: Group 1, Section 1

HEIGHT: 24–26 in. (61–66 cm)   WEIGHT: 60–75 lb. (27–34 kg)

OTHER NAMES: Scottish Collie, Collie

The Rough Collie is a distinctive-looking breed of dog, perhaps most commonly known as being the breed of the famous fictional dog, Lassie. Its origins are shared almost entirely with the closely related Smooth Collie, with the only difference being the texture and thickness of the coat. The Rough Collie became established in Scotland and is a descendent of the Borzoi, an ancient Russian sight-hound breed.

In more recent times, the Rough Collie has experienced a drastic change in its physical form. Since industrialization, ownership of this herding breed as a pet has increased in popularity and it appears frequently on the conformation show circuit. As a result, the height and weight of the breed has gradually decreased. It still retains strong working instincts and, as is typical of the majority of pastoral and herding breeds, is highly intelligent.

A Gentle Playmate

The Rough Collie is a good family pet that is adaptable and eager to please. It is not as intelligent as the Border Collie but does require stimulation to appeal to its ancient herding instincts. Generally calm in demeanor, it is easily excited if the general environment around it becomes so. It is not typically aggressive and any signs of aggression tend to point to behavioral problems or illness.

Around children the Rough Collie is gentle and affectionate. It is playful and agile but can adapt to a slower pace of life. Some Rough Collies can be particularly protective and territorial, but this rarely extends to aggression and is more commonly exemplified by restlessness. The Rough Collie is known for its loyalty and dedication to those immediately close to it, but it tends to make friends with new people quickly, provided it trusts them; around people it does not like it can be suspicious.

LEFT
The Rough Collie is related to the Borzoi and retains the distinguished demeanor, despite being a great family pet.

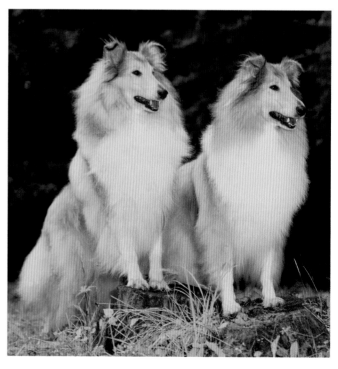

SMOOTH COLLIE

OFFICIAL CATEGORIZATION: UK: Pastoral, AKC: Herding, FCI: Group 1, Section 1

HEIGHT: 22–24 in. (56–61 cm) WEIGHT: 45–65 lb. (20.5–29.5 kg)

OTHER NAMES: None

COLOR: Sable and white, tricolor, or blue merle

COAT CARE: Minimal maintenance

DIET: High consumption

The Smooth Collie is distinct from the Rough Collie only in terms of appearance. The coat is noticeably smoother and easier to groom compared to that of the Rough Collie, but both coats are presented in the same colors and patterns—principally sable and white or tricolor varieties. The Smooth Collie, like the Rough Collie, has a robust and athletic physique that is often masked by the relatively long coat.

As a pet, the Smooth Collie is a popular choice, especially in Britain. With a gentle demeanor and eagerness to please almost identical to the rough-coated version, this breed has only one major difference when it comes to suitability as a pet. That difference is grooming—the Smooth Collie typically requires substantially less grooming than the Rough Collie and it is for this reason alone that pet owners will choose between the two breeds.

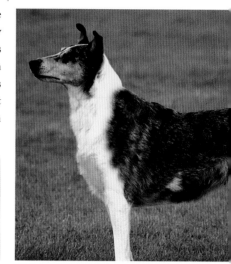

RIGHT
The Smooth Collie is considered a variety of the same breed as the Rough Collie in the United States and Canada, but as a separate breed in Britain and Australia.

BULL TERRIER

OFFICIAL CATEGORIZATION: UK: Terrier, AKC: Terrier, FCI: Group 3, Section 3

HEIGHT: 16–22 in. (40–56 cm) WEIGHT: 35–60 lb. (15–36 kg)

OTHER NAMES: None

COLOR: White, or white with tan or brindle markings

COAT CARE: Minimal maintenance

DIET: High consumption

The Bull Terrier is an English breed with a very distinctive and unusual appearance. Its triangular-shaped eyes and unusually shaped head marks it out as an individual, but it possesses the sturdy and muscular physique that is commonly associated with other Bull Terrier breeds, including the Staffordshire Bull Terrier and the American Pit Bull Terrier. It originated from bull-baiting circles in nineteenth-century England but was not a particularly successful fighter, lacking the overall strength required. It quickly became a popular pet in gentrified society and was used to work as a ratting terrier elsewhere.

The Bull Terrier of today makes an appealing pet. It is extremely friendly, even to strangers, which sometimes limits its suitability as a guard dog. It is gentle around children and displays tenacious loyalty to family members. The breed, particularly dogs solid white in color, is prone to deafness and should be checked by a vet when still a puppy.

LEFT
The English Bull Terrier's career in bull baiting during the nineteenth century did not last long because of its lack of strength.

CURLY-COATED RETRIEVER

COLOR: Black or liver

COAT CARE: High maintenance

DIET: High consumption

OFFICIAL CATEGORIZATION: UK: Gun Dog, AKC: Sporting, FCI: Group 8, Section 1

HEIGHT: 25½–28½ in. (65–72.5 cm)   WEIGHT: 80–100 lb. (36–45 kg)

OTHER NAMES: None

The Curly-Coated Retriever is a distinctive-looking English retriever breed. It is one of the longest-established retriever breeds and is extremely well-suited to working in and around water. The tightly curled coat enables the dog to remain warm in cold water, where it was often used to retrieve water fowl. It is less popular here than in Britain, despite having been exported to the United States early in the twentieth century. It is descended from the Newfoundland and the now-extinct Saint John's Water Dog.

The temperament of the Curly-Coated Retriever is distinctive to the breed. It is bold and confident but does not display the level-headedness associated with other more popular retriever breeds. It is noticeably brave and very eager to remain active for as long as possible if given the opportunity. It is, therefore, best suited to an active owner.

RIGHT
The curly coat of the Curly-Coated Retriever helps it to remain warm while wet, a useful attribute on a day out shooting.

AIREDALE TERRIER

COLOR: Body and neck black or grizzle; all other parts tan

COAT CARE: Moderate maintenance

DIET: Moderate/high consumption

OFFICIAL CATEGORIZATION: UK: Terrier, AKC: Terrier, FCI: Group 3, Section 1

HEIGHT: 23–24 in. (58–61 cm)   WEIGHT: 50–65 lb. (23–29 kg)

OTHER NAMES: Waterside Terrier, Bingley Terrier

The Airedale Terrier is most commonly known as a companion animal, but the breed has an impressively varied working history. Water work, vermin control, and even scenting are roles that the Airedale Terrier has managed to fulfill for man in the past. The breed has a tightly curled coat and large head on a small yet sturdy frame. It is energetic and agile with relatively strong terrier instincts. An Airedale Terrier used for work, or even one that has access to the countryside, will need daily grooming because the coat is prone to collecting burrs.

The Airedale Terrier is typical of many terrier breeds in that it is tenacious and hardy with strong ratting instincts. Around people it is loyal and bold, but it is unusual for an Airedale Terrier to be aggressive. It is intelligent and independent but takes to training eagerly and obediently.

OLD ENGLISH SHEEPDOG

OFFICIAL CATEGORIZATION: UK: Pastoral, AKC: Herding, FCI: Group 1, Section 1

HEIGHT: 22–24 in. (56–61 cm)　　WEIGHT: 70–100 lb. (31–45 kg)

OTHER NAMES: Bobtail, Dulux Dog

COLOR: Any shade of gray, grizzle, blue, or blue merle, with or without white markings

COAT CARE: High/very high maintenance

DIET: High consumption

The Old English Sheepdog is a distinctly shaggy well-known breed of English herding dog. In this country, the breed appears in the television series Sesame Street—Barkley is an Old English Sheepdog. In Britain and Australia, it is known for its association with the Dulux paint brand because of its appearance in the company's advertisements; in those countries, it is also referred to as the "Dulux Dog."

Traditionally, the Old English Sheepdog is a working pastoral dog with a strong ability for herding sheep. The breed is noted for its high levels of agility and ability to perform its role in particularly cold weather. It is believed that it is descended from Russian breeds of wolf hounds and also central European herding dogs, including the Bergamasco. As a pet, the breed is relatively popular, despite requiring a very high level of grooming.

Young at Heart

As with many pastoral breeds, the Old English Sheepdog is lively and intelligent. It has a strong working instinct but responds well to training in order to curtail any destructive or unwanted behavior associated with such instincts. The breed can be stubborn or disobedient if not given firm training.

ABOVE

If done professionally, the grooming of an Old English Sheepdog can be expensive; it is worth learning how to do it yourself.

The Old English Sheepdog displays impressive loyalty and courage, particularly in relation to its owner. Despite this it is generally well-mannered around other dogs and around new people. The Old English Sheepdog is considered unusual in the way it matures: the breed retains the behavior of a young dog for much of its life, then adopts a maturity very rapidly during the latter stages of its life. Because of this, it is considered to be a very fun and playful breed from puppyhood well into adulthood.

FLAT-COATED RETRIEVER

COLOR: Solid black or liver

COAT CARE: Moderate/high maintenance

DIET: High consumption

OFFICIAL CATEGORIZATION: UK: Gun Dog, AKC: Sporting, FCI: Group 8, Section 1

HEIGHT: 23–24 in. (58–61 cm)   WEIGHT: 60–80 lb. (27–36 kg)

OTHER NAMES: None

The Flat-Coated Retriever is an English gun-dog breed that counts North American breeds such as the Saint John's Water Dog among its closer ancestors. It became established in England as a breed around the middle of the nineteenth century. The characteristic flat coat sets it apart from other retrieving breeds and makes it a suitable dog to work both in water and on dry land.

The Flat-Coated Retriever is a friendly and kind breed but does display

particularly high levels of energy and exuberance, which can make it unsuitable as a pet for families with very young children. Although the breed is affectionate and gentle toward all, its playfulness can sometimes overwhelm it, leading to accidents—particularly around small children. The breed is intelligent and loves to be trained. It can become destructive if bored but will adapt its energy levels to suit its environment.

ENGLISH FOXHOUND

COLOR: Any recognized hound color and markings

COAT CARE: Minimal maintenance

DIET: High consumption

OFFICIAL CATEGORIZATION: UK: Hound, AKC: Hound, FCI: Group 6, Section 1

HEIGHT: 23–24 in. (58–64 cm)   WEIGHT: 65–70 lb. (29–32 kg)

OTHER NAMES: Foxhound

BELOW

Foxhounds can have difficulty settling to life in a house, having been bred to have strong pack instincts.

The Foxhound, or English Foxhound, is the original version of what is now two separate breeds: the English Foxhound and American Foxhound. The English Foxhound is heavier and slightly slower than the American. The Foxhound was bred to hunt foxes when concerns were raised over the numbers of deer that had been over-hunted. It was established using Greyhound, Fox Terrier, and Bulldog breeding stock. It is a relatively large hound, with a powerful nose and high levels of energy.

As a pet, the English Foxhound is a sociable and patient pack-orientated dog. It will adapt to its environment, but the breed is happiest when in green space in which it can run and chase. It is friendly and intelligent but is prone to giving a loud bay when stimulated, which can be very startling to people. It is particularly sociable around other dogs, especially other hounds.

OTTERHOUND

OFFICIAL CATEGORIZATION: UK: Hound, AKC: Hound, FCI: Group 6, Section 2

HEIGHT: 25½–28½ in. (65–72.5 cm)   WEIGHT: 80–115 lb. (36–54 kg)

OTHER NAMES: None

COLOR: Any color or combination of hound colors

COAT CARE: Moderate/high maintenance

DIET: High consumption

The Otterhound is an old and very rare breed of English hunting dog that was established by fishermen to control the otter population. It is descended from the Greyhound and rough-coated terriers, but displays a sturdy and solid physique under its shaggy coat that is atypical of its Greyhound ancestry. It is a hardy dog most commonly owned for working; the UK Kennel Club lists the breed as vulnerable because of its small numbers.

The Otterhound breed has not developed or become particularly established as a pet and, therefore, most Otterhounds are closely related to working animals and may struggle to adapt to domestic life. The breed is energetic, instinctive, and bold, but also loyal, friendly, and affectionate when given proper training and socialization. Some Otterhounds adapt better than others to the slow pace of domestic life and will exist happily in a relaxed and calm environment.

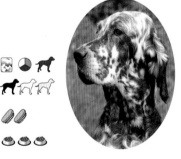

BELOW

Otterhounds are largely used as working dogs, having originally been bred to cull otters when fish stocks were getting too low.

ENGLISH SETTER

OFFICIAL CATEGORIZATION: UK: Gun Dog, AKC: Sporting, FCI: Group 7, Section 2

HEIGHT: 25–27 in. (65–69 cm)   WEIGHT: 55–80 lb. (25–36 kg)

OTHER NAMES: Lawerack

COLOR: Black and white (blue belton), orange and white (orange belton), lemon and white (lemon belton), liver and white (liver belton), or tricolor

COAT CARE: Moderate maintenance

DIET: High consumption

The English Setter is a traditional working gun-dog breed similar to the Irish Setter. It is an excellent bird dog, bred to locate game through scent and then to set it. (Setting is a method of pointing out game to a hunter.) Typically, the breed displays a speckled coat, with blue, white, and brown being common colors. It is medium sized and has a slender physique.

Setters in general have strong working instincts and the English Setter is no different. Although friendly and adaptable, the breed is happiest when given a degree of stimulation that appeals to its instincts. It is noted for its gentleness and affection and is considered to be a very tactile breed that enjoys human contact. The English Setter is also known as being very sensitive, with a keenness to please that is rarely slaked. Its activity level is typically adapted to its immediate environment.

BULLMASTIFF

OFFICIAL CATEGORIZATION: UK: Working, AKC: Working, FCI: Group 2, Section 2

COLOR: Red, fawn, or brindle

COAT CARE: Minimal maintenance

DIET: High/very high consumption

HEIGHT: 25–27 in. (64–69 cm)   WEIGHT: 110–130 lb. (50–59 kg)

OTHER NAMES: None

The Bullmastiff is an impressively strong and athletic breed with a sturdy yet agile body. It has a heavy jaw, as is typical of most breeds that are members of the Molosser family of dogs—from which the Bullmastiff descends. Its bloodline includes Bulldogs of the old type and other early Mastiff breeds. It was used originally as a hunting guard, meaning it would track down and hold poachers but would not bite them—rather it would scare them into submission with its bark.

In more modern times, the Bullmastiff has been used as a security dog, particularly in South Africa where it was a prominent feature around diamond mines. The breed then commonly presented with a brindle coat, but the popularity of this waned when the Bullmastiff was required less for the night work for which the coat was favored. It is now more common to see the Bullmastiff with a short and coarse light-fawn coat.

Strong But Calm

The Bullmastiff is a reliable breed in that the majority of examples exhibit uniform temperaments. It is routinely loyal, dependable, alert, sociable, and very friendly, despite its rather imposing appearance. The Bullmastiff is often a docile dog with a high tolerance for inactivity. It can often be seen attempting to excuse itself from high-energy situations in order to find a quiet spot in which to relax.

Although the Bullmastiff is generally friendly, its size and power allow it to become boisterous if not given adequate training and socialization. The Bullmastiff's appearance often suggests that it is a good fighter, but the reality is that the breed is instinctively averse to aggression, unless absolutely provoked, preferring instead to hold an aggressor and wait for its master. The Bullmastiff is well-known for being extremely sensitive to its owner's tone of voice.

BELOW
Impressive in stature, Bullmastiffs have been used as guard dogs in the diamond mines of South Africa.

POINTER

OFFICIAL CATEGORIZATION: UK: Gun Dog, AKC: Sporting, FCI: Group 7, Section 2

HEIGHT: 25–28 in. (63–71 cm)   WEIGHT: 55–75 lb. (25–34 kg)

OTHER NAMES: English Pointer

COLOR: Lemon and white, orange and white, liver and white, or black and white

COAT CARE: Minimal maintenance

DIET: High consumption

The term "pointer" can refer to many types of pointing breed but most frequently refers to the breed known as the English Pointer, with other breeds being differentiated by name. The English Pointer has a wide mix of genealogical heritage that includes sight hounds, scent hounds, the Bulldog, and the Newfoundland. It is a sturdy and well-proportioned member of

the gun-dog group and displays a strong yet not troublesome instinct for work.

As a pet, it is not uncommon for the working instincts of the Pointer to be prominent and desirable; many owners enjoy watching their pet strike a point position when it catches a scent. This instinct does not disrupt behavior, although it can

occasionally distract during training. The Pointer is an intelligent and lively breed with a fondness for company and activity. The Pointer is known for occasional mischievousness but is generally a gentle and loving breed of companion dog.

GORDON SETTER

OFFICIAL CATEGORIZATION: UK: Gun Dog, AKC: Sporting, FCI: Group 7, Section 2

HEIGHT: 24–27 in. (61–68.5 cm)   WEIGHT: 63–67 lb. (28.5–30.5 kg)

OTHER NAMES: None

COLOR: Black with tan markings, either of rich chestnut or mahogany color

COAT CARE: Moderate maintenance

DIET: High consumption

The Gordon Setter is a large breed of setter that is predominantly black and tan in color. It became established as the Gordon Setter during the eighteenth and nineteenth centuries, having descended from other setting breeds. The Gordon Setter is more hardy and versatile than typical setter breeds and

can work in many differing environments. It is well-liked for its high levels of stamina and keen sense of smell.

The Gordon Setter is considered to be a loyal, dependable, and sensible breed that is adept at its work and adapts well to

domestic life. It is highly intelligent and thrives when given the chance to hunt or come into contact with wildlife. Its instinctive setting is rarely a problem for owners and is often an impressive spectacle when the dog transforms from family pet to instinctive gun dog at the slightest hint of a scent.

GREYHOUND

COLOR: Various: black, white, red, blue, fawn, fallow, or brindle

COAT CARE: Minimal maintenance for smooth-haired, 2.5 brushers for wiredhaired

DIET: Moderate/high consumption

OFFICIAL CATEGORIZATION: UK: Hound, AKC: Hound, FCI: Group 10, Section 3

HEIGHT: 28–30 in. (71–76 cm)   **WEIGHT:** 65–70 lb. (29–32 kg)

OTHER NAMES: None

The Greyhound is an extremely popular and well-known member of the sight-hound family. Commonly used for racing, the Greyhound is arguably the fastest breed of dog in the world. It exhibits a sleek and lean physique with a slender head and almost stooping gait when running. It appears in various colors and patterns, with differing coat types ranging from smooth and short to wiry and long. The Greyhound was established as a breed in England, but descends from African and Arabian sight hounds.

Fascinating Facts

Greyhounds have a higher red blood cell count than any other breed. It is thought that this is one of the reasons that the breed can run so fast.

The Greyhound is a gentle and affectionate breed with little or no propensity for aggression. It is a loyal, intelligent, and dedicated breed that occasionally can be aloof toward new people and new dogs. It is easily trained and eager to please. In general, the breed is sweet natured with a fondness for people, especially people with whom the dog is familiar.

BELOW
With the lean muscular build typical of the sight hound, the Greyhound reacts quickly to chase small moving animals.

MASTIFF

COLOR: Apricot-fawn, silver-fawn, fawn, or dark fawn-brindle

COAT CARE: Minimal maintenance

DIET: High/very high consumption

OFFICIAL CATEGORIZATION: UK: Working, AKC: Working, FCI: Group 2, Section 2.1

HEIGHT: 28½–31½ in. (72.5–80 cm)   **WEIGHT:** 156½–161 lb. (71–73 kg)

OTHER NAMES: English Mastiff

The Mastiff, or English Mastiff as it is known in order to distinguish it from other Mastiff breeds, is a massive, heavy breed with an origin that predates Christianity. It was bred originally for fighting and guarding but has evolved into a gentle and sensitive pet dog. The Mastiff is powerfully built, with a huge head and short coat. It is one of the heaviest breeds of dog.

Despite its long history of fighting and guarding, the Mastiff of today makes a great pet for people with the space to accommodate one. A typical Mastiff is patient, loyal, intelligent, and confident. It is tolerant of overexcited children and gets on well with other dogs. The Mastiff is rarely known to bark but is alert and active if it is stimulated. It makes a good guard dog and will defend the home with its life if necessary. It is fearlessly protective over its family.

SCOTTISH DEERHOUND

OFFICIAL CATEGORIZATION: UK: Hound, AKC: Hound, FCI: Group 10, Section 2

HEIGHT: 30–32 in. (76–81 cm)   WEIGHT: 85–110 lb. (38–50 kg)

OTHER NAMES: None

COLOR: Dark blue-gray, darker and lighter grays or brindles, and yellows, sandy red, or red fawns with black points

COAT CARE: Low/moderate maintenance

DIET: High consumption

LEFT
Despite their large size, Deerhounds used to be kept in packs in former times to help with deerhunting.

The Scottish Deerhound is a large sight-hound breed that displays a characteristic wiry coat and lean physique. It is slightly larger than the Greyhound but smaller than the Irish Wolfhound. It retains certain working instincts and is stimulated by sight. The breed was created originally to hunt deer but is now a regular feature in conformation shows and is a relatively popular pet breed.

This quiet and reserved breed is fiercely loyal and brave. Despite being happy to watch the activity in a domestic household, the Scottish Deerhound will be the first to respond to a perceived threat or intruder. It is dignified and intelligent, while eager to please and fond of play. The breed is gentle with children and is considered to be willing to accept the presence of anyone, provided that person is accepted by the family. It can sometimes be slow to obey commands.

GLEN OF IMAAL TERRIER

OFFICIAL CATEGORIZATION: UK: Terrier, AKC: Terrier, FCI: Group 3, Section 1

HEIGHT: 14 in. (35–36 cm)   WEIGHT: 33–37½ lb. (15–17 kg)

OTHER NAMES: Irish Glen of Imaal Terrier

COLOR: Wheaten, blue, or brindle

COAT CARE: Low/moderate maintenance

DIET: Moderate consumption

The Glen of Imaal Terrier is an ancient Irish terrier breed of undetermined origin. It stands low to the ground and has a harsh coat, giving it a scruffy appearance. The breed is tenacious and lively with a keen terrier instinct. It was bred originally to hunt burrowing animals, such as badgers, and is well-known as a silent working terrier, as opposed to a terrier that barks or growls when working. Popular in The Republic of Ireland and some parts of Britain, it is relatively rare elsewhere.

As a pet, the Glen of Imaal Terrier is lively and friendly, but has a very strong working instinct. This is a breed of contrast, for the domestic dog is adaptable and gentle but when put to work becomes highly tenacious and tough. The breed rarely barks but has a habit for digging.

KERRY BLUE TERRIER

COLOR: Blue, with or without black points

COAT CARE: Moderate maintenance

DIET: Moderate/high consumption

OFFICIAL CATEGORIZATION: UK: Terrier, AKC: Terrier, FCI: Group 3, Section 1

HEIGHT: 18–19½ in. (46–48 cm)   WEIGHT: 33–40 lb. (15–18 kg)

OTHER NAMES: Irish Blue Terrier

The Kerry Blue Terrier is an Irish terrier breed that exhibits a distinctive wavy coat. It is born black, but this changes throughout infancy until the typical blue shade appears. It is a versatile and determined terrier that was bred originally for hunting.

The Kerry Blue Terrier is a popular pet breed in its native country of Ireland. It possesses a high sense of fun and enjoys rough play. The breed is intelligent but instinctive, with a natural attraction to anything small that moves. It displays an extremely high level of alertness that makes it a great watchdog. Challenging tasks are relished by the breed and help stave off boredom. In general, the Kerry Blue Terrier is an adaptable, slightly boisterous breed— typical of many terriers.

IRISH TERRIER

COLOR: Whole-colored— red, red-wheaten, or yellow-red

COAT CARE: Low maintenance

DIET: Moderate/high consumption

OFFICIAL CATEGORIZATION: UK: Terrier, AKC: Terrier, FCI: Group 3, Section 1

HEIGHT: 18–19½ in. (46–48 cm)   WEIGHT: 25–27 lb. (11–12 kg)

OTHER NAMES: Irish Red Terrier

The Irish Terrier is one of the oldest breeds of dog, believed to have been in existence for more than 2,000 years. It is a medium-sized, stocky terrier with distinctive wire hair and a tapered muzzle. Its triangular ears are folded forward and it has the appearance of wearing a moustache due to the coarse hair around the mouth. It is a versatile working breed with a history of hunting water rats and other vermin and even of retrieving.

The Irish Terrier is a popular pet breed but is widely considered to be something of a handful. It is instinctive, even reckless, with an apparent sense of abandon that makes it an exceptional playmate for young children. Despite its exuberance, it is loving and affectionate but does possess a strong will that can make it stubborn. The breed is extremely loyal and dedicated to its family.

LEFT
Irish Terriers can be very energetic but a lot of fun, providing you have the energy to cope.

SOFT-COATED WHEATEN TERRIER

OFFICIAL CATEGORIZATION: UK: Terrier, AKC: Terrier, FCI: Group 3, Section 1

HEIGHT: 18–19½ in. (46–49 cm)   WEIGHT: 35–40 lb. (16–18 kg)

OTHER NAMES: None

COLOR: Any shade of wheaten

COAT CARE: Moderate/high maintenance

DIET: Moderate/high consumption

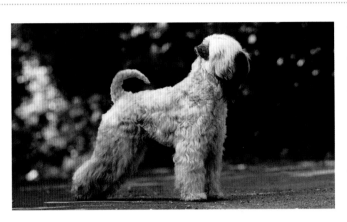

The Soft-Coated Wheaten Terrier is a medium-sized terrier with a square, sturdy physique and a distinctively soft coat. It is short legged and has a relatively large head that serves it well as a working vermin hunter. Bred in Ireland for work on farms, where it was used to catch vermin, the breed hunts small quarry and, to a lesser extent, herds livestock.

An excitable and lively terrier with a happy and playful disposition, the Soft-Coated Wheaten Terrier retains a puppylike personality for much of its adult life and will display an exuberance that belies its age. In general, the breed is friendly and sweet natured, with a particular affection for children. It tends to be aggressive toward other pets, with the exception of dogs. With proper training, these aggressive tendencies can be managed, but the Soft-Coated Wheaten Terrier is very much an instinctive breed.

IRISH WATER SPANIEL

OFFICIAL CATEGORIZATION: UK: Gun Dog, AKC: Sporting, FCI: Group 8, Section 3

HEIGHT: 23–24 in. (53–58 cm)   WEIGHT: 55–65 lb. (24–30 kg)

OTHER NAMES: Whiptail, Shannon Spaniel, Rat Tail Spaniel

COLOR: Solid liver

COAT CARE: High maintenance

DIET: High consumption

Recognized as one of the largest and rarest members of the spaniel family, the Irish Water Spaniel has a distinctive, tightly curled coat. It was first established in Ireland, but the ancestral origins of the breed are unclear. Because of its specially bred coat, it rarely sheds and is considered a suitable choice of pet for people who normally have allergic reactions to dog fur. The Irish Water Spaniel was originally bred to perform work in water, but it is now more often kept as a pet.

The Irish Water Spaniel is a lively and energetic breed with boundless energy. As its working history would suggest it is an excellent swimmer and loves the water. It is more suited to owners that pursue an active outdoor lifestyle, becuase the breed will become bored and restless if kept indoors for too long. It is generally friendly and intelligent.

LEFT
An intelligent, lively dog with a "waterproof" coat, the Irish Water Spaniel must get plenty of exercise.

KERRY BEAGLE

COLOR: Black and tan

COAT CARE: Minimal maintenance

DIET: High consumption

OFFICIAL CATEGORIZATION: UK: Not recognized, AKC: Not recognized, FCI: Not recognized

HEIGHT: 22–24 in. (56–61 cm) **WEIGHT:** 57½–62 lb. (26–28 kg)

OTHER NAMES: None

The Kerry Beagle is an old Irish hound breed. Typical of the Beagle type, with large ears and eyes, firm physique, and powerful nose, this breed was used originally for scenting and hunting. It is very rare outside of Ireland and has come close to extinction in the past. Its coloration is typically black and tan or black mottle. It is a noticeably athletic-looking dog with an alert expression.

The Kerry Beagle is an instinctive breed and retains many of its working instincts. Although not widely established as a pet

LEFT
The Kerry Beagle is popular throughout Ireland, where packs exist for drag hunting, for instance.

breed it has many attributes that make it a good domestic dog. It is friendly, sociable, and intelligent, and because of its history of working in a hound pack, it is particularly suited to living with other dogs.

It has high energy levels and can become overly interested in and distracted by scent, so good training is required.

IRISH RED-AND-WHITE SETTER

COLOR: White with solid red patches

COAT CARE: Moderate maintenance

DIET: High consumption

OFFICIAL CATEGORIZATION: UK: Gun Dog, AKC: Miscellaneous, FCI: Group 7, Section 2

HEIGHT: 24–26 in. (62–66 cm) **WEIGHT:** 50–70 lb. (27–32 kg)

OTHER NAMES: None

The Irish Red-and-White Setter has spent much of its existence being classed as an Irish Setter. Traditionally, Irish Setters could be red or red and white. The distinction became important when the red-and-white versions approached extinction. New breeding stock was introduced to preserve the red-and-white types, necessitating the need for a separate breed classification. The Irish Red-and-White Setter is predominantly a working gun dog.

An energetic and independent dog with a friendly and gentle demeanor, it makes a good pet and its instinctive behavior rarely causes any serious problems in the domestic environment. The breed is playful and active, which makes it most suitable for active owners with access to outdoor space. Although not an unintelligent breed, the Irish Red-and-White Setter can take time to become fully trained.

BELOW
The Irish Red-and-White Setter is not as old as the spaniel family, but is older than the pointer one.

IRISH SETTER

OFFICIAL CATEGORIZATION: UK: Gun Dog, AKC: Sporting, FCI: Group 7, Section 2

HEIGHT: 25–27 in. (64–69 cm)

WEIGHT: 60–70 lb. (27–32 kg)

OTHER NAMES: Red Setter

COLOR: Rich chestnut

COAT CARE: Moderate maintenance

DIET: High/very high consumption

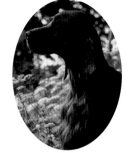

The Irish Setter is an active and energetic member of the gun-dog family. It is also known as the Red Setter, but coloration in relation to breed has been a controversial subject. In the nineteenth century, Irish Setters would display various colors, including red and white, and the predominantly red coloration was a rarity. Classification has, therefore, been somewhat confusing, but it is now agreed that the Irish Setter is all red and is thus distinguishable from the Irish Red-and-White Setter to which it is related.

The Irish Setter is a dependable pointing and setting breed, commonly used by hunters. Today, it makes a popular pet around the world. It is sturdy and relatively large, with a luxurious deep red coat, expressive face, and graceful carriage.

Impulsive But Gentle

The Irish Setter is friendly and gentle, making it a suitable family pet for certain homes. It is energetic and is best suited to an owner that can provide an active lifestyle. There are two lines of Irish Setter, field-bred and show-bred, and both can make excellent

ABOVE
Also known as the Red Setter, the Irish Setter must always be solely red.

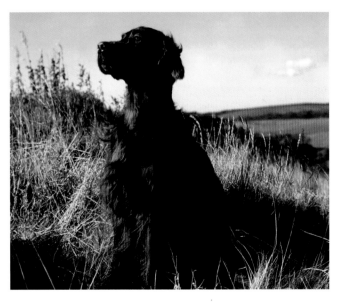

pets. The breed is known for being sensitive and on some occasions highly strung. Despite this, its temperament is considered generally to be relaxed and good natured.

The Irish Setter does tend to develop bad habits if not trained consistently, and it is certainly not a breed that is known for high intelligence. This does not mean that it is unintelligent, but rather that it is very impulsive and is governed by instinct over thought. However, the breed is not aggressive and should not display any aggressive tendencies—in fact, it is more common for an Irish Setter to seek out other dogs for play and companionship.

IRISH WOLFHOUND

COLOR: Gray, brindle, black, pure white, fawn, wheaten, or steel gray

COAT CARE: Low/moderate maintenance

DIET: High/very high consumption

OFFICIAL CATEGORIZATION: UK: Hound, AKC: Hound, FCI: Group 10, Section 2

HEIGHT: 32.5–35½ in. (82.5–90 cm) WEIGHT: 119–123½ lb. (54–56 kg)

OTHER NAMES: None

The Irish Wolfhound is an extremely tall breed of sight hound that originated in Ireland. It is the tallest breed in the world but arguably not the biggest, with the Saint Bernard and Mastiff breeds typically weighing more. It has a coarse and wiry coat, often giving the impression of old age, even in young dogs. It has a history of wolf hunting, but naturally this need is now extinct in Ireland and

hunting wolves is not permitted elsewhere due to their rarity. It is a popular breed on the show circuit as well as being a popular pet for those with the space.

LEFT

Many, many centuries ago, Irish Wolfhounds were used in war to haul the enemies from their horses.

The Irish Wolfhound is a gentle and docile breed, often displaying a bashful demeanor. It is unerringly loyal to its owner and is friendly to family and strangers alike. This slow-maturing breed does not make a particularly effective guard dog.

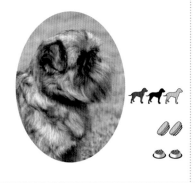

BRUSSELS GRIFFON

COLOR: Clear red, black or black and rich tan without white markings

COAT CARE: Moderate maintenance

DIET: Moderate consumption

OFFICIAL CATEGORIZATION: UK: Toy, AKC: Toy, FCI: Group 9, Section 3

HEIGHT: 7–8 in. (18–20 cm) WEIGHT: 8–10 lb. (3.6–4.5 kg)

OTHER NAMES: Belgium Griffon, Belgian Griffon, Griffon Bruxellois

The Brussels Griffon is a Belgian toy breed of dog with both terrier and toy ancestry. The immediate ancestor to the breed was kept as a ratting dog, but was latterly bred with an imported toy breed to create the Griffon. The breed is small with a distinctively flat face and well-coated

muzzle that gives the impression that the dog is wearing a beard.

The Brussels Griffon is a rare type of dog in that it is more suitable for single people than large families. This is due to the breed being exceptionally loyal and dedicated—once bonded its

interest in other people is minimal, although it is not aggressive toward or suspicious of new people. It is sensitive and affectionate due to its toy heritage, and it is rare that the modern Brussels Griffon dog displays any strong terrier instincts. However, it does display an air of self-confidence that belies its size.

SCHIPPERKE

OFFICIAL CATEGORIZATION: UK: Utility, AKC: Nonsporting,
FCI: Group 1, Section 1

HEIGHT: 10–13 in. (21–33 cm)   WEIGHT: 12–16 lb. (5.5–7.5 kg)

OTHER NAMES: Spitzke, Spits, Spitske

COLOR: Black

COAT CARE: Moderate/high maintenance

DIET: Moderate consumption

The Schipperke is a small Belgian breed of unconfirmed origin. Debate still flows over whether the dog is descended from terriers, herding dogs, northern European Spitz breeds, or a combination of all three. The dog traditionally was used to work as a ratter on canals and small boats, often kept as the captain's dog—the breed's name translates from Flemish as "Little Skipper." The most notable physical feature of the breed is its lack of tail.

Typically feisty but adaptable as a pet, the Schipperke is a popular breed in its home country and abroad. It is alert, energetic, and self-confident but with a warmth of character more often associated with hound breeds. Despite its small size, the breed is a good watchdog. It is inquisitive and can sometimes be willful, but with consistent and thorough training the Schipperke will prove to be a good all-round pet.

ARDENNES CATTLE DOG

OFFICIAL CATEGORIZATION: UK: Not recognized,
AKC: Not recognized, FCI: Group 1, Section 2

HEIGHT: 21½–24½ in. (55–63 cm)   WEIGHT: 62–77 lb. (28–35 kg)

OTHER NAMES: Bouvier des Ardennes

COLOR: Any color except white

COAT CARE: Moderate/high maintenance

DIET: High/very high consumption

The Ardennes Cattle Dog is a hardy herding breed originating from Belgium. It is predominantly a working breed and is not well-known outside of its home nation. It is kept as a pet by some but does not descend from any pet breed lines and, therefore, has a strong desire to work. It has a rustic temperament and is very happy to live by itself outdoors.

The Ardennes Cattle Dog is a tough, compact breed with a strong set of herding instincts. It is tenacious and protective, suspicious of strangers, and possessive. Its suitability as a mainstream pet is unknown due to the relative rarity of the breed, but the Ardennes Cattle Dog shows no particularly unsuitable characteristics. It is known for its loyalty and obedience, which makes it an adaptable pet, but it is not particularly numerous and so has not yet become established as a pet dog breed.

BELGIAN SHEPHERD (Groenendael)

COLOR: Black

COAT CARE: Moderate maintenance

DIET: High consumption

OFFICIAL CATEGORIZATION: UK: Pastoral, AKC: Herding, FCI: Group 1, Section 1

HEIGHT: 24–26 in. (61–66 cm)   WEIGHT: 65–75 lb. (29–34 kg)

OTHER NAMES: Chien de Berger Belge

The term "Belgian Shepherd" refers to any one of four varieties of dog. Confusingly, some varieties are recognized by certain authorities and some are not, while the four varieties are considered as separate breeds in certain territories. The main differences are superficial and relate to coat length, texture and color. They are all bred for herding but now perform in various other roles.

The Groenendael has a solid black coat and is the most popular of the four varieties. It is typically a very intelligent breed with strong working instincts. Strong-willed, confident, and energetic, it is best suited to a confident owner with training experience. It displays a natural inclination to control movement, and due to its strength and agility this can be problematic in the domestic environment.

BELGIAN SHEPHERD (Laekenois)

COLOR: Reddish fawn with black shading, principally in muzzle and tail

COAT CARE: Moderate maintenance

DIET: High consumption

OFFICIAL CATEGORIZATION: UK: Pastoral, AKC: Not recognized, FCI: Group 1, Section 1

HEIGHT: 24–26 in. (61–66 cm)   WEIGHT: 55–65 lb. (24–29 kg)

OTHER NAMES: Belgian Laekenois, Belgian Shepherd Dog, Chien de Berger Belge

The Laekenois variety of the Belgian Shepherd is the oldest version of the breed; it is also the variety that least resembles the other Belgian Shepherds. It has a distinctive woolly coat that goes some way to disguising its lean and powerful body. The face is covered to an extent with the woolly coat, which softens an otherwise angular and slender look. Bitches sometimes give birth to smooth-coated puppies, which can be classed as Malinois— a separate version of the Belgian Shepherd more commonly associated with police work in mainland Europe.

As with the other members of the Belgian Shepherd family, the Laekenois demonstrates excellent herding skills. It is a strong-willed and bold breed with a high degree of intelligence and independence. It has very few fundamental differences in temperament when compared to other Belgian Shepherds, but is the rarest of the four.

BELOW
The energetic and strong-willed Laekenois also goes by the easier name of Belgian Shepherd Dog.

BELGIAN SHEPHERD (Malinois)

OFFICIAL CATEGORIZATION: UK: Pastoral, AKC: Herding,
FCI: Group 1, Section 1

HEIGHT: 24–26 in. (61–66 cm)   WEIGHT: 65–75 lb. (29–34 kg)
OTHER NAMES: Belgian Malinois, Chien de Berger Belge,
Mechelaar, Mechelse Herder

COLOR: Gray, black, or rich fawn to mahogany

COAT CARE: Low/moderate maintenance

DIET: High/very high consumption

The Malinois is arguably the most well-known of the four Belgian Shepherd varieties. It can be distinguished by its short coat, which is typically gray, fawn, black, or a combination of any two. There is a large degree of variation in coat color and length in the Malinois due to the breeding techniques used, which favored function over appearance. Like the other three varieties, it is medium in size with an agile and well-proportioned body. The Belgian Shepherd is typically smaller than the German Shepherd.

The Malinios is bred almost exclusively for work and is an exceptional security and police dog. For this reason, it is suitable as a pet only for an experienced and confident owner. Its agility and speed, coupled with high intelligence and an instinct to protect, make it desirable for protection but relatively unsuitable as a family pet as it is happiest when at work.

LEFT
This breed needs extensive socialization from an early age, and firm, but not harsh, training.

BELGIAN SHEPHERD (Tervueren)

OFFICIAL CATEGORIZATION: UK: Pastoral, AKC: Herding,
FCI: Group 1, Section 1

HEIGHT: 24–26 in. (61–66 cm)   WEIGHT: 62–66 lb. (28–30 kg)

OTHER NAMES: Belgian Tervuren, Chien de Berger Belge

COLOR: Rich fawn to russet mahogany with black overlay

COAT CARE: High maintenance

DIET: High consumption

The Tervueren variety of Belgian Shepherd is distinguished by its longer coat that is well feathered around the neck, often giving the appearance that the dog is larger than the other varieties. (This is not the case, and all four of the Belgian Shepherd varieties are typically the same in terms of size.) The Tervueren is most similar to the Groenendael, distinct only by coat color, although the feathering on the Groenendael is less noticeable due to the solid black of its coat.

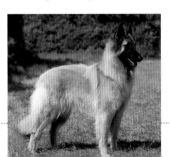

The Tervueren is comparable to the other three varieties of the breed but is the most prone to nervousness. With adequate and complete training, the Tervueren can adapt to domestic life reasonably well, but it is happiest when working. Typically, it is not used for security work, still being favored for traditional pastoral roles that it performs well with characteristic elegance.

Fascinating Facts

There is a law in the state of Illinois that makes it illegal to give whiskey to a dog.

BLOODHOUND

COLOR: Black and tan, liver and tan, or red

COAT CARE: Minimal maintenance

DIET: High/very high consumption

OFFICIAL CATEGORIZATION: UK: Hound, AKC: Hound, FCI: Group 6, Section 1

HEIGHT: 22½–25½ in. (57–65 cm) WEIGHT: 88–92½ lb. (40–42 kg)

OTHER NAMES: Chien de Saint-Hubert, Saint Hubert Hound

ABOVE

Bloodhounds have the best sense of smell of any breed, largely due to their sizeable nose.

The Bloodhound is an extremely large scent-hound breed originating in Europe. It is unknown which nation can officially take credit for the breed, because foundation breeding stock was moved about frequently by the monks that began the breeding. Its true origins are generally thought to be in Belgium, but other sources consider France as the ancestral home. The Bloodhound as it appears today was established in Britain, but the breed is rarely considered as English.

It is an ancestor of many scent-hound breeds, including the Bassett Hound and the Boxer. It has the strongest sense of smell of any breed, partially because of the sheer size of its nose. Despite its name, it was not bred specifically to scent blood. The reference to blood has two possible sources: it is considered by some to be linked to the name "hound of pure blood" that was given to the breed; while others claim it is linked to the breed's association with British aristocracy, who were colloquially referred to as "blue-blooded." Either source is feasible.

A Tolerant Pet

The Bloodhound of today is a popular pet. It is intelligent and alert, yet gentle and affectionate. The Bloodhound's patience is one of the reasons that it is so good with children. Many breeds cannot tolerate the overzealous attentions of young children, but the typical Bloodhound will passively endure unwanted attention even if it causes the dog pain.

A Bloodhound requires confident but respectful training. It is independently minded and that, combined with its intelligence, can make some specimens somewhat willful. As they grow older, Bloodhounds become more docile and passive, but as young pups they exhibit an exuberant and playful temperament. Some Bloodhounds are territorial and protective of the family home, but even these specimens are rarely aggressive toward new people.

Fascinating Facts

Despite their size and weight, Bloodhounds carry very little fat. The bones of the Bloodhound are extremely heavy in relation to their length.

BOUVIER DES FLANDRES

OFFICIAL CATEGORIZATION: UK: Working, AKC: Herding,
FCI: Group 1, Section 2

HEIGHT: 24½–27 in. (62–68 cm)   WEIGHT: 77–88 lb. (35–40 kg)

OTHER NAMES: Flanders Cattle Dog, Vlaamse Koehond

COLOR: Fawn to black,
passing through salt and
pepper, gray, and brindle

COAT CARE: Moderate maintenance

DIET: High consumption

The Bouvier des Flandres is a powerfully built Belgian herding breed. Displaying a very thick double coat with a shaggy texture, the breed is distinctive in appearance. The Bouvier des Flandres has straight legs and a well-muscled body; its tapered muzzle is accentuated by dense fur growth on the face, giving the impression that the dog has a moustache and beard.

Originally bred for herding cows in Belgium, they are now well-known as pets.

The Bouvier des Flandres is typical of most herding breeds in that it is intelligent, obedient, and agile. Training should be performed consistently and firmly, but not overly so. The breed responds well to human interaction and is known for being able to learn a command very quickly. Its friendly demeanor and gentleness marks it out as a suitable pet for most, but its high intelligence needs to be stimulated.

PAPILLON

OFFICIAL CATEGORIZATION: UK: Toy, AKC: Toy,
FCI: Group 9, Section 9

HEIGHT: 8–11 in. (20–28 cm)   WEIGHT: 6–10 lb. (3–5 kg)

OTHER NAMES: Continental Toy Spaniel

COLOR: White with patches: tricolors,
black and white with tan spots over
eyes; tan inside ears, on cheeks, and
under root of tail

COAT CARE: Moderate maintenance

DIET: Moderate consumption

The Papillon is an old toy breed that was bred in Europe. Its origins are split between various countries but it is thought to trace its ancestry back to Belgium. The breed has distinctive butterfly-shaped ears, hence the name Papillon. It has been bred exclusively for companionship, although it has an ancestry that includes various Spaniel breeds.

LEFT
Papillons are so-called from the French for butterfly (the shape of their dainty pricked-up ears).

The Papillon is a sweet natured and loyal breed. Despite its natural dedication and companionability, the dog is relatively hardy and independent—two traits more commonly associated with breeds outside of the toy group. There is less uniformity in temperament among Papillons than in other toy breeds, with some exhibiting extremely affectionate natures while others prefer to romp and play outdoors. The breed's intelligence is relatively high, but it does not possess any particularly disruptive instincts. However, a poorly trained Papillon may be aggressive toward other dogs.

PHALÈNE

COLOR: White with black markings

COAT CARE: Low/moderate maintenance

DIET: Low/moderate consumption

OFFICIAL CATEGORIZATION: UK: Toy (variety of Papillon), AKC: Not recognized, FCI: Not recognized

HEIGHT: 8–11 in. (21–28 cm)   WEIGHT: 8–10 lb. (3.5–4.5 kg)

OTHER NAMES: None

The Phalène is closely related to the Papillon. It predates the Papillon breed that we know today, but is now considered to be a version of that breed. The difference between the two is seen in the ears: the Papillon has pricked "butterfly" ears while the Phalène has dropped "moth" ears—hence the name. Otherwise the two breeds are almost identical in appearance and are often considered to be the same breed.

LEFT

Phalène are very similar to Papillon, the sole difference between the breeds being that the ears of the Phalène droop down, mothlike.

As with the Papillon, the Phalène is a gentle and sweet-natured dog on the whole, but there is a range of personalities within the breed. The Phalène can be anything from sensitive and gentle to unruly and boisterous. Much of the temperament depends on the environment in which the dog has developed. In certain countries, it is claimed that as two separate breeds the Phalène and the Papillon have distinct temperaments, but on the whole they are very similar.

TOY POODLE

COLOR: All solid colors

COAT CARE: Very high maintenance

DIET: Low/moderate consumption

OFFICIAL CATEGORIZATION: UK: Utility, AKC: Toy, FCI: Group 9, Section 2

HEIGHT: 9½–12½ in. (24–32 cm)   WEIGHT: 6–9 lb. (3–4 kg)

OTHER NAMES: None

The Poodle is a breed that has various distinctions due to size. Typically, ranging from smallest to largest, the Poodle is classed as Toy, Miniature, and Standard. The FCI also recognizes a medium-sized Poodle. The Toy Poodle is the smallest of the Poodle varieties and as such is considered a toy breed by some and a utility or nonsporting breed elsewhere. Poodle classification is particularly complex. In general, the Poodle breed is water-going and has a distinctive curly coat that reflects its origin. Many countries, including France and Germany, claim to be the ancestral home of the Poodle.

The Toy Poodle is intelligent and affectionate, although it can be a demanding breed. Despite its typically showy appearance, it is a hardy dog, retaining the toughness that served it well as a working animal. In the domestic environment, the Toy Poodle makes a friendly and adaptable pet.

LOWCHEN

OFFICIAL CATEGORIZATION: UK: Toy, AKC: Nonsporting, FCI: Group 9, Section 1

HEIGHT: 10–13 in. (25–33 cm)   WEIGHT: 11–18 lb. (4–8 kg)

OTHER NAMES: Little Lion Dog, Petit Chien Lion

COLOR: Any color or combination of colors

COAT CARE: Moderate maintenance

DIET: Moderate consumption

The Lowchen is an extremely rare breed and as such is expensive to buy as a purebred. It is considered French in origin, but this is unconfirmed. Its development has been traced through works of art dating back to the sixteenth century. The Lowchen is small and compact, typical of the Bichon-type breeds to which it is related. The breed is often referred to as the "little lion dog" due to its resemblance to a small lion.

has a high level of intelligence that makes it quite easy to train, although some examples of the breed can be wilful, verging on arrogant.

> RIGHT
> *The Lowchen (meaning "little lion") is so-called because of its resemblance to a lion. However, in size it is closer to a Bichon.*

The Lowchen is an energetic and enthusiastic pet that displays great loyalty, as do many toy breeds of similar ancestry. The breed has a toughness about it that belies its size and appearance, but is generally affectionate and sensitive and gets along well with children. The Lowchen

BASSET ARTESIENE NORMAND

OFFICIAL CATEGORIZATION: UK: Not recognized, AKC: Not recognized, FCI: Group 6, Section 1

HEIGHT: 10–14 in. (25–36 cm)   WEIGHT: 31–35 lb. (14–16 kg)

OTHER NAMES: None

COLOR: Bicolor (orange and white) or tricolor (orange, tan, and white)

COAT CARE: Minimal maintenance

DIET: Moderate/high consumption

The Basset Artesiene Normand is a squat scent-hound breed that originated in France. It has a distinctive appearance, with long ears, an unusually long body, short legs, a large head, and hound colorations. The breed has been bred specifically to be this shape to enable its owner to see over the top of it during a hunt.

with no particular instinct for defensiveness or territorialism. It is good with children due to its gentle and patient demeanor, but its loud bark can startle. The breed is generally sociable with other dogs thanks to its history of living in packs. The Basset Artesiene Normand's strong scenting

instinct can be a source of distraction during training and play.

This is a working hound breed but it also makes an adaptable pet. The Basset Artesiene Normand is generally friendly and intelligent but retains strong working instincts. It is commonly friendly to all,

MINIATURE POODLE

COLOR: All solid colors

COAT CARE: Very high maintenance

DIET: Moderate/high consumption

OFFICIAL CATEGORIZATION: UK: Utility, AKC: Toy, FCI: Group 9, Section 2

HEIGHT: 13½–16½ in. (34.5–42 cm)   WEIGHT: 15–17 lb. (7–8 kg)

OTHER NAMES: None

The Miniature Poodle, despite its name, is not the smallest of the Poodle varieties. It is typical of the other two Poodle varieties in that it has the distinctive curly coat and dainty gait that makes the Poodle breed so appealing. The Poodle's coat is hypoallergenic, meaning that it doesn't cause problems for people with allergies to dog fur. For this reason, the Miniature Poodle has been used as foundation breeding stock for certain new breeds, such as the Labradoodle, which is a Poodle and Labrador cross.

The Miniature Poodle is more commonly associated with work than the Toy Poodle, but is most established now as a pet breed. The Miniature Poodle is very adept at learning tricks due to its high intelligence and general obedience. It makes an extremely popular pet because of its outgoing personality, although some examples can exhibit shyness if not properly socialized from a young age.

FRENCH BULLDOG

Color: Brindle, fawn, white, or brindle and white, or any color with some exceptions

Coat Care: Zero maintenance

Diet: Moderate/high consumption

OFFICIAL CATEGORIZATION: UK: Utility, AKC: Nonsporting, FCI: Group 9, Section 11

HEIGHT: 10½–13½ in. (27–34.5 cm)   WEIGHT: 25½–30 lb. (11.5–13.5 kg)

OTHER NAMES: Bouledogue Français, Frenchie

The French Bulldog is a small breed of dog that descends from the older version of the Bulldog. Its existence came about due to the popularity of the original Bulldog combined with the general distaste for dog fighting, with which the original dog was associated—a smaller non-fighting breed was desired. The breed was developed in England but established in France. It is relatively small and as a result proved to be a useful farm dog, with a keen instinct for ratting. It has distinctively batlike ears.

The French Bulldog has a uniquely quirky personality that appeals to fanciers of the breed. It is alert, inquisitive, and affectionate with a penchant for funny and unusual behavior that is often magnified by its unusual appearance. It is valued for its ease of ownership and is very adaptable and companionable. To train a French Bulldog is relatively easy due to its alertness and high intelligence.

BASSET FAUVE DE BRETAGNE

OFFICIAL CATEGORIZATION: UK: Hound, AKC: Not recognized,
FCI: Group 6, Section 1

HEIGHT: 12½–15 in. (32–38 cm)   WEIGHT: 35–39½ lb. (16–18 kg)

OTHER NAMES: Fawn Brittany Basset

COLOR: Fawn, gold-wheaten or red-wheaten

COAT CARE: Moderate maintenance

DIET: Moderate/high consumption

The Basset Fauve de Bretagne is a breed of French hunting dog. It is a member of the hound family and bears a passing resemblance to the Basset Hound, although it is distinguished by its wiry coat. Unlike many French-bred hunting hounds, the Basset Fauve de Bretagne has a relatively well-proportioned back but characteristically short legs.

The Basset Fauve de Bretagne retains the hardiness that served it well as a hunting hound. It is a lively and energetic breed with a playful and happy demeanor. Its sense of smell is excellent and this can sometimes distract during training or play. The Basset Fauve de Bretagne is typically gentle around children but requires socialization. Around other dogs the breed is well-adapted because of its history of working within a hunting pack. An intelligent breed, this dog responds well to and really enjoys obedience training.

PETIT BASSET GRIFFON VENDEEN

OFFICIAL CATEGORIZATION: UK: Hound, AKC: Hound,
FCI: Group 6, Section 1

HEIGHT: 13–15 in. (33–38 cm)   WEIGHT: 25–40 lb. (15–20 kg)

OTHER NAMES: None

COLOR: White with any combination of lemon, orange, black, sable, tricolor, or grizzle markings

COAT CARE: Moderate maintenance

DIET: Moderate/high consumption

The Petit Basset Griffon Vendeen is a well-proportioned, stocky dog with a rustic appearance. It is similar to other French-bred hunting hounds in that it has a long body and short legs. It is a distant descendant of the Saint Hubert Hound, an ancestor of the Bloodhound. The Petit Basset Griffon Vendeen is a competent hunter in a pack and has a tough and hardy demeanor.

The breed is lively, energetic, and alert. Typical of some scent hounds, it is very vocal and likes to bay when stimulated by scent. It is good with children and displays a friendly and affectionate nature in the domestic environment but can have a stubborn nature that may impede obedience training. Although independently natured, the breed thrives when given plenty of exercise and attention. It is more motivated by reward than a will to please.

BASSET HOUND

COLOR: Any recognized hound color

COAT CARE: Minimal maintenance

DIET: High consumption

OFFICIAL CATEGORIZATION: UK: Hound, AKC: Hound, FCI: Group 6, Section 1

HEIGHT: 14–15 in. (35.5–38 cm)   WEIGHT: 53–65 lb. (23–29 kg)

OTHER NAMES: None

The Basset Hound is one of the most popular pet hound breeds. It originated in France as a pack hound and has a distinctive long body and large pendulous ears. The Basset Hound has a large, round skull and characteristic "sad" eyes, commonly associated with scent hounds. It displays a range of colors but sandy brown and white are typical.

The breed was established in France as a hunting hound and was used as a pack dog. It has an extremely powerful sense of smell, comparable to that of the Bloodhound and the Beagle. The Basset Hound's short legs make it a slow mover—a preferable quality for hunters who were traveling on foot instead of horseback because it meant that the dog could keep up easily with the hunt. The Basset Hound is prone to obesity and back problems; it should be prevented from jumping from any height, including the bottom step of a staircase.

A Popular Choice

The Basset Hound is a very popular pet around the world. The breed is typically friendly and affectionate but with an independent streak common in many hunting hounds. Its pack-hound origins make it a sociable and affable dog, well-suited to life with large families. It is typically very placid, with little or no propensity for aggressive behavior. Although not unintelligent, the Basset Hound has relatively slow reflexes, adding to an overall impression of slowness that can sometimes be mistaken for dim-wittedness.

The breed retains strong working instincts, but this is affected by the proximity of descent from working stock. Some Basset Hounds are active and energetic, while others have relatively low energy levels. Training requires patience and consistency from an owner, beccause the Basset Hound can sometimes forget—or perhaps choose to forget—certain commands.

BELOW LEFT
The short legs of the Basset Hound meant that it was ideal for accompanying people on foot, rather than horseback.

Fascinating Facts

The Basset Hound became popular as a pet breed after being featured in advertising campaigns for the shoe brand Hush Puppies.

BASSET BLEU DE GASCOGNE

OFFICIAL CATEGORIZATION: UK: Hound, AKC: Not recognized,
FCI: Group 6, Section 1

HEIGHT: 12–15 in. (30–38 cm)   WEIGHT: 35–40 lb. (16–20 kg)

OTHER NAMES: Blue Gascony Basset

COLOR: Black marked on a white base

COAT CARE: Minimal maintenance

DIET: Moderate/high consumption

The Basset Bleu de Gascogne is a French hunting hound with a very striking coat, exhibiting a tricolor coloration with ticked white to give it the blue appearance from which it gets its name. The breed is long-bodied but noticeably leaner than typical French hunting hounds. The legs are short, the ears long and pendulous, and the skull characteristically domed.

The breed is rare outside of its own country and is not particularly well-established as a pet breed. This is due to the small numbers of this rare breed, rather than any particular unsuitability in terms of temperament. The breed, while not exhibiting a range of uniform characteristics, is typically friendly and intelligent. Its hunting origins make it more instinctive than obedient, but with proper training the Basset Bleu de Gascogne will adapt well to domestic life. It is a slow mover, meaning any instinctive pursuits of scent can be thwarted by the owner.

PYRENEAN SHEPHERD

OFFICIAL CATEGORIZATION: UK: Pastoral, AKC: Miscellaneous,
FCI: Group 1, Section 1

HEIGHT: 16–19 in. (40–48 cm)   WEIGHT: 18–32 lb. (7–15 kg)

OTHER NAMES: Pyrenean Sheepdog, Petit Berger,
Berger des Pyrénées

COLOR: Various shades of fawn, with or without black hairs

COAT CARE: Moderate maintenance

DIET: Moderate/high consumption

The Pyrenean Shepherd, or Pyrenean Sheepdog as it is also known, is a small, hardy herding breed. It originates from the Pyrenees mountain range on the border of France and Spain, although it is considered to be a French breed. It is the smallest breed of French herding dog. It has either a smooth-faced coat, with finer hairs, or a thick, shaggy coat. Despite its slender frame it is agile and athletic. It has a special partnership with another breed—the Pyrenean Mountain dog, which was a guardian to the flocks herded by the Pyrenean Shepherd.

It is not a well-established pet breed outside of France, but its valor, agility, and intelligence make it, in theory at least, a very attractive pet dog. It has strong herding instincts and is still commonly used as a herding dog today, meaning that most examples of the breed that are kept as pets are either former or unused working dogs.

LEFT
The small Pyrenean Shepherd herded its flock, and worked in partnership with the Pyrenean Mountain Dog, which guarded the flock.

GRAND BASSET GRIFFON VENDEEN

COLOR: White, with any combination of lemon, orange, sable, grizzle, or black markings, or tricolor

COAT CARE: Moderate/high maintenance

DIET: Moderate/high consumption

OFFICIAL CATEGORIZATION: UK: Hound, AKC: Not recognized, FCI: Group 6, Section 1

HEIGHT: 15½–17½ in. (40–44 cm) WEIGHT: 40–44 lb. (18–20 kg)

OTHER NAMES: None

The Grand Basset Griffon Vendeen is one of three varieties of the Griffon Vendeen dog. It has a hardy and rustic appearance, accentuated by its shaggy and coarse coat, and is stocky in build but well-proportioned. It presents a variety of typical colors in its coat, with gray and white being relatively common. Unusually for a French hound breed, its body is not notably long and is much more in proportion than, for example, that of the Basset Hound.

This lively and confident breed makes an excellent pet and is particularly popular in French homes. It requires a high level of companionship and thrives in the company of other dogs. The Grand Basset Griffon Vendeen is a very sociable breed and becomes distressed and destructive if left alone for extended periods of time. It is relatively trainable but does require a good degree of firmness to avoid disobedience.

BEAGLE-HARRIER

COLOR: Tricolor

COAT CARE: Minimal maintenance

DIET: Moderate/high consumption

OFFICIAL CATEGORIZATION: UK: Not recognized, AKC: Not recognized, FCI: Group 6, Section 1

HEIGHT: 18–20 in. (45–50 cm.)   WEIGHT: 42–46 lb. (19–21 kg)

OTHER NAMES: None

Despite its name, the French-bred hunting hound known as the Beagle-Harrier is not a crossbreed and is considered to be a purebred by most authorities. Physically, it appears to be the perfect combination of both Beagle and Harrier, and its size is exactly in between the two. It is thought to share the same ancestry as the Beagle and the Harrier, rather than being a descendent of the two breeds combined, but this theory is frequently disputed.

The Beagle-Harrier is a friendly and gentle dog, well-adapted to domestic living. Its origins are in hound pack-hunting, which makes it a sociable and adaptable breed. It has a high level of loyalty and dedication to those around it and is generally cooperative in training. It requires a fair amount of space and exercise and can become unhappy if denied the chance to expend its energy.

RIGHT

The Beagle-Harrier is considered to be a breed in its own right, despite the double-barreled name, although it is not recognized by the UK and American Kennel Clubs.

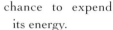

STANDARD POODLE

OFFICIAL CATEGORIZATION: UK: Utility, AKC: Nonsporting,
FCI: Group 9, Section 2

HEIGHT: 13½–16½ in. (34.5–42 cm)   WEIGHT: 45–70 lb. (20–32 kg)

OTHER NAMES: Pudle Caniche

COLOR: All solid colors

COAT CARE: Very high maintenance

DIET: Moderate/high consumption

The Standard Poodle is the largest of the Poodle varieties and displays the typically dense and curly coat for which the breed is known. It is a lean and well-proportioned dog with well-defined features, often accentuated with traditional clipping and grooming. The breed has a varied working past and this is reflected in the disparities of classification between countries. It is considered as a utility breed by the UK Kennel Club but has a history of retrieving; it was bred to work in water and on land. Poodles in general are adaptable and intelligent. In some instances, the Poodle can exhibit signs of being highly strung and oversensitive, but this is typically because of environment rather than breed temperament. The Standard Poodle is a confident and friendly breed, adept in training and keen to please. It enjoys human company and is sensitive to mood.

Fascinating Facts

The coat of the Poodle is hypoallergenic, which means that a Poodle can be kept by people who normally have allergic reactions to dogs.

LEFT

The clipping traditionally associated with a Poodle is thought to date back centuries, and was to protect the dog's joints when wet.

GRIFFON FAUVE DE BRETAGNE

OFFICIAL CATEGORIZATION: UK: Hound, AKC: Not recognized,
FCI: Group 6, Section 1

HEIGHT: 12½–15 in. (32–38 cm)   WEIGHT: 26½–42 lb. (12–19 kg)

OTHER NAMES: Fawn Brittany Basset

COLOR: Fawn, gold-wheaten, or red-wheaten

COAT CARE: Moderate maintenance

DIET: Moderate/high consumption

The Griffon Fauve de Bretagne is a particularly rare French hunting hound, slightly larger than its close relative the Basset Fauve de Bretagne. Prior to the French Revolution, hunting and hound ownership were an aristocratic privilege, but after these privileges were removed anyone could own a hound and hunt. Despite this, not everyone could afford horses and, therefore, these people were unable to keep pace with the hounds. This gave rise to the breeding of a range of short-legged hounds that were slow yet keen hunters.

RIGHT

A rare dog, unrecognized by the American Kennel Club, the Griffon Fauve de Bretagne is a French hunting hound.

The Griffon Fauve de Bretagne is similar in temperament to many low-standing French hunting hounds, although it is far less established as a pet breed compared to the Basset Hound or the smaller Basset Fauve de Bretagne. The breed is typically alert and active with a relatively high level of intelligence. Its instinct for hunting is also strong and so it requires a confident and firm owner.

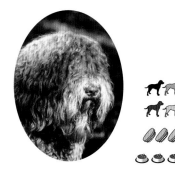

BARBET

COLOR: Black, gray, chestnut, tawny or sand

COAT CARE: High maintenance

DIET: High consumption

OFFICIAL CATEGORIZATION: UK: Not recognized, AKC: Not recognized, FCI: Group 8, Section 3

HEIGHT: 21–23½ in. (54–60 cm)   WEIGHT: 33–55 lb. (15–25 kg)

OTHER NAMES: French Water Dog

The Barbet is a breed of French water dog with ancient origins. It is generally considered to be the ancestor of modern water breeds, such as the Spaniel and the Portuguese Water Dog. The Barbet displays the dense, curly and woolly coat that is associated with a history of water retrieving. It is relatively large and has a sturdy yet well-proportioned body. It is typically presented with a solidly colored coat—patterns are not undesirable but they are rare.

The breed is not particularly well-known outside of France, but it is a moderately popular pet and working breed in its home country. It has a strong retrieving instinct, and responds well to play and training that is designed to stimulate this. It is a friendly and companionable breed that is fond of human company but can adapt well to sharing its home with other dogs given proper socialization.

LEFT
The Barbet, also known as the French Water Dog, has a hypoallergenic, non-shedding coat, like a Poodle.

BRITTANY

COLOR: Orange and white or liver and white

COAT CARE: Low/moderate maintenance

DIET: High consumption

OFFICIAL CATEGORIZATION: UK: Gun Dog, AKC: Sporting, FCI: Group 7, Section 1

HEIGHT: 17½–20 in. (45–51 cm)   WEIGHT: 30–40 lb. (14–18 kg)

OTHER NAMES: American Brittany, Brittany Spaniel, Epagneul Breton

The Brittany, also known as the Brittany Spaniel, is a French gun dog. Despite being commonly referred to as a spaniel, the breed is more closely associated with pointing and setting work. It exhibits colorations closely associated with spaniel breeds and has spaniel ancestry but its working history sets it apart from the traditional spaniel breeds. It is a well-proportioned breed that is athletically built but not heavy or stocky.

The Brittany is a highly intelligent and trainable breed. It is sensitive to mood, which means that it is aware when it disappoints its owner. An owner, therefore, needs to be careful to treat the dog kindly in order not to cause it distress. It is lively and exuberant, fond of children, and particularly playful. It requires a relatively high level of exercise but its boundless energy and willingness to be trained makes the Brittany a very rewarding breed of dog to own.

ANGLO-FRANÇAIS DE PETITE VÉNERIE

OFFICIAL CATEGORIZATION: UK: Not recognized, AKC: Not recognized, FCI: Group 6, Section 1

HEIGHT: 19–22 in. (48–55.5 cm)   WEIGHT: 35–44 lb. (16–20 kg)

OTHER NAMES: None

COLOR: Black and white, orange and white, or tricolor

COAT CARE: Minimal maintenance

DIET: High consumption

The Anglo-Français de Petite Vénerie is a scent-hound breed, predominantly used for working, that was established using French and English breeding stock. It is a large and lean breed with long pendulous ears. It has strong scenting abilities and a very strong prey drive, making it a formidable hunting dog. The breed is generally quick, agile, and possesses extreme stamina.

The Anglo-Français de Petite Vénerie is free-spirited and independent, with a keen desire to chase down small and medium-sized quarry. This makes the breed especially alert to movement, which can be a problem with other small pet animals. It is not established as a pet breed because of its relatively rarity, but it displays no particularly unsuitable attributes for domestication. However, it does retain strong working instincts and would be most suited to a confident and experienced owner who pursues an active lifestyle.

GRIFFON BLEU DE GASCOGNE

OFFICIAL CATEGORIZATION: UK: Hound, AKC: Not recognized, FCI: Group 6, Section 1

HEIGHT: 25–27½ in. (65–70 cm)   WEIGHT: 70½–77 lb. (32–35 kg)

OTHER NAMES: Blue Gascony Griffon

COLOR: Black marked on a white base, but covered entirely with black mottling

COAT CARE: Low maintenance

DIET: High consumption

The Griffon Bleu de Gascogne is one of a group of dogs referred to as Blue Gascony Hounds. It is closely related to the Grand Bleu de Gascogne and is distinguishable from the Basset, Grand, Petit, and Petit Basset by its size. Physically, the five varieties are almost identical in all but size and weight, but this difference has led to each breed being used for slightly differing working roles and has affected temperament. The Blue Gascony Hounds are an ancient group of scent hounds that are ancestors of the Blue Tick Coonhound.

The Griffon Bleu de Gascogne is an intelligent and highly driven breed. It is not widely established as a pet because it is still useful as a working hound in its native France. The dog is bred for stamina, endurance, and a willingness to hunt. It is highly unusual for a Griffon Bleu de Gascogne not to have strong working instincts.

BRAQUE FRANÇAIS (Type Pyrenean)

COLOR: No agreed colorations

COAT CARE: Minimal maintenance

DIET: High consumption

OFFICIAL CATEGORIZATION: UK: Not recognized, AKC: Not recognized, FCI: Not recognized

HEIGHT: Med.–large (no standard)   WEIGHT: Sturdy (no standard)

OTHER NAMES: None

The Braque Français is a name given to two types of French pointing breeds, distinguished by the region of France in which they became established. The Braque Français (Type Pyrenean) is the more well-known of the two breeds, but is not established outside of France. It has a strong and diverse set of working skills and is noted as a useful retriever and pointing breed. It is typically brown and white with ticked patches of white.

The breed is usually very affectionate and intelligent and is well-suited to family life. It is gentle with children but because of its size should always be supervised. The Braque Français (Type Pyrenean) does have strong working instincts that can over-power any level of obedience if the dog is not correctly and firmly trained.

RIGHT

The Braque Français (Type Pyrenean) is one of two types of Braque Français; the other is the larger Braque Gasgogne.

It has high energy levels and is suited to people with the same.

BRIQUET GRIFFON VENDÉEN

COLOR: Solid or mixed colors—fawn, light brown, white and orange, white and gray, or tricolor

COAT CARE: Moderate/high maintenance

DIET: Moderate/high consumption

OFFICIAL CATEGORIZATION: UK: Not recognized, AKC: Not recognized, FCI: Group 6, Section 1

HEIGHT: 20–22 in. (51–56 cm)   WEIGHT: 48–53 lb. (22–24 kg)

OTHER NAMES: None

The Briquet Griffon Vendéen is a breed of French hunting dog that is closely related to the larger Grand Basset Griffon Vendéen. It is a popular working breed, displaying a very thick double coat that gives the breed a rustic appearance. The head is short and domed, framed by long ears that are well coated. It is a sturdy but not stocky breed.

The breed is friendly and intelligent but retains a strong instinct for hunting. It is lively and energetic and requires dedicated and consistent training that stimulates its mind. When properly trained the Briquet Griffon Vendéen is a biddable and enthusiastic pet. The breed is prone to baying, which is not unusual for hunting hounds. Some people find this unacceptable and attempt to train it out of the dog, but it is a very instinctive behavior—almost a reflex for certain dogs bred from working stock.

PETIT BLEU DE GASCOGNE

OFFICIAL CATEGORIZATION: UK: Not recognized,
AKC: Not recognized, FCI: Group 6, Section 1

HEIGHT: 19½–23½ in. (50–60 cm)   WEIGHT: 42–46½ lb. (19–21 kg)

OTHER NAMES: None

COLOR: Blue mottled and black with tan markings

COAT CARE: Low maintenance

DIET: High consumption

The Petit Bleu de Gascogne is a French hunting hound and close relative of the Basset Bleu de Gascogne and the Grand Bleu de Gascogne. It is descended from ancient and now-extinct hounds that were popular for hunting in the Gascony region of France. Associated with aristocracy, its appearance and that of similar-looking breeds is often described as "noble" or "aristocratic." The Petit Bleu de Gascogne is smaller than the Grand Bleu because of selective breeding for working purposes.

Despite their obvious similarities, the Petit and the Grande are very different in terms of temperament. While they share many instinctive and houndlike behaviors, their work in the past differed according to the prey they hunted. The Petit Bleu de Gascogne is independently minded but loves the company of other dogs due to its pack origins. Training can be challenging for inexperienced owners.

RIGHT

The Petit Bleu de Gascogne, a working dog, was deliberately bred to be smaller than the Grand Bleu.

CHIEN D'ARTOIS

OFFICIAL CATEGORIZATION: UK: Not recognized,
AKC: Not recognized, FCI: Group 6, Section 1

HEIGHT: 20½–23 in. (52–58 cm)   WEIGHT: 61½–66 lb. (28–30 kg)

OTHER NAMES: Artois Hound

COLOR: Tricolor, dark tan, or white and black with big spots

COAT CARE: Low/moderate maintenance

DIET: High consumption

The Chien D'Artois, or Artois Hound, is a rare descendant of the Bloodhound that originates from France. It is a solidly built scenting hound with a sturdy body and noble head. It is typically of black, fawn, and white tricolor coloration. The Chien D'Artois has a typical scent-hound skull shape but lacks the looser facial skin commonly associated with other scent hounds. It possesses strong scenting abilities and has an insatiable working instinct.

The Chien D'Artois is not particularly established as a pet dog breed and is happiest when on the hunt.

Loyal and intelligent, with a high degree of independence, its energy and desire to work is impressive, but these characteristics do not bode well for domestic living. Despite this, the breed is sometimes kept as a pet in retirement, where it provides loyalty and companionship but requires ongoing training to remain happy.

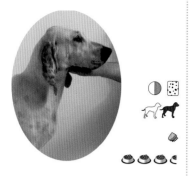

PORCELAINE

COLOR: White with orange spots

COAT CARE: Minimal maintenance

DIET: High/very high consumption

OFFICIAL CATEGORIZATION: UK: Not recognized, AKC: Not recognized, FCI: Group 6, Section 1

HEIGHT: 22–23 in. (56–58.5 cm)   WEIGHT: 55–62 lb. (25–28 kg)

OTHER NAMES: Chien de Franche-Comté

This ancient French scent-hound breed is so-called because of its distinguished white coat, which is said to resemble porcelain. It has a strikingly well-defined skull and large ears that are slightly off-colored in comparison to the rest of the coat color. The Porcelaine is well-proportioned and lean, giving the impression of speed and agility.

The breed is extremely instinctive and as a worker would hunt without instruction or command. It thrives in the company of other dogs and is typically friendly. On the hunt, the Porcelaine is fierce and unrelenting, which does make it an unsuitable pet for people with low activity levels. The breed is intelligent and has an excellent sense of smell. It also possesses an unusually expressive bay, which is characteristic of the breed. Unlike a lot of French hounds, the Porcelaine is reasonably well-established as a pet breed outside of France.

Fascinating Facts

Max is the most common name for male dogs in English-speaking countries.

FRENCH SPANIEL

COLOR: White with brown markings

COAT CARE: Moderate maintenance

DIET: High consumption

OFFICIAL CATEGORIZATION: UK: Not recognized, AKC: Not recognized, FCI: Group 7, Section 1

HEIGHT: 55–61 cm (22–24 in)   WEIGHT: 20–25 kg (44–55 lb)

OTHER NAMES: Epagneul Français

The French Spaniel, or Epagneul Français as it also known, is an ancient breed of gun dog that is thought be the forefather of many modern pointing breeds. It is typical of spaniel breeds in appearance but is notably heavier than most. It has a long history of work, dating back to the fourteenth century, but has evolved physically since then to become a more compact dog.

Although the French Spaniel is a rugged breed and hardy at work, it is a sensitive and gentle breed at home. Training should appeal to the breed's sweet nature. The French Spaniel is a good pet, although quite rare, and is very gentle and affectionate toward children. Its calmness and even temper makes it an easy pet to get along with. It is generally friendly to other dogs in the family home but some examples of the breed may initially resent a new dog.

BELOW
The forefather of some Pointer breeds, the French Spaniel can both point and retrieve, making it a versatile gun dog.

ARIEGEOIS

OFFICIAL CATEGORIZATION: UK: Not recognized, AKC: Not recognized, FCI: Group 6, Section 1

HEIGHT: 24–27 in. (61–68.5 cm) WEIGHT: 63–70 lb. (28.5–32 kg)

OTHER NAMES: None

COLOR: Tricolor with black and tan, primarily on the head; the body is essentially white

COAT CARE: Low/moderate maintenance

DIET: High consumption

The Ariegeois is a distinctive-looking French scent hound. Its head is atypical of other scent hounds in that it is narrow and lacking in loose skin and wrinkles. It has a lean, athletic body and a narrow tapering tail. The Ariegeois is predominantly mottled white with darker colors around the face and ears. Although the Ariegeois is a traditional hunting hound, it is much lighter boned than most scent hounds. This leaner physique was desirable for the work that the dog performed in the dry, rocky terrain of the Ariege region of France.

The Ariegeois is considered to be extremely friendly and sociable, even by scent-hound standards. It is not a commonly established breed but exhibits excellent pet-

RIGHT
Unlike other scent hounds, the Ariegeois has a smooth muzzle, without folds of skin for trapping scent.

dog characteristics. It is typically full of energy and can be extremely outgoing and playful. However, there is no uniform set of characteristics for the Ariegeois and some examples of the breed may be less outgoing.

GRIFFON NIVERNAIS

OFFICIAL CATEGORIZATION: UK: Not recognized, AKC: Not recognized, FCI: Group 6, Section 1

HEIGHT: 21–24 in. (53–61 cm) WEIGHT: 50–55 lb. (22.5–25 kg)

OTHER NAMES: None

COLOR: Blue-gray, dark gray, or wolf-gray

COAT CARE: Moderate/high maintenance

DIET: High consumption

The Griffon Nivernais is an ancient hound breed of French origin; its ancestry can be traced back to the thirteenth century. It has gradually decreased in size over generations in accordance with the type of quarry it was expected to hunt. The modern Griffon Nivernais is a relatively compact breed with a wiry outer coat. Its typical coloration is a "dirty" gray. The Griffon Nivernais, although not particularly established as a pet, has been exported from France numerous times and has been used for work in Greece, the United States, and Canada.

Although the breed exhibits a characteristically sad facial expression it is usually a lively and friendly animal. Its hunting instincts are strong but it is cooperative in training and has an eager desire to please. The Griffon Nivernais is known for having large reserves of stamina and can remain focused for long periods of time, which means it is less likely to become bored at home.

PETIT GASCON SAINTONGEOIS

COLOR: Tricolor, black on head and a few body spots, tan only on head, or black ticking throughout

COAT CARE: Low maintenance

DIET: High consumption

OFFICIAL CATEGORIZATION: UK: Not recognized, AKC: Not recognized, FCI: Not recognized

HEIGHT: 22–25 in. (56–63.5 cm) WEIGHT: 50–62 lb. (22.5–28 kg)

OTHER NAMES: None

This is a consistently rare breed of French hunting dog that has come close to extinction on more than one occasion. The Petit Gascon Saintongeois is a recently established and bred-down version of the large and powerful hunting breed Grand Gascon Saintongeois. It has common ancestry with the modern Bloodhound and bears a passing resemblance to the breed physically but is much smaller. It was originally bred for pack hunting and exhibits a strong sense of smell and a loud bay.

Because of its pack instincts the Petit Gascon Saintongeois is sociable and generally friendly. It has strong working instincts, particularly stimulated by movement of small game, which makes it an unsuitable choice of pet for owners of rabbits. It is energetic but somewhat serious and it requires a firm, confident owner to get the best out of it.

RIGHT
Captivated by the sight of small creatures moving, the Petit Gascon Saintongeois is not a good dog if you have a pet rabbit.

BRAQUE SAINT GERMAIN

COLOR: White with a few bright orange patches

COAT CARE: Minimal maintenance

DIET: High/very high consumption

OFFICIAL CATEGORIZATION: UK: Not recognized, AKC: Not recognized, FCI: Group 7, Section 1

HEIGHT: 20–24 in. (51–61 cm)   WEIGHT: 40–57 lb. (18–26 kg)

OTHER NAMES: Saint Germain Pointing Dog

The Braque St Germain is an old breed, having been established in the nineteenth century. It is believed that the founder of the breed was King Charles X of France. He was given two English Pointers, and after the male died the female was crossed with Braques Français. The Saint Germain is typically of white coloration with patches of orange—a distinctive coat that it inherited from the English Pointers. It is a rare breed, even in France, because of its relatively unknown suitability and adaptability as a pet.

The breed is considered to be a strong worker with good pointing instincts and an obedient nature. It is loyal, but typically to the one person it forms a bond with. This can result in certain examples of the breed exhibiting aloofness or suspicion toward those people with whom they are not familiar.

RIGHT
According to a contemporary writer, the early Pointer-Braque crossbreeds showed "a fine nose, great elegance of form, and an undeniable distinction."

BRAQUE D'AUVERGNE

OFFICIAL CATEGORIZATION: UK: Not recognized, AKC: Not recognized, FCI: Group 7, Section 1

HEIGHT: 22–24 in. (56–61 cm)   WEIGHT: 49–62 lb. (22.5–28 kg)

OTHER NAMES: Auvergne Pointer, Bleu d'Auvergne

COLOR: Black and white

COAT CARE: Minimal maintenance

DIET: High/very high consumption

The Braque d'Auvergne is an old breed of hunting dog originating in the Auvergne region of France. Despite being descended from scent hounds, the Braque d'Auvergne is considered to be a gun-dog breed. It is a large, strong, and athletically built dog, with a distinctive coat of white with either black spots or black roan. The coat is described in French as charbonnée, which means "charcoaled." Although the Braque d'Auvergne is a strong and well-built breed, it displays a lightness and delicacy in the chase that is unusual for its size.

The Braque d'Auvergne is a tough breed, used to working in mountainous terrain. At the side of a master it is a sensitive and loyal dog with a high level of intelligence combined with a strong working instinct. Some examples of the breed are notably affectionate and for this reason it is often kept as a pet in retirement.

RIGHT
Despite being a scent hound, the Braque d'Auvergne is classified as a gun dog by the FCI.

BERGER PICARD

OFFICIAL CATEGORIZATION: UK: Not recognized, AKC: Not recognized, FCI: Group 1, Section 1

HEIGHT: 21–25½ in. (53–65 cm)   WEIGHT: 50–70 lb. (23–32 kg)

OTHER NAMES: Berger de Picardie, Picardy Shepherd

COLOR: Fawn and gray with shade variations

COAT CARE: Moderate/high maintenance

DIET: High consumption

The Berger Picard is a French herding breed. It is rustic and rugged in its appearance and displays an impressive gray tousled coat that is not prone to matting. It is a solidly reliable working breed but is very rare. It has come close to extinction twice, after each of the two World Wars, during which breeding in its home region of northern France was disrupted. The Berger Picard is a close relative of the Briard.

As with most herding and pastoral breeds, the Berger Picard is intelligent and hard-working. Its loyalty and obedience are uniform characteristics born into the breed as instinctive behaviors. It is a sociable and generally friendly breed but can perform efficiently as a guard dog because of its self-confidence and dedication to protecting a flock. This alert breed is best suited to an owner who can spend ample time with their dog.

BRAQUE DU BOURBONNAIS

OFFICIAL CATEGORIZATION: UK: Not recognized,
AKC: Not recognized, FCI: Group 7, Section 1

COLOR: Liver or fawn

COAT CARE: Zero maintenance

DIET: High consumption

HEIGHT: 20–22½ in. (51–57 cm)   WEIGHT: 39½–55 lb. (18–25 kg)

OTHER NAMES: Bourbonnais Pointer

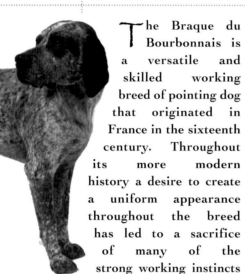

The Braque du Bourbonnais is a versatile and skilled working breed of pointing dog that originated in France in the sixteenth century. Throughout its more modern history a desire to create a uniform appearance throughout the breed has led to a sacrifice of many of the strong working instincts and damage to the overall health of the breed. Typically, this is a medium-sized, well-built dog with a brown-and-white flecked coat. Due to the history of overselective breeding many breeders are keen to see a variety of coats in the breed as a sign of diversity.

The breed has good working abilities, but these are not as instinctive as they are in many other breeds. It is friendly and affectionate and its intelligence is of a high level, which lends itself to training. The Braque du Bourbonnais is playful and gentle.

> LEFT
>
> *Braques du Bourbonnais are sometimes born with a short tail, or no tail at all.*

BLUE PICARDY SPANIEL

COLOR: Speckled gray-black, forming a bluish shade with some black patches

COAT CARE: Low maintenance

DIET: High consumption

OFFICIAL CATEGORIZATION: UK: Not recognized,
AKC: Not recognized, FCI: Group 7, Section 1

HEIGHT: 22–24 in. (56–61 cm)   WEIGHT: 43–47½ lb. (19.5–21.5 kg)

OTHER NAMES: Epagneul Blue de Picardie

This is a well-built breed of pointing dog. Despite being referred to by name as a Spaniel, the working history is in pointing. It is closely related to the Picard Spaniel and only experienced separation from that breed classification at the start of the twentieth century. The Blue Picardy Spaniel is gray with black ticking, which gives the coat a blue appearance.

The Blue Picardy Spaniel originated in France and is typical of French pointing and gun dogs. It is a lively and friendly breed that is affectionate to children and has a lot of energy. It is considered to be a very adaptable dog with an ability to match its activity levels with those around it, although the breed thrives in situations where it can access the scents and sights of the rural outdoors. Its instinctive pointing is impressive to see and does not disrupt any training or desired behavior patterns.

> BELOW
>
> *The Epagneul Bleu de Picardie goes by the easier name of Blue Picardy Spaniel, and has a gray coat with black ticking, giving it a bluish appearance.*

PICARDY SPANIEL

OFFICIAL CATEGORIZATION: UK: Not recognized,
AKC: Not recognized, FCI: Group 7, Section 1

HEIGHT: 22–24½ in. (56–61 cm)   WEIGHT: 42–46½ lb. (19–21 kg)

OTHER NAMES: Epagneul Picardie

COLOR: Liver, white, or tan,
with heavy ticking

COAT CARE: Low maintenance

DIET: High consumption

LEFT

*The Picardy Spaniel is a relaxed,
sociable dog, that would enjoy family
life, rather than life as a one-man dog.*

The Picardy Spaniel, or Epagneul Picard, is a close relative of the Blue Picardy Spaniel and exhibits many physical and behavioral similarities. However, it is older and more established than its relative and does not exhibit the blue coat. Despite its spaniel name, it has strong pointing instincts; the spaniel reference is due to the breeding stock and appearance of the dog. It is indeed a spaniel, but most pointing breeds have descended from spaniels and some were simply never named for their specific role.

The Picardy Spaniel is a relaxed, calm, and sociable breed. It is affectionate and gentle in nature to people and dogs, with an instinctive drive to show birds by striking its natural pointing pose. The dogs are generally active but are adaptable to most lifestyles. As a companion animal the Picardy Spaniel is loyal and dedicated to the whole family; it rarely singles out one person for particular favor.

BRIARD

OFFICIAL CATEGORIZATION: UK: Pastoral, AKC: Herding,
FCI: Group 1, Section 1

HEIGHT: 23–27 in. (58–69 cm)   WEIGHT: 75–79½ lb. (34–36 kg)

OTHER NAMES: Berger de Brie

COLOR: All uniform colors
except white

COAT CARE: High maintenance

DIET: High consumption

The Briard is a hardy and active herding breed that originated in France. It is a popular working dog with a rustic and tough exterior, of medium size, and well-proportioned, and fulfills a similar working role to the German Shepherd. It has a distinctively shaggy coat that covers much of the face; this coat is exhibited in a variety of colors but is typically one solid color. The Briard is one of the more well-known and well-established French herding breeds.

As with some herding dogs, the Briard can be overly protective and requires early socialization to engage it with lots of different people. It is intelligent, extremely loyal, and obedient. Its intelligence requires that training and play is stimulating, but it is generally not needy or overly sensitive. It tends to bond strongly with all members of a family and is uncomfortable in the absence of a companion.

ABOVE

*Being a herding dog, the Briard
can need special socialization
to ensure that it does not
become overprotective.*

BRAQUE FRANÇAIS (Type Gascogne)

COLOR: Maroon and white, strongly speckled

COAT CARE: Zero maintenance

DIET: High consumption

OFFICIAL CATEGORIZATION: UK: Not recognized, AKC: Not recognized, FCI: Group 7, Section 1

HEIGHT: 23–27 in. (58–69 cm)   **WEIGHT:** 55–65 lb. (25–30 kg)

OTHER NAMES: French Pointer

The Braque Français (Type Gascogne) is the larger of the two very French pointing breeds that have the Braque Français name. The Gascogne part of the name refers to the Gascony region of France where the dog is thought to have originated. The Braque Français (Type Gascogne) and its relative are traditional hunt, point, and retrieve breeds, meaning that they are versatile workers.

Despite their apparent usefulness in the field, this breed is rare, even in France. As a pet the breed is obedient, lively, and enthusiastic. Gentle and very affectionate around children of all ages and with a fondness for human company it is surprising that the breed is not more well-established as a pet. The breed is typically very adaptable and willing to limit its activity to match the environment, but it is at its happiest when given the chance to get out in the open and obey its natural working instincts.

ABOVE

An adaptable breed, the Braque Français Type Gascogne can hunt, point, and retrieve.

EPAGNEUL DE PONT-AUDEMER

COLOR: Liver or brown, or a mixture of liver or brown and white

COAT CARE: Moderate maintenance

DIET: Moderate/high consumption

OFFICIAL CATEGORIZATION: UK: Not recognized, AKC: Not recognized, FCI: Group 7, Section 1

HEIGHT: 20–23 in. (52–58 cm)   **WEIGHT:** 44–60 lb. (20–27 kg)

OTHER NAMES: Pont-Audemer Spaniel

This unique-looking breed is a multi-functional hunt, point, and retrieve dog. Its speciality is water retrieving, but its ancestry of poodles and spaniels enables it to vary its work. It is a distinctive-looking breed, with luxurious flowing locks atop a narrow and noble head.

It is a predominantly working breed but is very rare, and its numbers are limited to certain regions of its native France. It originated in the nineteenth century but has since experienced the introduction of new breeds in its bloodline in order to stabilize it.

It is a hardy and tough dog, typical of rustic working spaniels, but is considered gentle and friendly with its owner. It is affectionate toward those with whom it is familiar. It is not established as a pet breed because of its rarity but does not possess any attributes that suggest it would be an unsuitable pet dog.

BELOW

A rare and versatile spaniel, the Epagneul de Pont-Audemer is only found in certain regions in France.

DOGUE DE BORDEAUX

OFFICIAL CATEGORIZATION: UK: Working, AKC: Miscellaneous, FCI: Group 2, Section 2

HEIGHT: 23½–27 in. (60–68 cm)   WEIGHT: 108–112½ lb. (49–51 kg)

OTHER NAMES: None

COLOR: Shades of fawn, from mahogany to "Isabella"

COAT CARE: Minimal maintenance

DIET: High/very high consumption

LEFT
An extremely large breed, the Dogue de Bordeaux does not complete growing until two years of age.

The Dogue de Bordeaux is a large and powerful Mastiff breed native to France but popular and well-established throughout the world. It is typical of most descendents of early Molosser breeds in that it has a heavy jaw, strong body, and powerful bite. It was established in nineteenth-century France when dog fighting was popular, but is now bred for showing and companionship.

Fascinating Facts

The Dogue de Bordeaux is sometimes known as Atlas, in reference to the Greek God.

The coat of the Dogue de Bordeaux is typically light fawn. The breed will grow to an extremely large size, reaching its full proportions at around two years of age. It has an expressive face and as a puppy is considered to be uncommonly sweet-looking.

Despite its history of fighting and, latterly, as a formidable guard dog, the Dogue de Bordeaux is a popular pet because of its gentle and affectionate nature. The breed was featured in the Touchstone Pictures movie *Turner & Hooch,* which starred Tom Hanks as the owner of a lovable Dogue de Bordeaux.

Not Suited to Novices
The breed is fiercely loyal and dedicated to family members and makes a very useful guard dog because of its size, strength, and protective nature. The dog is naturally tenacious but in the domestic environment this is rarely exhibited. An owner must ensure that the dog is properly trained and socialized because any dog of this size exhibiting behavioral problems will become a serious concern.

The Dogue de Bordeaux typically exhibits calmness and patience with familiar people but can become aggressive and confrontational with newcomers that it perceives to be a threat to itself or those around it. Novice or inexperienced owners are not suited to this breed because it requires a firm, patient owner with a good knowledge of canine behavior. The Dogue de Bordeaux is known for snoring and drooling and can be quite a messy pet to have around the home.

BILLY

COLOR: Pure and off-white with orange or lemon spots on the head and body

COAT CARE: Minimal maintenance

DIET: High consumption

OFFICIAL CATEGORIZATION: UK: Not recognized, AKC: Not recognized, FCI: Group 6, Section 1

HEIGHT: 23½–27½ in. (60–70 cm)   WEIGHT: 52–70 lb. (23.5–32 kg)

OTHER NAMES: None

The Billy is a large hunting hound that originated in France. It is a very rare breed and is relatively unknown outside of its home country. It counts many breeds of hound among its ancestors, including the Harrier and the now-extinct Montemboeuf and Ceris breeds. The Billy is typically a pale-colored, short-coated dog displaying either white, off-white, or lemon colorations, with or without markings. It was bred originally to hunt large game, such as deer. It is a noticeably tall and thin breed of dog, giving the impression of clumsiness and ungainliness.

Despite its carriage, it is a quick, agile, and responsive hunting dog with a reputation for tenacity and enthusiasm in the hunt. Although it is a pack dog, its instinctive tenacity often results in the breed becoming overexcited when working, and it will often direct this excitement toward other pack members, which can lead to quarrels.

POITEVIN

COLOR: Tricolor or orange and white

COAT CARE: Minimal maintenance

DIET: High/very high consumption

OFFICIAL CATEGORIZATION: UK: Not recognized, AKC: Not recognized, FCI: Group 6, Section 1

HEIGHT: 24–28 in. (61–71 cm)   WEIGHT: 64–68½ lb. (29–31 kg)

OTHER NAMES: None

The Poitevin is a rare breed of French scent hound that was bred originally for hunting wolves. It was nearly extinct following a rabies outbreak in the mid-nineteenth century, but dedicated breeders worked hard to reestablish the breed, outcrossing remaining examples of the breed with the English Foxhound. It has an attractive, short coat that is typically orange, white, and black tricolor and it has noticeably small ears for a scent hound. Its scenting ability is strong, as is its stamina, which made it a very useful hunter.

The breed has always been rare, and when factors, such as the rabies outbreak and the controls imposed on wolf hunting, conspired against its numbers it was destined to remain rare. It is a hard-working, dedicated hound with an eager tenacity. It is rarely kept as a pet because of its speciality nature, but some examples of the breed have been exported to hound enthusiasts.

RIGHT
Almost extinct due to a rabies outbreak in the nineteenth century, some dedicated breeders set about building up the Poitevin numbers.

BRAQUE DE L'ARIEGE

OFFICIAL CATEGORIZATION: UK: Not recognized,
AKC: Not recognized, FCI: Group 7, Section 1

HEIGHT: 23½–26½ in. (60–67 cm)   WEIGHT: 55–66 lb. (25–30 kg)

OTHER NAMES: Ariege Pointer, Braque de Toulouse

COLOR: White with patches of orange or chestnut

COAT CARE: Low maintenance

DIET: High/very high consumption

The Braque de L'Ariege is an old breed of French pointing dog. It is also known as the Ariege Pointer and is a descendent of the Braque Saint Germain. The Braque de L'Ariege is a large, powerful breed with a deep chest and well-muscled but not heavy body, suitable for bird hunting. Its coat is typically white, mottled with orange or pale brown. It is noted for its elegance and graceful carriage in the hunt.

The breed is a skilled hunter and makes for a very versatile working companion. Away from the field it is a docile, gentle, and well-mannered dog that takes to training enthusiastically.

It has high intelligence and an eager working drive, which means the breed is certainly at its happiest when used for working, but, it will adapt to domestic life if given the right training and enough room to exercise.

LEFT
The Braque de L'Ariege is noted in the field for its elegant carriage.

GRAND GRIFFON VENDÉEN

OFFICIAL CATEGORIZATION: UK: Not recognized,
AKC: Not recognized, FCI: Group 6, Section 1

HEIGHT: 22–25 in. (56–63.5 cm)   WEIGHT: 66–77 lb. (30–35 kg)

OTHER NAMES: None

COLOR: Orange, gray, tawny, or black and tan

COAT CARE: High maintenance

DIET: High consumption

The Grand Griffon Vendéen is from a large family of French hunting dogs. It is related to the Petit Griffon Vendéen and the Basset Griffon Vendéen and is the eldest breed of the group. The Griffon Vendéen type of dog is presented in many varieties all with slightly differing working roles. They have been bred to be smaller, shorter legged, and with coarser coats in order to cope with various different environments. The Grand Griffon Vendéen is one of the more well-known members of the family.

The Grand Griffon Vendéen is instinctive and driven by the hunt. It is not an unsuitable pet but does require much stimulation and training if it is to be truly content. Its intelligence, while of a high level, does not naturally lend itself to obedience or housebreaking. It is most commonly kept as a pet by people with a rural home.

LEFT
The Grand Griffon Vendéen is related to the Petit Griffon Vendéen and the Basset Griffon Vendéen, all of whom have different coats.

GREAT ANGLO-FRENCH WHITE-AND-ORANGE HOUND

COLOR: White and relatively light orange or white and lemon

COAT CARE: Low maintenance

DIET: High consumption

OFFICIAL CATEGORIZATION: UK: Not recognized, AKC: Not recognized, FCI: Group 6, Section 1

HEIGHT: 23½–27½ in. (60–70– cm)   **WEIGHT:** 66–77 lb. (30–35 kg)

OTHER NAMES: None

The Great Anglo-French White-and-Orange Hound is a remarkably rare descendent of the Foxhound and the Billy breeds. It is considered to be a member of the Anglo-French Hound group of dogs, which is true, but is not directly related to other hounds. The breeds are classified together due to the breeding program between the French and the English, not because of common breeding stock, although there are some commonalities of ancestry between certain breeds.

To describe the breed's appearance is to simply say the name—it is a large scent-hound breed that has white-and-orange coloration. The breeds share similar temperaments because of their hunting history and the Great Anglo-French White-and-Orange Hound displays a typical combination of enthusiasm, vigor, tenacity, strong scenting instinct, and courage in the hunt. It is not well-suited to urban living environments and requires space and freedom to exercise.

ABOVE LEFT

If you live in a town, think carefully before buying a Great Anglo-French White and Orange Hound, because it requires considerable space.

Fascinating Facts

In the Belgian town of Ghent, public water fountains feature a water bowl for dogs, located at the bottom.

GRAND BLEU DE GASCOGNE

COLOR: Black marked on a white base, covered entirely with black mottling

COAT CARE: Minimal maintenance

DIET: High consumption

OFFICIAL CATEGORIZATION: UK: Hound, AKC: Not recognized, FCI: Group 6, Section 1

HEIGHT: 25–27½ in. (64–70 cm)   **WEIGHT:** 70½–77 lb. (32–35 kg)

OTHER NAMES: Great Gascony Hound, Great Gascony Blue

The Grand Bleu de Gascogne is a member of the large family of dogs known outside of France as the Blue Gascony Hounds. The members of the family are closely related and bear strong physical resemblance to each other, but were bred to fulfill different roles in the hunt. The Grand Bleu de Gascogne, as the name suggests, is the largest of the breeds and was used to track and hunt larger game.

The blue-coated appearance comes from light gray flecking against a white color. Some examples of the breed exhibit tan colorations in places, particularly around the muzzle. The Grand Bleu de Gascogne has strong hunting instincts but is relatively adaptable and can make a suitable pet in the right environment. It is loyal and dignified, often described as reliable in temperament. Although it is a rare breed, it has been exported to the United States by hound enthusiasts in the past.

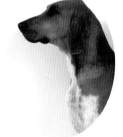

FRANÇAIS TRICOLORE

OFFICIAL CATEGORIZATION: UK: Not recognized, AKC: Not recognized, FCI: Group 6, Section 1

HEIGHT: 25–29 in. (63.5–73.5 cm) WEIGHT: 60–68 lb. (27–35.5 kg)

OTHER NAMES: None

COLOR: Broken tricolor pattern of tan, black, and white

COAT CARE: Minimal maintenance

DIET: High consumption

The Français Tricolore, not to be confused with the Grand Anglo-Français Tricolore, is a breed of hunting hound descended from various French hounds. It is distinct from the Grand Anglo-Français Tricolore in that the bloodline contains no English ancestry. It exhibits a tricolor of tan, black, and white; a black mantle and grizzled patches are sometimes seen. The breed is a fine example of a hunting hound, with a well-muscled, lean body that exhibits athleticism and grace in the hunt. The coat is fine in texture.

It is a rare breed outside of France and, therefore, is not particularly well-established as a pet beyond that country. The Français Tricolore is a well-adjusted and cooperative hunting companion. It has a good sense of smell and is a dedicated and obedient working dog. The working Français Tricolore should be even-tempered and confident but not overly boisterous or aggressive.

LEFT
The coat of the Français Tricolore comes in three colors, black, tan, and white.

FRANÇAIS BLANC ET NOIR

OFFICIAL CATEGORIZATION: UK: Not recognized, AKC: Not recognized, FCI: Group 6, Section 1

HEIGHT: 26–30 in. (66–76 cm) WEIGHT: 60–70 lb. (27–31.5 kg)

OTHER NAMES: French White-and-Black Hound

COLOR: Tricolor—black and white with tan marks on head and ears

COAT CARE: Minimal maintenance

DIET: High/very high consumption

The Français Blanc et Noir, or French White-and-Black Hound, is one of a group of French hunting hounds known as the "French Hounds." They are distinguished between themselves in color and coat pattern and are distinguished also from the Anglo-Français type of hounds in that they are descended from only French breeding stock. The Français Blanc et Noir, as the breed name suggests, is black and white in color. It is similar in size to the Français Tricolore and has a very similar working history. The Français Blanc et Noir is a sociable and pack-orientated working hound with strong scent abilities.

It is a strong and powerful breed with a well-balanced and muscular body. The French Hounds are descended from the Poitevin breed and this is reflected in their show type.

Any dog that displays evidence of English heritage in favor of Poitevin type is penalized in the show ring.

GRAND ANGLO-FRANÇAIS TRICOLORE

COLOR: Tricolor—black, white, and tan

COAT CARE: Minimal maintenance

DIET: High/very high consumption

OFFICIAL CATEGORIZATION: UK: Not recognized, AKC: Not recognized, FCI: Group 6, Section 1

HEIGHT: 24–28 in. (60–72 cm)   WEIGHT: 76–78 lb. (34.5–35.5 kg)

OTHER NAMES: Great Anglo-French Tricolor

The Grand Anglo-Français Tricolore is one of several varieties of dog that are known as Anglo-French Hounds (the others being the Great-Anglo French White-and-Orange Hound and the Grand Anglo-Français Blanc et Noir). The Grand Anglo-Français Tricolore have similarities to the French Hounds, but are descendents of the Poitevin and English Foxhounds. They were used as a pack dog to hunt large game.

The Grand Anglo-Français Tricolore, like the Grand Anglo-Français Blanc et Noir, displays a narrower head than the French Hounds, and is considered to be a more versatile hunter than its purely French counterparts. It is an eager and enthusiastic worker with a high degree of stamina and pace. The Grand Anglo-Français Tricolore and the Grand Anglo-Français Blanc et Noir are said to have inherited their distinctive sturdiness from the English Foxhound and their keen nose and impressive baying bark from the Poitevin. They require a great deal of exercise and are most suited to an outdoor life.

ABOVE

The Grand Anglo-Français Tricolore has a greater passion for hunting than its pure French counterpart.

FRANÇAIS BLANC ET ORANGE

COLOR: White and orange (can be yellow)

COAT CARE: Minimal maintenance

DIET: High consumption

OFFICIAL CATEGORIZATION: UK: Not recognized, AKC: Not recognized, FCI: Group 6, Section 1

HEIGHT: 24–28 in. (61–71 cm)   WEIGHT: 60–90 lb. (27–50 kg)

OTHER NAMES: French White-and-Orange Hound

The Français Blanc et Orange is the third variety of the French Hound type. It is distinguishable by its coloration, which is similar in shade to the Français Tricolore but lacks the black patches. The white of the coat can be either true white or lemon-white but the orange must not be redding in any place. The Français Blanc et Orange is typical of the French Hound family and any suggestion of English hound blood is undesirable.

Like the other two types of French Hound, the Français Blanc et Orange is a strong hunter with a powerful body and graceful carriage. In the hunt, it is enthusiastic and dedicated. It displays loyalty and obedience to the master but is instinctive and driven by its impressive scenting abilities. If kept as a pet, the breed is more comfortable outdoors and requires a large degree of exercise and stimulation.

RIGHT

Similar to the Français Tricolore, but the Français Blanc et Orange does not have the black coat markings.

GRAND ANGLO-FRANÇAIS BLANC ET NOIR

OFFICIAL CATEGORIZATION: UK: Not recognized,
AKC: Not recognized, FCI: Group 6, Section 1

HEIGHT: 27–30 in. (68.5–76 cm)   WEIGHT: 75–79½ lb. (34–36 kg)

OTHER NAMES: Great Anglo-French White-and-Black Hound

COLOR: Black and white, with occasional tan marks above eye and on thigh

COAT CARE: Low maintenance

DIET: High/very high consumption

The Grand Anglo-Français Blanc et Noir is the third type of Anglo-French Hound. It is most similar to the Grand Anglo-Français Tricolore but does not display any tan coloration in the coat except for occasional tan marks above the eye and on the thigh. The breed is typical of the Anglo-French Hound form in that it is athletic and strongly built with a sonorous bay and extremely keen scenting instinct.

The Anglo-French hounds come in two sizes, denoted by the presence or lack of either Grand or Great in the breed name, depending on which language is being used. Obviously, the Grand Hounds are the larger of the two varieties. The size reflects the type of game that the breed was expected to hunt—Grand Anglo-Français hounds were expected to deal with deer and wild boar, while their smaller relatives were used to hunt hare and other similar-sized quarry.

LEFT
The Grand Anglo-Français Blanc et Noir, like other breeds with "Grand" or "Great" in their name, were expected to hunt large prey, such as deer.

BEAUCERON

OFFICIAL CATEGORIZATION: UK: Working, AKC: Herding, FCI: Group 1, Section 1

HEIGHT: 24½–27½ in. (65–70 cm) WEIGHT: 66–85 lb. (30–38.5 kg)

OTHER NAMES: French Shorthaired Shepherd, Beauce Shepherd

COLOR: Black and tan

COAT CARE: Low maintenance

DIET: High/very high consumption

The Beauceron is a sturdy and strong herding breed that originated in France and, it is thought, became established around the sixteenth century. It is typically black and tan in coloration with a moderately thick coat. Commonly for most pastoral dog breeds, the Beauceron is intelligent and dedicated to its work. It carries itself with assured confidence and ease of movement. The dog is very versatile and has good guardian instincts that complement the more traditional herding that it was bred to do. The breed was also employed by the French in both World Wars as a messenger dog.

The Beauceron is a calm breed that displays obedience and cooperation in work and in the domestic environment. It can be trained in all types of activities from agility to obedience and tends to excel at whatever it is asked to do. It is typically lively and friendly.

GREAT PYRENEES

COLOR: White or white with markings of gray, badger, reddish brown, or varying shades of tan

COAT CARE: High maintenance

DIET: High/very high consumption

OFFICIAL CATEGORIZATION: UK: Pastoral, AKC: Working, FCI: Group 2, Section 2

HEIGHT: 26–29 in. (66–73.5 cm)   **WEIGHT:** 108–112½ lb. (49–51 kg)

OTHER NAMES: Pyrenean Mountain Dog, Chien des Pyrénées

The Great Pyrenees, or Pyrenean Mountain Dog as it is known in some countries, is a large herding breed established in France, although it is thought to have its origins either in Eastern Europe or Asia, with the Hungarian Kuvasz being one likely ancestor. The Great Pyrenees is similar in many ways to the Newfoundland but is less capable in water. The breed has a double, very thick coat that protected it from the cold of the mountain terrain in which it was put to work guarding and herding sheep. Despite being primarily a herding breed, the Great Pyrenees is a confident and willing guard of both the flock and home.

Affectionate and Devoted Pet

The Great Pyrenees makes an excellent, devoted family pet. However, it has the size and strength to be a genuine threat to the safety of any intruders and may exhibit suspicion of newcomers if not properly trained and socialized. Conversely, it is gentle and affectionate by nature, although some dogs will exhibit slight stubbornness. The Great Pyrenees has an aura of seriousness and calm confidence but can transform into a dedicated protector of the family if provoked.

BELOW LEFT
The Great Pyrenees takes two years to mature, so be prepared for life with a giant puppy for some months.

An owner will need to be firm but patient with the dog, because it tends to adapt to new commands and environments in its own time. A comfortable and secure Great Pyrenees will be a placid and easy-going pet, but the breed typically does not mature until at least two years old, so puppy exuberance from a large dog such as this may be a challenge to some. The Great Pyrenees is sociable when secure and is affectionate, patient, and gentle with children of all ages, as well as generally being tolerant of cats and other pets.

Fascinating Facts

The Great Pyrenees has a double dewclaw, a feature that makes the breed distinguishable from similar-looking breeds.

GRAND GASCON SAINTONGEOIS

OFFICIAL CATEGORIZATION: UK: Not recognized,
AKC: Not recognized, FCI: Group 6, Section 1

HEIGHT: 25½–28 in. (62–68 cm)   WEIGHT: 75–79½ lb. (34–36 kg)

OTHER NAMES: Virelade Hound

COLOR: White flecked with black spots

COAT CARE: Zero maintenance

DIET: High consumption

This large French hunting hound descends from the Grand Bleu de Gascogne and is a rare breed scarcely seen outside of its native France. It displays a powerful and agile physique, ideal for chasing and hunting large game. It has a distinctive coat of white with black ticks and tan colorations about the face.

As with many working hunt hounds, the Grand Gascon Saintongeois is sociable and thrives in the company of other dogs. Due to its rarity and strong working heritage, it does not display any uniformly petlike characteristics but is not unsuited to domestic living; in fact, the Grand Gascon Saintongeois is a popular pet in certain parts of France. It is loyal and biddable with a strong instinct for hunting, which suits it to a rural environment. It is typically more interested in tracking scent than settling down in front of the fire and will thrive when allowed frequent access to the outdoors.

KOOIKERHONDJE

OFFICIAL CATEGORIZATION: UK: Gun Dog,
AKC: Not recognized, FCI: Group 8, Section 2

HEIGHT: 14–16 in. (35–40 cm)   WEIGHT: 20–24 lb. (9–11 kg)

OTHER NAMES: Kooiker Hound, Small Dutch Waterfowl Dog, Dutch Decoy Dog

COLOR: Clear orange-red patches on white with black-tipped ears

COAT CARE: Moderate/high maintenance

DIET: Moderate consumption

The Kooikerhondje is a Dutch tolling dog that was bred to hunt waterfowl, especially ducks. It is a small, agile breed that is typically colored white and

tan with distinctive black-tipped ears. Some puppies are born in tricolor but these are ineligible for conformation. The breed's ancestry is traced back to the sixteenth century but it was not established formally until the mid-twentieth century. After World War II, the breed was nearly in danger of extinction. Due to the depletion of duck stocks in Europe after the war, the Kooikerhondje did not have a job and subsequently breeding declined.

As a pet, the Kooikerhondje is a popular choice for many and has been established as a pet breed for centuries. It is confident, friendly, and generally interested in what is going on around it. It is typically suspicious of new people, but once happy with their presence will be a loyal and dedicated friend.

LEFT
The Kooikerhondje was bred to hunt ducks, but following World War II there was not much call for this breed.

DUTCH SMOUSHOND

OFFICIAL CATEGORIZATION: UK: Not recognized,
AKC: Not recognized, FCI: Group 2, Section 1

COLOR: Straw yellow

COAT CARE: High maintenance

DIET: Moderate consumption

HEIGHT: 14–17 in. (35–42 cm)   WEIGHT: 20–22 lb. (9–10 kg)

OTHER NAMES: Hollandse Smoushond

The Dutch Smoushond is a rare breed of terrier that displays a thick double coat on a sturdy and compact body. The breed's origins are in the Netherlands, where it was bred as a ratting dog. Never widely popular as a breed, the Dutch Smoushond has been subject to breeding programs to save it from almost total extinction. The modern Dutch Smoushond is a friendly intelligent breed with strong working instincts.

As a lively, alert, and eager-to-please breed, the Dutch Smoushond does make an excellent pet, but there is little interest in it outside of its

RIGHT
A rare ratting terrier, the Dutch Smoushund has never become widely popular as a breed.

native Netherlands. It is intelligent and feisty, but gentle and compassionate around children. The breed sometimes displays shyness around strangers but the degree to which this manifests itself differs between individual dogs. It is generally companionable and, once comfortable in the presence of a new person, will be a lively and involved pet dog.

SCHAPENDOES

COLOR: All colors accepted—black or gray preferred

COAT CARE: High maintenance

DIET: Moderate/high consumption

OFFICIAL CATEGORIZATION: UK: Not recognized,
AKC: Not recognized, FCI: Group 1, Section 1

HEIGHT: 17–20 in. (43–51 cm)   WEIGHT: 31–35 lb. (14–16 kg)

OTHER NAMES: None

The Schapendoes is a shaggy sheepdog native to the Netherlands. It has a distinctive thick and curly coat and well-proportioned physique. The Schapendoes is relatively unknown, especially outside of its native country. It is descended from the same breeding stock as the Briard and does bear a slight resemblance to that French breed. Certain Dutch breeds have associations with royalty, but the Schapendoes has long been associated with the working classes of the Netherlands and is considered something of a "people's dog."

The Schapendoes is thought to be a good herder but is often overlooked in favor of the Border Collie. As a pet, the Schapendoes makes a good companion, with natural intelligence and an obedient nature. Like many other pastoral breeds, it is prone to attempting to "herd" family members, so good training is important to prevent unsociable or inappropriate behavior.

KEESHOND

OFFICIAL CATEGORIZATION: UK: Utility,
AKC: nonsporting, FCI: Group 5, Section 4

HEIGHT: 16½–19½ in. (42–49.5 cm)   WEIGHT: 35–40 lb. (16–18 kg)

OTHER NAMES: Dutch Barge Dog, Smiling Dutchman, Wolfsspitz

COLOR: Mixture of gray, black, and cream

COAT CARE: High/very high maintenance

DIET: High consumption

The Keeshond is officially a German breed but with a very Dutch heritage. It was the official canine mascot of the Dutch rebellion against the House of Orange and is named in honor of the leader of the rebellion, Cornelis (Kees) de

Gyselaer. It is a descendent of the Samoyed and displays a resemblance to that breed. The Keeshond is typically dark gray in color, with luxurious, thick fur. It is compact and relatively small but not lightweight.

The breed's working history is as a barge dog, often performing all types of roles required on

the waterways of the Netherlands. It is lively and very intelligent and has a willingness to please.

The Keeshond is gentle and affectionate toward children and is generally adaptable in most domestic environments. It is known for its tendency to stick close to members of the family—this is a sign not of dependence but of dedication and affection.

STABYHOUN

OFFICIAL CATEGORIZATION: UK: Not recognized,
AKC: Not recognized, FCI: Group 7, Section 1

HEIGHT: 19½–22½ in. (49–57 cm)   WEIGHT: 50–55 lb. (23–25 kg)

OTHER NAMES: Stabij, Frisian Pointing Dog, Beike

COLOR: Black, brown, and orange with white markings

COAT CARE: Low/moderate maintenance

DIET: High consumption

The Stabyhoun is a versatile working gun dog native to the Netherlands. It is currently experiencing an increase in popularity as a pet, but its origin is as a dog of all trades. The Stabyhoun is a skilled pointer, retriever, and even mole catcher. It is a medium-sized breed, typically black and white in

color although orange and white or brown and white are also displayed. The breed has a medium-length sleek coat.

The Stabyhoun is an affectionate and somewhat tactile dog that displays great tenderness toward those close to it. Its intelligence and will

to please make it an excellent dog to train. It can function as a guard dog but will not become aggressive easily. It is even tempered and consistent in its behavior, but training needs to be ongoing to ensure that the Stabyhoun remembers all of its commands. The breed is easygoing and adaptable to many different lifestyles.

FRISIAN WATER DOG

COLOR: Black and white, liver and white, solid black, or solid liver

COAT CARE: Moderate maintenance

DIET: Moderate/high consumption

OFFICIAL CATEGORIZATION: UK: Not recognized, AKC: Not recognized, FCI: Group 8, Section 3

HEIGHT: 21½–23 in. (55–59 cm)   WEIGHT: 33–44 lb. (15–20 kg)

OTHER NAMES: Dutch Spaniel, Wetterhoun

The Frisian Water Dog, or Wetterhoun, is a Dutch breed of working gun dog that is closely related to the Stabyhoun. It is distinct from its relative due to its curly coat and generally hardier appearance, but is descended from the same breeding stock as the Stabyhoun. Although the Frisian Water Dog was bred initially as an all-purpose gun dog, is particularly useful in water and as a hunter of polecats. It is a strongly built breed and appears to show no fear when being faced with large or vicious opposition.

The Frisian Water Dog is a brave, watchful, and intelligent breed with strong protective instincts. It is independently minded and very eager to fend off any imposing animals in its territory. It is not suitable for inexperienced dog owners, however, it does display devotion and loyalty to its family. The Frisian Water Dog is a breed that demands a respectful approach during training.

DUTCH SHEPHERD DOG

COLOR: Silver brindle and gold brindle

COAT CARE: Low/moderate maintenance

DIET: High consumption

OFFICIAL CATEGORIZATION: UK: Not recognized, AKC: Not recognized, FCI: Group 1, Section 1

HEIGHT: 22–25 in. (56–64 cm)   WEIGHT: 55–67 lb. (29–30 kg)

OTHER NAMES: Hollandse Herder

The Dutch Shepherd Dog is a breed that is becoming increasingly popular as a working dog. It is well-known for its robust health and even temperament and is gaining popularity among police forces in the United States and Europe. It is a well-built, medium-sized dog that displays either a long, short or wirehaired coat. It has a very symmetrical frame and a proud stance. Like most pastoral and herding breeds, it is a versatile worker and can adapt to new and differing requirements. It is very similar physically to the Belgian Shepherd, but also has an amount of German Shepherd Dog blood.

This is a breed of supreme intelligence and temperament. It is outgoing and friendly with a keen will to obey. It has an even temper and is rarely flustered. Around people the Dutch Shepherd Dog is gentle and sometimes affectionate, but always friendly. It is protective over territory and family.

RIGHT
The Dutch Shepherd Dog, being very intelligent, is becoming ever more popular among police forces in the United States and Europe.

DRENTSE PARTRIDGE DOG

OFFICIAL CATEGORIZATION: UK: Not recognized,
AKC: Not recognized, FCI: Group 7, Section 1

HEIGHT: 22–25 in. (55–63 cm)   WEIGHT: 44–55 lb. (20–25 kg)

OTHER NAMES: Drentse Patrijshond, Dutch Partridge Dog

COLOR: White with brown or orange markings

COAT CARE: Low/moderate maintenance

DIET: High consumption

In sixteenth-century Netherlands, hunting was a privilege rarely enjoyed by commoners. Those that were permitted to hunt could rarely afford a pack of dogs, each with its speciality, so various multi-purpose breeds were created that could function in different roles. The **Drentse Partridge Dog, or Drentse Partijshond as it is also known, was bred from spaniels to perform on hunts. It still has a loosely spaniel-like appearance, but to those familiar with the breed it is easily distinguished. It is fast, strong, and agile with a good instinct for many working roles.**

As a pet the Drentse Partridge Dog is an even-tempered, loyal companion — generally intelligent and eager to please. The breed displays an unusual ability to adopt a domestic temperament when at home and a working temperament when in the field. It is gentle and affectionate to family members and particularly fond of children.

SAARLOOS WOLFDOG

OFFICIAL CATEGORIZATION: UK: Not recognized,
AKC: Not recognized, FCI: Group 1, Section 1

HEIGHT: 23–29 in. (60–75 cm)   WEIGHT: 66–77 lb. (30–35 kg)

OTHER NAMES: Saarlooswolfhond, Saarloos Wolf Hound

COLOR: Wolf gray, white, brown, or cream

COAT CARE: High/very high maintenance

DIET: High consumption

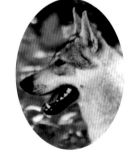

The Saarloos Wolfdog is now an established breed that is a direct descendent of the European Wolf and the German Shepherd Dog. It has a distinctly lupine appearance and exhibits various wild behaviors that are instinctive. It is named in honor of its Dutch creator, Leendert Saarloos. **The breed in some instances is indistinguishable from a wolf and as such has many admirers and owners. It is not a breed that is suited to all situations, but the ever-versatile German Shepherd Dog blood has enabled** the breed to perform as an assistance dog and on the conformation circuit.

The Saarloos Wolfdog is distinctively quiet and is quick to recognize weakness in a pack and assume leadership — a survival instinct inherited directly from the wolf. Although semi-wild in origin, the Saarloos Wolfdog is affectionate and friendly toward those with whom it is close. It exhibits wolf and dog body language simultaneously.

POMERANIAN

COLOR: All colors, patterns, and variations

COAT CARE: High maintenance

DIET: Moderate consumption

OFFICIAL CATEGORIZATION: UK: Toy, AKC: Toy, FCI: Group 5, Section 4

HEIGHT: 7–12 in. (18–30 cm)   WEIGHT: 3–7 lb. (1–3 kg.)

OTHER NAMES: Deutscher Zwergspitz, Toy German Spitz, Zwers

The Pomeranian is a popular toy breed of dog that is descended from northern European Spitz breeds. Its origins are in the region of Pomerania, which borders eastern Germany and northern Poland. The breed is small but has typical Spitz characteristics, including the thick coat and upwardly pointing ears. The Pomeranian is a well-proportioned, lightly boned breed. It is deceptive in appearance, often seeming larger due to its thick double coat.

The Pomeranian descends from companion breeds and other, larger herding and sledding breeds. It has been bred down to suit the

RIGHT

A descendant of other sledding varieties of Spitz, the Pomeranian has been bred to be small to suit its companion role.

companion role for which it was intended. The breed is lively and affectionate, but certain examples can be overly sensitive and demanding. It is the ideal dog for an owner who can devote a lot of attention, affection, and time. This agile and alert breed can function very well as a watchdog but is best suited to the role of cherished pet.

GERMAN SPITZ (Klein)

COLOR: All varieties

COAT CARE: High/very high maintenance

DIET: Moderate consumption

OFFICIAL CATEGORIZATION: UK: Utility, AKC: Not recognized, FCI: Group 5, Section 4

HEIGHT: 9–11½ in. (23–29 cm)   WEIGHT: 18–22 lb. (8–10 kg)

OTHER NAMES: Deutscher Spitz, Kleinspitz

The German Spitz (Klein), or Kleinspitz, is one of a number of German Spitz breeds. The Klein is small and is similar in appearance to the Pomeranian, which is also sometimes classed as a German Spitz. It is well-proportioned with a distinctively foxy face, thick, woolly fur, and the pointed ears that are typical of almost all Spitz-type dogs. It is generally seen in many solid colors but does also display sable and bicolor. It is descended from the Samoyed, which is believed to have been introduced to Germany by the Vikings. It is part of a very large family of dogs that are popular all over the world.

The German Spitz (Klein) is an intelligent and vivacious breed with a very loving and affectionate temperament. It is intelligent, bold, and always alert. It may be wary of strangers at first but is generally sociable.

AFFENPINSCHER

OFFICIAL CATEGORIZATION: UK: Toy, AKC: Toy,
FCI: Group 2, Section 1

HEIGHT: 9½–11½ in. (24–28 cm)   WEIGHT: 6½–9 lb. (3–4 kg)

OTHER NAMES: Monkey Dog

COLOR: Black, gray, silver, red, or black and tan

COAT CARE: Moderate maintenance

DIET: Moderate consumption

The Affenpinscher is a unique-looking dog. The name translates from German as "Monkey Dog" and it is easy to see why—the distinctive facial shape and shaggy growth of fur give this breed a curious expression. It is considered to be a descendant of the Brussels Griffon but this is unconfirmed. Originally kept as a ratting dog, the Affenpinscher has typical terrier-like qualities and is a tenacious dog.

The breed is now smaller than it was in its working days. This is due to a deliberate process of down breeding that has made the once-large and active ratting breed into a more manageable domestic companion. The Affenpinscher is alert, lively, and exhibits an eager working instinct. It tends to be a very sociable dog with an affectionate disposition toward children. However, it can become very excitable and is prone to exhibiting protective behavior around toys and food.

MINIATURE PINSCHER

OFFICIAL CATEGORIZATION: UK: Toy, AKC: Toy,
FCI: Group 2, Section 1

HEIGHT: 10–12 in. (25–30 cm)   WEIGHT: 9–13 lb. (4–6 kg)

OTHER NAMES: Zwergpinscher

COLOR: Red, stag red (red flecked with black), or black and tan/rust

COAT CARE: Minimal maintenance

DIET: Moderate consumption

The Miniature Pinscher is a German dog that is classified as a toy breed, despite the word Pinscher meaning "terrier." Originally, the breed was a working terrier but has since been classified as a companion breed. It is relatively large compared to other toy breeds, exhibiting a sleek frame, short red or black-and-tan coat, and pricked ears. The dog is a bred-down version of its close relative the Pinscher and has a notably high-stepping gait. Despite a resemblance to the Doberman the two breeds are not related.

Today's Miniature Pinscher is dainty yet tenacious and still retains strong ratting instincts. It is a lively and agile breed of dog with a vivacious personality. It can be highly strung but this is mostly due to environment rather than uniform breed characteristics. It is loyal and dedicated but does not tolerate being pestered if seeking solitude.

LEFT
Despite resembling a Doberman, the Miniature Pinscher is unrelated, instead descending from terriers.

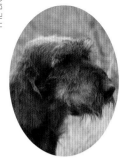

DACHSHUND

OFFICIAL CATEGORIZATION: UK: Hound, AKC: Hound, FCI: Group 4, Section 1

COLOR: All colors

COAT CARE: Low/moderate maintenance

DIET: Moderate consumption

HEIGHT: 14 in. (35 cm)

WEIGHT: 20–26 lb. (9–12 kg)

OTHER NAMES: Sausage Dog

There are essentially six types of Dachshund because they come in two sizes and each size exhibits three different coat types. The sizes are miniature and standard/normal and the coat types are shorthaired, wire-haired, and longhaired. These distinguishing factors are enough to warrant a breed variation but not significant enough for there to be separate breed classifications, as seen with Norwich Terriers and Norfolk Terriers, despite the belief that the wirehaired Dachshund is typically more outgoing than the other varieties. The breed has a distinctive head shape, with long pendulous ears and large, alert eyes.

ABOVE
Dachshunds' coats can be shorthaired, wirehaired, or longhaired.

A Hunter
The Dachshund is a long-bodied dog, originally bred for hunting. Its first quarry was badger, from which the Dachshund derives its name—*dachs* translated from German into English means "badger" and *hund* means "dog." The miniature Dachshund was bred to have shorter legs in order for it to be able to enter badger sets and, latterly, to hunt and kill smaller prey, such as hare and stoat.

An Independent Nature
The breed is typically tenacious and alert, with strong hunting instincts. Around people it is loyal and protective but can be very eager on doing its own thing. It is lively, curiou,s and sometimes mischievous, with a knack for finding trouble. The Dachshund is sociable to a degree but does better with children who are old enough to read the dog's body language and leave it alone if necessary because it can be sensitive. Despite being very intelligent, it is difficult to train and will only respond to stimuli as and when it is so inclined. Despite this, the breed is a good companion animal and offers much joy and fun to the family.

GERMAN SPITZ (Mittel)

OFFICIAL CATEGORIZATION: UK: Utility, AKC: Not recognized,
FCI: Group 5, Section 4

HEIGHT: 12–15 in. (30–38 cm)   WEIGHT: 15½–24 lb. (7–11 kg)

OTHER NAMES: Mittelspitz, Standard German Spitz

COLOR: All varieties

COAT CARE: High maintenance

DIET: Moderate consumption

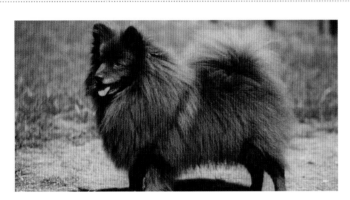

The German Spitz (Mittel), or Standard German Spitz, is a member of the German Spitz group of dogs and is the middle-sized variety. Like its close relatives, it is typical of the Spitz-type dogs from which it descends. The breed shares the distinctive facial characteristics of the Samoyed and displays the thick double coat that is associated with many northern European Spitz breeds. Unlike the Klein variety, the Mittel has been used for work in the past, mainly as a farm worker, where it was expected to deal with vermin and perform general watchdog work.

As a pet, the breed is popular in its native Germany (while its close relative the Pomeranian is popular outside of Germany). The breed generally is even tempered but can become uncomfortable if not left alone when required. It is important that children are aware of and respect the independent nature of this breed.

WESTPHALIAN DACHSBRACKE

OFFICIAL CATEGORIZATION: UK: Not recognized, AKC: Not
recognized, FCI: Group 6, Section 1

HEIGHT: 11–15 in. (30–38 cm)   WEIGHT: 31–35 lb. (14–16 kg)

OTHER NAMES: None

COLOR: Red to yellow with a black saddle or mantle, plus typical white hound markings

COAT CARE: Minimal maintenance

DIET: Moderate consumption

The Westphalian Dachsbracke is a short-legged hunting breed native to Germany. It was once a favorite of German royalty and still has regal associations today. The breed was used to hunt fox, hare, and boar in the snow and has an excellent sense of smell. It is a descendant of the Dachshund and displays a white, black, and tan tricolor. Unlike many scent hounds, the nimble and agile Westphalian Dachsbracke has quite a slender and noble head.

The breed is predominantly associated with working and is not particularly well-distributed as a pet dog. Its nature is loyal and affable but with strong hunting instincts that are inclined to take over. The Westphalian Dachsbracke is obedient and eager to work and generally is considered friendly and smart. The breed, if kept as a pet, would need firm training because it can be obstinate and strong-willed, especially when exposed to a scent.

LEFT
The Westphalian Dachsbracke was bred to hunt prey of varying sizes: fox, hare, and boar.

MINIATURE SCHNAUZER

COLOR: Salt and pepper, black and silver, or solid black

COAT CARE: Moderate/high maintenance

DIET: Moderate/high consumption

OFFICIAL CATEGORIZATION: UK: Utility, AKC: Terrier, FCI: Group 2, Section 1

HEIGHT: 12.5–15½ in. (32–39½ cm)   WEIGHT: 15½–20 lb. (7–9 kg)

OTHER NAMES: Zwergschnauzer

The Miniature Schnauzer is the smallest of the three Schnauzer varieties. The Schnauzer breed gets its name from the German word *schnauze*, which means "snout"—this is in reference to its elongated and pronounced muzzle. It was established as a breed in its own right in the nineteenth century after selective down breeding from the then-Standard Schnauzer and various Poodle varieties. It has a distinctive, tightly curled coat, which is indicative of the Poodle breeding stock. The breed is very popular worldwide.

The Miniature Schnauzer has a compact and sturdy little body with a very characteristic and unusual growth of fur on its face, which gives the impression that it has a beard, moustache, and bushy eyebrows. It also has very folded, triangular ears that frame the face in a distinctive manner.

Independent But Protective

The Miniature Schnauzer has a working history of vermin control in rural Germany. However, as a pet it is a useful watchdog and guard dog. It is naturally protective over its home territory and will question the presence of any new people or animals until it is confident that they are welcomed by its owner. It has a natural affection for children but can become irritated by incessant fussing, so it is important for children to be aware of the dog's limitations.

Certain examples of the breed can display a degree of neediness—this is often a sign of boredom or under-stimulation and should be addressed with training and play. The Miniature Schnauzer is an intelligent breed and will not be happy if left alone for extended periods of time. However, it is quite independent and capable of indicating when it wants to socialize and when it wants to be left to its own devices.

ABOVE

The Miniature Schnauzer's name comes from the German schnauze *meaning "snout" on account of its longhaired muzzle.*

KROMFOHRLÄNDER

OFFICIAL CATEGORIZATION: UK: Not recognized,
AKC: Not recognized, FCI: Group 9, Section 10

HEIGHT: 15–18 in. (38–46 cm)   WEIGHT: 22–31 lb. (10–14 kg)

OTHER NAMES: Länder, Krom

COLOR: White with brown markings ranging from dark to light

COAT CARE: Low maintenance

DIET: Moderate consumption

The Kromfohrländer is a relatively new breed of dog originating in Germany in the mid-twentieth century. It was the result of an accidental breeding of two crossbreeds but, due to a careful process of breeding and outbreeding, has become established as a breed in its own right, despite criticism that the dog is lacking any uniformity associated with recognized breeds. It is believed that the original parents were a Grand Basset Griffon Vendeen and a Fox Terrier.

Used for hunting by its founder, it is not a particularly well-established breed outside of Germany due to the short length of time that it has been in existence, but it is very popular among hunters in some parts of that country. The Kromfohrländer is easy to train and generally friendly toward most people, although it is not overly affectionate with very young children.

GERMAN SPANIEL

OFFICIAL CATEGORIZATION: UK: Not recognized,
AKC: Not recognized, FCI: Group 8, Section 2

HEIGHT: 19–21½ in. (48–54 cm)   WEIGHT: 42–46½ lb. (19–21 kg)

OTHER NAMES: Deutscher Wachtelhund, German Quail Dog

COLOR: Solid dark brown with white spots on the chest and toes or with tan markings

COAT CARE: Low/moderate maintenance

DIET: High consumption

The German Spaniel, or Deutscher Wachtelhund as it is known in its native land, is a large-boned, sturdy working spaniel. The name *wachtelhund* translates as "quail dog," in reference to the game that the dog was associated with during its early working days. It is descended from numerous water-spaniel breeds but is closely associated with field work. It is well-built and strong, especially for its size, which is slightly larger than the English Springer Spaniel.

This breed is a versatile worker, adept at retrieving large prey, flushing, and even tracking. It has a very good scenting ability and is skilled in the hunt. It is hardy and rustic, able to work in all weathers and terrains; it has been used to work in thick swampland in the past, which is a difficult environment for any breed. It is intelligent and obedient but requires firm and consistent training.

LEFT
The German Spaniel, or Deutscher Wachtelhund, is descended from several breeds of water spaniel.

GERMAN HUNTING TERRIER

COLOR: Black, with brown or reddish tan markings

COAT CARE: Minimal maintenance

DIET: High consumption

OFFICIAL CATEGORIZATION: UK: Not recognized, AKC: Not recognized, FCI: Group 3, Section 1

HEIGHT: 13–15½ in. (33–40 cm)   WEIGHT: 20–22 lb. (9–10 kg)

OTHER NAMES: Deutscher Jagdterrier, German Jagdterrier

The German Hunting Terrier is an exceptionally skilled working breed native to Germany. It was bred using Fox Terrier and Welsh Terrier breeding stock; it is also believed that the Dachshund contributed to the bloodline latterly. Typically, it is black and tan in color, with a stocky and well-proportioned body. It is an agile, tenacious, and **relentless hunting breed and is considered to be one of the best hunting terriers.**

Unlike the vast majority of terrier breeds, the German Hunting Terrier is not considered to be a suitable pet breed. Its tenacity, work drive, and high level of instinctive behavior mean that the breed would be unhappy in a domestic environment. It is loyal, courageous, and intelligent but is only stimulated by the hunt. Although occasionally the breed may show affection to its owner, it is a fearless animal and will not back down, which makes it extremely difficult to domesticate.

GERMAN HOUND

COLOR: Dark reddish fawn, may be slightly smoky with black tips, or black and tan

COAT CARE: Minimal maintenance

DIET: Moderate/high consumption

OFFICIAL CATEGORIZATION: UK: Not recognized, AKC: Not recognized, FCI: Group 6, Section 1

HEIGHT: 14½–15 in. (37–38 cm)   WEIGHT: 42–46½ lb. (19–21 kg)

OTHER NAMES: Deutsche Bracke

The German Hound is an ancient breed but it did not become standardized until 1955. Until then there was little uniformity within the breed and the dog was bred for function over form. It is hardy and solidly built but not overly heavy. The coat is typically black, red, fawn, white, or a combination of **these. The German Hound has large, pendulous ears and a face that is characteristic of many scenting hounds.**

The breed was used originally for chasing down game in mountainous areas and consequently was bred to be athletic and possess high levels of stamina. The German Hound is an enthusiastic and conscientious hunter, tackling large game with style and grace. Its even and affable temperament make it a suitable pet but it retains a strong working instinct and is particularly happy when out in the open, although it is adaptable.

BELOW
The Deutsche Bracke is a hardy, athletic dog, suitable for pursuing game across mountainous regions.

GERMAN SPITZ (Giant)

OFFICIAL CATEGORIZATION: UK: Not recognized,
AKC: Not recognized, FCI: Group 5, Section 4

COLOR: Black, white or brown

COAT CARE: Moderate/high maintenance

HEIGHT: 16–17 in. (40.5–41.5 cm) WEIGHT: 38½–40 lb. (17.5–18.5 kg)

OTHER NAMES: Deutscher Grossespitz

DIET: Moderate/high consumption

The German Spitz (Giant), or Grossespitz, is the largest of the German Spitz breeds. It is solid in color, exhibiting either brown, black, or white, and bears the typical look of a northern European Spitz breed. It has a thick double coat, erect ears, and a solid but not heavy body. It has large eyes and short hair about the head and a curled-over tail typical of the majority of Spitz-type dogs.

The breed is playful and energetic. It makes a good watchdog because it is alert and instinctively territorial but this does not extend to instant aggression toward strangers. It is a lively dog and is always interested in interacting with people or other dogs—it rarely sits by itself out of the way. Although not unintelligent, the breed is not easy to train and requires consistent and conscientious training.

GERMAN PINSCHER

OFFICIAL CATEGORIZATION: UK: Working, AKC: Working,
FCI: Group 2, Section 1

COLOR: Fawn (Isabella) to stag red in various shades, or black and tan

COAT CARE: Zero maintenance

HEIGHT: 17–19 in. (43–48 cm) WEIGHT: 25–35 lb. (11–16 kg)

OTHER NAMES: Deutscher Pinscher

DIET: High consumption

The German Pinscher is an old breed that is present in the bloodlines of some of the more well-known German dog breeds, including the Doberman, Miniature Pinscher, Affenpinscher, and all three varieties of Schnauzer. It is typically lean and well-muscled with a short coat and erect ears. The face is slender, but not to the extent that is typical of the Doberman. The German Pinscher typically exhibits a solid coloration—commonly tan, black, brown, red, or blue. It was worked as a hunting terrier breed but has adapted to become a reliable companion animal.

Although highly intelligent and sociable, the German Pinscher exhibits willfulness on occasion and training must counteract this undesirable trait. While of hunting origin, the breed can be trusted in the open. The typical German Pinscher will be a friendly and adaptable dog, but some examples are instinctively quiet and watchful, making for effective guard dogs.

LEFT
The German Pinscher has been used to develop several new breeds, including the Doberman Pinscher.

SCHNAUZER

COLOR: Pepper and salt or pure black

COAT CARE: Moderate/high maintenance

DIET: Moderate/high consumption

OFFICIAL CATEGORIZATION: UK: Utility, AKC: Working, FCI: Group 2, Section 1

HEIGHT: 17.5–20½ in. (44½–52 cm)   WEIGHT: 30–45 lb. (14–20 kg)

OTHER NAMES: Mittelschnauzer, Standard Schnauzer

The Schnauzer, or Standard Schnauzer as it is also known, is the median-sized variety of the popular German herding breed. It is a well-proportioned and solid breed with a distinctively harsh and wiry coat. The face is well-furnished with fur, giving the dog a "beard" and "eyebrows." The Schnauzer, like the other two varieties within the breed, is a heavy-boned dog. The ears are angular, cropped in some countries but left natural in others.

The Schnauzer is a popular pet throughout the United States and Europe. It is intelligent, retaining many of its original herding instincts, but it is also an adaptable and even-tempered breed, making it suitable for most family environments. It is friendly, sociable, and affectionate and thrives on interaction with family members—which means it may become distressed if isolated for too long. Although generally friendly, the Schnauzer may initially be reserved around new people.

Fascinating Facts

The Dutch artist Rembrandt was a fan of the Standard Schnauzer and featured the breed in his works.

SMALL MUNSTERLANDER

COLOR: Large patches of brown on a ticked or solid white background

COAT CARE: Low/moderate maintenance

DIET: High consumption

OFFICIAL CATEGORIZATION: UK: Not recognized, AKC: Not recognized, FCI: Group 7, Section 1

HEIGHT: 45–50 in. (18–20 cm)   WEIGHT: 33–37½ lb. (15–17 kg)

OTHER NAMES: Kleiner Münsterländer, Kleiner Munsterlander Vorstehund

The Small Munsterlander is a German breed of dog descended from traditional working pointer breeds, including the English Setter and German Pointer. It is the smaller of the Munsterlander type and is the more popular breed. It became established as a breed in the nineteenth century and is a popular working and pet dog today. It is well-built but not overly heavy, with a coat typically of white with brown patches of grizzled hair; the face and head are black.

The Small Munsterlander is a skilled and valued hunt, point, and retrieve breed. It is well-known for keeping close to the huntsman and having an especially reliable point. As a pet, the breed is eager and enthusiastic about its family—playful and energetic, but not overly so. It is conscientious in training and rarely behaves out of turn. It is an intelligent and skilled animal that will adapt to domestic life.

LEFT
The Small Munsterlander is a popular working dog and renowned for its particularly accurate point.

EURASIA

OFFICIAL CATEGORIZATION: UK: Utility, AKC: Not recognized,
FCI: Group 5, Section 5

HEIGHT: 20½–23½ in. (52–60 cm)   WEIGHT: 51–70 lb. (23–32 kg)

OTHER NAMES: Eurasian

COLOR: Any

COAT CARE: Moderate/high maintenance

DIET: High consumption

The Eurasia, or Eurasian as it is sometimes called, is a newly established dog breed. It was created by crossing the Chow Chow and the Wolfspitz, although it resembles the latter more closely. It also has Samoyed contributions in its bloodline, which emphasizes an appearance that is typical of the Spitz type. It is a striking breed with a large, proud stance and thick double coat. The face is proud and dignified while retaining an expression of alertness that is commonly associated with the Siberian Husky.

As a pet, the Eurasia is friendly, calm, and even-tempered. It is notably clean and becomes uncomfortable if left ungroomed. The Eurasia has little or no tendency toward aggression but will defend itself if provoked. It is generally a welcoming dog, especially toward those with whom it has become familiar. With children the breed typically forms strong bonds of friendship that are exhibited through gentleness and affection.

ABOVE LEFT
The Eurasia, or Eurasian, is a clean-living dog that likes to be kept well groomed.

BAVARIAN MOUNTAIN HOUND

OFFICIAL CATEGORIZATION: UK: Not recognized,
AKC: Not recognized, FCI: Group 6, Section 2

HEIGHT: 18½–20½ in. (47–52 cm)   WEIGHT: 44–55 lb. (20–25 kg)

OTHER NAMES: Bayrischer Gebirgsschweisshund

COLOR: Black-masked fawn or brindle

COAT CARE: Moderate maintenance

DIET: Moderate/high consumption

The Bavarian Mountain Hound is a rare breed of impressive appearance. Well-built, giving the impression of athleticism and strength, the breed displays an attractive solid fawn or dark-brown colored coat, with darker coloration about the muzzle. The breed was established to work in tough terrain in the mountains of the German province of Bavaria and as a result is hardy and rugged.

The breed, while skilled in the hunt and highly instinctive, is docile and calm when not at work. It is an obedient and fast-learning dog with a high degree of intelligence. The Bavarian Mountain Hound is happiest when at work but will adapt to the domestic environment, particularly if given consistent and firm training from an experienced owner. The breed displays strong loyalty to its owner and is courageous in defending itself and those to whom it is close.

GERMAN SHORTHAIRED POINTER

COLOR: Solid liver or a combination of liver and white

COAT CARE: Minimal maintenance

DIET: High/very high consumption

OFFICIAL CATEGORIZATION: UK: Gun Dog, AKC: Sporting, FCI: Group 7, Section 1

HEIGHT: 23–25 in. (58–64 cm)   WEIGHT: 50–75 lb. (25–32 kg)

OTHER NAMES: Deutscher Kurzhaariger Vorstehhund, Kurzhaar

The German Short-Haired Pointer is a popular working gun-dog breed that is descended from the Spanish Pointer. It became established as a breed during the eighteenth century, but its popularity as a pet has increased greatly in recent years. It is a well-proportioned breed with a short coat, commonly exhibited in liver roan, solid liver, white with ticked liver, or white with liver saddle. The head typically is solid liver in color.

The breed makes an excellent family pet despite its very strong working instincts. It is typically very friendly and playful with a natural protectiveness toward children. When young it can be exuberant but it usually grows out of this behavior before full maturity. It is loyal and intelligent, with a very affectionate nature that makes it suitable for most family environments. The German Shorthaired Pointer requires patience but is intelligent and not difficult to train.

LEFT

This breed needs plenty of vigorous activity, so it must be well-trained to control its hunting instincts.

HANOVERIAN HOUND

COLOR: Light to dark reddish fawn

COAT CARE: Zero maintenance

DIET: High/very high consumption

OFFICIAL CATEGORIZATION: UK: Not recognized, AKC: Not recognized, FCI: Group 6, Section 2

HEIGHT: 19½–21½ in. (50–55 cm) WEIGHT: 66–77 lb. (30–35 kg) stocky

OTHER NAMES: Hanoverian Scenthound

The Hanoverian Hound is a large and rare descendent of the Bloodhound and Saint Hubert Hound. It is strong and well-proportioned with a distinguished short coat of dark reddish or fawn brindle. Some examples of the breed have a darker mask while others have consistent coloration throughout. The Hanoverian Hound has a large, slightly domed skull, giving the breed the impression of heaviness around the head.

The Hanoverian Hound is not typically a pack hound, more often seen working alone or in a pair. It is relentless in the hunt and is capable of catching deer and wild boar by itself. It has a keen sense of smell and a strong instinct and drive for its work, which makes it a very useful dog. To its owner it is loyal and obedient, with some examples of the breed showing more affection than others.

RIGHT

A Hanoverian Hound is such a dedicated hunter that it can catch a deer or wild boar by itself.

BOXER

OFFICIAL CATEGORIZATION: UK: Working, AKC: Working, FCI: Group 2, Section 2

HEIGHT: 23–25 in. (57.5–63 cm)   WEIGHT: 66–70 lb. (30–32 kg)

OTHER NAMES: None

COLOR: Fawn and brindle

COAT CARE: Minimal maintenance

DIET: High consumption

The Boxer is a very popular and well-known breed of dog, native to Germany. It is a descendent of the Bulldog and other now-extinct Molosser breeds. It has a short coat, commonly presented in white, fawn, and tan—either solid or brindled. The Boxer has a characteristically flat face that is very expressive. It is solidly proportioned and strongly built but should be lean and muscular, not heavy. The head is well-domed and a protruding lower jaw magnifies the distinctive face. In some parts of the world the ears are customarily cropped but in other places this is illegal.

The Boxer is descended from traditional fighting breeds and it too has a history of being used for fighting. Throughout history the Boxer has been used as a guard dog and was used during World War I by the German army.

Today, the breed is most commonly seen as a pet, although it does still play a small role in police forces around the world. Boxers, particularly those of solid-white coloration, are prone to certain cancers and deafness.

A Loving Companion

The breed is highly affectionate and loving, which contributes to its immense worldwide popularity. It has a tender nature toward its family and but would be problematic if presented by a full-grown adult. As a typically is playful and docile. A Boxer may greet a stranger at the door with suspicion but will await the response of other family members before exhibiting any protective behavior.

The Boxer is alert, energetic, and self-confident, but rarely aggressive without due provocation. It exhibits exuberance as a puppy that is endearing guard dog the Boxer is effective but not infallible.

Its loyalty and dedication to its family is extremely high and it will defend them tenaciously.

BELOW
Descended from some fighting breeds, and occasionally used in guard dog and police dog roles, Boxers today are more commonly kept as pets.

Fascinating Facts

The first examples of the Boxer breed were unveiled in 1895, at a show that was being staged to exhibit Saint Bernards.

PUDELPOINTER

COLOR: Liver, chestnut, and occasionally black

COAT CARE: Low/moderate maintenance

DIET: High consumption

OFFICIAL CATEGORIZATION: UK: Not recognized, AKC: Not recognized, FCI: Group 7, Section 1

HEIGHT: 21–26 in. (53–66 cm)   WEIGHT: 44–66 lb. (20–30 kg)

OTHER NAMES: None

The Pudelpointer is a breed of gun dog native to Germany that descends from the Poodle, English Pointer, and French Barbet. It is a medium-sized, well-proportioned dog with a dense and wiry coat. The intention was to create a hard-working and versatile gun-dog breed that was adept at tracking, pointing, and retrieving. Despite having been established since the nineteenth century, it is not a hugely stable breed and there is not great uniformity in working ability.

The breed has inherited a keen scenting ability and hunting instinct from the English Pointer and intelligence and a love of water from the Poodle. The breed is relatively popular as a pet and is friendly and biddable, typically showing affection to its owner.

WEIMARANER

COLOR: Shades of mouse gray to silver-gray

COAT CARE: Minimal maintenance

DIET: High consumption

OFFICIAL CATEGORIZATION: UK: Gun Dog, AKC: Sporting, FCI: Group 7, Section 1

HEIGHT: 25–27 in. (63.5–69 cm)   WEIGHT: 55–70 lb. (25–32 kg)

OTHER NAMES: Weimaraner Vorstehhund

With its silver coat and elegant face the Weimaraner is an instantly recognizable and striking breed of dog. It is a multi-purpose gun dog, medium in size with a short coat that exhibits a distinctive silver-gray or browny gray coloration, typically lighter about the ears. The breed is lean and athletic, well-proportioned, and agile. The Weimaraner has a noble head with large ears.

As a pet the breed is particularly popular. It is fiercely loyal, with the ability to defend itself and family members adequately. It is typically playful, bordering on the boisterous, and is noted for its spirited and energetic demeanor. Although the Weimaraner is intelligent and generally biddable, it can demonstrate an exuberance that, while good-spirited and friendly, may be destructive if left uncorrected for too long. The breed is generally affectionate and gentle toward children.

RIGHT
Despite its elegant good looks, the Weimaraner enjoys family life, children, and play.

GERMAN SHEPHERD DOG

OFFICIAL CATEGORIZATION: UK: Pastoral, AKC: Herding, FCI: Group 1, Section 1

HEIGHT: 23½–26½ in. (59.5–67.5 cm) **WEIGHT:** 75–95 lb. (34–43 kg)

OTHER NAMES: Alsatian, Deutscher Schäferhund

COLOR: Black or black saddle with tan, or gold to light gray markings

COAT CARE: Moderate/high maintenance

DIET: High/very high consumption

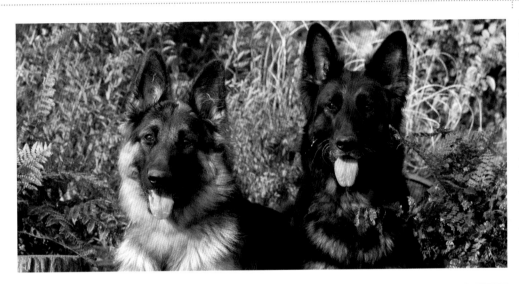

The German Shepherd Dog is a large, agile, and powerful herding breed, originating in the late nineteenth century and an extremely popular working and pet breed today. It displays either a longhaired or shorthaired coat in a variety of colors, ranging from dark brown and black, red and black, and black and tan to, less commonly, blue and black, and in some cases solid white. It is a well-built, lean dog with extreme agility and power. It is a popular breed for security and police work but, as the name suggests, it was developed initially for herding.

Due to its popularity, there are various genetic lines of the breed, each with their own typical characteristics. The American line of German Shepherd Dogs is distinct from eastern European lines in that the European lines have a characteristic prewar appearance that includes a notably straight back. The breed varies in size, with larger specimens being popular in the working environment and more manageable sizes selected for domestic life. It has a thick, normally black tail and a graceful yet very deliberate gait. It is intelligent and forthright, with a strong herding and protecting instinct; it is also an excellent tracking dog.

Fascinating Facts

The first ever German Shepherd Dog of modern type was born in 1899 and was called Horand von Grafrath.

ABOVE
The German Shepherd Dog's coat can be long- or shorthaired and can come in a variety of colors, although the tail tends to be black.

An Intelligent Protector
The breed is popular as a pet for many reasons. It is fearless and determined, with a high degree of intelligence. It is friendly with those that it knows and keen to defend its family and home from those that it does not. Gentle around children, the breed is playful and willing to please, with an adaptable nature that makes it easy to install into most environments. Its courage and reliability as a guard dog make it a popular choice for security work but also make it an excellent pet in a large home, as its natural instinct is to patrol its environment to keep it free from unwanted visitors.

ROTTWEILER

OFFICIAL CATEGORIZATION: UK: Working, AKC: Working, FCI: Group 2, Section 2

COLOR: Black with tan to mahogany markings, or solid black

COAT CARE: Minimal maintenance

DIET: Very high consumption

HEIGHT: 24–27 in. (60.5–69 cm) WEIGHT: 108–112½ lb. (49–51 kg)

OTHER NAMES: None

LEFT
Rottweilers have had some bad press, because, unfortunately, if they do turn on a human, their size and strength cause considerable injury.

The Rottweiler is a large and powerful breed native to Germany. It was bred as a herd guard and a traveling guard that would protect traders from robbery in between towns. It is well-built and heavy-set, yet athletic, with a short coat. The Rottweiler is typically black with a tan muzzle or all black. The jaw is strong, as is typical for breeds descended from the ancient Molosser types of dog. It has a proud stance and large head with a curious and interested expression. The breed is an extremely popular pet throughout the world.

A Bad Press
In more recent times, the Rottweiler's reputation has been damaged. The breed has been subject to political debate relating to dangerous dogs, notably in Britain. This is due mainly to irresponsible ownership of the breed, which has sadly led to incidents of biting.

Fascinating Facts

If Rottweilers are unhappy or feel that they are neglected, they often lose their appetite.

The Rottweiler is not an inherently aggressive breed, but if provoked to bite, it can and will inflict a lot of damage on the victim. Partly because of its power and strength, the breed is often attractive to the very people who should not own it.

Loyal and Affectionate
As a pet, the Rottweiler is an ambassador for large breeds. It is loyal, dedicated, and affectionate, with some exhibiting a confident and self-assured aura that borders on arrogance. It is not known to be as intelligent as a herding breed, but it does possess a sharp mind and alert nature. The Rottweiler is typically playful with familiar people but suspicious of those it does not know. It is rarely aggressive without due reason and in many cases the breed is docile and placid, even in tense situations. Its size makes it an effective deterrent to would-be intruders, but its guarding ability is somewhat hindered by its affectionate and gentle nature.

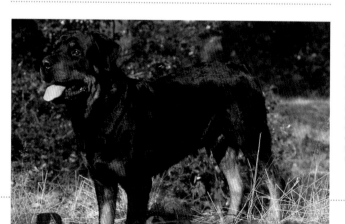

LARGE MUNSTERLANDER

OFFICIAL CATEGORIZATION: UK: Gun Dog,
AKC: Not recognized, FCI: Group 7, Section 1

HEIGHT: 23½–25½ in. (60–65 cm)   WEIGHT: 64–68½ lb. (29–31 kg)

OTHER NAMES: Grosser Munsterlander

COLOR: White or blue roan with black
patches—flecked, ticked, or
a combination of these

COAT CARE: Low/moderate
maintenance

DIET: High consumption

The Large Munsterlander is the less common variety of Munsterlander dog. The Munsterlander breed was established in the nineteenth century, but the small and large variations

were not denoted until the twentieth century. Descended from English pointing and setting breeds, the Large Munsterlander is square-built and powerful without being overly heavy. It has a dignified expression and a powerful and pronounced muzzle. Typically, it is colored black and white but occasionally exhibits fawn or brown markings.

It is a reliable and consistent working breed with a good pointing and tracking instinct. As a pet, it is gentle and affectionate. This breed was commonly kept by the hunt master even when used predominantly for work, so typically it is well-adjusted to the domestic environment. The Large Munsterlander is intelligent and refined with an ability to adapt to the environment around it.

HOVAWART

OFFICIAL CATEGORIZATION: UK: Working,
AKC: Not recognized, FCI: Group 2, Section 2

HEIGHT: 25–27½ in. (63–70 cm)   WEIGHT: 66–88 lb. (30–40 kg)

OTHER NAMES: None

COLOR: Black, black/gold,
or blonde

COAT CARE: Moderate/high
maintenance

DIET: High consumption

The Hovawart is an old breed of guardian dog native to the Black Forest region of Germany. It is considered to be a shining

example of diligent German breeding. The Hovawart bears a striking resemblance to the Golden Retriever, with which the modern Hovawart does share some ancestors, but the breeds have very different origins. The Hovawart was bred as an estate guard and, despite having a long heritage, it

went unnoticed for years, only to be reestablished in the mid-twentieth century.

The Hovawart is well-proportioned for agility and has a feathered coat. It is a versatile worker with good swimming skills, agile of body and mind and ever watchful. As a pet, the breed is friendly

and warm natured but often quiet; a barking Hovawart is a good indication that the dog is concerned about something. The breed is typically intelligent and very eager to take instruction.

LEFT
Native to the Black Forest region of Germany, the Hovawart is a traditional guard dog.

GERMAN ROUGH-HAIRED POINTING DOG

COLOR: No standard

COAT CARE: Moderate/high maintenance

DIET: High consumption

OFFICIAL CATEGORIZATION: UK: Not recognized, AKC: Not recognized, FCI: Group 7, Section 1

HEIGHT: No standard

WEIGHT: No standard

OTHER NAMES: None

The German Rough-Haired Pointing Dog is an old breed of working pointer very similar in appearance to the German Wirehaired Pointer—it even shares the same distinctive coat. The two breeds are distinguished due to the work that they were expected to perform, but they are of common ancestry. This breed is well-proportioned and athletic with strong pointing instincts. It is a considerably rare breed and is not recognized by the German Kennel Club authorities.

The German Rough-Haired Pointing Dog is similar in many ways to other pointing breeds and displays a keen sense of smell. Typical of pointers, the German Rough-Haired Pointing Dog makes a good domestic pet. It is eaager to please and is generally of high intelligence. The breed is considerate of and affectionate toward children and those with whom it is familiar. It is best suited to an owner with an active outdoor lifestyle.

> **RIGHT**
> *The German Rough-Haired Pointing Dog has strong working instincts, and a particularly strong point.*

GERMAN LONGHAIRED POINTER

COLOR: Solid brown with white markings, dark brown roan with brown patches, or white ticked with brown patches

COAT CARE: Moderate/high maintenance

DIET: High consumption

OFFICIAL CATEGORIZATION: UK: Gun Dog, AKC: Not recognized, FCI: Group 7, Section 1

HEIGHT: 24–28 in. (60–70 cm)

WEIGHT: 64–68½ lb. (29–31 kg)

OTHER NAMES: Deutscher Langhaariger

The German Longhaired Pointer is a breed of working gun dog. It is relatively rare when compared to the German Shorthaired Pointer or the Wirehaired Pointer, but is considered now to be a useful working dog. Early in the breed's development it was thought too slow, and English Setter blood was introduced to the breed to help improve its speed. It has a relatively thick and quite wavy coat, feathered ears, and typically is solid chocolate or brown in color.

The breed is friendly and affectionate and is known for being gentle toward children. It is an energetic, lively, and instinctive breed and, therefore, needs to be exercised adequately to avoid boredom and depression. The German Longhaired Pointer is a very social dog, both with people and other dogs, so is quite prone to suffering separation anxiety if left alone for extended periods of time.

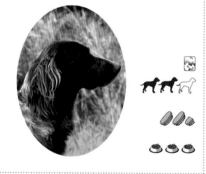

GIANT SCHNAUZER

OFFICIAL CATEGORIZATION: UK: Working, AKC: Working,
FCI: Group 2, Section 1

HEIGHT: 25½–27½ in. (65–70 cm)   WEIGHT: 70–99 lb. (32–45 kg)

OTHER NAMES: Riesenschnauzer, Russian Bear Schnauzer

COLOR: Pure black or pepper and salt

COAT CARE: Moderate maintenance

DIET: High consumption

The Giant Schnauzer is the largest variety of the Schnauzer breed and is a solidly built and distinctive-looking dog. It is a descendant of the Standard Schnauzer and was bred using the Great Dane to create a dog with desirable Schnauzer attributes but with more power and strength. The Giant Schnauzer has a coarse wiry coat that either is clipped very short or left to grow to a medium length. It was originally used to work as a herding and droving breed but is a versatile and adaptable dog that has been of use to many, including various police forces, throughout its working history.

The breed's loyalty and affection sometimes causes it to become very attached to its owner, often following them around the home. The Giant Schnauzer is a popular pet and is very intelligent. It is open to training early on but, while generally obedient, can be independently minded at times.

GERMAN WIREHAIRED POINTER

OFFICIAL CATEGORIZATION: UK: Gun Dog, AKC: Sporting,
FCI: Group 7, Section 1

HEIGHT: 23½–26½ in. (60–67 cm)   WEIGHT: 55–75 lb. (25–34 kg)

OTHER NAMES: Deutsch Drahthaar

COLOR: Liver and white, solid liver, or black and white

COAT CARE: Moderate maintenance

DIET: High consumption

The German Wire-haired Pointer is a skilled working dog that has been bred to work in cold weather and water. It is a well-built, athletic dog that possesses a strong hunting instinct. It is typical of many hunt, point and retrieve breeds and is thus a versatile hunting companion. It became established as a breed in the twentieth century and is a descendant of the English Foxhound. The coat is coarse and wiry, making it water-resistant, and typically is of liver and white roan or ticked coloration.

LEFT
German Wirehaired Pointers have been bred for a coat that can withstand water and still keep the dog warm in cold temperatures.

The German Wirehaired Pointer is an intelligent and skilled working breed that has adapted well to domestic life. It is a lively and active pet with an alert nature, which makes it a useful watchdog. The breed requires a good level of stimulation to prevent it from becoming bored and roaming off; it has the potential to become is very boisterous.

DOBERMAN PINSCHER

COLOR: Black, red, blue, or fawn (Isabella)

COAT CARE: Minimal maintenance

DIET: High consumption

OFFICIAL CATEGORIZATION: UK: Working, AKC: Working, FCI: Group 2, Section 1

HEIGHT: 25½–28½ in. (65–72.5 cm) WEIGHT: 75–90 lb. (34–50 kg)

OTHER NAMES: Doberman

The Doberman Pinscher is a lean and athletic dog, originally bred by a tax collector for his protection. The breeding stock used included the Manchester Terrier, German Pinscher, Greyhound, and Rottweiler, giving it a winning combination of intelligence, tenacity, strength, and speed. It is either black and tan or brown and tan in color and has a short, smooth coat and slender, elongated face. It is a popular pet throughout the world.

Since its original working days, the Doberman Pinscher has been subject to breeding practices that have diluted its original tenacity and highly protective instincts. Although it is still a competent and willing guardian, this is not as pronounced as in earlier specimens. The Doberman Pinscher makes a good pet for confident owners and is highly intelligent and willing to please. The typical Doberman Pinscher is very friendly and loyal to family members, while remaining assertive and absolutely fearless in the face of strangers.

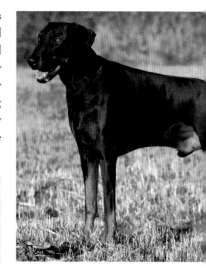

RIGHT

The Dobermans of today have had their highly protective instincts diluted, but they are still fearless of strangers.

LEONBERGER

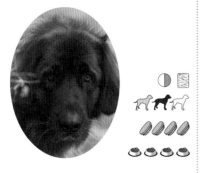

COLOR: Lion gold, red, reddish brown, sandy (fawn or cream), or combinations thereof

COAT CARE: Very high maintenance

DIET: Very high consumption

OFFICIAL CATEGORIZATION: UK: Working, AKC: FSS, FCI: Group 2, Section 2

HEIGHT: 28½–31½ in. (72–80 cm) WEIGHT: 198½–203 lb. (90–92 kg)

OTHER NAMES: None

The Leonberger is a majestic and striking breed of dog that descends from the Great Pyrenees, the Saint Bernard, and the Newfoundland. It is a large breed with a thick coat and a distinctive black mask that contrasts with the lighter brown of the body coat. It was bred in the German town of Leonberg to the specification that it must in some way resemble a lion in honor of the town's coat of arms. It is an excellent swimmer and possesses great strength.

Because of its size and food consumption, ownership of the breed declined rapidly during World War II, but numbers have increased since then. The Leonberger is a docile, intelligent, loyal, and gentle pet with an affectionate and sweet nature. It is extremely unlikely to become aggressive but will bark to warn of danger. The breed gets along well with children and has an extremely generous nature.

GREAT DANE

OFFICIAL CATEGORIZATION: UK: Working, AKC: Working,
FCI: Group 2, Section 2

HEIGHT: 30–32 in. (76–81 cm)   WEIGHT: 117–121 lb. (53–55 kg)

OTHER NAMES: Deutsche Dogge, Granddanois

COLOR: Brindle, fawn, blue, or black

COAT CARE: Minimal maintenance

DIET: High/very high consumption

Fascinating Facts

Former President Franklin D. Roosevelt had a Great Dane named President.

The Great Dane is an exceptionally large breed of dog, native to Germany. The breed is often mistakenly referred to as Danish in origin, but the name came about due to English noblemen who were traveling in Denmark wrongly thinking the breed was Danish and naming it thus. The Great Dane is an ancient breed and has played a large part in the history of northern and central Europe, having fought in many ancient wars. It is typically sandy in color, but also displays a distinctive Harlequin coloration.

most famous portrayal of the Great Dane is that of the cartoon character "Scooby-Doo," who, while looking like a Great Dane, displays none of the courage and alertness of the breed. The Great Dane is typically resolute and reliable with little incidence of undue excitement; it is a very steady and even-tempered dog.

The Great Dane is an intelligent and versatile breed that combines working and

domestic instincts. It is a loyal companion and typically likes to be involved in family life. The breed displays a quiet dignity but never aloofness, and its gentleness and patience with children is uncommonly vast. The Great Dane, despite its size, is not docile but alert and interested. It responds to perceived threats with confidence and poise, rather than instant tenacity and guile. Those that are familiar with the breed note its elegance and extremely social nature as reasons for its huge popularity. However, because of its size any boisterousness or disobedience can become problematic, so thorough training is essential.

Proud and Dignified
The Great Dane stands very tall and proud, with a well-muscled and strong body. It has been used for tracking, guarding and hunting in the past, so is versatile when at work. In some countries, the ears of the Great Dane traditionally are cropped, but this is becoming less common. The

RIGHT
Great Danes can come with a sandy-colored coat, as shown, or with a more unusual Harlequin coloring.

AUSTRIAN SHORTHAIRED PINSCHER

COLOR: Various

COAT CARE: Minimal maintenance

DIET: High consumption

OFFICIAL CATEGORIZATION: UK: Not recognized, AKC: Not recognized, FCI: Group 2, Section 1

HEIGHT: 14–20 in. (36–51 cm)   WEIGHT: 20–40 lb. (12–18 kg)

OTHER NAMES: Österreichischen Kurzhaanigen Pinscher, Austrian Pinscher

Sometimes simply called the Austrian Pinscher, the Austrian Shorthaired Pinscher is a breed of livestock guardian dog that is descended from the German Pinscher. It has a short dense coat and a sturdy and well-proportioned body. It is typically of red, brown, black, or tan solid coloration, and less commonly brindle or black and tan. The head is distinctively pear shaped. This breed is larger and stockier than the German Pinscher and its origins can be traced back to the eighteenth century.

It is mainly a working dog and has been bred to have a tendency to bite, which is desirable in some working farm breeds for controlling herds but not desirable in a pet. It is a lone worker and is unsociable toward other dogs and can be fierce in reinforcing this. The breed is intelligent and dedicated to guarding, displaying a suspicious nature.

Fascinating Facts

The word *pinscher* is German for "terrier." The Doberman was originally called Dobermann Pinscher due to the presence of terriers in the bloodline, but is now sometimes called simply Doberman because the breed is established as a working dog.

ALPINE DACHSBRACKE

COLOR: Black and tan, brown, or most popular is red with or without black

COAT CARE: Moderate maintenance

DIET: High consumption

OFFICIAL CATEGORIZATION: UK: Not recognized, AKC: Not recognized; FCI: Group 6, Section 2

HEIGHT: 13–16 in. (34–42 cm)   WEIGHT: 33–40 lb. (15–18 kg)

OTHER NAMES: Alpenländische Dachsbracke

The Alpine Dachsbracke is an ancient breed of German or Austrian hunting dog that is similar in appearance to the more popular Dachshund. The

RIGHT

Similar to the Dachshund, the Alpine Dachsbracke has a stronger muzzl, for hunting, and can even track a cold trail.

Alpine Dachsbracke is short-legged and muscular, exhibiting a thick double coat in red and black or dark red with patches of black. It is distinct from the Dachshund facially as it has a stronger muzzle. The breed was used originally for hunting in the Alps on the Austrian and German borders. It has an excellent scenting ability and can track a scent even after the trail has gone cold.

The breed is primarily a working hound; it is typically very affectionate toward its master but will display this affection only when not on a scent. It is a breed that is dedicated to its work. Around children and other dogs, the Alpine Dachsbracke is typically sociable and friendly but remains instinctive when it picks up a scent.

STYRIAN COARSE-HAIRED HOUND

OFFICIAL CATEGORIZATION: UK: Not recognized,
AKC: Not recognized, FCI: Group 6, Section 1

HEIGHT: 17½–21 in. (45–53 cm)   WEIGHT: 33–40 lb. (15–18 kg)

OTHER NAMES: Peintingen Bracke

COLOR: Red or fawn, with or without white mark on chest

COAT CARE: Low maintenance

DIET: High consumption

The Styrian Coarse-Haired Hound is a hardy, rough-coated scent hound used to hunt boar and is of eighteenth-century Austrian origins. It is medium sized and has a sturdy and well-proportioned body, and typically a coat of red or fawn with darker ears. It is a serious-looking dog with strong working instincts; it can work for extended periods of time without becoming tired or weak.

This breed is predominantly a working dog and is not kept as a pet. It is dominant and sometimes unwilling to socialize with people or other dogs. As a working dog it is efficient, reliable, and obedient, often showing friendliness to its master. It is rare that this breed will demonstrate affection, although it is not unapproachable or aggressive. It prefers to live outside and may

Fascinating Facts

The Styrian Coarse-Haired Hound is able to work in very high altitudes.

become destructive if restricted indoors. The breed is not well-known outside of Europe.

TYROLEAN HOUND

OFFICIAL CATEGORIZATION: UK: Not recognized,
AKC: Not recognized, FCI: Group 6, Section 1

HEIGHT: 17–20 in. (44–50 cm)   WEIGHT: 42–46½ lb. (19–21 kg)

OTHER NAMES: Tiroler Bracke, Austrian Brachet

COLOR: Red or black and tan, both of which may have white markings

COAT CARE: Low/moderate maintenance

DIET: High consumption

This is an ancient breed that has a long working history but it became standardized only in the nineteenth century. It originated as a scent hound in Austria, where it was bred to track large but wounded game, such as deer and boar. The breed is slightly longer than it is tall but it is well-proportioned, with a slightly domed skull. The breed is thought to descend from ancient and now extinct Celtic Hounds.

LEFT
The Tyrolean Hound was bred centuries ago in Austria to track large wounded game, such as deer.

The Tyrolean Hound is an adept hunting dog with a good sense of smell and insatiable desire to complete every hunt. It is hard-working and energetic, which makes it suitable as a pet only for owners with the ability to give it sufficient exercise. It is a loyal companion and will display affection to those with whom it is familiar. The breed is even tempered and reliable and is rarely provoked into undue excitement.

261

AUSTRIAN BLACK-AND-TAN HOUND

COLOR: Black with small, clearly defined light- to dark-tan markings

COAT CARE: Low maintenance

DIET: High consumption

OFFICIAL CATEGORIZATION: UK: Not recognized, AKC: Not recognized, FCI: Group 6, Section 1

HEIGHT: 19–22 in. (48–56 cm)   WEIGHT: 42–46½ lb. (19–21 kg)

OTHER NAMES: Ostreichische Tan Hound

The Austrian Black-and-Tan Hound is a working scent hound that is descended from ancient Celtic Hounds. It has a short coat, large ears, and a distinctive broad chest that gives the impression of strength and agility. It has an excellent scenting capacity and is instinctive in its work. The breed requires little encouragement to give chase or track a scent, but may need instructions to stop working.

It is predominantly a hunting hound and is rare outside of its native Austria, but the Austrian Black-and-Tan Hound makes a good companion. It is intelligent and obedient, often forming a strong bond with those close to it. It is a good-natured and well-tempered breed, not easily excited but also not aloof. It has a graceful calmness about it. The breed is not known for being overly affectionate but is generally friendly and sociable when secure and comfortable.

RIGHT
The Austrian Black-and-Tan Hound needs little encouragment to track a scent; you may find it difficult to make it leave a trail!

SMALL SWISS HOUND

COLOR: No agreed standard

COAT CARE: Minimal maintenance

DIET: Moderate consumption

OFFICIAL CATEGORIZATION: UK: Not recognized, AKC: Not recognized, FCI: Group 6, Section 1

HEIGHT: No agreed standard   WEIGHT: No agreed standard

OTHER NAMES: None

The Small Swiss Hound is one of two (sometimes three, depending on classification) dog breeds referred to as "Swiss Hound." It is an ancient and

RIGHT
The Small Swiss Hound, like other Swiss Hounds, comes from purely Swiss lines of which the Swiss are very proud.

traditional Swiss breed and has the distinction of being "pure" Swiss. Unlike the many French hounds, the Swiss Hounds have no English breed blood—they are composed entirely of native breeding stock, making them a source of pride for Swiss breeders. The Small Swiss Hound is typically athletic and lean, with long, pendulous ears and a keen nose for scenting.

The breed is commonly used to hunt small game, such as hare, and does so with grace and style. It is noted for its pleasant-voiced bay, which it exhibits when hunting. The breed is intelligent, considered, and calm with an even temper and distinctively unflappable personality. It loves to run and requires good space in which to exercise as it has a great deal of stamina.

ENTLEBUCHER MOUNTAIN DOG

OFFICIAL CATEGORIZATION: UK: Not recognized,
AKC: Not recognized, FCI: Group 2, Section 3

HEIGHT: 19–20 in. (48–50.5 cm) WEIGHT: 45–65 lb. (20.5–29.5 kg)

OTHER NAMES: Entlebucher Sennenhund, Entlebucher Cattle Dog

COLOR: Tricolor—black, tan, and white

COAT CARE: Minimal maintenance

DIET: Moderate/high consumption

The Entlebucher Mountain Dog is a small breed of herding dog native to Switzerland. It is of compact and sturdy build with an attractive and distinctive coat, normally of black, tan, and white tricolor pattern. It is a close relative of the Appenzell Cattle Dog and was established to drove and herd livestock in the mountainous region of Entlebuch, in its native Switzerland. It is a strong and agile breed with good working instincts.

The breed is a valued worker but also makes an adaptable and rewarding pet. It is sociable and friendly and thrives in human company. Like many herding breeds, the Entlebucher Mountain Dog is highly intelligent and mentally agile; it may get bored easily if left unattended. The breed is known for its self-confidence and independence, but certain specimens can exhibit a huge desire for closeness and affection. It is gentle with children and loving to all.

LEFT
Bred to work in the mountainous Entlebuch region of Switzerland, the Entlebucher Mountain Dog is sturdy and agile.

SWISS HOUND

OFFICIAL CATEGORIZATION: UK: Not recognized,
AKC: Not recognized, FCI: Group 6, Section 1

HEIGHT: 11½–21½ in. (30–55 cm)   WEIGHT: 33–44 lb. (15–20 kg)

OTHER NAMES: Schweizerischer Laufhund

COLOR: White with orange-fawn spots or an orange-fawn saddle, sometimes very lightly speckled

COAT CARE: Minimal maintenance

DIET: Moderate/high consumption

The Swiss Hound is the larger-legged relative of the Small Swiss Hound. It is believed to have originated in the sixteenth century, with early examples of the breed thought to have become established near to the Swiss–French border. It is a well-balanced and sturdy dog with a strong hunting instinct and sensitive nose. The Swiss Hound has a great deal of stamina and is an impressive hunter. Like the smaller version of the breed, the Swiss Hound is considered to have a pleasant bay when in the hunt.

As with certain other working breeds, the Swiss Hound is most content when it can put its natural instincts to use. Despite this, it is an adaptable and friendly companion that displays great loyalty to its master. The Swiss Hound is gentle, docile, and affectionate. The breed requires solid training from an experienced owner to ensure it adapts to domestic life.

APPENZELL MOUNTAIN DOG

COLOR: Black or brown with symmetrical white-and-rust markings

COAT CARE: Minimal maintenance

DIET: High consumption

OFFICIAL CATEGORIZATION: UK: Not recognized, AKC: Not recognized, FCI: Group 2, Section 3

HEIGHT: 22–23 in. (56–58.5 cm)   WEIGHT: 59–70 lb. (22–32 kg)

OTHER NAMES: Appenzeller Sennenhund, Appenzell Cattle Dog

The Appenzell Mountain Dog, otherwise known as the Appenzell Cattle Dog, is a well-built yet compact breed of dog native to Switzerland. It displays the distinctively Swiss symmetrical black, copper, and white tricolor that is seen in the more common Bernese Mountain Dog. The breed has an alert expression, which is typical of flock-guarding breeds such as this.

The dog is intelligent, active, and eager to work. It is similar in many ways to the Border Collie, especially in relation to intelligence and the need for stimulation. The Appenzell Mountain Dog is unhappy if not able to exercise its strong herding instincts, whether through work or structured play and training. In the right environment, the Appenzell Mountain Dog is a friendly and obedient dog with a calm and reliable demeanor that often radiates charm and confidence in equal measure.

RIGHT
Whether through work or play the Appenzell Cattle Dog likes to utilize its herding instincts.

BERNESE MOUNTAIN DOG

COLOR: Tricolor: black, tan, and white

COAT CARE: Moderate maintenance

DIET: High/very high consumption

OFFICIAL CATEGORIZATION: UK: Working, AKC: Working, FCI: Group 2, Section 3

HEIGHT: 25–27½ in. (64–70 cm)   WEIGHT: 65–120 lb. (29.5–54.5 kg)

OTHER NAMES: Berner Sennenhund, Bouvier Bernois, Dürrbächler

The Bernese Mountain Dog is one of the most popular Swiss dog breeds. It is a strikingly handsome breed—strong but not massive, with a distinctive symmetrical tricolor and well-muscled body. It is solidly built but not heavy, with a thick and luxuriously feathered coat. The head is dignified and symmetrically patterned and the gaze is alert and watchful. It was bred originally for herding and droving in the mountains of the Swiss region of Canton. It is noticeably of Mastiff descent, but bears some physical hallmarks of other droving breeds.

The Bernese Mountain Dog is a friendly and affectionate breed that displays a high level of intelligence and playfulness. It is considered to be an extremely good pet as it is gentle with children, patient and eager to please. The breed exhibits a combination of exuberance and calmness and is adaptable to the atmosphere of its immediate environment.

SAINT BERNARD

OFFICIAL CATEGORIZATION: UK: Working, AKC: Working,
FCI: Group 2, Section 2

HEIGHT: 26–29 in. (66–73.5 cm)   WEIGHT: 110–200 lb. (50–91 kg)

OTHER NAMES: Saint Bernhardshund, Alpine Mastiff

COLOR: White with red, or red with white

COAT CARE: Low maintenance

DIET: 4.5 bowls

This is one of the largest dog breeds—heavy-set and extremely strong it was bred by monks and named after a lodge located at Saint Bernard's Pass in the Alps, bordering Switzerland and Italy. Saint Bernard's Pass was a notorious hazardous part of the mountain face where climbers regularly became stranded.

The Saint Bernard was used predominantly to rescue those trapped out on the mountains, but also as a farming dog and watchdog. The breed descends from the Greater Swiss Mountain Dog but also experienced the introduction of Newfoundland blood into the bloodline, which gave rise to some Saint Bernards exhibiting thick, long coats. The breed was originally smooth coated and the new thick coats were impractical because they collected snow, but both coats are now common. The breed is an excellent tracking dog and is still used for mountain rescue.

Reliable Companion

The Saint Bernard is gentle and caring with a high degree of intelligence. Owners and breeders of the breed attest that the dog has the ability to sense an impending change in weather and will become distressed before a storm or avalanche. The breed has a natural inclination to protect those close to it and will do so whatever the risk to itself.

The Saint Bernard is a patient breed, very slow moving but not docile. It exhibits a peaceful, sometimes solemn persona but is generally a happy and friendly beast. It is receptive to training and likes to play, but due to its size and boisterous tendencies it needs to be controlled. The breed makes a good watchdog and its size may deter any would-be intruders. However, it is rare that the Saint Bernard becomes aggressive—if it does it is usually a sign that it is feeling intimidated or is unwell.

RIGHT
Saint Bernard's were bred by monks near a particularly difficult Alpine pass, where travelers frequently needed rescuing.

Fascinating Facts

During the early development of the breed, the Saint Bernard was nearly wiped out because of an avalanche that killed most of the original breeding stock.

GREATER SWISS MOUNTAIN DOG

COLOR: Black topcoat with rich rust and white markings

COAT CARE: Minimal maintenance

DIET: High/very high consumption

OFFICIAL CATEGORIZATION: UK: Not recognized, AKC: Working, FCI: Group 2, Section 3

HEIGHT: 25½–27½ in. (65–72 cm)   WEIGHT: 132–154 lb. (60–70 kg)

OTHER NAMES: Großer Schweizer Sennenhund

The Greater Swiss Mountain Dog is the largest of the Swiss Mountain Dog family, bred for herding in the Swiss mountains. It is an ancient breed and is almost certainly of Molosser descent. It bears a slight resemblance in form to the Rottweiler but typically has a much denser coat. The breed displays the black, white, and copper tricolor that is so greatly associated with Swiss dog breeds. The Greater Swiss Mountain Dog is an ancestor of the Saint Bernard, but is not nearly so large.

The breed is confident, watchful, and vigilant. It is a good guard dog and will act as such if called upon to do so. The Greater Swiss Mountain Dog is friendly and smart, with an outgoing yet calm personality. It is gentle and patient, making an exceptionally good friend for children, but will be assertive if harassed or pestered.

LEFT
The Greater Swiss Mountain Dog is a herder and one of the ancestors of the Saint Bernard.

BICHON FRISE

COLOR: White

COAT CARE: High/very high maintenance

DIET: Moderate consumption

OFFICIAL CATEGORIZATION: UK: Toy, AKC: nonsporting, FCI: Group 9, Section 1

HEIGHT: 9–11 in. (23–28 cm)   WEIGHT: 7–12 lb. (3–5 kg)

OTHER NAMES: Bichon Tenerife, Bichon à Poil Frisé

The Bichon Frise, despite its French name, is a Spanish breed with some Belgian heritage. The breed has a very distinctive curly, almost "puffy," coat that is usually solid white in color. It is a small breed, classified as a toy dog, and is a descendent of the Poodle, from which it inherited its coat. The breed has ancient origins and is thought to have been in existence for more than 2,000 years. It is well-traveled and was used as currency by sailors, which explains its wide distribution. It became established as a breed in Spain around the fourteenth century.

It is a feisty and playful dog, typical of many toy breeds. It loves attention and is very sociable. The breed is energetic and affectionate, prone to sudden bursts of energy that see the dog racing around at high speed and then stopping suddenly. It is quite intelligent and offers good companionship.

SPANISH WATER DOG

OFFICIAL CATEGORIZATION: UK: Gun Dog,
AKC: Not recognized, FCI: Group 8, Section 3

HEIGHT: 17½–19½ in. (44–50 cm)   WEIGHT: 40–48 lb. (18–22 kg)

OTHER NAMES: Perro de Agua Español, Andalusian Turk

COLOR: Solid black, brown, or white of various shades; black and white or brown and white

COAT CARE: Moderate/high maintenance

DIET: High consumption

The Spanish Water Dog is a versatile working breed that has performed as a herder and as a useful retriever in and out of water. It has a curly, water-resistant coat set against a sturdy and well-proportioned body. The head is covered in curls that will require sheering at least once a year. Although it has a varied working past its behavior is most typical of a herding breed.

The Spanish Water Dog is hard-working, enthusiastic, and is still in possession of some very dominant working instincts. It is an adaptable breed and will function well as a pet, a herder, or a retriever. It is friendly and playful, showing dedication to its family and affection toward children. As with most herding breeds, it may try to control the movement of its family, and it can be wary of strangers; it will exhibit suspicion until confident and secure about new people.

CATALAN SHEEPDOG

OFFICIAL CATEGORIZATION: UK: Not recognized,
AKC: Not recognized, FCI: Group 1, Section 1

HEIGHT: 17–21 in. (45–55 cm)   WEIGHT: 45–60 lb. (20–27 kg)

OTHER NAMES: Catalonian Shepherd, Gos d'Atura Català, Perro de Pastor Catalán

COLOR: Fawn to dark sable and light to dark gray

COAT CARE: Moderate/high maintenance

DIET: Moderate/high consumption

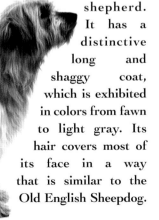

The Catalan Sheepdog is descended from the ancient Pyrenean shepherd. It has a distinctive long and shaggy coat, which is exhibited in colors from fawn to light gray. Its hair covers most of its face in a way that is similar to the Old English Sheepdog. It is a talented and keen herding breed, with a well-proportioned and athletic body.

The breed is agile, intelligent, and enthusiastic. It works under no instruction from the master—rather it is instinctive in its herding and is dedicated to controlling the flock. It is a versatile breed and makes a good pet in the right environment. It adapts well to domestic life, particularly if given sufficient exercise and mental stimulation. Without a flock to herd, the Catalan Sheepdog will be a calm and even-tempered pet that exhibits friendliness and affection to all.

SPANISH HOUND

COLOR: White with large, rounded orange or black spots of varying intensity

COAT CARE: Zero maintenance

DIET: High consumption

OFFICIAL CATEGORIZATION: UK: Not recognized, AKC: Not recognized, FCI: Group 6, Section 1

HEIGHT: 20–22 in. (51–56 cm)   WEIGHT: 53–57½ lb. (24–26 kg)

OTHER NAMES: Sabueso Espanol

The Spanish Hound has an agile appearance and a grace of movement, with a straight back and broad chest. There are two variants and both are judged exactly the same except for size—one is small, the other is large. The coat of this breed is short and typically white with large red or black spots. The Spanish Hound was bred to hunt hare but is adept at hunting both larger and smaller game.

This is a working breed, not well-known outside of its native country. Although it is even tempered, obedient, and reliable, it does not thrive well in the domestic environment because of its strong working instincts. It is not an established pet breed and, therefore, only working dogs are available. The Spanish Hound is loyal and affectionate but is simply not suited to domestic living and should be treated as a working dog.

BELOW
The Spanish Hound is powerful and long. It has a strong neck with a dewlap.

CANARY WARREN HOUND

COLOR: Red and white, with red ranging from orange to mahogany

COAT CARE: Zero maintenance

DIET: High consumption

OFFICIAL CATEGORIZATION: UK: Not recognized, AKC: Not recognized, FCI: Group 5, Section 7

HEIGHT: 21–25 in. (54–64 cm)   WEIGHT: 53–57½ lb. (24–26 kg)

OTHER NAMES: Podenco Canario, Canarian Warren Hound

The Canary Warren Hound, or Canarian Warren Hound as it is sometimes called, is an ancient breed thought to be descended from Egyptian breeds, because remains of the Canary Warren Hound's ancestors have been found in the tombs of the ancient Pharaohs. It is a slender dog, with a lean body and narrow head; it was worked as a hunter of rabbits and other small game. Its origins are in the Spanish Canary Islands, which themselves take their name from the Latin for "dog"—*canis*.

The breed is tenacious and vivacious, with a strong hunting instinct and keen nose for scent. The breed is a dedicated worker but makes a peaceful pet. If unstimulated, the breed will not exhibit strong hunting instincts unless it picks up a scent—it is not a dog constantly on the search for scent. The Canary Warren Hound, while intelligent, is not watchful and does not make a good guard dog.

LEFT
The Canary Warren Hound comes from the Canary Islands. It is an intelligent hunter, but not a good watchdog.

MAJORCA MASTIFF

OFFICIAL CATEGORIZATION: UK: Not recognized,
AKC: Not recognized, FCI: Group 2, Section 2

HEIGHT: 21–24 in. (53.5–61 cm)   WEIGHT: 77–83½ lb. (35–38 kg)

OTHER NAMES: Dogue de Mallorca, Perro Presa Mallorquin,
Ca de Bou, Mallorcan Bulldog

COLOR: Brindle, tan, and black

COAT CARE: Low maintenance

DIET: High consumption

This fighting breed is known by many Spanish and English names, including Perro Presa Mallorquin, Ca de Bou, and Mallorcan Bulldog. It is a heavy-set and very strong breed, with a powerful jaw and extremely heavy bite. It was bred for bull baiting and has a distinctive fighting style, wherein it uses its powerful jaws to grip its victim. It is not used for fighting so often today due to public distaste for the sport, but it still has an intimidating presence. The breed comes in many colors and has a short, coarse coat.

Although the breed is in possession of a powerful physique and strong fighting instincts it can be trained for companionship. However, it is not suitable for inexperienced or unconfident pet owners, because it requires firm handling and competent training. This alert and lively breed makes an excellent guard dog due to its tenacity and agility.

LEFT
Bred for bull baiting, the Majorca Mastiff has an unusually tenacious bite and will not let go.

IBIZAN HOUND

OFFICIAL CATEGORIZATION: UK: Hound, AKC: Hound,
FCI: Group 5, Section 7

HEIGHT: 22–29 in. (56–74 cm)   WEIGHT: 42–55 lb. (19–22 kg)

OTHER NAMES: Ibizan Podenco, Ibizan Warren Hound,
Podenco Ibicenco

COLOR: White or red (from light, yellowish red called "lion" to deep red), solid, or in any combination

COAT CARE: Zero maintenance

DIET: High consumption

Although this breed looks like an ancient hound, possibly descended from the Pharaoh Hound, genetic research has revealed that it is a relatively new breed, bred to resemble older hound breeds. It is lean and slight with erect ears and either a short, smooth coat or a longer, coarse, and wiry coat, depending on variety. It is normal for this breed's ribs to be visible. This fast breed is capable of hunting by sight or scent.

The Ibizan Hound typically is intelligent and sociable, with a gentle and affectionate nature toward children, young and old. It is lively and agile and requires a good degree of attention, but it is willing when trained and will cooperate when positive training measures are used—although it does not respond well to punishment. Despite its generally sociable nature toward people and dogs, some examples are independently minded and enjoy their own space.

BURGOS POINTING DOG

COLOR: White with liver spots or flecks

COAT CARE: Zero maintenance

DIET: High consumption

OFFICIAL CATEGORIZATION: UK: Not recognized, AKC: Not recognized, FCI: Group 7, Section 1

HEIGHT: 25½–29½ in. (65–75 cm)   WEIGHT: 64–68½ lb. (29–31 kg)

OTHER NAMES: Perdiguero de Burgos

The rare Burgos Pointing Dog is descended from old Spanish Pointing breeds. It is very pure of blood and has remained the same for centuries. It is not a popular working dog today and is close to extinction; it is relatively unknown outside of its native Spain. It is a large and well-proportioned dog with pendulous lips and ears.

The coat of the Burgos Pointing Dog is white with liver ticks or liver-colored spots.

This is a working breed of dog and is adaptable as a hunt, point, and retrieve dog or as a traditional hunting dog. It is obedient and loyal but is not established as a pet breed because of its low numbers. The breed is intelligent and willing to be trained, although such training should be firm and consistent. The Burgos Pointing Dog is a tough breed and reflects its hardy and rugged working style in its personality.

RIGHT
The Burgos Pointing Dog is very rare and can be found only in Spain.

PYRENEAN MASTIFF

COLOR: White with well-defined mask

COAT CARE: Low/moderate maintenance

DIET: High/very high consumption

OFFICIAL CATEGORIZATION: UK: Not recognized, AKC: Not recognized, FCI: Group 2, Section 2

HEIGHT: 30–32 in. (77–81 cm)   WEIGHT: 120–160 lb. (53–73 kg)

OTHER NAMES: Mastín del Pirineo

Large flock-guarding dogs have been present in Spain for more than 2,000 years, but only relatively recently have these breeds become standardized and established. The Pyrenean Mastiff is one such breed. It is large and powerful, of Molosser descent with a thick, warm coat and large, typically Mastifflike head. It

also has a characteristically large and loose dewlap.

The modern Pyrenean Mastiff is a gentle dog within its own family but a formidable guard dog with strong and dominating protective instincts. It treats strangers with restrained caution but is happy to socialize when it can sense that the stranger is welcome. The breed is intelligent and dedicated and shows a particular affection to children but is assertive when harassed or pestered. It is self-confident, with an intent watchfulness, and is apparently very aware of its size and strength, unlike some other large breeds.

SPANISH GREYHOUND

OFFICIAL CATEGORIZATION: UK: Not recognized,
AKC: Not recognized, FCI: Group 10, Section 3

HEIGHT: 24½–27½ in. (62–70 cm)   WEIGHT: 55–66 lb. (25–30 kg)

OTHER NAMES: Galgo Espanol

COLOR: Fawn and brindle, black, spotted black (dark and light), burnt chestnut, cinnamon, yellow, red, or white

COAT CARE: Minimal maintenance

DIET: Moderate/high consumption

The Spanish Greyhound is an ancient sight-hound breed dating back to the ninth century. It is believed to be descended from African sight-hound stock, brought to Spain by the Moors and established in the country for sport and hunting. It is an extremely lean and agile breed, similar in physique to the Whippet. It exhibits many different coat colorations but fawn and brindle is the most common.

The breed is tough and hardy, with a keen chasing instinct that it retains from its days as a working sight hound. Its scenting ability is unusually weak, with extremely strong sight evolving in its place. The Spanish Greyhound is noticeably affectionate and becomes attached to its owner, which is typical of many sight-hound breeds that were established to work and hunt alongside one master. It is a loyal and dedicated dog with a lot of energy.

MAJORCA SHEPHERD DOG

OFFICIAL CATEGORIZATION: UK: Not recognized,
AKC: Not recognized, FCI: Group 1, Section 1

HEIGHT: 19–22 in. (48–56 cm)   WEIGHT: 86–90½ lb. (39–41 kg)

OTHER NAMES: Ca de Bestiar

COLOR: Black

COAT CARE: Minimal maintenance

DIET: High consumption

The Majorca Shepherd Dog is a working livestock guardian that will also function as a herding dog. It is well-built and extremely athletic with an intensely strong guardian instinct. It has existed for centuries throughout the Balearic Islands and Western Mediterranean regions and is of pure blood. It has a short, smooth coat, typically a solid black color. The breed is well-known and valuable for being able to work through intense heat and humidity.

The Majorca Shepherd Dog is predominantly a working dog and is not established as a companion breed. It is fiercely protective over its flock and is quick to become aggressive if the flock is threatened. It is strong, agile, quick, and instinctive, making it a formidable guardian of the flock but unsuitable as a domesticated pet. The Majorca Shepherd Dog is loyal to its master and displays a high degree of reliability and consistency in its temperament.

LEFT

Also known as the Ca de Bestiar, the Majorca Shepherd Dog came from the Balearic Islands and Western Mediterranean.

SPANISH MASTIFF

COLOR: Reddish or fawn, brindle, black, or "wolf"-colored

COAT CARE: Minimal maintenance

DIET: High/very high consumption

OFFICIAL CATEGORIZATION: UK: Not recognized, AKC: Not recognized, FCI: Group 2, Section 2

HEIGHT: 28½–31½ in. (72.5–80 cm) WEIGHT: 110–140 lb. (50–65 kg)

OTHER NAMES: Mastín Español

The Spanish Mastiff is a large and powerful flock guardian and herding breed. It has distinctive loose skin and a double dewlap. This gives the impression of weightiness—in fact, the breed is powerfully built but without excessive heaviness. It is descended from ancient Mastiff breeds. The Spanish Mastiff has been used in dog fighting in the past but is normally associated with pastoral duties. The breed has existed on the Iberian Peninsula for thousands of years but was not standardized and established as a breed until the mid-twentieth century.

The breed is somewhat serious and independent, not affectionate and occasionally aloof. It is a dependable guardian dog and is reliable in its temperament. It does not require much attention and typically is unconcerned about human company, often more happy to look after its flock and protect it from predators. Despite this, the Spanish Mastiff is extremely loyal and will defend its family tenaciously.

RIGHT

While it can be aloof and is not very affectionate, the Spanish Mastiff will conscientiously look after its family members.

PORTUGUESE PODENGO

COLOR: Yellow, fawn, or black (diluted or faded), with or without white markings

COAT CARE: Low/moderate maintenance

DIET: Moderate consumption

OFFICIAL CATEGORIZATION: UK: Hound, AKC: Not recognized, FCI: Group 5, Section 7

HEIGHT: 8–12 in. (20–30 cm) WEIGHT: 9–11 lb. (4–5 kg)

OTHER NAMES: Podengo Portugues, Warren Hound

The Portuguese Podengo is an ancient hound breed of which there are three sizes of dog, with two differing coat variations. There is a large, medium, and small size and each can exhibit either a smooth- or a wirehaired coat. It is a versatile hound, able to hunt with sight or scent. Typically small, it was put to work hunting rabbits, which led to its alternative name "Warren Hound." The breed is relatively rare outside of its native Portugal, with the exception of the United States, where the breed has been imported by immigrants who used it to work in rural areas.

RIGHT

The Portuguese Podengo can be found in its native Portugal, and in the United States, where it was transported by migrants.

The breed is active, watchful, and alert. It makes a useful watchdog and will bark if suspicious. The Portuguese Podengo is a loyal and friendly companion with a slightly boisterous nature. It is sociable and friendly toward children, making it an excellent all-round family pet.

PORTUGUESE SHEEPDOG

OFFICIAL CATEGORIZATION: UK: Not recognized, AKC: Not recognized, FCI: Group 1, Section 1

HEIGHT: 17½–21½ in. (45–55 cm)   WEIGHT: 26½–29½ lb. (12–18 kg)

OTHER NAMES: Monkey Dog

COLOR: Yellow, brown, fawn, gray/wolf gray, or black; with tan; with or without a mixture of white hairs

COAT CARE: Moderate/high maintenance

DIET: Moderate/high consumption

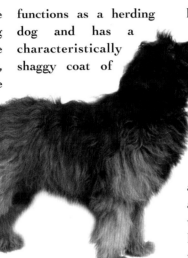

Breeds resembling the Portuguese Sheepdog have been in existence in Portugal for centuries, but the modern Portuguese Sheepdog became established only in the twentieth century. It is likely to be a descendant of the Briard but has distinct similarities to the Great Pyrenees as well. It functions as a herding dog and has a characteristically shaggy coat of long, normally black and gray fur. It is a particularly rare breed outside of Portugal.

The Portuguese Sheepdog is an effective flock herder and flock guardian. It is adaptable as a pet due to its intelligence and obedience, but it retains very strong guarding and herding instincts that give the dog a tendency to be aggressive toward strangers. It is fiercely protective over its family and home territory, exhibiting an alert watchfulness at all times. Solid training is required for this loyal and sociable breed to integrate fully into the domestic setup.

LEFT

A new breed, only established in the twentieth century, the Portuguese Sheepdog needs diligent training to make it domesticated.

PORTUGUESE WATER DOG

OFFICIAL CATEGORIZATION: UK: Working, AKC: Working, FCI: Group 8, Section 3

HEIGHT: 20–23 in. (51–58 cm)   WEIGHT: 42–55 lb. (19–25 kg)

OTHER NAMES: Cão de água Português

COLOR: Black, white and various tones of brown

COAT CARE: High/very high maintenance

DIET: High consumption

The Portuguese Water Dog is a breed of working retriever that is believed to descend from the Standard Poodle. It was used for assisting fishermen in bringing in trawler nets, swimming between ships as a courier, and even chasing fish into areas where they could be caught. It has a thick curly coat that is similar to that of the Standard Poodle and is well-muscled and compact with webbed toes, typical of many water working dogs. It is relatively rare today but was once an extremely popular sight up and down the coastlines of Portugal.

The breed is intelligent, hard-working, tough, and friendly. It exhibits strong working instincts but these can be controlled with sufficient training. The Portuguese Water Dog is an extremely loyal and affectionate dog, likely to bond with one family member over another. It displays unfettered loyalty and will stick close to the side of its master at all times.

CÃO DE FILA DE SÃO MIGUEL

OFFICIAL CATEGORIZATION: UK: Not recognized, AKC: Not recognized, FCI: Group 1, Section 2

COLOR: Reddish yellow or gray

COAT CARE: Low/moderate maintenance

DIET: High/very high consumption

HEIGHT: 19½–24 in. (50–61 cm)   WEIGHT: 55–90 lb. (25–41 kg)

OTHER NAMES: Azores Cattle Dog

The Cão de Fila de São Miguel is a large herding breed with a strong, medium-sized physique and powerful head. It is native to the Portuguese island of São Miguel, where it was developed to herd wild cattle in very thick and hard-to-penetrate vegetation. It is far larger than is typical for a cattle dog and has an unusual, reddish yellow brindle coat.

The Cão de Fila de São Miguel is a rustic and hardy breed, often worked outside all year round herding cattle.

It is intelligent and quick to learn but has strong working instincts that can often dominate the dog's behavior. It is a superb guard dog due to its large and powerful body combined with a tenacious herding and protective instinct. It exudes a calm confidence wherever it is and tends to be alert and very watchful. With children, the breed is patient and tolerant, but is not demonstrably affectionate.

CASTRO LABOREIRO DOG

OFFICIAL CATEGORIZATION: UK: Not recognized, AKC: Not recognized, FCI: Group 2, Section 2

COLOR: Black, chestnut, or mahogany

COAT CARE: Low/moderate maintenance

DIET: High consumption

HEIGHT: 20–24 in. (51–60 cm)   WEIGHT: 50–75 lb. (45–75 kg)

OTHER NAMES: Portuguese Cattle Dog

The Castro Laboreiro Dog is a breed of unknown heritage that is native to Portugal. It is named for the village Castro Laboreiro where it was bred.

It is likely a descendant of a Molosser-type dog and displays a typically strong jaw and body. The breed is a particular source of pride for the locals of its native village, who describe the breed as being "the best in the world." It is a courageous and hard-working flock guardian and hunter, typically of thick black coat to enable it to work outside all year round.

The Castro Laboreiro Dog is an adaptable pet breed and is gentle with those it is close to but wary of strangers. Because of its great herding ability, the breed makes a fine watchdog and guard dog while displaying extremely high intelligence and obedience—making it a rewarding pet, too.

PORTUGUESE POINTER

OFFICIAL CATEGORIZATION: UK: Not recognized,
AKC: Not recognized, FCI: Group 7, Section 1

HEIGHT: 20–22 in. (50–56 cm)   WEIGHT: 44–59 lb. (20–27 kg)

OTHER NAMES: Perdigueiro Português

COLOR: Yellow or light brown,
with or without white markings

COAT CARE: Minimal maintenance

DIET: High consumption

The Portuguese Pointer is a hardy and rustic breed of pointing dog, bred for hunting partridge and other game. It is short coated, typically light brown or sandy, and is a well-muscled, medium-sized specimen with a high level of stamina and strength. The Portuguese Pointer is a versatile worker and can adapt to hunting on many different terrains. It is not a well-known breed outside of Portugal and is considered rare by national kennel club authorities.

The breed is hard-working and intelligent, with strong hunt, point, and retrieve abilities. It is a rugged dog that prefers the outdoors and being able to work but will adapt to domestic life if given adequate training and socialization.

The breed is friendly and affectionate and enjoys the company of people and other dogs. It is a companionable dog and will adapt its energy and activity level to suit its immediate environment.

ESTRELA MOUNTAIN DOG

OFFICIAL CATEGORIZATION: UK: Pastoral, AKC: Not
recognized, FCI: Group 2, Section 2

HEIGHT: 25½–28½ in. (65–72 cm)   WEIGHT: 66–110 lb. (30–50 kg)

OTHER NAMES: Portuguese Shepherd, Cão da Serra da Estrela

COLOR: Fawn, brindle, or wolf gray

COAT CARE: Moderate/high
maintenance

DIET: High consumption

The Estrela Mountain Dog is a flock guardian breed of distinctive appearance. It comes in two varieties, namely long- and short-haired. The breed is ancient and its origins are unclear, but the Estrela Mountain Dog has been evolving and changing for centuries to meet the needs of the mountain shepherds it was bred to serve. It has a sturdy physique, possibly inherited from the ancient Mastiff breeds that are believed to be ancestors of the Estrela Mountain Dog. It is a tough and hardy breed, capable of negotiating difficult mountain terrain. It is a versatile herder and guardian.

As a pet, the breed is relatively popular, especially in its native Portugal. It is of even temperament and is typically affectionate and friendly toward family, while remaining indifferent to those it does not know. It has a strong protective instinct that it exercises clearly when it detects a threat to flock or family.

LEFT
The Estrela Mountain Dog is an ancient breed, but one that is constantly evolving, too.

RAFEIRO DO ALENTEJO

OFFICIAL CATEGORIZATION: UK: Not recognized, AKC: Not recognized, FCI: Group 2, Section 2

COLOR: Black, tawny, yellow, or wolf

COAT CARE: Moderate maintenance

DIET: High/very high consumption

HEIGHT: 26–29½ in. (66–75 cm)　　**WEIGHT:** 110–132 lb. (50–60 kg)

OTHER NAMES: Alentejo Mastiff

The Rafeiro do Alentejo is a powerful and strong descendent of the Tibetan Mastiff. It is a Portuguese breed that was established in order to protect the mountain sheep flocks. It was also used as a

drover to take the flocks from the mountain to the fields in winter, and as a result the breed has developed a thick coat and hardy demeanor to cope with this grueling work.

It is a loyal and reliable breed but not suitable for an inexperienced owner. Its work has shaped its temperament and it is considerably independent. Although intelligent, obedient, and fond of children, the breed is not overly interested in showing affection or socializing, preferring to exhibit an air of alert watchfulness. If the Rafeiro do Alentejo detects a threat, it will spring into action and defend either flock or family tenaciously, and with its strength and territorialism it makes an exceptional guard dog.

BOLOGNESE

OFFICIAL CATEGORIZATION: UK: Toy, AKC: Not recognized, FCI: Group 9, Section 1

COLOR: Pure white

COAT CARE: Moderate/high maintenance

DIET: Moderate consumption

HEIGHT: 10½–12 in. (27–30.5 cm)　　**WEIGHT:** 9–10 lb. (4–5 kg)

OTHER NAMES: Bichon Bolognese

The Bolognese is a small dog and member of the Bichon family of dogs native to Italy. Like the pasta sauce, it is named for the city of Bologna, but it is unclear if this is the true place of the breed's origin. It is a toy breed, typically displaying a white, almost woolly coat. The breed's origins can be traced back to the sixteenth century through various works of art depicting almost identical-looking dogs in the company of royalty. The artist Goya was fond of the Bolognese dog.

As a pet, the breed is extremely popular. It is loyal, dedicated, and affectionate. The Bolognese is lively, energetic, and sociable. It is not as energetic as its relative the Bichon Frise, but still makes a thoroughly willing playmate and companion for young children. The breed will develop a strong bond with its family but may be wary of strangers.

VOLPINO ITALIANO

OFFICIAL CATEGORIZATION: UK: Not recognized,
AKC: Not recognized, FCI: Group 5, Section 4

HEIGHT: 10½–12 in. (27–30 cm)   WEIGHT: 6½–11 lb. (3–5 kg)

OTHER NAMES: Cane de Quirinale, Florentine Spitz, Italian Spitz

COLOR: White

COAT CARE: High maintenance

DIET: Moderate consumption

The Volpino Italiano is a small breed of Spitz origin that is native to the Swiss–Italian border area, although it is established as an Italian breed. It is typical of northern European Spitz breeds, except for being notably small in comparison to certain types. It bears a striking resemblance to the German-bred Pomeranian but is a much older breed. It is typically white in color with a dense and fluffy coat.

The Volpino Italiano is a suitable pet for most domestic environments. It is friendly, lively, alert, and intelligent. It displays loyalty to its owner and is often very affectionate toward people with whom it is familiar. It was originally used as a guard dog and watchdog, despite its small size. It is thought to have decreased in size since the days of performing guard-dog duties, but the Volpino Italiano retains some working instinct and is an effective watchdog for the family.

LAGOTTO ROMAGNOLO

OFFICIAL CATEGORIZATION: UK: Gun Dog,
AKC: Not recognized, FCI: Group 8, Section 3

HEIGHT: 17–19 in. (43–48 cm)   WEIGHT: 28½–35 lb. (13–16 kg)

OTHER NAMES: Romagna Water Dog

COLOR: Solid off-white, white with brown or orange markings, brown roan, solid brown, or solid orange

COAT CARE: Moderate maintenance

DIET: Moderate/high consumption

This Italian-bred gun dog is a very valuable and versatile worker. The Lagotto Romagnolo is a medium-sized yet very sturdy breed that is able to retrieve on land or in water. It has a distinctive water-resistant coat that is thick and curly. The coat is either solid in color or exhibits large patches, and the colors range from yellow to dark brown. It is a very old breed and there is artwork depicting the dog that dates back to the fifteenth century.

This intelligent and adaptable breed has strong working capabilities but also makes a very good family pet. Its intelligence and mental agility demands that it be trained and stimulated, but the breed is known for being affectionate, sociable with people and other dogs, friendly, and gentle. It is a high-energy dog and requires a good degree of exercise but it is suited to most family environments.

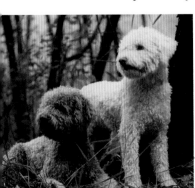

LEFT

This Italian gun dog, Lagotto Romagnolo, is depicted in paintings that date back to the fifteenth century.

CIRNECO DELL'ETNA

OFFICIAL CATEGORIZATION: UK: Not recognized, AKC: Not recognized, FCI: Group 5, Section 7

COLOR: Tan

COAT CARE: Zero maintenance

DIET: Moderate/high consumption

HEIGHT: 17–20 in. (43–51 cm)

WEIGHT: 22–26 lb. (10–12 kg)

OTHER NAMES: Sicilian Greyhound

This is a breed of small sight hound that originates in Sicily and is often referred to as the Sicilian Greyhound. Superficially, it resembles a miniature Pharaoh Hound, but differs very substantially from that breed in the ideal breed standards. The Cirneco dell'Etna was bred originally for hunting rabbits and is very quick and athletic. It is still found all over Sicily and particularly in the area surrounding Mount Etna, where the dogs hunt on volcanic terrain. It is small compared to other sight-hound breeds from the Mediterranean but is agile and keen in the hunt. It is short-coated and has distinctive bat-like ears. It is believed to have been established for more than 3,000 years, having been brought to Sicily by Phoenician traders.

As a pet the dog is lively, energetic, loyal, and friendly. As is typical of so many sight hounds, the Cirneco dell'Etna is a loyal and dedicated companion. The breed is intelligent and those specimens bred from working lines have very strong prey drives, which can disrupt training and behavior. It is generally gentle around children and enjoys the company of people.

SEGUGIO ITALIANO

OFFICIAL CATEGORIZATION: UK: Hound, AKC: Not recognized, FCI: Group 6, Section 1

COLOR: Black and tan or any shade from deep red to wheaten

COAT CARE: Minimal maintenance

DIET: High consumption

HEIGHT: 20½–23 in. (52–59 cm)

WEIGHT: 44–50½ lb. (20–23 kg)

OTHER NAMES: None

The Segugio Italiano is an ancient scent-hound breed. Unlike most scent hounds, it has a slender skull, but due to Mastiff blood that was introduced to the bloodline centuries ago it is otherwise stocky and well-built. It is an energetic and active breed used originally for hunting a wide variety of game, displaying a notable interest in the prey once captured. It is popular in northern Italy as a companion and as a worker but is relatively unknown outside of its homeland.

As a pet the Segugio Italiano is gentle and affectionate. It is particularly suitable for a person living on their own as the dog tends to be fiercely loyal to one companion. This does not mean it is aloof with others—it is generally friendly and sociable—but as with many hunting hounds it is considered by some familiar with the breed to be a "one-man dog."

RIGHT
The Segugio Italiano is popular in Northern Italy, but largely unheard of outside the country.

BERGAMASCO

OFFICIAL CATEGORIZATION: UK: Pastoral,
AKC: Not recognized, FCI: Group 1, Section 1

HEIGHT: 23–25 in. (58–62 cm)   WEIGHT: 70–84 lb. (32–38 kg)

OTHER NAMES: Bergamasco Shepherd Dog, Bergermaschi,
Cane da pastore Bergamasco

COLOR: Solid gray, or with patches of all shades of gray through to black

COAT CARE: Very high maintenance

DIET: High consumption

The Bergamasco is an Italian herding breed native to the Alpine region near to the border with Switzerland and has been in existence for more than 2,000 years. It is a unique-looking breed, with an unusual felted coat that occurs through matting of the fur. This gives the dog protection against the climate and against predators. It is a medium-sized, well-built dog with strong herding instincts.

As a pet, the Bergamasco is a willing and sociable companion, useful as guardian of flock and home, but special consideration must be given to grooming. The unusual coat is naturally matted and shabby but care must be taken to keep it free from dirt and parasites. The breed's herding heritage and naturally high intelligence make it a rewarding dog to own. Training is taken willingly but the Bergamasco does need a moderate level of stimulation to remain happy.

LEFT
The matted coat of the Bergamasco not only keeps it warm in the Alps, but also acts as a protective layer against attackers.

BRACCO ITALIANO

OFFICIAL CATEGORIZATION: UK: Gun Dog,
AKC: Not recognized, FCI: Group 7, Section 1

HEIGHT: 22½–26½ in. (58–67 cm)   WEIGHT: 55–88 lb. (25–40 kg)

Other Names: Italian Pointer

COLOR: White or white with orange, amber, or chestnut markings

COAT CARE: Minimal maintenance

DIET: High consumption

Bracco Italiano is the name given to two similar dogs. Both are pointers bred for hunting work in northern Italy: one originates from the Piedmont region and the other from Lombardy. Both are now considered to be the same breed and have a common ancestry of ancient Mastiff breeds and the Segugio Italiano. The Lombardy version of the breed is darker and heavier than the Piedmont-bred version. The Bracco Italiano is a stocky yet well-balanced pointing breed that was used to hunt birds. It has a relatively large head, long ears, and pendulous lips.

The domesticated Bracco Italiano is a sociable, loving dog that is happiest when at the side of its master. It is intelligent and relatively easy to train but can sometimes be stubborn. Although the breed adapts well to domestic life it very much enjoys exercising its strong hunting instincts when given the opportunity.

CANE CORSO

COLOR: Black or fawn

COAT CARE: Low maintenance

DIET: High/very high consumption

OFFICIAL CATEGORIZATION: UK: Not recognized, AKC: Not recognized, FCI: Group 2, Section 2

HEIGHT: 23½–26½ in. (60–68 cm)   WEIGHT: 88–110 lb. (40–50 kg)

OTHER NAMES: Cane da Macellaio, Italian Corso Dog, Italian Mastiff

The Cane Corso is a large and powerful breed descended from the Molosser and bred for guarding. It is lean yet very strong with a powerful jaw. The breed exhibits two colorations, black and fawn. The coat is short and smooth while the skin around the dewlap and face is looser. The Cane Corso has a very strong guarding instinct and is more than capable of defending against large predators. It has also been used as a hunting dog and until very recently was a rare breed. It has been subject to specialized breeding programs to make the breed's status more stable.

Although the Cane Corso is a very powerful dog and exhibits self-confidence, it can also be sensitive and suffer from separation anxiety. The breed is intelligent, sociable, and generally friendly. It is naturally protective of children, however, is not overtly aggressive or suspicious of new faces unless it has a distinct reason to be.

RIGHT
With a stocky build, the Cane Corso can have either a black or fawn coat.

ITALIAN SPINONE

COLOR: Solid white, white and orange, orange roan with or without orange markings, white with brown markings, or brown roan with or without brown markings

COAT CARE: Moderate maintenance

DIET: High consumption

OFFICIAL CATEGORIZATION: UK: Gun Dog, AKC: Sporting, FCI: Group 7, Section 1

HEIGHT: 23½–27½ in. (60–70 cm)   WEIGHT: 75–86 lb. (34–39 kg)

OTHER NAMES: Italian Griffon, Italian Coarse-Haired Pointer

The Italian Spinone is a versatile working gun-dog breed. It is of square build and has a wiry, relatively strong coat that is short and close to the dog's body. It is of medium size with a well-balanced and athletic physique. It is a well-established hunting breed and is in common usage in its native Italy and other parts of the world. It is known for its hard-working nature and obedience.

The Italian Spinone is a loyal and submissive working companion, with high intelligence and a working drive that is still very prominent today. It has been used by man for the same purpose for many centuries and the breed has an instinctive rapport with people. The dog is friendly, sociable and a little docile. Patient and affectionate with children, the Italian Spinone is a suitable and popular family pet for many differing domestic environments.

MAREMMA SHEEPDOG

OFFICIAL CATEGORIZATION: UK: Pastoral,
AKC: Not recognized, FCI: Group 1, Section 1

HEIGHT: 25½–28½ in. (65–73 cm)   WEIGHT: 77–99 lb. (35–45 kg)

OTHER NAMES: Pastore Abruzzese, Cane da Pastore
Maremmano-Abruzzese

COLOR: White

COAT CARE: Moderate/high maintenance

DIET: High/very high consumption

The Maremma Sheepdog is a large and powerful flock guardian native to Italy. The breed is ancient and has been established as a versatile and very reliable pastoral guardian for centuries. Its breeding origins are in the Tuscany region of Italy. The breed **has a thick, slightly woolly coat that is only exhibited in solid white. Little is known about the ancestry of the breed but it is likely that it is descended from the Anatolian Shepherd dog.**

The Maremma Sheepdog is dignified, noble, and intelligent, with excellent guarding abilities. It is not prone to undue excitement and is a particularly watchful and alert breed. It is less popular in areas where sheep farming has declined but is often kept as a pet in Italy and elsewhere. It is naturally gentle with anything smaller than itself, such as children or lambs, and is extremely protective over its territory.

LEFT
With its thick woolly coat, the Maremma Sheepdog guards its flock carefully and gently.

NEAPOLITAN MASTIFF

OFFICIAL CATEGORIZATION: UK: Working, AKC: Working,
FCI: Group 2, Section 2

HEIGHT: 25½–29½ in. (65–75 cm)   WEIGHT: 110–154 lb. (50–70 kg)

OTHER NAMES: Mastino Napoletano, Mastino

COLOR: Black, blue, all shades of gray, or brown from fawn to red

COAT CARE: Minimal maintenance

DIET: Very high consumption

The Neapolitan Mastiff is a huge and very powerful breed of dog native to Italy. It is an ancient breed and is thought to be a direct and immediate descendant of the ancient Molossus breed, from which all Mastiff breeds descend. It has been used throughout history as a guardian breed,

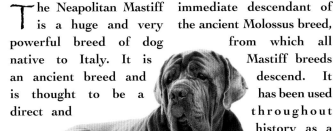

but during Roman times was often pitted against leopards for public entertainment. It has loose skin around the body, dewlap, and face, often to the point that it hangs down. The breed is normally dark in color—commonly black, dark brown, or a dark brindle.

The Neapolitan Mastiff is a very protective breed and is instinctive in guarding. It is friendly and very relaxed around people with whom it is familiar and once it is used to the presence of a new person will accept them, too. The breed is famously gentle, tolerant, and protective of children.

MALTESE

OFFICIAL CATEGORIZATION: UK: Toy, AKC: Toy,
FCI: Group 9, Section 1

COLOR: Pure white

COAT CARE: High maintenance

DIET: Low/moderate consumption

HEIGHT: 10 in. (25 cm)   **WEIGHT:** 4–6 lb. (1.8–2.7 kg)

OTHER NAMES: Bichon Maltaise, Couton

The Maltese is thought to be one of the oldest dog breeds in the world, with some historians placing its origins as far back as nearly 8,000 years ago. It is descended from root breeding stock from Asia and Central Europe but became established in Malta where it was standardized. It is a toy breed and is typically very small with long, silky white hair. The breed is considered to have been a companion breed for most of its existence, accompanying Roman conquests throughout Europe, but in the early stages of its development it was an effective vermin catcher.

Sweet But Feisty

The breed has a very sweet appearance, with large eyes and an almost teddy-bear-like nose. It is very small and has never been much use as a guard dog but it is extremely alert and quick to signal danger. Legend has it that the breed used to be kept alongside Rottweiler-type dogs. If the Maltese heard a sound or saw something untoward, it would yap, prompting the Rottweiler into action to deal with the problem.

The breed is sweet natured but feisty. It is quick to bark if it thinks it is necessary. Very intelligent and mentally agile, the Maltese is quite easy to train. It is sociable and affectionate but can be overly boisterous in the company of young children. In most cases a well-socialized Maltese is friendly and affectionate with children but it is necessary to supervise initial introductions.

The Maltese is a social animal but does not crave or seek a lot of attention—it is happy to take it when it is offered and will act independently otherwise. Its natural inclination for playfulness does not diminish with age and even senior dogs are very eager to play with anyone who is willing. The breed is loyal to its family and will readily adapt to its environment.

ABOVE

A pretty little dog, the Maltese is also extremely alert, yapping to let everyone know of an intruder.

PHARAOH HOUND

OFFICIAL CATEGORIZATION: UK: Hound, AKC: Hound,
FCI: Group 5, Section 6

HEIGHT: 23–25 in. (58.5–63 cm)   WEIGHT: 40–60 lb. (18–27.5 kg)

OTHER NAMES: Kelb Tal-Fenek

COLOR: Tan or chestnut with white markings

COAT CARE: Zero maintenance

DIET: High consumption

The ancient Pharaoh Hound is a distinguished sight hound that is native to Malta. It is sometimes classified as a Pariah Dog, but its working origins are in hunting rabbit. It combines the appearance of strength and power with grace and dignity. It is lean and athletic with a short, very fine coat that is commonly light brown in color ranging from tan to chestnut. The coat is normally one solid color across the body, face, and feet. The Pharaoh Hound has large, erect ears that are typical among dogs of ancient sight-hound descent.

The Pharaoh Hound is quite a rare breed, moderately more popular in Malta but generally small in numbers around the world. It has a strong hunting instinct that it retains from its days as a working dog but it remains a very suitable pet. It has high levels of energy and alertness, with a playful and highly affectionate temperament.

KARST SHEPHERD DOG

OFFICIAL CATEGORIZATION: UK: Not recognized,
AKC: Not recognized, FCI: Group 2, Section 2

HEIGHT: 22–25 in. (57–63 cm)   WEIGHT: 58–88 lb. (26–40 kg)

Other Names: None

COLOR: Iron gray or silver-gray

COAT CARE: Moderate maintenance

DIET: High consumption

The Karst Shepherd Dog is a herding breed that originated in Slovenia. It is an ancient breed and is considered by some to represent the middle point between the Molosser descendants, such as the Mastiff and the Shepherd Dog descendants, such as the German Shepherd Dog. It is a long-coated, rugged breed of dog that is hardy and very tough. It was bred to function as a flock guardian and as such is very instinctive in its suspicion of strangers.

The Karst Shepherd Dog is a popular family pet in Slovenia and is very well-suited to domestic living. It is intelligent and obedient with a keen and instinctively protective nature of the family. The breed is generally friendly and affectionate with family and typically wary of newcomers. It is receptive to training and when well-socialized will be happy to welcome familiar faces into the family home.

LEFT
The Karst Shepherd Dog is popular in Slovenia, and is thought to have similarities to the German Shepherd Dog.

CROATIAN SHEEPDOG

OFFICIAL CATEGORIZATION: UK: Not recognized,
AKC: Not recognized, FCI: Group 1, Section 1

COLOR: Black

COAT CARE: Low/moderate maintenance

HEIGHT: 16–21 in. (40–53 cm)   WEIGHT: 29–43 lb. (13–20 kg)

DIET: Moderate/high consumption

OTHER NAMES: Hrvatski Ovcar

The Croatian Sheepdog is an old breed of herding dog, with its origins in fourteenth-century Europe. It is a medium-sized, sturdily built dog with a rich and thick coat that typically is slightly shaggy. The breed is increasing steadily in size as it is bred more for companionship, but working lines produce compact, solid-black-colored herders of distinction. The breed is agile, energetic, and highly valued by Croatian farming communities.

The Croatian Sheepdog is unerringly loyal and displays great affection to its master. It is a breed that absolutely thrives in the company of a master who can send it to work. The breed is notably healthy, with very high resistance to viruses and little incidence of inherited disorders. This is due to the breed being bred mostly for function and ability rather than form. The Croatian Sheepdog is friendly and intelligent while being naturally and instinctively cautious of strangers.

RIGHT
Typically healthy and fond of a hard day's work, the Croatian Sheepdog has been bred since the fourteenth century.

POSAVAZ HOUND

OFFICIAL CATEGORIZATION: UK: Not recognized,
AKC: Not recognized, FCI: Group 6, Section 1

COLOR: Tricolor

COAT CARE: Minimal maintenance

HEIGHT: No standard   WEIGHT: No standard

DIET: Moderate/high consumption

OTHER NAMES: Posovac Hound, Posavatz Hound, Posavski Gonic

The Posavaz Hound is a rare breed of dog native to the former Yugoslavia. It is named after the region of Posavina where it became established. It is a versatile and hard-working scent hound that was originally used to hunt deer, rabbit, and hare. It has a good nose and a good level of stamina.

The breed is practically unknown outside of its native land, which now geographically consists of Croatia, Serbia, Slovenia, and Bosnia and Herzegovina. The Posavaz Hound is known by different names and by many different spellings of the same name.

It is a loyal and affectionate hound that is skilled and dedicated in the hunt. The breed

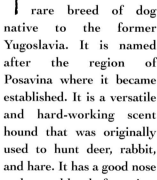

is a versatile and tough hunter, able to work in many differing environments. It is companionable and friendly, displaying great loyalty to its master. The breed is gentle and affectionate with all people and is of very even and reliable temperament.

ISTRIAN SHORTHAIRED HOUND

OFFICIAL CATEGORIZATION: UK: Not recognized, AKC: Not recognized, FCI: Group 6, Section 1

HEIGHT: 18–21½ in. (45.5–53.5 cm) WEIGHT: 35–52 lb. (16–23.5 kg)

OTHER NAMES: Istrian Smooth-Haired Hound

COLOR: White with tan or brown markings, tricolor

COAT CARE: Zero maintenance

DIET: Moderate/high consumption

The Istrian Hound is the name given to two variations of a breed. The short-haired and coarse-haired varieties are distinct physically only by their coat. The reasons for the difference in coat have also given rise to slight differences in working instinct and temperament. The Istrian Shorthaired Hound, sometimes referred to as the Istrian Smooth-Haired Hound, is sometimes slightly smaller than the longhaired variety. Both dogs are distinct from other hounds originating in the Istrian region of Europe due to their orange and white colorations.

The breed is of unclear origin but it is likely that it descended from ancient sight hounds and European scent hounds. The breed is a skilled tracker and is extremely competent in the hunt. It is said to have a peaceful temperament when not working, which, combined with a calm and even demeanor, makes it a suitable pet.

LEFT
The Istrian Shorthaired Hound originates from the Istria region in Europe (west Croatia).

ISTRIAN COARSE-HAIRED HOUND

OFFICIAL CATEGORIZATION: UK: Not recognized, AKC: Not recognized, FCI: Group 6, Section 6

HEIGHT: 17–23 in. (44–58 cm) WEIGHT: 25–56 lb. (16–26 kg)

OTHER NAMES: Istrian Rough-Coated Hound

COLOR: White with yellow or orange markings

COAT CARE: Moderate/high maintenance

DIET: High consumption

The Istrian Coarse-Haired Hound is the second variety of Istrian Hound. It is sometimes slightly larger than its shorthaired relative but both varieties are judged using the same standard and the height differences usually fall well within prescribed standards. The Istrian Coarse-Haired Hound has a much thicker and warmer coat than the shorthaired variety, but it too displays the distinctive and easily identifiable orange and white colorations.

The Istrian Coarse-Haired Hound is gentle and peaceful when not in the hunt. The coarse-haired version of the breed is more popular as a pet but displays a very similar temperament to the short-haired variety, so this popularity is most likely to be due to its appearance. The breed, as is typical with many hounds, is a loyal and dedicated companion with a high level of intelligence. It is instinctive but willing to obey if given adequate training.

DALMATIAN

OFFICIAL CATEGORIZATION: UK: Utility, AKC: nonsporting, FCI: Group 6, Section 3

COLOR: White with black or liver spots

HEIGHT: 21½–24½ in. (54.5–62 cm) WEIGHT: 45–70 lb. (20–32 kg)

COAT CARE: Zero maintenance

DIET: High consumption

OTHER NAMES: Carriage Dog, Dalmatiner, Dalmatinac, Plum Pudding Dog, Spotted Coach Dog, Firehouse Dog

Fascinating Facts

Dalmatian puppies are born pure white; their characteristic spotted coats develop as the dogs mature.

The Dalmatian is one of the most distinctive-looking breeds of dog in the world. No other breed exhibits the unique spotted coat, which comes in either black and white or liver and white and makes the breed instantly recognizable the world over.

The Dalmatian is thought to have originated in the region of Dalmatia, which is now in modern-day Croatia, although many people believe that the dog is of German heritage. There is no proof either way and because the Dalmatian is such an ancient breed it is hard to dispute either argument. In more recent times, the breed was used as a carriage dog and was bred to run alongside and ahead, guiding the horses that pulled chariots and carriages carrying noblemen and women. It was also used in the United States as a fire dog to run ahead of horse-drawn fire carts.

Prone to Deafness

The Dalmatian is a medium-sized dog, well-proportioned and athletic-looking. The standard head shape varies quite considerably throughout the breed, with shorter-muzzled dogs and more slender-faced dogs both being considered to be within the standard. The breed is susceptible to deafness, which is particularly prevalent in the rare examples that are born with a predominantly white coat with fewer spots. In the early stages of the dog's modern development, deafness was not identified and the dog's inability to respond to an owner gained it a reputation as being unintelligent. Of course, this is now known to be untrue but the misconception is still a common one.

The breed is lively and friendly, with a playful and affectionate nature. It is extremely sociable and becomes distressed if isolated from human or animal company. The breed is well-known for its unusual habit of "smiling."

LEFT
The only dog to have such a distinctive spotted coat, it is easy to recognize a Dalmatian.

BOSNIAN COARSE-HAIRED HOUND

OFFICIAL CATEGORIZATION: UK: Not recognized, AKC: Not recognized, FCI: Group 6, Section 1

HEIGHT: 18–22 in. (46–55 cm)   WEIGHT: 35–53 lb. (16–24 kg)

OTHER NAMES: Bosanski Oštrodlaki Goniã-Barak, Bosnian Rough-Haired Hound, Bosnian Rough-Coated Hound, Bosnian Coarse-Coated Hound

COLOR: Wheaten, reddish yellow, earthy gray, or blackish with white markings, or bi- or tricolored

COAT CARE: Moderate/high maintenance

DIET: High consumption

The Bosnian Coarse-Haired Hound is a compact and well-proportioned scent hound that was bred for hunting small to medium-sized game. It has a distinctively rough coat that gives rise to the many names by which the breed is known, which include Bosnian Rough-Haired Hound, Bosnian Rough-Coated Hound, and Bosnian Coarse-Coated Hound. It is descended from old Griffon breeds and inherits their long body shape. It is believed but not confirmed that Molosser breeds may also have contributed to the breed's bloodline.

This breed is relatively uncommon outside of its native land. It is a hardy and tough hound able to hunt for long periods of time without tiring. It is also a very adaptable dog and can work over many types of terrain. It is typically loyal and sociable with people and other dogs, displaying affection to its master when not stimulated by the hunt.

SERBIAN HOUND

OFFICIAL CATEGORIZATION: UK: Not recognized, AKC: Not recognized, FCI: Group 6, Section 1

HEIGHT: 17–21 in. (43–53 cm)   WEIGHT: 42–46 1/2 lb. (19–21 kg)

OTHER NAMES: Balkan Hound, Balkanski Goniã

COLOR: Red or tan with a black saddle

COAT CARE: Zero maintenance

DIET: High consumption

The Serbian Hound, previously known as the Balkan Hound, is a hard-working hunting hound that was bred to track wounded animals, such as deer and hare. The Serbian Hound is short coated and sturdy, normally exhibiting either black-and-tan or black-and-red colorations. It has a relatively slender head and large ears. The breed is considered to be a serious and dedicated hunter with a very strong prey drive and instinct for the chase.

Although a formidable working dog and not particularly well-established as a pet breed, the Serbian Hound has a warm and friendly nature. The breed is of high intelligence with a great degree of loyalty to its master. It requires firm training because it can be hot-tempered and feisty. However, when not in the hunt it will generally become quite docile and calm.

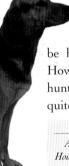

SERBIAN TRICOLOR HOUND

COLOR: Black and tan with a white front

COAT CARE: Zero maintenance

DIET: High consumption

OFFICIAL CATEGORIZATION: UK: Not recognized, AKC: Not recognized, FCI: Group 6, Section 1

HEIGHT: 18–22 in. (46–56 cm)   WEIGHT: 44–55 lb. (20–25 kg)

OTHER NAMES: Srpski Trobojni Goniã

The Serbian Tricolor Hound is a very rare breed. It is very similar to the Montenegrin Mountain Hound but is distinguishable from its close relative by the white patch on its front, which gives it the black, tan, and white tricolored pattern. It is a sturdy yet compact breed with a well-balanced and graceful carriage. A skilled and instinctive hunter, the Serbian Tricolor Hound was used for tracking medium-sized and some-times large game, such as deer and boar. The breed has a strong nose for the hunt and is known for its dedication and vigour when hunting.

The hound is remarkably friendly and affectionate, often quick to form a close bond with its owner. Intelligent and alert, with a strong hunting instinct, the breed is often happier when in the hunt, but does make an adaptable and willing domestic pet. The Serbian Tricolor Hound requires solid training in order to control its hunting instincts.

LEFT

This breed was formerly known as the Yugoslavian Tricolor Hound; the FCI changed the name in 1996.

MONTENEGRIN MOUNTAIN HOUND

COLOR: Black with tan markings

COAT CARE: Low maintenance

DIET: Moderate/high consumption

OFFICIAL CATEGORIZATION: UK: Not recognized, AKC: Not recognized, FCI: Group 6, Section 1

HEIGHT: 19–19½ in. (49–50 cm)   WEIGHT: 55–60 lb. (20–25 kg)

OTHER NAMES: Crnogorski Planinski Goniã, Serbian Mountain Hound

The Montenegrin Mountain Hound, or Serbian Mountain Hound as it is also known, is a hunting dog native to Serbia and Montenegro. It is very similar to the Serbian Tricolor Hound with the only difference being the coat, which lacks the white color and thus the tricolor pattern. The breed is compact and evenly balanced with a graceful and smooth carriage. The Montenegrin Mountain Hound was bred, like the Serbian Tricolor Hound, for hunting medium to large game ranging in size from hare and fox to wild boar and roe deer.

The breed is affectionate and friendly, normally forming a close bond with its master. It is intelligent but very instinctive and requires good training for the owner to be able to control its urge to hunt. The breed is relatively unknown outside of its native country.

LEFT

Like the countryside around it, the Montenegrin Mountain Hound has had many changes of name in recent history.

YUGOSLAVIAN SHEPHERD DOG

OFFICIAL CATEGORIZATION: UK: Not recognized,
AKC: Not recognized, FCI: Group 2, Section 2

HEIGHT: 23–26 in. (58.5–66 cm)   WEIGHT: 65–88 lb. (29.5–39 kg)

OTHER NAMES: Sharrplaninatz, Sharplanina

COLOR: Tan, gray, white, or black

COAT CARE: Moderate maintenance

DIET: High consumption

The Yugoslavian Shepherd Dog, which is also known by the native name Sharplanina, is a breed so rare that it faces a very real threat of extinction. It was bred originally to herd cattle on the steep and snowy slopes of the Macedonian mountains, but in recent years has had very little work, due to the disappearance of much of the livestock from that

region of Europe. The breed is large and strong, with a very thick coat that is similar in appearance and color to that of the Leonberger.

The breed is very hardy and used to enduring extremely cold conditions. It is a tolerant yet very protective breed and is instinctive in its flock-guarding behavior. The breed is loyal and affectionate with family and curious of strangers. It is a formidable guardian of home and flock, but is tender and gentle when in the domestic environment.

ITALIAN GREYHOUND

OFFICIAL CATEGORIZATION: UK: Toy, AKC: Toy,
FCI: Group 10, Section 3

HEIGHT: 13–15 in. (32–38 cm)   WEIGHT: 8–10 lb. (3.5–4.5 kg)

OTHER NAMES: Piccolo Levriero Italiano

COLOR: Black, blue, cream, fawn, red, or white

COAT CARE: Zero maintenance

DIET: Moderate/high consumption

The Italian Greyhound is the smallest of the sight-hound breeds. Despite its name, its origins are in Turkey and Greece. It gets its name from its popularity in Italian Renaissance art and culture, where it featured prominently as a companion dog for the rich. It is predominantly a pet breed today but has been used for hunting in the past, often alongside birds of prey. The breed is slight and agile, with a typical sight-hound shape—lean and well-balanced. It is exceptionally quick on its feet and still retains strong hunting instincts.

The Italian Greyhound is a popular pet but it does have a notably mischievous streak. It is intelligent but is rarely motivated to please its owner; instead it is affectionate and friendly without seeking to be obedient. It can be trained, but rewards are by far the most successful way to secure the breed's cooperation and favor.

LEFT
The Italian Greyhound is affectionate, but not very biddable.

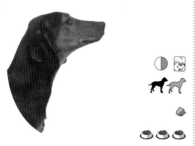

HELLENIC HOUND

COLOR: Black with tan markings

COAT CARE: Minimal maintenance

DIET: High consumption

OFFICIAL CATEGORIZATION: UK: Not recognized, AKC: Not recognized, FCI: Group 6, Section 1

HEIGHT: 18–22 in. (45–55 cm)   WEIGHT: 38–44 lb. (17–20 kg)

OTHER NAMES: Hellenikos Ichnilatis

The Hellenic Hound is a rare breed native to Greece. It is thought that it descended from northern African hound breeds taken to Greece by traders more than 2,000 years ago. It is not a well-known breed outside of Greece but is relatively popular within its native country. This black-and-tan scent hound has a delicate and sophisticated nose. It is an enthusiastic and dedicated hunter with an instinctive drive for chasing small to medium-sized game.

RIGHT
A keen working dog, the Hellenic Hound would find the lack of occupation as a pet distressing.

The Hellenic Hound is predominantly a working dog, with a powerful and dominant hunting instinct. It is not generally considered to be a suitable pet due to its preference for work over domestic living. The breed is lively and intelligent and these characteristics are only truly exploited in the hunt. Although the dog is friendly and obedient it simply does not adapt well to domestic living and would become distressed if restricted.

CESKY TERRIER

COLOR: Gray-blue or light brown with yellow markings

COAT CARE: Low/moderate maintenance

DIET: Moderate consumption

OFFICIAL CATEGORIZATION: UK: Terrier, AKC: Not recognized, FCI: Group 3, Section 2

HEIGHT: 9½–12½ in. (25–32 cm)   WEIGHT: 13–22 lb. (6–10 kg)

OTHER NAMES: Czesky Terrier, Bohemian Terrier

The Cesky Terrier is a breed native to the Czech Republic but of very British heritage. This new breed was established in the 1960s by crossbreeding the Sealyham Terrier and the Scottish Terrier. It is a small and robust breed of dog with an excellent ratting ability and instinct. It is a popular pet and is now established as a purebred in many countries. It is a short-legged and long-bodied breed with a wavy and bushy coat.

The Cesky Terrier is sweet natured and friendly. It is noted for lacking certain terrier attributes, such as dog aggression and tenacity, but certainly retains the typical terrier-like vivacious-ness and lively demeanor. The breed is feisty and brave but outgoing and extremely sociable, especially with children. It is typically welcoming and not suspicious of new people, with an even temper and reliable, consistent temperament.

BOHEMIAN WIREHAIRED POINTING GRIFFON

OFFICIAL CATEGORIZATION: UK: Not recognized,
AKC: Sporting, FCI: Group 7, Section 1

COLOR: Dark roan with or without brown blotches, brown with ticking, or solid brown with no markings

HEIGHT: 23½–26 in. (60–66 cm)   WEIGHT: 62–75 lb. (28–34 kg)

COAT CARE: Low/moderate maintenance

OTHER NAMES: Cesky Fousek, Czech Coarse-Haired Pointer, Slovakian Wirehaired Pointer

DIET: High consumption

The Bohemian Wirehaired Pointing Griffon is an ancient breed of gun dog originating from Bohemia, which is now part of the modern-day Czech Republic. It is a versatile worker, able to perform hunt, point, and retrieve duties, as well as being competent in water for duck hunting. The breed evolved during the fourteenth century but was not standardized until the nineteenth century. It is an ancestor of the Slovakian Rough-Haired Pointer.

The breed is also known as the Cesky Fousek, which references firstly the country of origin and secondly the "flowing" of the hair around the face. The breed is strong and firmly built, with high stamina. The Bohemian Wirehaired Pointing Griffon is an instinctive and competent working dog that is still in use in its native land. It is an intelligent, alert, and very active breed.

CZECHOSLOVAKIAN WOLFDOG

OFFICIAL CATEGORIZATION: UK: Not recognized,
AKC: Not recognized, FCI: Group 1, Section 1

COLOR: Yellow-gray to silver-gray with a light mask

HEIGHT: 24½–27½ in. (62–70 cm)   WEIGHT: 55–59½ lb. (25–27 kg)

COAT CARE: Low/moderate maintenance

OTHER NAMES: Československý vlčák

DIET: High/very high consumption

The Czechoslovakian Wolfdog is a controversial new breed of wolf-dog hybrid. Like the Saarloos Wolfdog, it was bred using domestic canine (German Shepherd) and wild lupine (Carpathian Wolf) stock. The purpose of the breeding was to create a breed of dog that combined the temperament and intelligence of the German Shepherd Dog with the appearance and robust health of a wild wolf. The breed resembles a wolf more than it does a dog, but it is far more trainable. It has been subject to controversy in the past due to the breed's perceived status as being wild and dangerous.

Due to its immediate wild ancestry, the Czechoslovakian Wolfdog is particularly pack orientated. With its intelligence and highly instinctive nature, it is a challenging yet very rewarding pet. Special consideration must be given to training, which can not revolve around repetitive games and drills—rather it must stimulate the wild intelligence of this intriguing breed.

ABOVE RIGHT
The Czechoslovakian Wolfdog is a controversial breed, crossing the Carpathian Wolf and a German Shepherd.

SLOVAKIAN HOUND

COLOR: Black with brown to mahogany markings

COAT CARE: Minimal maintenance

DIET: High consumption

OFFICIAL CATEGORIZATION: UK: Not recognized, AKC: Not recognized, FCI: Group 6, Section 1

HEIGHT: 17½–19½ in. (45–50 cm)   WEIGHT: 33–44 lb. (15–20 kg)

OTHER NAMES: Slovensky Kopov, Black Forest Hound

The Slovakian Hound is an ancient breed of scent hound native to the Czech Republic. It is distinct from other similar Eastern European hounds by its black-and-tan markings. It is a sturdy and well-balanced dog of medium size with a hard yet smooth coat. It was bred for pack hunting and is believed to be a descendent of now-extinct pack hounds.

In the hunt, the Slovakian Hound is sleek, fast, and quick-witted. As with many breeds originating in the Czech Republic region, the Slovakian Hound is known by many other names, most notably the Black Forest Hound.

The Slovakian Hound is an intelligent and dedicated hunter, with powerful instincts and a determination in the chase that makes it an extremely valuable working companion. It is friendly with its master and is patient and affectionate with children if properly socialized but is prone to shyness.

RIGHT
Native to the Czech Republic the Slovakian Hound is a descendant of pack hounds that are now extinct.

SLOVAKIAN CHUVACH

COLOR: White

COAT CARE: Moderate/high maintenance

DIET: High consumption

OFFICIAL CATEGORIZATION: UK: Not recognized, AKC: Not recognized, FCI: Group 1, Section 1

HEIGHT: 22–27½ in. (50–70 cm)   WEIGHT: 66–99 lb. (30–45 kg)

OTHER NAMES: Slovak Cuvac

The Slovakian Chuvach is a large and powerful flock guardian breed that can trace its origins back to the seventeenth century. It is exclusively white in color, with a thick coat. The Slovakian Chuvach was originally used to protect mountain flocks from wolves in its native Slovakia, but as the wolf population declined in Europe so did the breed. Without a job to perform, the breed faced extinction but was resurrected by dedicated breeding that led to it becoming internationally standardized in the late 1960s.

The breed is commonly used in its native country as a border patrol dog, but is also kept as a pet. It is a protective and dedicated breed that is quick to defend flock or family if required. The Slovakian Chuvach is known for its affectionate nature, often seeking closeness with family members. It is patient and kindly with children but fearless and dominant of any perceived predators or intruders.

SLOVAKIAN ROUGH-HAIRED POINTER

OFFICIAL CATEGORIZATION: UK: Not recognized,
AKC: Not recognized, FCI: Group 7, Section 1

HEIGHT: 24½–26½ in. (62–68 cm)   WEIGHT: No standard

OTHER NAMES: Slovensky Hrubosrsky Stavac (Ohar), Slovakian Wirehaired Pointer, Slovakian Wirehaired Pointing Dog, Slovakian Pointing Griffon

COLOR: Gray-brown or
pewter silver

COAT CARE: Moderate maintenance

DIET: High consumption

This breed is known by many very similar names, including Slovakian Wirehaired Pointer, Slovakian Wire-haired Pointing Dog, and Slovakian Pointing Griffon. This confusion is due to the relatively new status of this purpose-bred dog. The Slovakian Rough-Haired Pointing dog originated from a breeding program that incorporated the Weimaraner, the Cesky Fousek, and the German Wirehaired Pointer as root stock. It was intended that the resultant dog would be a versatile hunt, point, and retrieve animal that could function on land or in water. It has a noticeably harsh coat, which occasionally exhibits the distinctive silver coloration of the Weimaraner.

The breed is energetic and brave with a high level of intelligence. Its friendliness and social tendencies make the Slovakian Rough-Haired Pointer a suitable breed of dog for many families. Its instincts are very strong and require competent and consistent training, but in general the breed is keen to please.

Fascinating Facts

The Great Pyrenees is highly sensitive to anaesthetic.

POLISH LOWLAND SHEEPDOG

OFFICIAL CATEGORIZATION: UK: Pastoral,
AKC: Herding, FCI: Group 1, Section 1

HEIGHT: 17–19½ in. (43–50 cm)   WEIGHT: 39½–44 lb. (18–20 kg)

OTHER NAMES: Valee Sheepdog

COLOR: Any

COAT CARE: High maintenance

DIET: High consumption

The Polish Lowland Sheepdog is a well-known and valuable herding dog originating in the thirteenth century and is an ancestor of the Bearded Collie. A Polish merchant took his Polish Lowland Sheepdog to Scotland to move a herd that he was selling. When a Scottish shepherd noticed the breed's excellent abilities he bought a dog and two bitches for breeding; the puppies were bred with local dogs and eventually

became established as Bearded Collies. Like its descendents, the Polish Lowland Sheepdog is well-balanced and muscular, with a shaggy coat.

The Polish Lowland Sheepdog is highly intelligent with strong herding abilities. It is a suitable companion for almost all environments because it is friendly, trainable, generally affectionate, and sociable. Some dogs may attempt to dominate weak family members, so consistent training is very important. This adaptable and even-tempered breed is noted for having an excellent memory.

POLISH HOUND

COLOR: Black and tan or black and tan saddled

COAT CARE: Minimal maintenance

DIET: High consumption

OFFICIAL CATEGORIZATION: UK: Not recognized, AKC: Not recognized, FCI: Group 6, Section 1

HEIGHT: 22–26 in. (56–65 cm)   WEIGHT: 55–70½ lb. (25–32 kg)

OTHER NAMES: Ogar Polski

The Polish Hound is an ancient breed of working hound with a very striking appearance. Although it is thought of as indigenous to Poland, some say it is descended from Austrian or German strains. It is black and tan in color, with tan coloration on the face. In some specimens, the tan is almost a gold shade, giving the breed an unusual look. The Polish Hound is well-built, evenly balanced and very strong. It is a versatile hunter, with a keen sense of smell and able to cover a lot of differing terrain in harsh weather. Dedicated and resilient, this breed is a valuable hunter that will not give up on a scent.

The Polish Hound is an extremely popular hunting companion in its native land. The breed is sociable and enjoys the company of children and adults equally. However, its tenacity and highly sensitive scenting instinct means that the breed is happiest at work. Fortunately its outgoing and self-confident nature makes the Polish Hound an exceptionally good dog to train for such work.

TATRA SHEPHERD DOG

COLOR: White

COAT CARE: Moderate/high maintenance

DIET: High/very high consumption

OFFICIAL CATEGORIZATION: UK: Not recognized, AKC: Not recognized, FCI: Group 1, Section 1

HEIGHT: 25½–27½ in. (65–70 cm)   WEIGHT: 99–132 lb. (45–60 kg)

OTHER NAMES: Polski Owczarek Podhalanski

The Tatra Shepherd Dog is a strong and powerful herding dog with a noticeably heavy white coat and is an ancestor of the Great Pyrenees. The breed originated in the

RIGHT
The Tatra Shepherd Dog of Poland is an ancestor of the Great Pyrenees, or Pyrenean Mountain Dog.

mountainous regions of Poland, where it was used as a herder and flock guardian. Mountain herding breeds were typically expected not only to herd and guard their flock but also to find lost flock members and to guide them home. The Tatra Shepherd Dog is an intelligent and strong breed that is capable of defending its flock from wolves. The breed is instinctive and, because it was left to work on its own, it is very independent.

This intelligent breed is not well-known outside of Poland. However, it is an exceptional pet in the right circumstances. High intelligence, loyalty, and dedication to the family are just three attributes that make this dog so companionable.

POLISH GREYHOUND

OFFICIAL CATEGORIZATION: UK: Not recognized,
AKC: Not recognized, FCI: Group 10, Section 3

HEIGHT: 27½–31½ in. (70–80 cm) WEIGHT: 86–90½ lb. (39–41 kg)

Other Names: Chart Polski

COLOR: Any

COAT CARE: Minimal maintenance

DIET: High consumption

The Polish Greyhound is a powerful and muscular sight hound bred for hunting hare and fox in rough terrain. It is an ancient breed descended from Asian sight-hound breeds. It is slightly more robust than is typical for sight hound breeds but is still lean and well-balanced. The coat comes in a variety of textures, lengths and colors.

As is common with most sight hounds, the Polish Greyhound makes a good companion. Its loyalty and affection are directed to its master but the breed is sociable and friendly toward all. It is an instinctive breed, with excellent eyesight and an urge to chase whatever stimulates it. Despite being athletic and extremely fast on foot, this breed requires no more exercise than other breeds of similar size, and is very adaptable to the domestic environment. The breed is tough and resilient, requiring firm, consistent training from its owner.

ABOVE
A very instinctive breed, the Polish Greyhound has a strong desire to give chase.

PUMI

OFFICIAL CATEGORIZATION: UK: Not recognized,
AKC: Not recognized, FCI: Group 1, Section 1

HEIGHT: 14–17 in. (35–44 cm) WEIGHT: 18–29 lb. (8–13 kg)

OTHER NAMES: Hungarian Pumi

COLOR: Any shade of gray

COAT CARE: Moderate maintenance

DIET: Moderate/high consumption

The Pumi is a breed of farm dog native to Hungary. It is a descendant of French and German herding and terrier breeds and is a close relative of the Puli. The Puli and the Pumi were considered to be the same breed until as recently as the 1920s. The Puli was a freely bred farm dog, with no specific standard for appearance. The breeds were separated by their coat, with the Pumi exhibiting a shorter, wirier coat. The Pumi was used as an all-purpose farm dog, adept at herding all types of livestock as well as catching vermin and guarding flocks.

The Pumi is an intelligent and vivacious breed. It is considered remarkably daring and alert—very content to tackle perceived intruders alone without much consideration for its safety. It is affectionate and sociable, but does require training to help it adapt to the domestic environment.

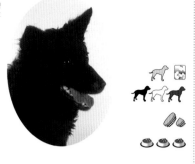

MUDI

Color: Black, white, brown, fawn, or black merle

COAT CARE: Low/moderate maintenance

DIET: High consumption

OFFICIAL CATEGORIZATION: UK: Not recognized, AKC: Not recognized, FCI: Group 1, Section 1

HEIGHT: 14–18½ in. (35–40 cm)   WEIGHT: 18–29 lb. (8–13 kg)

OTHER NAMES: Hungarian Mudi, Canis Ovilis Fenyesi

The Mudi is a rare breed of herding dog native to Hungary with a diverse working history. The breed is descended from the Hungarian Puli, and Spitz breeds, having become established in the nineteenth century. It has worked as a herding dog, a flock guardian, and less commonly as a hunting companion. It is a medium-sized breed that bears some physical typicalities of the Spitz breeds, such as erect ears and alert facial expression. The coat is usually black, white, brown, fawn, or black merle.

This breed is intelligent and hardy. It has a strong working instinct but is adaptable to domestic life, subject to strong and confident training. As with some herding breeds, the Mudi has a tendency to nip at the heels of anything it deems to be part of the flock, which can include family members. The Mudi is sharp of mind and alert, making it a useful guard dog.

RIGHT
The Mudi is a rare Hungarian herding breed with Spitz ancestry.

HUNGARIAN PULI

COLOR: Rusty black, black, all shades of gray, or white

COAT CARE: Moderate/high maintenance

DIET: Moderate/high consumption

OFFICIAL CATEGORIZATION: UK: Pastoral, AKC: Herding, FCI: Group 1, Section 1

HEIGHT: 16–17½ in. (40–44 cm)   WEIGHT: 29–33 lb. (13–15 kg)

OTHER NAMES: Hungarian Water Dog

This Hungarian breed of herding dog is distinctive in its appearance due to its corded and shaggy coat. The breed has a woolly undercoat and long feltlike cords of hair on the outside. It is a sturdy and robust dog that was bred originally around the eleventh century to herd livestock but adapted to become a useful flock guardian. Its close relative the Pumi does not exhibit the distinctive coat, but they are physically similar in other respects.

The Hungarian Puli is a brave and dedicated flock guardian, hardy and rustic with an independent streak. It has strong herding and protective instincts that it will display in the domestic environment; it is also known as being possessive. The breed is alert and watchful, suspicious and curious of unusual sounds. Friendly and affectionate with family members, the breed may initially be suspicious of new people, but will take the lead from its master.

HUNGARIAN VIZSLA

OFFICIAL CATEGORIZATION: UK: Gun Dog, AKC: Sporting, FCI: Group 7, Section 1

HEIGHT: 22½–25 in. (57–64 cm)   WEIGHT: 44–66 lb. (20–30 kg)

OTHER NAMES: Magyar Vizsla, Hungarian Pointer

COLOR: Solid golden rust of various shades

COAT CARE: Minimal maintenance

DIET: High consumption

The original Hungarian Vizsla is an ancient breed that can trace its origins as far back as the ninth century. It was used first for ratting but developed to be a proficient hunt, point and retrieve breed. It is the ancestor of many popular breeds, including the Weimaraner. The Hungarian Wirehaired Vizsla is the descendant of the Hungarian Vizsla and the German Wirehaired Pointer. It is slightly larger than its ancestor and has a thicker coat enabling it to work in colder conditions.

An Excellent Pet

The Hungarian Vizsla is a good worker with a keen instinct to obey commands. Both varieties of the breed are considered to make excellent pets due to their friendly and demonstrably affectionate natures. They are considerate and patient with children, often bonding particularly strongly with youngsters. The Hungarian Vizsla is an intelligent and sociable breed that thrives on interaction; it gets on with other dogs and is always keen to be involved with the family. It does not like being separated from its pack or family and may misbehave if left alone for too long.

The Hungarian Vizsla is a gentle, docile, and placid breed that is prone to bouts of excitement and energy. Its charming and bashful persona makes it a very appealing pet and it is well-suited to many different domestic environments. Training should be conducted patiently—the Hungarian Vizsla is eager to learn and to please.

ABOVE

Interestingly the smooth- and the wirehaired varieties of Vizsla come from different ancestral lines.

LEFT

The coat of the Hungarian Wirehaired Vizsla allows it to work in colder climates than the smooth-haired variety.

TRANSYLVANIAN HOUND

COLOR: Reddish brown or black

COAT CARE: Minimal maintenance

DIET: Moderate/high consumption

OFFICIAL CATEGORIZATION: UK: Not recognized, AKC: Not recognized, FCI: Group 6, Section 1

HEIGHT: 17½–19½ in. (45–50 cm)   WEIGHT: 66–77 lb. (30–35 kg)

OTHER NAMES: Erdelyi Kopo

The Transylvanian Hound is an ancient breed of hunting hound originating in ninth-century Hungary. It is a breed that has two varieties—the short-legged and standard. The short-legged Transylvanian Hound was used for hunting small game, such as fox and hare, while the standard version was used to hunt wild boar and deer. The short-legged variation of this breed is also commonly found with slightly shorter hair. The coat is typically reddish in the short-legged variety and black with other colors in the standard variety.

tends to be governed by its urge and drive to hunt. When away from the hunt it is docile and placid, loyal, and affectionate toward its owner and generally sociable and friendly toward others.

RIGHT
The Transylvanian Hound is a dedicated hunter, with great senses of both smell and direction.

The Transylvanian Hound is a dedicated and tireless hunter, with a strong nose and remarkable sense of direction. It is intelligent but highly instinctive and

KOMONDOR

COLOR: White

COAT CARE: 4.5 brushes

DIET: High consumption

OFFICIAL CATEGORIZATION: UK: Pastoral, AKC: Working, FCI: Group 1, Section 1

HEIGHT: 27½–30 in. (70–76 cm)   WEIGHT: 110–135 lb. (50–61 kg)

OTHER NAMES: Hungarian Komondor, Hungarian Sheepdog

The Komondor is a striking and distinctive-looking herding dog originating in ninth-century Hungary. Its coat develops from thick and fluffy during puppyhood to dense and corded in maturity, described as resembling dreadlocked hair. The coat serves to keep the dog warm in the cold and cool in the heat, but is uncomfortable when wet. This indicates that the Komondor became established as a breed in a climate where there were weather extremes but little rain. The Komondor is a working herder with a hardy and rugged persona.

Although popular as a pet, the Komondor is not particularly affectionate. It is a serious working breed with a dedication and instinct for herding and protecting. The breed can make a formidable guard dog and adaptable pet, gentle and tolerant of children and sociable in general.

Despite this, the breed prefers to work and protect the flock.

HUNGARIAN KUVASZ

OFFICIAL CATEGORIZATION: UK: Pastoral, AKC: Working,
FCI: Group 1, Section 1

HEIGHT: 28–29½ in. (71–75 cm)   WEIGHT: 88–115 lb. (40–52 kg)

OTHER NAMES: Kuvasz

COLOR: Pure white

COAT CARE: Moderate maintenance

DIET: High consumption

The Hungarian Kuvasz is an ancient breed often cited as originating from Hungary, but while the breed did become established in Hungary it was moved around eastern Europe by the nomadic Magyar tribe. As a result, it has a diverse gene pool and counts many ancient and extinct Asian and European breeds as ancestors. After World War II, this large and powerful herding breed was close to extinction in Hungary. Recently, the breed has been stabilized by dedicated breeding but, the Great Pyrenees—a large dog with a thick white coat—has been introduced to the bloodline to help diversify the gene pool.

The Hungarian Kuvasz is a dedicated flock guardian and has extremely strong protective instincts. This intelligent breed is constantly alert and aware, quick to respond to any unusual noise or movement. It is patient and affectionate with children, loyal and friendly to its master, but suspiciously curious of strangers.

LEFT
As its name indicates, the Hungarian Kuvasz was established in Hungary, but it did also migrate with its Magyar tribal owners.

HUNGARIAN GREYHOUND

OFFICIAL CATEGORIZATION: UK: Not recognized,
AKC: Not recognized, FCI: Group 10, Section 3

HEIGHT: 25½–27½ in. (65–70 cm)   WEIGHT: 64–68½ lb. (29–31 kg)

OTHER NAMES: Magyar Agar

COLOR: All colors—solid, spot, or brindle

COAT CARE: Minimal maintenance

DIET: Moderate/high consumption

The Hungarian Greyhound is an ancient sight hound descending from old Asian sight-hound breeds. It became established as a breed around the ninth century but has evolved physically since then into a faster specimen. It is predominantly a working hunter, bred for tracking and killing hare and fox. The breed is not particularly quick when compared to the Greyhound, but is tireless and bold with a lot of stamina. The Hungarian Greyhound is a breed of robust health, with a lean physique and all types of coat colors.

The Hungarian Greyhound is a gentle and affectionate dog when not in the hunt. It has a strong independent streak that is related to its working history. The breed is known for having a particularly weak scenting ability, but it has extremely sharp eyesight to compensate. It is a calm and even-tempered dog with an adaptable and relaxed temperament.

SAMOYED

COLOR: White, white and biscuit, or cream

COAT CARE: Moderate/high maintenance

DIET: Moderate/high consumption

OFFICIAL CATEGORIZATION: UK: Pastoral, AKC: Working, FCI: Group 5, Section 1

HEIGHT: 21–22 in. (51–56 cm)   WEIGHT: 44–65 lb. (20–32.5 kg)

OTHER NAMES: Samoiedskaya Sobaka, Nenetskaya Laika

The Samoyed is an ancient northern Spitz breed that is named after the Arctic tribe that bred it. It is a distinctive and easily recognized breed, with a snow-white thick coat, erect ears, noble expression, and alert gaze. It is one of the oldest breeds of dog in the world and is an ancestor to many modern Spitz-type breeds. The Samoyed tribe used this dog to guard their herds, pull carts, and hunt large game such, as walrus.

as appearing to smile the breed is extremely friendly—so friendly that most attempts at using a Samoyed as a guard dog have failed. The breed is highly intelligent and sociable; it is gentle and affectionate to all and displays a special loyalty toward its master.

Training a Samoyed can be a challenge, because the breed is prone to willfulness. It is suited to gentle persuasion as opposed to firm training. It is extremely companionable and thrives in the company of people and other dogs. Its disposition is typically alert, watchful, and active. Despite being a poor choice for guarding duties, the ever-aware Samoyed is normally the first to respond to a strange noise.

BELOW

The Samoyed tribe used this breed to guard its flocks and help it hunt game, and so this ancient Spitz breed became known as Samoyed.

In the late nineteenth century, the breed was taken to Britain by the explorer Robert Falcon Scott, who was impressed by the Samoyed's strength and pulling ability. The Samoyed has a special place in exploration history: Norwegian explorer Roald Amundsen was the first person to reach the South Pole and he did so using a team of sled dogs led by a Samoyed.

The "Smiling" Dog

The breed is strong, well-muscled, and covered in a thick white coat. Samoyeds are known as "smiling dogs" due to the way the mouth opens when the dog is panting. As well

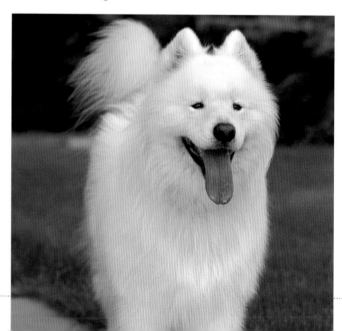

SIBERIAN HUSKY

OFFICIAL CATEGORIZATION: UK: Working, AKC: Working, FCI: Group 5, Section 1

COLOR: All colors, from black to pure white

HEIGHT: 21–23½ in. (53–60 cm)   WEIGHT: 45–60 lb. (20–27 kg)

COAT CARE: Moderate maintenance

OTHER NAMES: Chukcha, Chuksha, Keshia

DIET: High consumption

LEFT

Associated with Polar exploration, Huskys provided the ideal transportation aid in the race for the Pole.

Like the Samoyed, the Siberian Husky is one of the oldest breeds of dog in the world. Commonly associated with dog-sled racing and polar exploration, the Siberian Husky is a well-known breed. It originated on the Siberian Peninsula, now part of Russia, centuries ago and led a relatively isolated existence until the late nineteenth century, when it was exported from Siberia for use in sledding.

It is a member of the Spitz genetic family and is thought to be one of the closest relatives of the wild wolves from which modern dog breeds have evolved. To look at the Siberian Husky is to look at a very certain point in the evolution of the domesticated dog. The breed is large and wild-looking, with an almost wolflike face and a distinctive thick coat. Coloration is normally silver, gray, red, or black, or a combination of color and white, or, in less common instances, solid white.

A Sociable Talker

Due to the harsh conditions in which the breed evolved, only those dogs with a strong prey drive and the ability to exercise it survived, meaning that the Siberian Husky of today is descended from only the strongest and most intelligent dogs. The modern Siberian Husky, despite its wild roots, is a gentle and compassionate breed, often fond of children and very sociable. It retains strong wild instincts but is obedient and biddable.

The breed is very vocal and often howls or "talks" to its owner. The Siberian Husky, despite being friendly and adaptable, may simply decide to ignore certain commands, so reward-based training is often the most successful path to obedience. The breed is generally even tempered and reliable but it can be prone to bouts of high activity where it may jump, howl, and run until exhausted.

Fascinating Facts

A statue in New York City's Central Park was erected in honor of a Siberian Husky that carried diphtheria medicine 674 miles (1,084 km) across Alaska during an epidemic.

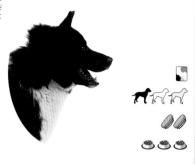

RUSSIAN EUROPEAN LAIKA

COLOR: Black, gray, white, or salt and pepper

COAT CARE: Moderate maintenance

DIET: High consumption

OFFICIAL CATEGORIZATION: UK: Not recognized, AKC: Not recognized, FCI: Group 5, Section 2

HEIGHT: 20½–23 in. (52–58 cm)   WEIGHT: No standard

OTHER NAMES: Russko-Evropeiskaia Laika

The Russian European Laika is the smallest of the three Laika breeds. The term Laika refers to Russian hunting breeds and translates as "barker." The Russian European Laika originated in the vast expanse of land between the Finnish border and the Ural Mountains, where

it was used to hunt very small game, such as squirrel. Like most northern European breeds, the Russian European Laika has a dense and thick coat and erect ears. The coat comes in a small variety of colors ranging from gray to black with patches of white. The Russian European Laika is a friendly and reliable breed of dog. It is not prone to aggression but is still in possession of a strong hunting instinct. It is loyal and affectionate, and particularly good with children due to its patient and tolerant disposition. It is a highly territorial breed and will respond protectively toward dogs and people entering the home.

WEST SIBERIAN LAIKA

COLOR: Black, white, tan, gray, or red

COAT CARE: Moderate maintenance

DIET: High consumption

OFFICIAL CATEGORIZATION: UK: Not recognized, AKC: Not recognized, FCI: Group 5, Section 2

HEIGHT: 20–24 in. (50–60 cm)   WEIGHT: 40–55 lb. (18–25 kg)

OTHER NAMES: None

The West Siberian Laika is an agile and versatile hunting dog. Slightly larger than the Russian European Laika, it was bred to hunt a variety of prey from birds to foxes. It is of medium size with a sturdy build. The coat is thick and dense, normally of light gray to dark gray coloration. The breed originated on the European side of Siberia and has been used predominantly for hunting.

The West Siberian Laika is noted as being the calmest and most even tempered of the three Laika breeds.

It is instinctive and eager to hunt with a tireless and dedicated attitude to its work. The breed displays a warm and sociable persona, with little tendency toward aggression. It is a patient breed with a lot of charm—welcoming to all and affectionate toward its family. It displays a protective instinct toward children and is keen to be trained.

SOUTH RUSSIAN SHEPHERD DOG

OFFICIAL CATEGORIZATION: UK: Not recognized,
AKC: Not recognized, FCI: Group 1, Section 1

HEIGHT: 24–27 in. (61–68.5 cm)   WEIGHT: 53–57½ lb. (24–26 kg)

OTHER NAMES: South Russian Ovtcharka,
Ovtcharka de Russie Meridionale

COLOR: White, white and yellow, straw, gray, or dark gray

COAT CARE: Moderate/high maintenance

DIET: High consumption

The South Russian Shepherd Dog is an ancient breed of herding dog that is descended from a mixture of northern European herders. It is a very large, muscular breed but its physical form is well-hidden by its thick and dense coat. The coat is normally solid in color, ranging from pure white through light yellow to dark gray. Its appearance is more typical of European herding breeds than of Siberian breeds.

The breed is powerful, active, and intelligent. It has a strong working instinct and as such it can be distrustful of new people. With sufficient socialization, the breed can adapt to act independently of this instinct, but, as with many pastoral breeds, it is bred specifically to be highly protective and wary; therefore, to attempt to negate this trait would be to ignore the dog's original purpose. It is not known for being demonstrably friendly but is exceptionally loyal and courageous.

EAST SIBERIAN LAIKA

OFFICIAL CATEGORIZATION: UK: Not recognized,
AKC: Not recognized, FCI: Group 5, Section 2

HEIGHT: 22–25 in. (50–62.5 cm)   WEIGHT: 40–50 lb. (18–22.5 kg)

OTHER NAMES: None

COLOR: Black, tan, or white

COAT CARE: Moderate maintenance

DIET: High consumption

The East Siberian Laika is the largest of the three Laika varieties. It was bred for hunting in snowy forests, with birds and large game, such as moose and boar, among the commonly tracked quarry. It is a strong and purposefully agile dog with a thick coat that is typical of northern European breeds. It comes in a wide variety of colors, which is a sign of genetic diversity and robust health.

The breed is calm, even tempered, and very considered in its actions. Not prone to instinctive bursts of activity, it is watchful and reserved in new situations. Among family it is a warm and affectionate breed with a tendency toward protectiveness. It is perfectly capable of defending itself against attack but is unlikely to display aggressive behavior. The breed is intelligent and an excellent hunter. To train it well it is important for the owner to remain patient and gentle.

LEFT
The East Siberian Laika is a hefty dog used for hunting moose and boar, but has an affectionate domestic disposition.

CENTRAL ASIAN SHEPHERD DOG

COLOR: Various

COAT CARE: Low/moderate maintenance

DIET: High/very high consumption

OFFICIAL CATEGORIZATION: UK: Not recognized, AKC: Not recognized, FCI: Group 2, Section 2

HEIGHT: 27–32 in. (65–78 cm)   WEIGHT: 121–176 lb. (55–79 kg)

OTHER NAMES: Central Asian Ovcharka

This large and powerful Molosser breed is one of the oldest and most genetically diverse breeds of dog. As the breed was becoming established, it occupied a vast expanse of land that reached from northern Turkey to central Russia and toward the Chinese border. It is a descendant of many different breeds but is typical of the Molosser type, with a powerful body, large head, and heavy jaw. Due to its genetic diversity, its color and the degree of conformation to type is wide ranging, and because of this the breed is robustly healthy.

As a livestock guardian, the Central Asian Shepherd Dog is naturally protective of anything smaller than itself. This instinct extends to family pets, children, and, in some cases, adults. It is a gentle breed when with family, but is a bold and fearless protector when instinct takes over. Its even temper means it will react protectively only when necessary.

Fascinating Facts

The heaviest ever dog was an English Mastiff named Zorba. Zorba reached a weight of 343 lb. (156 kg) in 1989.

LEFT

As its name suggests, the Central Asian Shepherd Dog has a gene pool stretching from Turkey via Russia toward the Chinese border.

RUSSIAN BLACK TERRIER

COLOR: Black

COAT CARE: Moderate/high maintenance

DIET: High consumption

OFFICIAL CATEGORIZATION: UK: Working, AKC: Working, FCI: Group 2, Section 1

HEIGHT: 27–30½ in. (68–77 cm)   WEIGHT: 80–143 lb. (36–65 kg)

OTHER NAMES: Tchiorny Terrier, Chornyi, Russian Bear Schnauzer

The Russian Black Terrier is a dog of unique and unusual heritage. It was purpose-bred by the Russian state to function as a guard and police dog. The breeders, who occupied a state-owned facility, imported breeds, including the Giant Schnauzer, Rottweiler, Newfoundland, and Airedale Terrier and used them as root breeding stock. The resulting breed is large and muscular, with a hard and dense black coat.

Despite its formal origins, breeding of the Black Russian Terrier has been opened up and, as a result, the standard for temperament and appearance is changing. The breed was

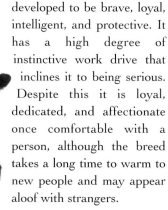

developed to be brave, loyal, intelligent, and protective. It has a high degree of instinctive work drive that inclines it to being serious. Despite this it is loyal, dedicated, and affectionate once comfortable with a person, although the breed takes a long time to warm to new people and may appear aloof with strangers.

CAUCASIAN SHEPHERD DOG

OFFICIAL CATEGORIZATION: UK: Not recognized,
AKC: Not recognized, FCI: Group 2, Section 2

HEIGHT: 25–28 in. (64–72 cm)   WEIGHT: 99–154 lb. (45–70 kg)

OTHER NAMES: Gampr, Nagazi nagazi, Kavkaski Ovcar,
Sage Ghafghazi

COLOR: Gray, fawn, tan, brindle, or white

COAT CARE: Moderate/high maintenance

DIET: High/very high consumption

The Caucasian Shepherd Dog is one of the oldest living descendants of the ancient Molosser-type dog. It is a product of its initial environment, bred by people who needed to protect their flocks from large predators. It is for that reason that the Caucasian Shepherd Dog is such a large, brave, and powerful dog. Despite being named as a shepherd dog, the breed is a true flock guardian. The term *ovcharka*, which is Russian for "shepherd dog" "is often applied to the name of this breed and taken as an insult by breeders.

The breed is intelligent and considered, often consciously ignoring commands and favoring instinct. It is neither gentle nor affectionate, but is tolerant. Around children it is patient and forgiving but will not reciprocate demonstrable affection. The breed has quick and serious protective reflexes; it will protect its flock or family in any situation and will do so tenaciously.

LEFT
A Caucasian Sheepdog puppy and its father. This breed often favors instinct over obedience.

BORZOI

OFFICIAL CATEGORIZATION: UK: Hound, AKC: Hound,
FCI: Group 10, Section 1

HEIGHT: 27½–30½ in. (70–77 cm)   WEIGHT: 97–101½ lb. (44–46 kg)

OTHER NAMES: Barzoï, Russian Wolfhound,
Russkaya Psovaya Borzaya, Psovoi

COLOR: Any

COAT CARE: Moderate maintenance

DIET: High consumption

The Russian name Borzoi means "quick dog." The Borzoi is an old sight hound breed with disputed origins: typically it is accepted as having been established in Russia, but its genetic and ancestral origins are thought to be in Asia. The breed is large, slender, and has a long, thick coat in many varying colors and patterns. Despite its size, it has the appearance of a slender, graceful, and powerful hunter.

The Borzoi is a gentle, polite, and kindly breed of dog, rarely barking or exhibiting unwanted activity. It harbors a natural respect for people and is loyal, with a warm and welcoming temperament. Although independent and intelligent, the Borzoi is naturally submissive to people and very obedient. It can be somewhat nervous around new people, especially children, but with proper training and socialization it becomes a friendly and confident dog that is willing and cooperative.

OTHER EUROPEAN BREEDS

Crossbreeding and two world wars have caused some of Europe's dog breeds to become marginalized. A modern trend of breeding "designer dogs" has given rise to certain new hybrids that are fast on their way to becoming established, but are yet to fully meet breed registration criteria. Other breeds are isolated by geography or by the niche appeal of the work they can do, which explains why certain breeds never make it out of their own country.

Schnoodle

The Schnoodle is a popular crossbreed of the Poodle and the Schnauzer. It is fast becoming a more uniform type and breeding results are becoming more predictable, although there is still no standard. The dog is popular in Europe, as are many Poodle hybrid breeds. Poodles are used frequently in establishing new breeds as they have many desirable physical qualities, notably their hypoallergenic fur.

Swedish Lapphund

The Swedish Lapphund is a rare breed of Spitz origin. It is considered to be Sweden's version of the more well-known Finnish Lapphund. It is a popular pet in Sweden but is relatively unknown outside of its native country. Physically, it is very similar to its Finnish relative—short, with a dense, bushy coat and alert expression. The breed makes an excellent pet because of its friendly and obedient nature.

Finnish Reindeer Herder

The Finnish Reindeer Herder, or Lapponian Herder as it is sometimes known, is a rare and primitive breed that is relatively unheard of outside of its native Finland. It is descended from northern European Spitz-type dogs and has many physical

---

characteristics that reflect this origin, such as erect ears, a thick coat, and alert expression.

Finnish Hound

The Finnish Hound is a working hound that is popular in Finland and Sweden but rare elsewhere. It is descended from a mixture of northern European hounds and displays a coloration that normally includes black, tan, and white. It is a strong and athletic breed with a friendly and obedient demeanor. It is rarely entered into conformation shows because of its strong working heritage.

ABOVE

Finnish Hounds are rare outside Finland and not often shown, being bred for their working characteristics.

Griffon d'Arret a Poil dur Korthals

This breed is also known as the Wirehaired Pointing Griffon. It is of Franco-Dutch origin and was bred to serve as a gun dog in swampy terrain. The coat is harsh and very protective, suitable for work in mud and muddy water. The breed is an excellent worker but is very rare. It is an obedient and affectionate dog with a high level of working instinct and intelligence.

Raibs Suns

The Raibs Suns is a rare breed of unknown heritage. It is believed to have originated in or near to the Baltic state of Estonia, but its exact lineage is disputed. Some claim that the breed is little more than a mongrel, while others maintain that it is a deliberate crossbreeding of various German Spitz breeds and other European dogs. It is a small to medium-sized dog, very lively and intelligent, with a thick, heavy coat.

Jagdterrier

The resurgence in numbers of the Jagdterrier is the result of the strong German patriotism that occurred between the two world wars. Terrier enthusiasts set out with a goal to recreate

extinct German breeds. The Jagdterrier was the result of a process known as back breeding, whereby established breeds that may have descended from the target breed are used and selected based on their physical and working likeness to the desired result. The Black-and-Tan Terrier was used, and its coloration is still present in the Jagdterrier today, but its working ability was not strong enough. The modern Jagdterrier is said to resemble the Patterdale Terrier.

ABOVE RIGHT

Between World Wars I and II, German breeders attempted to retrace the breeding steps and rediscover the Jagdterrier.

LEFT

The Griffon d'Arret a Poil dur Korthals, more simply known as the Wirehaired Pointing Griffin, is an ideal gun dog in swampy conditions.

Africa

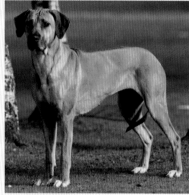

Africa is home to only nine native dog breeds. Because of the hot climate and arid landscape that covers much of Africa, there has been less opportunity to breed dogs here compared to other, more forgiving environments. If, historically, there is no grass for animals to graze on, then there is no need for herding dogs, guarding dogs, or even hunting dogs, which partly explains the small number of African breeds. Poverty and war have also made dog breeding difficult.

Influential Ancestry

Despite there being only nine native African breeds, without these nine there are many other breeds that would not be in existence today. Some of the world's oldest and most genetically influential breeds originated in northern Africa.

The cooler northern parts of Africa are home to four of the continent's nine dog breeds. The Canary Islands are home to the Perro de Pressa Canario, a powerful and imposing Mastiff breed used for protecting livestock. Move east onto the mainland and into Morocco—the home of the Aidi and Sloughi. These two compatriot breeds were developed for very different functions, the Aidi to protect livestock and the Sloughi to hunt. The northeast of Africa is the ancestral

breeding ground of the Saluki, another hunting hound and one of the oldest breeds of dog on the earth.

Ancient Breeds

Western Africa has also provided a climate conducive to dog breeding. The Azawakh hound, a dog bred by a nomadic tribe, became established in Mali, where it is still popular today. Central Africa is home to only one breed, the Basenji, which was bred to work in the thick bush of the Congo.

The smallest African breed is the Coton du Tulear, native to the island of Madagascar located off the southwest coast. Southern Africa is famous for two dogs: the Rhodesian Ridgeback of Zimbabwe and the Boerboel of South Africa—both large, powerful breeds.

PERRO DE PRESA CANARIO

OFFICIAL CATEGORIZATION: UK: Not recognized,
AKC: Not recognized, FCI: Group 2, Section 2

HEIGHT: 23½–25½ in. (60–64.5 cm) WEIGHT: 110–130 lb. (50–59 kg)

OTHER NAMES: Canary Dog, Presa Canario

COLOR: Fawn, brindle, or black

COAT CARE: Minimal maintenance

DIET: High/very high consumption

The Perro de Presa Canario is a large and imposing Mastiff breed native to the Canary Islands. The breed is of undetermined origin but it is believed that it started life as a farm and home guardian, with occasional usage as a herding breed. It later went on to become involved in dog fighting in its native country, but is now more commonly kept as a pet. The breed is exceptionally powerful and has a crushing bite. Typically, it has a very coarse, short coat that is brindle patterned and black or fawn colored.

> **RIGHT**
> *Thought to have started out as a guard dog, the Perro de Presa Canario (Canary Dog) has a dreadful crushing bite.*

The Perro de Presa Canario is a formidable and extremely able guard dog. It is self-confident and very aware of its own power. It requires a dominant and experienced owner to deliver consistent and firm training. The breed is intelligent, tolerant, and loyal, but is quick to become protective and defensive if stimulated.

AIDI

OFFICIAL CATEGORIZATION: UK: Not recognized,
AKC: Not recognized, FCI: Group 2, Section 2

HEIGHT: 21–25 in. (53–63.5 cm)   WEIGHT: 53–57½ lb. (24–26 kg)

OTHER NAMES: Chien de l'Atlas, Atlas Shepherd Dog

COLOR: White, black, black and white, pale red, or tawny

COAT CARE: Moderate maintenance

DIET: High consumption

This Moroccan breed was established as a flock guardian. Unusually for an African breed, it has a thick coat and bushy tail. The coat is either white, black and white, pale red, or tawny and is always heavy, despite the heat. The Aidi is lean and agile with a strong protective instinct. The dog has an alert, watchful expression that is typical of many guardian breeds.

This is an intelligent and sensitive breed and as such is prone to responding badly to firm or strict training. It is agile of mind and body, instinctive and eager to please. The Aidi can become distressed and distracted if it thinks it has displeased its master. It is an excellent watchdog and guard dog and instinctive in its will to protect the flock. In a domestic environment, it retains all of its natural guarding instinct and treats the family as its own flock.

SLOUGHI

COLOR: Light sand to red sand (fawn)

COAT CARE: Zero maintenance

DIET: High consumption

OFFICIAL CATEGORIZATION: UK: Hound, AKC: Not recognized, FCI: Group 10, Section 3

HEIGHT: 26–28½ in. (66–72 cm)   WEIGHT: 66–70 lb. (30–32 kg)

OTHER NAMES: Arabian Greyhound, Sloughi Moghrebi

The Sloughi is an ancient sight-hound breed native to northern Africa. It is extremely lean, giving the impression of speed, grace, and agility. It is entirely normal for the breed to have prominent ribs due to its athletic frame. It was bred for hunting in the wide open plains of northern Africa and is extremely skilled at hunting and catching large prey. Depictions of dogs resembling the Sloughi have been found in artifacts dating back more than 5,000 years.

The Sloughi is unusual for a sight hound in that it is not demonstrably affectionate and is very reserved. Although loyal, friendly, and biddable, it is subtle in its demonstration of emotion. The breed is sensitive and eager to please, responding best to kind reassurance rather than firm correction. The Sloughi is a very dedicated companion, often showing far greater favor to one person over others.

LEFT
The Sloughi originates from Morocco.

SALUKI

COLOR: Any color other than brindle

COAT CARE: Low maintenance

DIET: High consumption

OFFICIAL CATEGORIZATION: UK: Hound, AKC: Hound, FCI: Group 10, Section 1

HEIGHT: 23–28 in. (58–71 cm)   WEIGHT: 29–66 lb. (13–30 kg)

OTHER NAMES: Gazelle Hound, Royal Dog of Egypt, Persian Greyhound, Tazi

The Saluki was arguably the first breed of dog to diverge from the wolf species. The breed is actually more correctly described as an Afro-Eurasian or Asian dog that originated in the Middle East. It was established more than 5,000 years ago by nomadic tribes traveling from Arabia into northern Africa. It is an extremely fast sight hound, capable of catching a gazelle. A tall, long-bodied breed with long, feathered ears and tail, the Saluki has a graceful and elegant appearance, sleek movement, and flowing gait.

The breed retains typical sight-hound hunting instincts and is easily stimulated by sudden movement. In the domestic environment, it is quiet, gentle, and sensitive. It shows affection toward children and family members but will be assertive in its need for solitude. As a breed it is common for the Saluki to become very attached to one person above others and this often leads to the dog becoming distressed if separated from that person for too long.

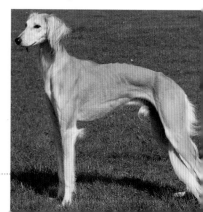

AZAWAKH

OFFICIAL CATEGORIZATION: UK: Not recognized,
AKC: Not recognized, FCI: Group 10, Section 3

HEIGHT: 25–29 in. (64–74 cm) WEIGHT: 44–55 lb. (20–25 kg)

OTHER NAMES: Tuareg Sloughi

COLOR: Fawn with slight patching

COAT CARE: Zero maintenance

DIET: High consumption

The Azawakh is a north-African sight-hound breed. It is believed to have been bred by the nomadic Tuareg tribe, but despite a strong association between the breed and the tribe this is not confirmed. In modern times, the Tuareg still use the Azawakh to chase and trip gazelle in order for mounted hunters to complete the kill. The breed is lean and short coated, with an agile and graceful carriage. It is valued for its hardiness and toughness.

The Azawakh is a brave and tireless hunter, more commonly used as a pack hound than a lone hunter. It is selective to whom it gives affection and can be reserved with people it does not know. Instinctively compelled by the hunt, the breed is typically vigilant, alert, watchful, and quick to react to danger. As a result, it is a popular watchdog in north African countries.

Fascinating Facts

The hunting attempts of African wild dogs are successful 70–90 percent of the time. In comparison, Sumatran tigers catch their prey only 10 percent of the time.

LEFT
Azawakh is another of the native African breeds, originating in Mali.

BASENJI

OFFICIAL CATEGORIZATION: UK: Hound, AKC: Hound,
FCI: Group 5, Section 6

HEIGHT: 15½–18½ in. (39.5–47 cm) WEIGHT: 22–26½ lb. (10–12 kg)

OTHER NAMES: African Bush Dog, Ango Angari, Avuvi,
Congo Dog, Zande Dog

COLOR: Pure black and white, red and white, black, tan, and white with tan melon pips and mask, black, or tan and white

COAT CARE: Minimal maintenance

DIET: Moderate/high consumption

The Basenji, a breed well-known for its lack of bark and hatred of water, is a central African hound. It is not typical of scent hounds in terms of appearance or behavior, but is often classified as one. The Basenji is small and elegant, with a short coat, tightly curled tail, wrinkled forehead, and pricked ears. It is often described as having a gazellelike elegance. It was bred to live and work in bushy areas, often as a village guard and as a hunter. Despite its lack of bark, it does vocalize when happy—emitting an unusual yodel-type sound.

The Basenji is watchful and very alert. Often credited with having unusually feline behavior, the Basenji is fond of high perches. The breed is exceptionally friendly and affectionate, with a strong fondness for children. It is independently minded and intelligent but is cooperative in training and is typically eager to please.

RHODESIAN RIDGEBACK

COLOR: Light wheaten to red wheaten

COAT CARE: Minimal maintenance

DIET: High consumption

OFFICIAL CATEGORIZATION: UK: Hound, AKC: Hound, FCI: Group 6, Section 3

HEIGHT: 25–27 in. (63–69 cm)   WEIGHT: 78–82½ lb. (35.5–37.5 kg)

OTHER NAMES: African Lion Hound

The Rhodesian Ridgeback is a large hunting dog that originated in eighteenth-century Africa. It was established by European settlers in Zimbabwe and was used to hunt lions in packs. The breed descends from the Great Dane, Bloodhound, and Scottish Deerhound. It has a very distinguishing ridge of hair that runs along the spine, caused by backward hair growth beginning at the top of the back and extending various lengths along the spine. The Rhodesian Ridgeback is a large breed, with a strong yet lean physique. Typically it is light brown in color, but the exact shade may vary.

breed. It is loyal and affectionate but occasionally can be mischievous or boisterous. Some examples of the breed are wary of strangers, while others are noticeably friendly toward everyone. The breed is also particularly sensitive, especially during training. If a Rhodesian Ridgeback senses it has caused displeasure, it may attempt to get back in favor with its

owner through a combination of affection and "charm."

Around children the breed is kind and gentle, although occasionally clumsy, but never spiteful. The breed is often noted for its calmness and even temper, which enables it to adapt well to domestic life. Despite its rather impressive working history as a lion-hunting breed, the Rhodesian Ridgeback is not inherently keen for the hunt. Although it does have hunting instincts at the fore, its calmness is the more pronounced characteristic.

Fascinating Facts

Some Rhodesian Ridgeback puppies are born without the distinctive ridge. Normally, these puppies are sterilized to prevent them from breeding.

The breed is notable for the degree of diversity in physical appearance that is allowed for within the standard. While some breed standards require strict uniformity, the standard of the Rhodesian Ridgeback allows for examples to

have fuller or more slender faces. The breed standard is considered to be similar in its flexibility to that of the Dalmatian.

Calm and Kind

The Rhodesian Ridgeback is an intelligent and instinctive

COTON DE TULEAR

OFFICIAL CATEGORIZATION: UK: Toy, AKC: Not recognized,
FCI: Group 1, Section 1

HEIGHT: 10–12½ in. (25–32 cm)   WEIGHT: 9–13 lb. (4–6 kg)

OTHER NAMES: None

COLOR: White

COAT CARE: High maintenance

DIET: Moderate consumption

The Coton de Tulear is a toy breed that was established in Madagascar. Ancestors of the breed, particularly members of the Bichon family of dogs, were brought to Madagascar by pirates, sailors, and merchants and were bred with local dogs. The breed is named partly for its cottonlike coat and partly in honour of the Madagascan town of Tulear, where it originated. It was a popular breed among seafarers due to its size, lively and friendly personality, and ability to catch vermin. The breed is compact and small, with a fine and fluffy coat.

The Coton de Tulear is a lively, curious, and dedicated companion. Sometimes shy and prone to separation anxiety, the breed is gentle and playful when happy and secure in its environment. It responds well to new people and generally is sociable.

SOUTH AFRICAN BOERBOEL

OFFICIAL CATEGORIZATION: UK: Not recognized,
AKC: Not recognized, FCI: Not recognized

HEIGHT: 25–28 in. (64–70 cm)   WEIGHT: 154–200 lb. (70–90 kg)

OTHER NAMES: South African Mastiff

COLOR: Cream white, pale tawny, reddish brown, brown, or all shades of brindle

COAT CARE: Minimal maintenance

DIET: High/very high consumption

ABOVE
Originally bred to be a guard dog, the South African Boerboel is not an aggressive dog.

The South African Boerboel is a large Mastiff-type breed that was established by European settlers in South Africa. It descends from the Mastiff and certain bull breeds, such as the Bulldog, and was bred with the sole intention of guarding property. It is a strong and powerful, well-proportioned breed with even balance. Its short coat is typically tan with a black muzzle. The breed is physically comparable to a large Rottweiler.

Despite the intention of the original breeders to produce a guard dog, the breed is not aggressive. Rather, it is curious and sensitive, able to detect the reaction of its master to a visitor. It does not react protectively to all visitors but will deal with any intruders or unwelcome guests on command. It is a popular pet and will adapt to a role of companionship very happily. It is calm and even tempered with a deeply affectionate approach toward children.

OTHER AFRICAN BREEDS

Many of today's modern breeds can be traced back to Africa, but the continent has few native dogs to call its own compared to Europe, Asia, and the Americas. This is partly due to the climate in the majority of Africa—grass does not grow and flocks cannot graze, meaning the need for herding dogs is limited. Many African nations are poor and the lifestyle of the inhabitants is not conducive to pet dog ownership, which is another reason for the low number of dogs.

Africanis

"Africanis" is the umbrella name for the southern African native dog. The name (also written "AfriCanis") was formulated in 1998 by the Africanis Society of Southern Africa, which has carried out scientific research on the history of these dogs. It is not a selectively bred breed but prevails as a land race. Over the ages it adapted to various ecological niches in response to natural selection.

Archaeological findings indicate that the domestic dog first entered the African continent 6,700 years ago. It arrived from the Middle East in the company of migrating herdsmen and spread to the west and the south. To cross the equator and to populate subequatorial Africa, it had to wait for the Early Iron Age Bantu migration, which started 2,000 years ago. Africanis still prevail deep in the tribal lands, where they remain untouched by exotic (western) breed imports.

Africanis is a medium-sized dog of slender to average build, generally well-muscled. It gives the impression of

ABOVE
The Africanis is a descendant of the dogs that are depicted on the Egyptian murals inside the pyramids.

swiftness, endurance, and efficiency. Natural selection has adapted these dogs to their environment and made them tolerant of parasites and resistant to common diseases. Africanis displaying a kind of spinal ridge will occasionally occur. Selective breeding has endeavored to generalize and per-petuate this feature in the Rhodesian Ridgeback.

LEFT
Africanis exist to this day deep in tribal lands, undiluted with new breeds.

ABOVE

Egyptian Pariah Dogs are opportunists, hunting or scavenging for food.

Egyptian Pariah Dog

There are numerous individual groups of dogs in Egypt that are referred to as Egyptian Pariah Dogs. They exist on the fringes of communities and settlements, occasionally interacting with humans but normally living independently of people. The typical Egyptian Pariah Dog is sleek and lean and will hunt for food alone, as well as scavenge. Unlike feral dogs, the Egyptian Pariah Dogs can become integrated into human communities relatively easily and are often taken in by families and kept as pets or trained as hunting dogs. The appearance of the Egyptian Pariah Dog is not standardized, but it is typical for these dogs to have large, erect ears, smooth coats, and slender heads.

Sulimov Dog

The Sulimov Dog is a new breed of canine hybrid. The breed was established in Russia, using Siberian Huskies and Golden Jackals native to Africa. Despite the fact that the breed was created on Russian soil, its African ancestry is considered by some as enough to render the dog an "African breed," despite the fact that the Sulimov Dog has never been established on that continent.

The breed was developed to create a specimen that had an extremely advanced sense of smell that could operate in both hot and cold climates. The breeder was employed by a Russian airline to create a dog to work across the various airports in Russia; due to the country's size, the airports in Russia are subject to a wide variety of climates. The Siberian Husky was used in the breeding mix so that the offspring would be tolerant of the cold and able to detect scent in snow, while the Jackal genetic influence enabled the dogs to tolerate high temperatures and detect scents as they became more volatile in the heat.

BELOW (LEFT & RIGHT)

The desire for a new breed able to work in conditions of extreme heat and cold was the impetus for the breeding of the Husky-Jackal crossbreed, the Sulimov Dog, which is a combination of the Golden Jackal (left) and the Sibrian Husky (right). The Sulimov Dog is an African breed, but bred in Russia.

Asia

From the Turkish border to Japan, Asia is home to many different and unusual breeds. The variety of Asia's dogs is considerable, from companion animals (bred for ancient Chinese dynasties and retained in their native countries for centuries) to large, powerful guarding breeds. Asia is a place of genetic diversity. Mountains, grasslands, palaces, and deserts are all home to ancient Asian dog breeds. Throughout history, Asia has produced some of the most impressive and unusual dog breeds man has seen.

A Dog For Every Occasion

The Anatolian Shepherd dog, originating near to the European border, is the most westerly bred dog of Asia. From Anatolia, look south to Israel and the home of the Canaan Dog—an ancient and treasured Pariah. Then move into the Middle East—the home of the Afghan Hound.

The further east one moves through Asia, the smaller the dog breeds become. Bhutan, China, and Tibet have all contributed popular small breeds, from the Pekingese to the Pug. China's contribution to the canine population is notably unusual and includes hairless breeds, dogs bred for royal fancy, and dogs bred for guarding temples. Moving through Tibet and China toward Korea, the native breeds become

larger again. The Tibetan Mastiff, a powerful and extremely competent guard dog, is the largest Tibetan breed.

Korea's canine population is small, with only one recognized breed—the Korean Jindo. Conversely, Japan has established many dog breeds, both large and small. From the diminutive Japanese Terrier to the Tosa Inu, Japan has bred a dog for almost every function and desire. Companion dogs, herding dogs, and ferocious and fearless guarding dogs form just a portion of Japan's native canine heritage. The Hokkaido, Akita, and Shikoku are all breeds named after their native provinces in Japan, spreading these ancient names across the world as the breeds were exported.

ANATOLIAN SHEPHERD DOG

OFFICIAL CATEGORIZATION: UK: Pastoral, AKC: Working,
FCI: Group 2, Section 2

HEIGHT: 29–32 in. (74–81 cm)   WEIGHT: 110–141 lb. (50–64 kg)

OTHER NAMES: Coban Köpegi, Karabash

COLOR: All colors and patterns

COAT CARE: Moderate maintenance

DIET: High/very high consumption

The Anatolian Shepherd Dog is a large flock guardian breed from the now-Turkish region of Anatolia. This powerful and very strong dog was bred to protect sheep from predators, such as wolves, and, in cases of the breed being exported to Africa, it was used to guard against attacks from big cats, such as cheetahs. It has a thick, short coat that comes in many colors and patterns, commonly tawny and fawn with black around the mask.

The breed is an instinctive guardian with a good degree of confidence and has the power and ability to protect a flock against even the most formidable predator, but it is also intelligent and obedient. Although gentle and caring around children and family members, the Anatolian Shepherd is fearless and tenacious in the face of threat and is curious or even suspicious of new people. The breed requires strong leadership and a confident owner.

LEFT

The most westerly of all the Asian breeds, the Anatolian Shepherd Dog originated from the region that is now Turkey.

CANAAN DOG

OFFICIAL CATEGORIZATION: UK: Utility, AKC: Herding,
FCI: Group 5, Section 6

HEIGHT: 20–24 in. (50–60 cm)   WEIGHT: 40–55 lb. (18–25 kg)

OTHER NAMES: Kelev K'naani

COLOR: Sand or red-brown, white, black, or spotted, with or without a symmetrical black mask

COAT CARE: Moderate maintenance

DIET: High consumption

The Canaan Dog is an immediate descendent of Israeli pariah dogs. It is a wild and ancient breed with a long history of working to serve nomadic Israelite tribes. Although its immediate ancestors were pariah dogs, roaming wild in the desert, it has inherited blood from ancient Spitz breeds and displays many physical similarities to the type, including the erect ears and alert expression. It is a robustly

built and generally healthy breed that displays a range of coat colorations.

The breed was and still is used as a guard and defense dog. The working origins of the breed suggest that it was developed to guard settlements from intruders, both people and animals. It is not an inherently aggressive breed but is considered and watchful, sensitive to threat and danger. The breed has a fierce loyalty and dedication to its owner and will display affection toward and socialize with those in its family.

AFGHAN HOUND

COLOR: Any

COAT CARE: Moderate/high maintenance

DIET: High consumption

OFFICIAL CATEGORIZATION: UK: Hound, AKC: Hound, FCI: Group 10, Section 1

HEIGHT: 27–29 in. (68–74 cm)   WEIGHT: 45–60 lb. (20–27 kg)

OTHER NAMES: Baluchi Hound, Sage Baluchi, Ogar Afgan

The Afghan Hound is an ancient and distinctive-looking hunting hound that is now more common as a pet and show dog. It stands tall, with a lean physique and luxuriously long and silky coat. It is built for speed and endurance, acquiring the coat in the cold mountainous regions of Afghanistan where it was established to hunt deer and other large game. The Afghan Hound typically is a light brown shade, but all colors are accepted by the various breed standards.

Intelligent and dignified, the Afghan Hound has a noticeable and character-istic independent streak that often leads it to appear aloof or disobedient. The breed is playful, energetic, and friendly with a fondness of high-energy pursuits. It is gentle, loyal, and dedicated, but some specimens can be difficult to train due to their willfulness. The Afghan Hound is always lively and sociable but equally able to function as a watchdog.

DAMCHI

COLOR: Black, white, or tricolor

COAT CARE: Moderate maintenance

DIET: Moderate/high consumption

OFFICIAL CATEGORIZATION: UK: Not recognized, AKC: Not recognized, FCI: Not recognized

HEIGHT: No standard   WEIGHT: No standard

OTHER NAMES: None

The Damchi is a rare breed of dog originating in Bhutan. It is small to medium-small in size and resembles the Tibetan Spaniel, but is slightly larger and stockier by comparison. Because of its remoteness and isolation in Bhutan, not many people are aware of the breed's existence. There are two theories surrounding the etymology of the breed's name: one proposes that the breed is named after a small Himalayan village in which it may have originated; the other suggests that the name Damchi means "tied-dog" and that this explains the breed's purpose as a guard dog. Neither theory has been confirmed.

The breed is well-loved in its native country and is kept as a guard or watchdog and as a pet; it has even been featured on national postage stamps. It is thought that the only specimens of the Damchi breed outside of Bhutan are to be found in Germany.

RIGHT
A rare breed, the Damchi is found largely in its native country, Bhutan, where it is much loved.

THAI RIDGEBACK

OFFICIAL CATEGORIZATION: UK: Not recognized,
AKC: Not recognized, FCI: Group 5, Section 8

HEIGHT: 20–22 in. (56–61 cm)   WEIGHT: 51–75 lb. (23–34 kg)

OTHER NAMES: None

COLOR: Blue, black, fawn, or beige

COAT CARE: Minimal maintenance

DIET: High consumption

The Thai Ridgeback is a rare and unusual breed of ancient origin. Its precise history and development are unknown, but there is a strong likelihood that the breed was used as a cattle and flock guardian. It is a medium-sized, very strong, and athletically built breed with a short coat, loose skin, and a distinctive ridge. It is one of only two pure-bred dogs to have the ridge, which is caused by a portion of hair on the spine growing in the opposite direction to the rest. The Thai Ridgeback has a short, strong muzzle and erect ears.

Native to eastern Thailand, this protective and intelligent breed is only just beginning to experience popularity outside of its country of origin. It is considered by many to remain undomesticated—that is to say that it is yet to become standardized as a pet breed. It is an independent breed that is most suited to an experienced owner.

PEKINGESE

OFFICIAL CATEGORIZATION: UK: Toy, AKC: Toy,
FCI: Group 9, Section 8

HEIGHT: 6–9 in. (15–23 cm)   WEIGHT: 7–14 lb. (3–6 kg)

OTHER NAMES: Foo Dog, Peking Palasthund

COLOR: Any

COAT CARE: Moderate maintenance

DIET: Moderate consumption

This ancient Chinese breed is an unusual-looking and highly popular dog originating in the Chinese city of Beijing, formerly known as Peking, from where the breed takes its name. It was considered sacred by the Chinese and was thought to have divine powers to drive away evil spirits. It is small, with a long flowing coat. The face is flat and the large, bulbous eyes are set wide apart, giving the dog a characteristic and unique expression. The legs of the Pekingese are bowed, which gives the dog a rolling gait.

Bred as a companion for Chinese emperors, the Pekingese is a very social and friendly breed. It is lively, energetic, and somewhat stubborn; usually loyal to one person, it is known for happily disobeying that person regardless of training. Despite this, the breed is a very popular pet due to its boundless enthusiasm for human companionship.

LEFT
The Pekingese is named after the capital of China—now Beijing, but formerly called Peking; this little dog is widely popular.

SHIH TZU

COLOR: Any

COAT CARE: Moderate maintenance

DIET: Moderate consumption

OFFICIAL CATEGORIZATION: UK: Utility, AKC: Toy, FCI: Group 9, Section 5

HEIGHT: 10½ in. (27 cm)   WEIGHT: 10–18 lb. (4.5–8 kg)

OTHER NAMES: Chinese Lion Dog, Chrysanthemum Dog

The Shih Tzu is an historic breed that originated in China as a descendant of the Lhasa Apso and the Pekingese. Despite appearing to have all of the physical characteristics associated with toy breeds, it is classed by the UK Kennel Club as a Utility breed. It is considered by many to be ornamental in its appearance—a reflection of its small size, diminutive yet sturdy frame, and silky, fine hair. The Shih Tzu tail is carried high in a very distinctive way. Like the Pekingese, the Shih Tzu was bred for the comfort and companionship of Chinese emperors. It was so revered by the Chinese that traders refused to trade or sell the breed to anyone outside of China.

Popular Show Dog

The breed has a snub nose and a particularly flat face, lending it quite an eye-catching expression. Due to the appeal of small dogs, demand is growing for smaller variations of the Shih Tzu breed. Although this is discouraged in principle by

ABOVE

The Chinese revered their little Shih Tzu companions and refused to sell them to anyone outside China.

many organizations, certain breeders are attempting to meet this demand, which is leading to instances of careless breeding.

In the show ring, the Shih Tzu is a popular and successful breed. Due to its form and appearance, it has particular appeal to hobby breeders and conformation competitors, but this has led to certain health problems being associated with the breed, such as breathing difficulties.

The Shih Tzu's loyal and lively personality is one of the reasons that the breed is so popular. It is an alert, intelligent companion that suits many differing domestic environments. It is a good friend to children, provided that they are educated to understand the various needs and aversions that this cheerful and hardy breed may have.

CHINESE CRESTED

OFFICIAL CATEGORIZATION: UK: Toy, AKC: Toy,
FCI: Group 9, Section 4

HEIGHT: 11–13 in. (28–33 cm)　　WEIGHT: 10–14½ lb. (4.5–6.5 kg)

OTHER NAMES: None

COLOR: Any

COAT CARE: Zero maintenance for
hairless, moderate/high for powder puff

DIET: Moderate/high consumption

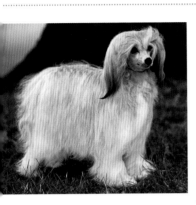

The Chinese Crested is an unusual breed of dog. It comes in two varieties: one with no hair except on top of the head and on the feet, known as "hairless"; and one with hair all over the body, known as "powder puff." Both types can be born in the same litter. The breed, despite its name, is almost certainly of African origin having become established as a standardized breed in China some time after its initial development. It is not related to the Mexican Hairless, despite the common trait. It is relatively small and slender with a broad skull and long muzzle.

The breed is loyal and sociable, displaying warmth and friendship to family members. It is a dedicated companion that thrives on and almost craves human company. The Chinese Crested has a definite sense of fun, exhibited in an alert and energetic manner that is characteristic of the breed.

ABOVE
The unusual Chinese Crested can give birth to a "hairless"-variety puppy (as shown) and to one with hair all over its body in the same litter.

LHASA APSO

OFFICIAL CATEGORIZATION: UK: Utility, AKC: Nonsporting,
FCI: Group 9, Section 5

HEIGHT: 8½–11½ in. (21.5–29 cm)　　WEIGHT: 14–18 lb. (6.5–8 kg)

OTHER NAMES: Lhassa Terrier

COLOR: Any

COAT CARE: High maintenance

DIET: Moderate consumption

The Lhasa Apso is an ancient companion and watchdog breed native to Tibet, where it is considered sacred. The breed is kept in monasteries and temples and is thought to be a spiritual protector. It is a small dog with luxurious long hair that is often styled by the owner. This healthy, long-living and hardy breed has been in existence for thousands of years, but only as recently as the twentieth century were specimens taken out of Tibet. The Dalai Lama was strongly associated with the breed due to his fondness for traveling with a Lhasa Apso.

The breed is naturally happy and playful, with an energetic and alert disposition, and bonds well with both children and adults.

The Lhasa Apso's alertness, coupled with a strong sense of hearing, makes it a useful watchdog, able to distinguish between everyday and unusual sounds. The breed is known for barking only when there is due cause.

PUG

COLOR: Silver, apricot fawn, or black

COAT CARE: Minimal maintenance

DIET: Moderate consumption

OFFICIAL CATEGORIZATION: UK: Toy, AKC: Toy, FCI: Group 9, Section 11

HEIGHT: 10–13 in. (25.5–33 cm)   WEIGHT: 14–18 lb. (6.5–8 kg)

OTHER NAMES: Carlin, Chinese Pug, Mops, Puggu

A Favorite of royalty and emperors, the Pug is a well-known breed native to China with a rich and varied history. Marie Antoinette, William of Orange, and Queen Victoria all kept Pugs, and the breed was established originally as a lap dog for emperors of the Chinese Shang Dynasty. It is famous for its extremely squashed face and compact, square-shaped, and tightly knit body. The tail curls over on to the back, which is covered with a sleek and soft coat. The coat comes in many varieties of color, including fawn, black, and apricot.

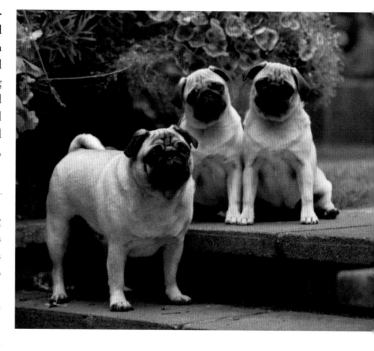

Bred to Type

The Pug of today is dramatically different in appearance to the Pug that became famous during the seventeenth and eighteenth centuries. The modern Pug is stocky and small, contrasting with the rather lean and athletic-looking Pug of times gone by. This is due to the preferences of various kennel-club authorities around the world, which prescribe the standards for each breed. Breeding to type has caused many inherent health problems for the Pug, including having a particularly injury-prone face, breathing difficulties, and an intolerance of heat. The breed is also highly prone to obesity and regularly encounters mobility problems as a result.

ABOVE
Originally bred for the emperors of China, the Pug has been popular with European monarchs, too.

A Demanding but Fun-Loving Pet

Despite its health problems, the breed is a popular pet. It is friendly and charming, with a sometimes willful attitude toward training. The breed is intelligent and curious, making it adept at obedience training provided that its interest can be maintained before boredom sets in. The Pug can be a demanding pet, requiring a lot of attention and exhibiting jealousy if left unattended for long periods of time. It is also a particularly sensitive breed that is prone to becoming distressed if it thinks it has upset or displeased its owner. The Pug is typically a friendly and fun-loving breed.

TIBETAN SPANIEL

OFFICIAL CATEGORIZATION: UK: Utility, AKC: Nonsporting,
FCI: Group 9, Section 5

HEIGHT: 8½–11½ in. (21.5–29 cm)

WEIGHT: 9–15 lb. (4–7 kg)

OTHER NAMES: None

COLOR: Any

COAT CARE: Moderate/high maintenance

DIET: Moderate consumption

The Tibetan Spaniel is an ancient breed strongly associated with the monks and monasteries of Tibet and, latterly, China. The breed was kept by monks as a watchdog, but was so valued and highly prized that it was given as a gift between monasteries and palaces. Despite its rather misleading name, the Tibetan Spaniel has no history or physical similarity with spaniel-type dogs. In contrast to gun-dog breeds, the Tibetan Spaniel is small and flat-faced, with a compact, sturdy body. The coat is exhibited in any color or combination of colors.

The Tibetan Spaniel is a very suitable pet due to its history of companionship in its country of origin. It is lively and friendly, with a playful and energetic disposition. Affectionate with family members, especially children, the Tibetan Spaniel makes a competent guard dog because of its alert and watchful nature, coupled with keen eyesight.

> **LEFT**
> *The Tibetan Spaniel makes an ideal pet, having been bred as a guard dog and with a long history of companionship.*

TIBETAN TERRIER

OFFICIAL CATEGORIZATION: UK: Utility, AKC: Nonsporting,
FCI: Group 9, Section 5

HEIGHT: 14–16 in. (36–41 cm)

WEIGHT: 18–30 lb. (8–14 kg)

OTHER NAMES: Tsang Apso

COLOR: Any

COAT CARE: High maintenance

DIET: Moderate/high consumption

The Tibetan Terrier is not a true terrier; the misleading name of this and other Asian breeds is most likely due to European travelers making loose comparisons with their own breeds and then exporting the dogs under new names. The Tibetan Terrier has an unclear and rather mixed heritage, thought to have worked as a farm dog and as a sacred temple dog—both theories are probable. The breed is small to medium-sized, with a square-shaped body, a fine outercoat and thick woolly undercoat. The Tibetan Terrier is very rare in Europe and breeding stock is limited.

This energetic, spirited, and vigilant breed makes an exceptional watchdog in the domestic environment. It is dedicated to its owner and family and has a playful yet often stubborn temperament that can present a challenge in training. The Tibetan Terrier is typically an affectionate and loving dog that is wary of strangers.

SHAR PEI

COLOR: All colors except white

COAT CARE: Minimal maintenance

DIET: Moderate/high consumption

OFFICIAL CATEGORIZATION: UK: Utility, AKC: Nonsporting, FCI: Group 2, Section 2

HEIGHT: 18–20 in. (46–51 cm)   WEIGHT: 42–46½ lb. (19–21 kg)

OTHER NAMES: Chinese Shar Pei, Chinese Fighting Dog

The Shar Pei is an unusual-looking breed that originated in China during the time of the Han Dynasty (206 B.C. to A.D. 220). It was used originally as a farm dog but later became a popular breed for dog fighting. The characteristically loose and wrinkled skin was thought advantageous because it allows the breed to turn around in its own skin and be able to deliver a bite to the head of any dog that has its jaws around the Shar Pei's back or rump.

The breed is stocky, muscular, and powerful. Because of the novelty of the breed's wrinkly face, the Shar Pei has been subject to irresponsible and careless breeding that has led to serious health problems. The Shar Pei is a confident and assured breed, loyal to its family and naturally wary of strangers until it is familiar with them. It is strong willed yet affectionate and friendly, with a watchful nature and strong independent streak.

Fascinating Facts

Because of careless breeding, some examples of the Shar Pei breed are so wrinkled that they cannot see.

CHOW CHOW

COLOR: Black, red, blue, fawn, cream, or white

COAT CARE: High/very high maintenance

DIET: Moderate/high consumption

OFFICIAL CATEGORIZATION: UK: Utility, AKC: Nonsporting, FCI: Group 5, Section 5

HEIGHT: 19–22 in. (48–56 cm)   WEIGHT: 44–55 lb. (20–25 kg)

OTHER NAMES: None

ABOVE

A natural guard dog, the Chow Chow likes to keep watch on its territory.

The Chow Chow is an old Chinese breed with two very distinctive physical features: it has a blue-black tongue and unusually straight hind legs that cause the dog to have a stilted gait. The breed comes in two coat varieties, one is extremely thick, dense, and smooth, the other thick, dense, and rough. It is **a sturdy, well-built breed with a slightly wrinkled face and broad muzzle.**

Originally used as a guardian dog, the Chow Chow is now a popular pet breed. It has a somewhat serious and independent persona, often very content to sit and watch the outside world through a window on watch for the arrival of any unwanted visitors. It is generally friendly with family but can be overtly unwelcoming toward new people. The breed has a strong territorial instinct that is typical of dogs that were used for herding and guarding in their working days.

TIBETAN MASTIFF

OFFICIAL CATEGORIZATION: UK: Working, AKC: Working, FCI: Group 2, Section 2

HEIGHT: 24½–27½ in. (62–70 cm) WEIGHT: 100–160 lb. (45–72 kg)

OTHER NAMES: Do-Khyi, Tsang-khyi

COLOR: Black, brown, or blue-gray, with or without tan markings

COAT CARE: Moderate maintenance

DIET: High consumption

The Tibetan Mastiff is a large, powerful, and particularly rare breed of dog. It is typical of many Mastiff breeds in that it has a large body, massive head, and powerful jaws. The coat of the breed is thick and warm. Some specimens of the breed have notably wrinkled heads. It was bred as a livestock guardian and is thought to be one of the forefathers of the Mastiff type and an ancestor of the Leonberger, Saint Bernard, and even Pug.

As is common among former working flock guardians, the Tibetan Mastiff has a very pronounced protective instinct that makes it prone to exhibiting suspicion around new people. It is typically friendly toward its family with a gentle and affectionate approach to young children, over whom it will be particularly watchful and protective. The Tibetan Mastiff is a highly intelligent and sometimes stubborn breed that requires solid training. The native strain of dog, which still exists in Tibet, and the Westernized breed can vary in temperament, with the former being more ferocious and aggressive.

TIBETAN KYI APSO

OFFICIAL CATEGORIZATION: UK: Not recognized, AKC: Not recognized, FCI: Not recognized

HEIGHT: 8–12 in. (20–30 cm)   WEIGHT: 9–14 lb. (4–6.5 kg)

OTHER NAMES: None

COLOR: Black and white or gold and white

COAT CARE: Moderate maintenance

DIET: Moderate consumption

The Tibetan Kyi Apso is an extremely rare breed native to the mountainous regions of Tibet. Its name translates as "bearded dog," which is a reference to the long hair that grows around its mouth. It was used originally as a herding and flock guardian breed and is large enough to make most predators think twice about confrontation. Its bark is said to be able to travel as far as the eye can see. The Tibetan Kyi Apso coat should be thick and weather-resistant; native dogs have differing coat lengths depending on their geographical distribution.

The Tibetan Kyi Apso is highly intelligent, alert, and loyal. Primarily a watch- and guard dog, the breed has strong protective instincts coupled with a profound independent streak that can make it appear aloof. It is confident and calm when indoors but watchful and always ready for action when guarding.

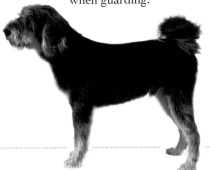

KOREAN JINDO

COLOR: White, black and tan, or various shades of red

COAT CARE: Moderate maintenance

DIET: Moderate/high consumption

OFFICIAL CATEGORIZATION: UK: Utility, AKC: Not recognized, FCI: Group 5, Section 5

HEIGHT: 19–21 in. (48–53 cm)   WEIGHT: 35–40 lb. (16–18 kg)

OTHER NAMES: Chindo, Jindo, Jindo Gae

The Korean Jindo is a rare and ancient breed that existed in isolation for centuries on the Korean island of Jindo, where it was guarded and protected from export. The first litter to be born off the island were bred near the English city of Bristol. The Korean Jindo is a Spitz-type breed, typically white, red, or black and tan in color with erect ears and an alert expression.

extremely intelligent and independent. It has a strong hunting instinct that is still likely to be exercised in the domestic environment. The breed is exceptionally loyal to its owner.

The breed is considered to be a Korean national treasure and even has its own research institute on the island, where the dogs are assessed for quality and health. In the ancient past, the Korean Jindo was left to fend for itself, which has caused the breed to become

LEFT

The Korean Jindo's intelligence can be too much for some — it is a dog that is able to think for itself, and that will find its own entertainment if left alone for too long.

JAPANESE CHIN

COLOR: Black and white, red and white, or black and white with tan points

COAT CARE: Moderate maintenance

DIET: Moderate consumption

OFFICIAL CATEGORIZATION: UK: Toy, AKC: Toy, FCI: Group 9, Section 8

HEIGHT: 8–11 in. (20–27 cm)   WEIGHT: 4–7 lb. (2–3 kg)

OTHER NAMES: Japanese Spaniel

The Japanese Chin is considered by most to be of Japanese origin, but doubt surrounds its true origin and it is plausible that the breed originated in China. Archaeological research proposes that it is of the same genetic ancestry as the Pekingese and the Tibetan Spaniel. The breed is very small with long and fine hair; the face is flat, with an upturned muzzle and large, wide-set eyes.

The Japanese Chin is quiet, affectionate, and gentle. It is independent and watchful but thrives in human company. The breed is considered to be rather catlike in some of its characteristics, particularly in the way it washes its face with its paws. The Japanese Chin can become uncomfortable and distracted in unfamiliar surroundings. Typically, the breed is even tempered and adaptable, noted for its quiet demeanor and relaxed, easy-going nature.

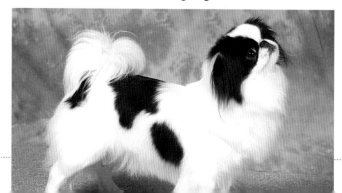

JAPANESE SPITZ

OFFICIAL CATEGORIZATION: UK: Not recognized,
AKC: Not recognized, FCI: Group 5, Section 5

HEIGHT: 12½–15 in. (32–38 cm)　　WEIGHT: 11–22 lb. (5–10 kg)

OTHER NAMES: Nihon Supittsu

COLOR: White

COAT CARE: Moderate/high maintenance

DIET: Moderate consumption

The Japanese Spitz is a descendant of the Samoyed, German Spitz, and American Eskimo dog.

It is relatively small, pure white, and typical of the Spitz form, with erect ears, alert expression, and thick coat. The Japanese Spitz became established as a breed in the nineteenth century after a specific breeding program. Due to Japan's fluctuating temperatures it has a double coat— the outer layer stands off from the body and insulates the dog, while the undercoat is thick and dense.

The breed was developed as a companion dog because it is loyal and affectionate. It does not respond well to being ignored and can resort to destructive behavior as a means of getting attention if left alone. The Japanese Spitz is a protective breed that displays a great affection to children, adults, and even visitors, provided the dog is comfortable in their presence.

Fascinating **F**acts

The white fur of Japanese Spitz dogs has a nonstick texture often described as being similar to Teflon.

LEFT
The luxurious pure white, double coat of the Japanese Spitz has evolved to insulate it during cold winters.

JAPANESE TERRIER

OFFICIAL CATEGORIZATION: UK: Not recognized,
AKC: Not recognized, FCI: Group 3, Section 2

HEIGHT: 12–13 in. (30–33 cm)　　WEIGHT: 6½–8½ lb. (3–4 kg)

OTHER NAMES: Nippon Terrier, Nihon Terrier, Nihon Teria

COLOR: Tricolor

COAT CARE: Minimal maintenance

DIET: Moderate consumption

The Japanese Terrier is a rare breed, even in its native country. It is a descendent of the Smooth Fox Terrier, to which it bears a slight resemblance in terms of shape. The Japanese Terrier originated in the early twentieth century but was not standardized until the 1930s. The breed exhibits a

black, white, and tan tricolor pattern with white and tan on the body and black on the head. The coat is short and smooth.

The Japanese Terrier is a lively and energetic breed, displaying typical terrier characteristics, such as tenacity, vigilance, and

playfulness. It is affectionate and extremely spirited, not prone to aggression or wariness of strangers. The breed is noticeably cheerful and happy, often curious and eager to be in the company of its family. It does not have a working history and is a good companion, although it has inherited the typical terrier vivaciousness.

JAPANESE SHIBA INU

COLOR: Red, black and tan, white, or cream

COAT CARE: Moderate maintenance

DIET: Moderate/high consumption

OFFICIAL CATEGORIZATION: UK: Utility, AKC: Nonsporting, FCI: Group 5, Section 5

HEIGHT: 14–17 in. (35.5–43 cm)   WEIGHT: 20–24 lb. (9–11 kg)

OTHER NAMES: Shiba Ken

The Japanese Shiba Inu is an old hunting breed that is descended from Spitz-breed dogs. It is similar in appearance to the Japanese Akita Inu but markedly

smaller. It is one of the oldest distinct Japanese dog breeds. The Japanese Shiba Inu was worked as a hunter of small game, and as such is extremely agile and fleet of foot. The breed has a thick double coat that is typically red, white, black and tan, or cream.

The breed is noted for its fastidious attitude toward cleanliness—it is very

LEFT
This hunting dog is the oldest breed native to Japan; the Shiba Inu is intelligent and affectionate and a pleasureable pet.

averse to becoming messy and will avoid mud and dirt at all costs. This makes it quite easy to housebreak. This ancient breed is highly intelligent and very independent, but is sociable and keen to be involved with the family. It is noted for its affection.

KISHU KEN

COLOR: White, brindle, or sesame

COAT CARE: Low/moderate maintenance

DIET: Moderate/high consumption

OFFICIAL CATEGORIZATION: UK: Not recognized, AKC: Not recognized, FCI: Group 5, Section 5

HEIGHT: 17–22 in. (43–56 cm)   WEIGHT: 30–60 lb. (13.5–27 kg)

OTHER NAMES: Kishu , Kishu-Inu

The Kishu Ken, or simply Kishu as it is more commonly known, is an ancient Japanese hunting breed. It is an agile, well-balanced, medium-sized dog with great hunting skills. It was established thousands of years ago to hunt boar and other medium-sized game, but is more common as a pet

today. It is typical of the Spitz type and bears a strong resemblance to the Hokkaido. The Kishu Ken is normally white, but less common specimens exhibit coats in shades of red and also brindle.

The breed is an intelligent, quiet, and watchful type.

It rarely barks—a retained characteristic that served it well as a silent hunter. A barking Kishu Ken is a sign that the dog has detected a perceived threat to its own or its family's safety. It is a sociable and friendly breed, but retains a degree of toughness from its working days.

SHIKOKU

OFFICIAL CATEGORIZATION: UK: Not recognized,
AKC: Not recognized, FCI: Group 5, Section 5

HEIGHT: 19–21.5 in. (49–55 cm)   WEIGHT: 33–44 lb. (15–20 kg)

OTHER NAMES: Kochi-Ken

COLOR: Sesame variations

COAT CARE: Low/moderate maintenance

DIET: High consumption

The Shikoku is a primitive Japanese hunting breed native to and named after Shikoku Island. It is similar in appearance to other notable Japanese breeds and is considered to be the intermediate in form and size between the Japanese Akita Inu and the Shiba Inu. This rare breed has a distinctively lupine face and coat, giving it a somewhat wild appearance. It is well balanced and agile with a sturdy but not heavy physique. The Shikoku is a graceful and elegant hunter and was declared a "natural monument" by Japan in 1937.

The breed has strong hunting instincts, a lot of stamina, and tremendous enthusiasm. It is persistent and tough, reflecting its working heritage, but will adapt to domestic life if given sufficient stimulation and exercise. Highly intelligent, the Shikoku is able to make up its own mind about commands and can seem somewhat independent—almost disobedient—at times.

LEFT
Named after Shikoku Island, the Shikoku has a long history of hunting.

HOKKAIDO

OFFICIAL CATEGORIZATION: UK: Not recognized,
AKC: Not recognized, FCI: Group 5, Section 5

HEIGHT: 18–22 in. (46–56 cm)   WEIGHT: 45–65 lb. (20–30 kg)

OTHER NAMES: Ainu dog, Ainu-Ken

COLOR: Sesame, brindle, black, wolf gray, red, brown, or white

COAT CARE: Low/moderate maintenance

DIET: Moderate/high consumption

The Hokkaido is a hardy and tough hunting breed with an ancient heritage in the mountainous regions of Hokkaido Island, from where it takes its name. It was used originally for hunting large game and was prized for its ability to withstand the cold due to its thick and dense coat, as well as its innate homing instinct. This medium-sized, well-proportioned breed exhibits many coat colors, including wolf gray, black, white, and red.

Faithful and loyal, the Hokkaido is typical of a number of ancient hunting breeds in that it has retained many of the basic instincts of the past and put them to good use in the domestic environment. It is an extremely intelligent and alert breed, suited to families with a lot of space. The Hokkaido will be affectionate and gentle with children, provided that it is used to them and is socialized.

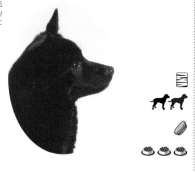

KAI KEN

COLOR: Black brindle, red brindle, or brindle

COAT CARE: Low maintenance

DIET: High consumption

OFFICIAL CATEGORIZATION: UK: Not recognized, AKC: Not recognized, FCI: Group 5, Section 5

HEIGHT: 19½–22½ in. (49.5–57 cm) WEIGHT: 53–57½ lb. (24–26 kg)

OTHER NAMES: None

The Kai Ken is considered to be Japan's purest breed of dog. It is a medium-sized, typically black or brindle member of the Spitz family of dogs. The medium-length harsh coat and strong hind limbs are reflective of the dog's ancestry as a mountain breed. The ears, as is typical in Spitz breeds, are erect and the tail is commonly curled over the back. The ancestors of this breed are now extinct but, like the Kai Ken, were used for hunting boar and deer. Like many other Japanese breeds, it was named by the Japanese Ministry of Education as a "natural monument."

The breed is hardy and alert with strong working instincts. It is courageous and bold, with a lively and active demeanor.

It gets along with children and other dogs but will display a suspicious curiosity toward strangers. As it is watchful, the Kai Ken makes a good guard dog.

RIGHT
The Kai Ken is Japan's purest Japanese breed, but is nevertheless a hardy strain.

TOSA

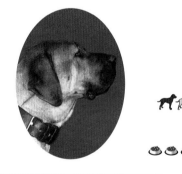

COLOR: Red, brindle, or fawn

COAT CARE: Minimal maintenance

DIET: High consumption

OFFICIAL CATEGORIZATION: UK: Banned under the Dangerous Dogs Act 1991, AKC: Not recognized, FCI: Group 2, Section 2

HEIGHT: 24½–32 in. (62–82 cm) WEIGHT: 80–120 lb. (36.5–54.5 kg)

OTHER NAMES: Tosa Inu, Tosa Ken, Tosa Tijken

The Tosa, also known as the Tosa Inu or Tosa Ken, is a large and powerful breed native to Japan. The modern Tosa has been interbred with other large breeds including the Great Dane, Bull Dog, Mastiff, and Bull Terrier. The Tosa has a large head and body and a short, dense coat that is typically solid red in color. In the past, the breed has been used for organized dog fights and in Britain the Tosa is banned under the Dangerous Dogs Act. This is not due to the breed being inherently dangerous but to discourage its importation for the express purpose of dog fighting.

Despite its fighting associations and subsequent ban in Britain, the breed is a popular pet elsewhere. The Tosa is intelligent and sometimes stubborn but typically gentle and affectionate. It lacks the fearsome look of other breeds once used for fighting and is generally a friendly companion.

AKITA

OFFICIAL CATEGORIZATION: UK: Utility, AKC: Working, FCI: Group 5, Section 5

HEIGHT: 26–28 in. (66–71 cm)   WEIGHT: 77–121 lb. (35–55 kg)

OTHER NAMES: Japanese Akita Inu, Akita Ken, Akita Inu, Japanese Akita

COLOR: Any color, including white, brindle, or pinto

COAT CARE: Low/moderate maintenance

DIET: High/very high consumption

LEFT
The Akita is a large breed, weighing up to a hefty 121 lb. (55 kg).

T he Akita is an ancient Japanese breed that descends from now-extinct hunting dogs. Great Dane blood is thought to have been introduced into the Akita bloodline at some point in the twentieth century. The Akita is a large, noble, and extremely strong breed that was originally used for hunting and guarding.

as the Akita Ken or Akita Inu. In some parts of the world, the two are considered one breed, but in other countries, notably Britain, there is a distinction between the Akita and the Japanese Akita Inu and both are recognized. Japan refuses to recognize the American version—using markings and face color as a sign of Americanization. All colors and patterns are allowed in American Akitas, whereas the Akita Inu can only come in red, fawn, sesame, brindle, and pure white.

Traditionally, the breed is large, with the American version being typically larger. Both types have thick fur and powerful bodies.

Excellent Guard Dog
The Akita is an intelligent yet very dominant and confident breed—this dominance must be kept under control by a strong master. It is selflessly devoted to its family, especially children. Quiet and watchful, only barking or becoming excited when there is good cause, it makes an excellent guard dog.

Fascinating Facts

The Akita is a symbol of loyalty in its native country of Japan.

A Complicated History
The classification of the Akita breed is controversial. The Akita is an ancient Japanese breed named after the Japanese prefecture of the same name. It was already a diverse breed in Japan, with a mixed ancestry. However, it has been subject to large-scale export since World War II. As a result different bloodlines and different types of Akita have become established outside of Japan, giving rise to a divergence of the breed that has necessitated the distinction between the Akita and the Japanese Akita, the latter also known

OTHER ASIAN BREEDS

Asia has a long history of producing popular and universally valued dog breeds. In some more remote parts of the continent, certain breeds have remained isolated from the rest of the world, particularly those breeds that were established for roles specific to their native countries. Many Asian breeds are yet to become recognized worldwide and remain relatively obscure. In other cases, the dogs are so valued by those that breed them that their export has been limited or prohibited, meaning that the breeds have been unable to become established.

Chong Qing Dog

The Chong Qing Dog is a rare Chinese breed of dog native to the province of Chong Qing. It is not recognized by any major kennel clubs or authorities and is subject to conservation measures by fans of the breed who are concerned about its vulnerable status. The breed is known for being very healthy and free from inbreeding-related problems that are commonly associated with purebred dogs. Physically, it bears a passing resemblance to the Boxer, but this is not an indication of ancestry, because the breed is thought to have descended from now-extinct Mastiff breeds.

Alangu Mastiff

The Alangu Mastiff is a large and powerful breed that is descended from the ancient and extinct Molosser-type dog. It has been used predominantly for fighting and guarding in southern India and also in Pakistan. This history has given the dog a rather aggressive and protective temperament that is more suited to guarding work than a role as a pet. It is typical of many Mastiff breeds and has a short, coarse coat that comes in many colors, commonly red, fawn, and brindle.

Bakharwal Dog

The Bakharwal Dog is a descendent of the Molosser but is substantially leaner than many modern breeds of similar descent. It is a heavy-boned and broad-chested breed that was used in India and Kashmir as a sheep herder and guardian. The typical coloration of the Bakharwal Dog is black and tan, but some specimens exhibit a black,

tan, and white tricolor pattern. It is a loyal breed that has ferocious protective instincts.

Indian Spitz

The Indian Spitz is an ancient and rare breed. It is recognized by the Kennel Club of India but not by any other major kennel-club organizations. The breed was established to function as a versatile farm

worker but has since reverted to being used mostly as a pet dog. It is almost identical to the Pomeranian in appearance, but is of differing heritage.

Kanni

The Kanni is an ancient and extremely rare breed of hunting hound established in India and is a descendent of the Saluki. It is lean and graceful, with sleek lines, a dignified head and usually black and tan in coloration. Despite its ancestry, the breed is less typical of the hound type and is often mistaken as a relative of the Doberman by people who are unfamiliar with the breed.

Sapsali

The Sapsali, or Sapsaree as it is sometimes known, is a Korean breed that was traditionally thought to have been able to dispel ghosts from a person's home. It is an abundantly furry dog of medium size and build, similar in appearance to various pastoral and herding breeds. Despite its apparent link to herding breeds, the Sapsali was bred exclusively for use as a pet and companion dog. It is gentle and peaceful, with boundless affection. Not prone to or skilled at aggression, it is favored for its even temper and sweet nature.

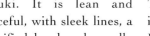

ABOVE

Now primarily a pet dog, the Indian Spitz was originally bred as a working breed.

BELOW

The Sapsali is an affectionate breed, bred purposefully to be a pet.

BELOW LEFT

There also exists a cream-colored variety of the Kanni breed, which is known as "Paalakanni."

Australia

Australia is the world's smallest continent and, as such, has only four recognized native breeds. Before European settlers arrived in Australia, the Aboriginal people kept and used dogs but are thought not to have bred for type but for function. Typically, these dogs were limited to parts of the land that were cooler. Of the four recognized native Australian breeds, all are descended from British breeds.

Working Dogs

Australia's dog breeds are generally working breeds. Herding and terrier breeds are by far the most popular types of dogs bred in Australia. The Australian Cattle Dog, also known as the Queensland Heeler, is arguably the most well-known Australian breed, having been established to herd on the vast ranches and farms of northeastern Australia. It is believed to be an ancestor of the Dingo, which is a semiwild or feral dog that has been native to Australia for generations. The Dingo is abundant throughout much of Australia. In its pure form, it is found mainly in northern Australia, but Dingo hybrids are more commonly found on the southwest and southeast coastal regions.

A Warm Climate

Due to the consistently warm temperatures in the center of mainland Australia, no recognized dog breeds have become established in that part of the continent because there is little work available for dogs there. Only the Dingo has a notable population throughout the whole of the country, but that too is more suited to the cooler coastal areas. Of the Australian breeds that are not recognized, the Kangaroo Dog is thought to be the breed with the strongest Australian lineage.

Pet dog ownership in Australia is popular, but throughout the nation's relatively short history of dog breeding, dogs have been bred predominantly for work.

AUSTRALIAN SILKY TERRIER

OFFICIAL CATEGORIZATION: UK: Toy, AKC: Toy, FCI: Group 3, Section 4

HEIGHT: 7½–10½ in. (19–26.5 cm)   WEIGHT: 8–10 lb. (3.5–4.5 kg)

OTHER NAMES: None

COLOR: Blue and tan

COAT CARE: Moderate/high maintenance

Diet: Moderate consumption

The Australian Silky Terrier is a small breed of dog that is classed in some countries as a terrier breed and in others as a toy breed. It is generally accepted that the breed is the descendent of a Yorkshire Terrier and Australian Terrier crossbreeding, but debate still surrounded the status of the Australian Terrier breed at the time of the emergence of the Silky, which did not become standardized until the twentieth century. The Australian Silky Terrier is similar in appearance to a Yorkshire Terrier but typically has a longer head and an especially silky coat.

The Australian Silky Terrier was bred as a companion animal and as such has a strong instinct for socialization. It tends to be friendly and sociable with all of the family but will attach itself to one person above all others. The breed has an instinctive wariness of strangers but will relax once familiar with them.

AUSTRALIAN TERRIER

OFFICIAL CATEGORIZATION: UK: Terrier, AKC: Terrier, FCI: Group 3, Section 2

HEIGHT: 8½–11½ in. (21.5–29 cm)   WEIGHT: 12–16½ lb. (5.5–7.5 kg)

OTHER NAMES: None

COLOR: Blue, steel blue, or dark gray-blue, with rich tan

COAT CARE: Low/moderate maintenance

DIET: Moderate consumption

The Australian Terrier is a descendent of various British terrier breeds, including the Yorkshire Terrier, Cairn Terrier, and Scottish Terrier. It was bred to be a working terrier but is now a popular pet. It resembles the Yorkshire Terrier and was used as root breeding stock for the Australian Silky Terrier. The breed is small, well proportioned, and agile, with a rugged appearance that is distinctive of the breed. It became established as a breed in the nineteenth century and was the first native Australian dog breed to be recognized outside of the country.

The Australian Terrier was bred to control rodents and snakes in rural Australia and is still a popular working breed today. It has strong terrier instincts and is a hard worker with noticeable tenacity. It is dedicated in the domestic environment—feisty, friendly, and outgoing, generally keen to please and exceptionally loyal to the family.

LEFT

The first native Australian breed to be recognized outside the country was the Australian Terrier.

AUSTRALIAN CATTLE DOG

OFFICIAL CATEGORIZATION: UK: Pastoral, AKC: Herding, FCI: Group 1, Section 2

COLOR: Blue, mottled, or speckled, black and tan or red

COAT CARE: Moderate maintenance

DIET: High consumption

HEIGHT: 18–20 in. (46–51 cm)   **WEIGHT:** 25–33 lb. (12–18 kg)

OTHER NAMES: Australian Heeler, Blue Heeler, Queensland Heeler, Hall's Heeler

The Australian Cattle Dog is a member of the herding dog family and was bred and developed in Australia during the nineteenth century. It is descended from the Bull Terrier, ancestral Collie-type dogs, wild Dingo, and a now-extinct breed called the Smithfield, which was a relative of the Old English Sheepdog. It is a traditional herding breed that gets its Heeler nick-name due to its habit of nipping at the heels of rogue flock members.

Because of the hot climate in Australia, this breed has a short, light coat and large upward-pointing ears. The coat is exhibited in many colors—most commonly in blue, blue mottle, black, and tan and red. It is still put to good use today in rural

Australia but also makes a popular pet dog breed all around the world. The Australian Cattle Dog is a dedicated and tyrannical herder; it rarely lets any rogue sheep or cow get too far away before it delivers a nip to the back of the legs. During the evolution of the working Australian Cattle Dog, any that bit too hard were not used for breeding in order to encourage only light nipping tendencies that would not injure any livestock.

Not for the Novice Owner
Like most herding and pastoral breeds of dog, the Australian Cattle Dog is intelligent, energetic, and determined. Suited to active

families, the breed requires a relatively high amount of interaction and stimulation to be happy and well adjusted. It is generally a happy and sociable dog, loyal to its master and eager to please. The Australian Cattle Dog seeks a dominant and power-ful leader, therefore, the owner must be able to fulfill this need or the dog may bond too closely with other dogs. It is common for packs

Fascinating Facts

The oldest dog ever recorded was an Australian Cattle Dog that lived to the age of 29.

ABOVE
Nicknamed the Heeler, the Australian Cattle Dog gets this name from its habit of nipping the lower legs of the cattle.

that include the Australian Cattle Dog to experience occasional scuffles in order to establish dominance.

KELPIE

OFFICIAL CATEGORIZATION: UK: Not recognized,
AKC: Not recognized, FCI: Group 1, Section 1

HEIGHT: 16–24 in. (40–61 cm)   WEIGHT: 25–65 lb. (11–30 kg)

OTHER NAMES: Australian Sheep Dog

COLOR: Various

COAT CARE: Minimal maintenance

DIET: High consumption

The Kelpie is an Australian herding breed that is very popular both as a working and pet dog in its native country. It is named after a mythological water horse. There are two distinct types of Kelpie: show-bred Kelpies, which have a reduced working instinct, and work-bred Kelpies, which are less uniform in their appearance but more adept at herding. The working Kelpies generally tend to enjoy better health, due to the lack of focus on breeding for a precise physical type.

The Kelpie is a rugged and hardy dog with an athletic, agile frame, erect ears, and coarse coat. Working Kelpies exhibit most colors and patterns, but show-bred Kelpies are restricted to solid colors. The show-bred Kelpie is typically shorter and heavier than the working variety.

The breed is thought to have become established with the use of wild Dingo blood alongside Collie and native-dog breeding stock, but this is often denied by custodians of the breed. Evidence exists that the practice of using Dingoes to populate the Kelpie gene pool is ongoing, but this is denied by most breeders who claim that it is absurd to breed a known sheep-killer with a herding dog.

Agile and Intelligent

The Kelpie is an intelligent and independent dog. It has a curious and tireless nature and is reluctant to give up on a challenge. In general the breed is friendly, loyal, and protective, as is common with all herding breeds. Working specimens are more inclined to follow their herding instincts in the domestic environment than show-bred dogs, which are more relaxed and docile.

The Kelpie is physically and mentally agile and will not be happy if both characteristics are not catered for. Working Kelpies in particular are keen to be stimulated, which can be achieved with a long walk and some solid training.

ABOVE AND LEFT
Australian Kelpies come in show and working varieties, the latter having far fewer medical conditions.

OTHER AUSTRALIAN BREEDS

A ustralia is a country where dogs are predominantly bred to meet a specific working function. There are many parts of Australia in which dogs are uncommon, specifically in the hot, arid outback where there is little call for any canine work. Most of the Australian breeds that have become established are from a working background, and only recently have Australian breeders begun to develop pet breeds of their own. There is a large amount of British breed ancestry in Australia's newer native breeds.

Australian Stumpy-Tail Cattle Dog

The Australian Stumpy-Tail Cattle Dog is a breed that is still in development. It is similar in many ways to its relative, the Australian Cattle Dog, but also exhibits some very important differences. It is naturally prone to having a bob or stumpy tail and is generally lighter and more agile than the Australian Cattle Dog, which serves it well for herding cattle. The breed also presents a wider

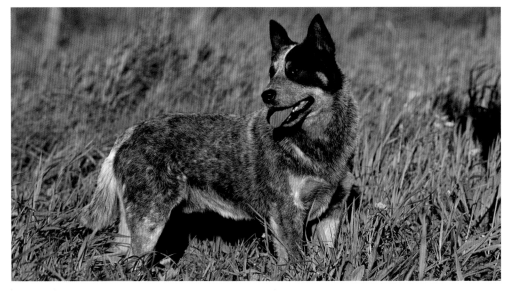

ABOVE RIGHT
The Australian Cattle Dog is very similar to the Australian Stumpy-Tail Cattle Dog, but has a full tail, among other differences.

BELOW
Despite its appearance, the tail of the Australian Stumpy-Tailed Cattle Dog is not docked; it grows like that.

range of coat coloration, length, texture, and pattern.

Kangaroo Dog

The Kangaroo Dog is not an established breed but is considered to be a type of dog, more precisely a type of working sight hound. It is descended from British sight hounds, such as the Scottish Deerhound and the Greyhound, and was established to hunt medium-sized game and prey. Despite the name, the Kangaroo Dog is bred mainly for hunting rabbit, feral pig, Dingo, and fox. The Kangaroo Dog is large and powerful, with great speed, stamina, persistence, and highly sensitive eyesight. It is most common in remote rural communities and, so

BELOW
The Kangaroo Dog is a large, powerful sight hound, used for hunting Dingoes among other things.

far, the main breeders have expressed little interest in seeing it standardized and recognized by any major kennel clubs.

Coolie

The Coolie, or German Coolie as it is sometimes known, is a working breed of cattle dog. It is still evolving and breeders are regularly introducing new blood into the bloodline to diversify and protect the breed. The history of the breed is unclear, but a likely theory is that the Coolie descends from the Border Collie, which was introduced to Australia when European settlers arrived. It is a rustic and tough cattle dog of good balance and medium size that exhibits little uniformity other than a strong herding instinct and inconsistent coat pattern and coloration.

Miniature Fox Terrier

The Miniature Fox Terrier, or Mini Foxie as it is commonly called in Australia, is a relatively new breed that descends from European terriers. Manchester Terriers and Fox Terrier breeds have been used to develop the breed to its current status. It is a small, tenacious, and friendly breed that has been put to work throughout Australia as a vermin catcher. Its affectionate and kindly nature, coupled with its bold and confident demeanor, make the Miniature Fox Terrier a popular pet in its native country, although it is relatively unknown outside of Australia.

Tenterfield Terrier

The Tenterfield Terrier is a small working terrier that descends from the Rat Terrier and certain other English terrier breeds. Its origins beyond its genetic ancestry are unclear, except that it was developed in the town of Tenterfield, New South Wales. It is similar to the Miniature Fox Terrier but is predominantly kept as a pet. The Tenterfield Terrier, like the Miniature Fox Terrier, is still a breed under development. It is not standardized and many litters include dogs that are physically distinct from their litter mates. Unlike the breeders of the Miniature Fox Terrier, Tenterfield Terrier breeders are keen to establish a uniform type for their breed and are also extremely careful to ensure the good overall health of the dog.

Useful Addresses

Kennel Clubs and Associations

American Kennel Club
260 Madison Ave.
New York, New York 10016
Tel: (919) 233–9767
www.akc.org

National Canine Association
6734 Huntsman Blvd.
Springfield, Virginia 22152
www.nationalcanine.com

American Canine Association
200 Lincoln Ave.
Suite 119
Phoenixville, Pennsylvania 19460
Tel: (800) 651–8332
www.acacanines.com

United Kennel Club
100 E. Kilgore Rd.
Kalamazoo, Michigan 49002
Tel: (269) 343–9020
www.ukcdogs.com

United Canine Association
P.O. Box 2600
Tehachapi, California 93581
Tel: (661) 822–5482
www.ucadogs.com

World Wide Kennel Club
P.O. Box 62
Mount Vernon, New York 10552
Tel: (914) 654–8574
www.worldwidekennel.qpg.com

Continental Kennel Club
P.O. Box 1628
Walker
Los Angeles, California 70785

Tel: (800) 952–3376
www.continentalkennelclub.com

American Dog Owners Association
P.O. Box 186
Castleton, New York 12033
Tel: (888) 714–7220
www.adoa.org

American Dog Breeders Association
P.O. Box 1771
Salt Lake City, Utah 84110
Tel: (801) 936–7513
www.adbadogs.com

American Rare Breed Association
9921 Frank Tippett Road
Cheltanham, Maryland 20623
Tel: (301) 868–5718
www.arba.org

Mixed Breed Dog Clubs of America
13884 State Route 104
Lucasville, Ohio 45648
Tel: (740) 259–3941
www.mbdca.org

United States Canine Registry/ Coalition of Dog Registries
www.uscanines.org

World Canine Organization (Federation Cynologique Internationale)
www.fci.be

The Canadian Kennel Club
89 Skyway Ave.
Suite 100
Etobicoke, Ontario M9W 6R4
Canada
Tel: (416) 675–5511
www.ckc.ca

The Kennel Club
1–5 Clarges St
London W1J 8AB
UK
Tel: +44 (0)870 606 6750
www.thekennelclub.org.uk

Federation Cynologique Internationale
Place Albert 1er, 13
B-6530
Thuin
Belgique
Tel: +32 71 59 12 38
www.fci.be

Care & Management

American Kennel Club Canine Health Foundation
P.O. Box 900061
Raleigh, North Carolina 27675
Tel: (888) 682–9696
www.akcchf.org

American Holistic Veterinary Medical Association
2214 Old Emmorton Road
Bel Air, Md 21015
Tel: (410)-569-0795
www.ahvma.org

Academy for Veterinary Homeopathy (AVH)
1283 Lincoln Street
Eugene, OR 97401
Tel: (503)-342-7665
www.theavh.org

American Canine Sports Medicine Association
P.O. Box 07412

Fort Meyers, Florida 33919
www.acsma.org

Healthy Dogs
www.healthy-dogs.net
I Love Dogs
(includes veterinarian directory)
www.i-love-dogs.com

**American Boarding Kennels
Association**
1702 East Pikes Peak Ave
Colorado Springs, Colorado 80909
Tel: (877) 570–7788
www.abka.com

Deaf Dog Education Action Fund
P.O. Box 2840
Oneco, Florida 34264
www.deafdogs.org

Canine Obedience Unlimited
11140 Rockville Pike
Rockville, Maryland 20852
Tel: (240) 793–5787
www.canineobedienceunlimited.com

Dog Training USA
www.dog-training-usa.com

Welfare Organizations

**American Society for the Prevention
of Cruelty to Animals (ASPCA)**
424 E. 92nd St.
New York, New York 10128–6804
Tel: (212) 876–7700
www.aspca.org

Humane Society of the United States
HSUS Headquarters
2100 L. St. NW

Washington D.C. 20037
Tel: (202) 452–1100
www.hsus.org

National Animal Interest Alliance
P.O. Box 66579
Portland, Oregon 97290
Tel: (503) 761–1139
www.naiaonline.org

Dogs Deserve Better, Inc
P.O. Box 23
Tipton, Pennsylvania 16684
Tel: +1 877 636 1408
www.dogsdeservebetter.com

Animal Placement Bureau
P.O. Box 80146
Lansing, Michigan 48908
Tel: (800) SAVE A PET
www.apbpets.com

Smiley Dog Rescue
P.O. Box 2728
Oakland, California 94602
Tel: (510) 496–3484
www.smileydogrescue.org

**The Animal Welfare
Foundation of Canada**
Suite 616
410 Bank St.
Ottawa, Ontario K2P 1Y8
Canada
Email: info@awfc.ca
www.awfc.ca

**Canadian Federation of
Humane Societies**
102-30 Concourse Gate
Ottawa, Ontario, K2E 7V7
Canada
Tel: (888) 678–CFHS
www.cfhs.ca

Agility and Trials

**United States Dog
Agility Association**
P.O. Box 850955
Richardson, Texas 75085
Tel: (972) 487–2200
www.usdaa.com

North American Dog Agility Council
P.O. Box 1206
Colbert, Oklahoma 74733
www.nadac.com

**Association of American Working
Trials Societies**
2016 Rowe Loop
Pflugerville, Texas 78660
Tel: (512) 990–2016
www.waggin-tails.com

Support Dogs

Association of Guide Dog Users
55 Delaware Avenue
Somerset, Massachusetts 02726
Tel: (508) 673–0218
www.nfb-nagdu.org

Canine Companions for Independence
P.O. Box 446
Santa Rosa, California 95402
Tel: (800) 572–BARK
www.caninecompanions.org

Miscellaneous

The Dog Museum
1721 South Mason Road
Saint Louis, Missouri
Tel: (314) 821–364

Further Reading

Abrantes, Roger *The Evolution of Canine Social Behavior*, Dogwise Publishing (Washington, USA), 2003

Acker, Randy; Fergus, Jim; Smith, Christopher, *Dog First Aid: Emergency Care for the Hunting, Working, and Outdoor Dog (A Field Guide)*, Wilderness Adventure Press (Michigan, USA), 1994

Alderton, David, *Top to Tail: The 360 Degrees Guide to Picking Your Perfect Pet*, David & Charles (Devon, UK), 2004

American Kennel Club, *The Complete Dog Book: 20th Edition*, Ballantine Books (New York City, USA), 2006

American Rescue Dog Association, *Search and Rescue Dogs: Training Methods*, Prentice-Hall (London, UK), 1991

Atkinson, Eleanor, *Greyfriars Bobby*, Puffin Classics (London, UK), 1995

Bailey, Gwen, *Choosing the Right Dog For You: Profiles of Over 200 Dog Breeds*, Hamlyn (London, UK), 2004

Becker, Marty; Spadafori, Gina, *Why Do Dogs Drink Out of the Toilet?: 101 of the Most Perplexing Questions Answered about Canine Conundrums, Medical Mysteries & Befuddling Behaviors*, Health Communications (Florida, USA), 2006

Chance, Paul, *Learning and Behavior*, Wadsworth Publishing Co. Inc. (Connecticut), 2002

Fennel, Jan, *The Seven Ages of Man's Best Friend: A Comprehensive Guide to Caring For Your Dog Through All the Stages of Life*, Collins (London, UK), 2007

Fergus, Charles, *Gun Dog Breeds: A Guide to Spaniels, Retrievers and Pointing Dogs*, The Lyons Press (Connecticut, USA), 2003

Finder Harris, Beth J., *Breeding a Litter: The Complete Book of Prenatal and Postnatal Care*, John Wiley & Sons (New Jersey, USA), 1993

Goody, Peter C., *Dog Anatomy: A Pictorial Approach to Canine Structure*, J.A. Allen & Co. Ltd (California, USA), 1999

Grogan, John, *Marley & Me: Life and Love with the World's Worst Dog*, William Morrow (New York City, USA), 2006

Hynes, Bruce, *The Noble Newfoundland Dog: A History in Stories, Legends, and the Occasional Tall Tale*, Nimbus Publishing (Nova Scotia, Canada), 2005

Knight, Eric *Lassie Come Home*, Holt, Rinehart and Winston (Austin, Texas, USA), 1940

Lane, Dick; Ewart, Neil, *A–Z of Dog Diseases and Common Health Problems*, Ringpress Books Ltd (Gloucestershire, UK), 1996

Lane, Marion S., *The Humane Society of the United States Complete Guide to Dog Care: Everything You Need to Know to Keep Your Dog Healthy and Happy*, Little, Brown and Company (London, UK), 2001

London, Jack, *The Call of the Wild*, Aladdin Classics (Ontario & New Jersey, USA; London, UK), 2003

Pryor, Karen, *Don't Shoot the Dog!: The New Art of Teaching and Training*, Ringpress Books Ltd. (Gloucestershire, UK), 2002

Rice, Dan, *Small Dog Breeds*, Barron's Educational Series (New York, USA), 2002

Saunders, Marshall, *Beautiful Joe: A Dog's Own Story*, Book Jungle (Illinois, USA), 2006

Secord, William, *Dog Painting 1840–1940: A Social History of the Dog in Art*, Antique Collectors' Club Ltd (Suffolk, UK), 1999

Serpell, James, *The Domestic Dog: Its Evolution, Behavior, and Interactions with People*, Cambridge University Press (Cambridge, UK), 1995

Stilwell, Victoria, *It's Me or the Dog: How to Have the Perfect Pet*, Collins (London, UK), 2005

Stone, Ben; Stone, Peal, *The Stone Guide to Dog Grooming for All Breeds*, John Wiley & Sons (New Jersey, USA), 1981

Tanner, Michael, *The Legend of Mick the Miller*, Highdown (London, UK), 2004

Taylor, David, *The British Veterinary Association Guide to Dog Care*, Dorling Kindersley Publishers Ltd (London, UK), 1989

Thomson, Laura, *The Dogs: A Personal History of Greyhound Racing*, High Stakes Publishing (Harpenden, UK), 2003

Thurston, Mary Elizabeth, *The Lost History of the Canine Race: Our 15,000-Year Love Affair With Dogs*, Andrews Mcmeel Publishing (New Jersey, USA), 2006

Glossary

action
The way in which a dog runs or moves when working. This term is normally applied when dogs are being judged at work or in conformation.

athletic
Describes the look or carriage of a lean, strong dog. Typically sight hounds and working breeds are described as athletic.

basset
A type of dog originating in France, typified by short legs. Examples are Basset Hound, Grand Basset Griffin Vendeen, and Basset Fauve de Bretagne.

belton
White and colored hairs growing together to give the appearance of other colors, such as lemon.

blaze
White stripe separating other colors, typical of tricolor coloration, as exemplified by the Bernese Mountain Dog.

bite
The position in which a dog's teeth naturally come to rest.

bob tail
A naturally short tail.

bold
Describes the typical character of an outgoing, confident breed. Terrier breeds can often be described as bold.

boisterous
Describes the typical character of a curious and fearless dog breed. Certain terrier breeds and some pointer breeds can be described as boisterous.

bracco
Italian term for pointer type.

braque
French term for pointer type.

breed
Name used to identify dogs of a distinct type and bloodline. Labrador Retriever, Doberman, or English Springer Spaniel are all names of breeds.

breed, to
The process by which owners intentionally encourage two dogs to mate under controlled conditions in order to create offspring of the same breed.

breed standard
Document outlining parameters of size, color, and appearance of a dog breed.

breed true, to
The process by which a new breed begins to display uniformity of physical characteristics.

breeding stock
Individual dogs that are used for mating in order to generate offspring of a certain breed.

brindle
A striped coat pattern.

canid
Taxonomical reference to members of the dog family, including wolves, dogs, and foxes.

carriage
The identifiable way in which a dog holds its head, moves its legs and stands.

coat
The fur of a dog in its entirety, used when describing length, texture, and color.

conformation
A type of competition in which an individual dog is judged on its closeness to its type.

crop
Cosmetic procedure performed on a dog's ears to make them stand on end.

cur
Generic American term for a dog of unidentifiable heritage, commonly used to describe semiwild dogs.

demeanor
Describes the typical way in which a dog interacts with humans and other dogs presuming there are no mitigating behavioral or environmental factors.

dewclaw
Fifth digit found at the back of the pastern on some breeds. Depending on breed

and circumstances this is often removed by a vet.

dewlap
Growth of fur below the jaw, particularly pronounced in certain breeds, notably Mastiff types.

dock
To shorten the length of a dog's tail by removing a portion of it, normally performed by a vet for cosmetic or practical working reasons. This procedure is illegal in Britain.

dominant
Descriptive of either an individual dog or breed that is likely to assert superiority over other dogs and people. Normally describes an individual member of a litter or pack.

down breed, to
To deliberately decrease the standard size of a breed by using smaller breeds or smaller examples of the same breed in order to create a smaller type.

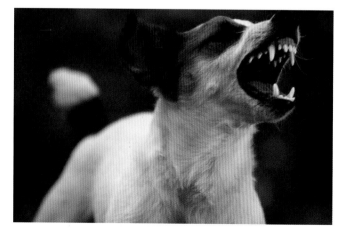

drive
Instinctive desire or action found in all dogs. Can refer to prey drive, play drive, hunt drive, or defense drive.

drop
Describes long, pendulous ears. Scent Hounds typically have drop ears.

erect
Describes ears that naturally stand on top of the head.

even temper
An even-tempered breed is unlikely to respond excitedly or unpredictably to the majority of standard stimuli.

family
Normally refers to a collection of breeds descended from the same type. For example, "Northern European Spitz Family."

ferocious
Describes a dog that is typically adept at fighting, hunting, or protecting.

gait
The distinctive manner in which a dog mobilizes or moves. This can aid identification of ancestry in crossbreeds, or mixed breeds, of undetermined ancestry.

group
A group, or breed group, is the means of categorizing breeds by using criteria such as function or form.

guardian
Describes the natural attributes or personality of a breed established to protect people or livestock.

gun shy
Describes the tendency of some dogs to exhibit fear in the proximity of gun fire, particularly relevant to sporting and gun-dog breeds.

hardy
Describes the physical and behavioral nature of a dog bred to demonstrate a high tolerance for cold, exhaustion, discomfort, or solitude.

herding
Descriptive of dogs bred to control the movement of livestock.

jowls
Folds of skin about the mouth and jaw, particularly pronounced in Molosser-type dogs.

mask
Used to describe the face of a dog or breed when the face is a different color, normally black, compared to the rest of the body.

merle
Describes a coat coloration that displays a marbled effect of dark fur against lighter fur.

mixed breed
A dog with more than two breeds in its ancestry. For example, the offspring of two crossbreeds.

molosser
Describes a type of heavy, powerfully built dog with a large head that is thought to descend from the ancient Molossus.

muzzle
The part of a dog's face where a muzzle would be placed. It is used as a term to describe the nature of the face, for example "wide muzzle."

non-pedigree
A dog that does not have a pedigree to confirm its ancestry. Crossbreeds and mixed breeds are non-pedigree dogs.

outcross, to
To introduce the blood of another breed or variation in order for a breed to acquire certain attributes. This is often done when new breeds are being established or as a means to strengthen the gene pool of an existing breed.

pastoral
A description of a dog's instincts or the name of a breed group as governed by a kennel club. It is analogous with the term "herding."

pedigree
A document that confirms and details the genetic ancestry of a dog. It is also a term used to denote pure breeding.

pointer
A type of gun dog or sporting breed that is trained to indicate the location of game or prey to its master by standing in a point position.

recognized
For a breed to be recognized, a kennel club or similar authority must agree to the standard for that breed. There are a lot of breeds that are recognized in certain parts of the world and not in others.

retriever
A type of gun-dog breed that was established to be soft of mouth, in order to return game and prey carefully to its master.

rustic
A breed that typically displays characteristics that are suitable to outdoor living, particularly challenging environments, such as hills. It is a general and intangible term that encompasses the overall appearance and temperament of a dog or breed.

sable
A type of coat coloration defined by black-tipped hairs on a paler background.

saddle
An area of a dog's coat that is of different color to the main color. The saddle is in the area near the bottom of the back where a saddle would be fitted to a horse.

setter
A type of gun dog that is bred and trained to indicate the location of game, particularly birds.

show-bred
A show-bred dog is a variation of a breed that is distinct from its counterpart working variety because it was bred to conform to the breed standard rather than for its working ability. Show-bred dogs can differ a lot from work-bred versions of the same breed—the Cocker Spaniel is a good example of this.

spitz
A family of dogs or type of breed that includes the Samoyed, Pomeranian and Finnish Spitz. The breeds typically have thick coats, erect ears, and alert facial expressions.

standardized
A breed becomes standardized when each litter displays a uniform set of characteristics and attributes. The offspring of standardized breeds are of predictable appearance.

temperament
A general means of describing the likely reactions of an individual dog or breed to certain stimuli. For example, a dog that is protective in its temperament may respond suspiciously to the presence of a stranger in its home.

terrier
A type of dog breed that is descended from dogs that were bred to catch vermin. More modern terrier breeds have been established as companion and guarding breeds.

terrier instinct
Refers to stimulation by small moving animals and, in some cases, objects. It describes an action that is closely associated with terrier breeds but can apply to certain other dogs.

toy breed
A breed that was bred specifically to provide companionship. Certain toy breeds started life as working breeds but have adapted to domestic companionship. Toy breeds are typically small.

tricolor
A type of coat coloration that has three colors. Typically tricolor comes in black, white, and tan.

type
Used in conjunction with another word, such as "Mastiff" or "Spitz," to describe the appearance of an individual dog or breed.

watchdog
A breed or individual dog that is required to alert its owner to the presence of potential intruders. It is also used to distinguish between guard dogs, which are watchdogs that are also required to deal with intruders, and dogs that are incapable of dealing with an intruder except for signaling their presence.

working
Describes any breed that is or was used predominantly to fulfill a function other than companionship.

Picture Credits

Illustrations by **Ann Biggs**: 52 (c, b), 53 (t), 54, 55, 56 (tr), 57 (t, cr)

Pictures courtesy of:

Animal Photography: Sally Anne Thompson: 243 (cr, bl), 262 (tl, cr), 338 (tl), 339 (tr); R.T. Willbie: 306 (tl), 307 (b)

Ardea: John Daniels: 63 (br); Jean Michel Labat: 263 (tr, ct), 291 (cr)

Bridgeman Art Library: Private Collection, Photo © Bonhams, London, UK: 49 (b); Private Collection, Archives Charmet: 48 (tr); The Trustees of the Goodwood Collection: 30 (bl); Private Collection, The Stapleton Collection: 17 (t); Private Collection: 115 (t)

Chen Chao: 332 (cl, cr)

Cogis: Alexis: 232 (cl, br); Devis: 261 (cr, bl); Francais: 134 (tl, cr); Gehlhar: 156 (tl, cr)

Corbis: 12 (c); Archivo Iconografico, S.A.: 32 (br); Arte & Immagini srl: 38 (tr, b); Yann Arthus-Bertrand: 194 (br), 217 (cbr, b), 270 (tr, c), 289 (tr, c); Ricardo Azoury: 22 (c); Dmitri Baltermants: 40 (bl); The Barnes Foundation, Merion Station, Pennsylvania: 38 (tl); Bettmann: 13 (b), 31 (br), 36 (t), 40, 41 (b), 50 (t); Bohemian Nomad Picturemakers: 16 (b); Michael Brenan: 32 (tl), 41 (t); Bureau L.A. Collection: 46 (tl), 51 (br); Burstein Collection: 32 (c); Carlos Carrion: 21 (t); Gopal Chitrakar/Reuters: 39 (t); Christie's Images: 37 (t), 49 (t); Peter Dench: 32 (t); DLILLC: 70 (tr), 344; Nir Elias: 22 (bl); Robert Eric: 25 (tr); Andrew Fox: 42 (tr); Gallo Images: 45 (b); Paul Hilton/epa: 10, 29 (t); Historical Picture Archive: 15 (t); Dave G. Houser: 46 (c); Rob Howard: 88 (tl), 89 (tl); Hulton-Deutsch Collection: 31 (bl), 44 (tl, bc), 45 (t, cr), 47 (br); Richard Hutchings: 34 (br); Mike Kemp: 39 (b); Layne Kennedy: 129 (cr, b); Araldo de Luca: 32 (bl), 37 (c); LWA/Dann Tardif: 83 (br); Tom Nebbia: 19 (bl); Elder Neville: 74 (c), 75 (t); Kay Nietfeld/epa: 14 (b); Paper Rodeo: 29 (b); Philadelphia Museum of Art: 48 (tl); PoodlesRock: 44 (bl); Reuters: 12 (b); John Springer Collection: 50 (c); Darren Staples/Reuters: 22 (bl); Stapleton Collection: 44 (cl), 48 (b); Trolley Dodger: 42 (tl); Gary Trotter/Eye Ubiquitous: 315 (tr); Dung Vo Trung: 94 (br); Seth Wenig/Reuters: 282 (cl); Heiko Wolfraum: 102 (b);Michael S. Yamashita: 43 (t); David Michael Zimmerman: 11 (c), 63 (tc)

Juliette Cunliffe: 97 (br), 99 (b), 116 (tr), 117 (tl), 332 (tl), 333 (t)

DK: 5 (tl, cr), 69 (tl, tr), 70 (tl), 79 (br), 82 (br), 84 (cr), 85 (t), 90 (cl), 90 (b), 90 (tc, tl), 91 (bl, br), 93 (tr, b), 96 (t, b), 97 (bl), 101 (t, b), 102 (t), 103 (b), 104 (c), 105 (tl, b), 114 (cl, b), 124 (br), 132 (tl, cr), 135 (cl), 137 (cr, br), 138, 139 (tcr, bcr, br), 141, 143 (tr, tcr), 145 (cr), 146, 149 (t, c), 151 (bl, cbr), 152, 153 (tr, cl, cbr), 154, 155 (tr, cbr, br), 156 (cl, bl), 157 (br), 158 (cl), 159 (cr, br), 160 (bl), 163 (cr), 165 (br), 166 (b), 166 (cl, br), 170 (bcl, br), 171 (ctr, cbr), 174 (tl, br), 176 (br), 179, 183 (br), 184 (tl), 193 (tr, ctr), 195 (tl, ct), 197 (tr, cr), 200 (tl, tcl), 202 (br), 203 (tr), 208 (ctl), 209 (ctr, cbr, br), 213 (cr, bl), 215 (cr, br), 217 (tr, ctr), 218 (cl, bl), 219, 220 (tl, ctl, cbl), 222 (cl, br), 224 (tl, ctl), 225 (tr, cl), 226 (tl, cr), 229, 230 (br), 231, 232 (tl, cr), 233 (tr, cl), 235 (tr, cl), 236 (tl, cr), 238, 239 (bl), 240 (cl), 243 (tr), 245 (tr, cl), 247 (cl), 248 (tl, b), 249 (bl), 252 (tl, c), 257 (bl), 260, 261 (tr, ct), 263 (bl), 264 (tl, cr), 266 (t), 267 (cr, bl), 268 (cl, cr, b), 270 (cl, b), 272 (b), 273 (c), 274 (cl, br), 275, 276 (tl, cl, cr), 277 (tr), 278 (c, cl, br), 279 (b), 280 (c), 281 (tr, cr, b), 284, 285, 287, 288, 290, 291 (c), 292 (tl, cr), 293 (tr, c), 294 (tl, c), 295 (cr), 296 (tl, br), 298 (tl), 299 (tr, c), 302 (cl, b), 304 (cl, b), 305 (c), 306 (bl, br), 307 (tl, tr), 309 (tcr), 310 (tl), 317 (tr, cl, b), 320 (b), 325, 327 (tr, bl), 329 (cr, bl), 330 (tl, cbl), 341 (l)

FLPA: Rolf Bender: 112 (b); Neil Bowman: 315 (bl); Hugh Clark: 178 (b); David Dalton: 33 (t), 63 (cl), 67 (t), 129 (cl), 165 (tr, cl), 211 (br), 230 (cl), 265 (b), 280 (c), 296 (cl), 300 (c), 317 (cr); Dirk Enters: 57 (cl); Foto Natura Collection: 24 (tl), 25 (b), 176 (cl), 206 (c), 209 (tr), 244 (b), 313 (tr), 331 (b); David T. Grewcock 100 (tl), 101 (c); Angela Hampton: 19 (bl), 26 (tl), 194 (bl); David Hosking: 34 (bl), 86 (tl), 99 (c), 276 (tr); Simon Hosking: 92 (b); Wayne Hutchinson: 58 (t), 182 (c); Mitsuaki Iwago: 5 (cl), 61 (t), Rob Jones: 265 (c); Michael Krabs: 334 (c), 336 (bl); Gerard Lacz: 24 (tr), 67 (br), 117 (b), 177 (cr), 202 (tl), 207 (bl), 213 (cl), 279 (cl), 321 (bl); Frank W Lane: 103 (c); R P Lawrence: 110 (c); Phil McLean: 11 (l), 20 (t); Catherine Mullen: 113 (br); Elliott Neep: 110 (tl), 112 (t); Panda Photo: 281 (cl), 310 (tcl); Mandal Ranjit: 113 (t); Mark Raycroft: 4, 11 (r), 18 (tl), 24 (b), 59 (bl, br), 60 (tr), 62, 63 (bl), 64 (t), 64 (cr), 65 (tr, cl, bl), 68 (tl), 71 (bl, br), 107 (r), 107 (c), 114 (cr), 127 (t), 128 (c), 131 (b), 132 (cl, br), 133 (b, tr), 136 (bcl, b), 142 (br), 144 (cr), 181 (bl), 191 (cr), 195 (bl), 212 (cr), 242 (c), 252 (cl, br), 253 (br), 256 (tl, cr), 300 (b), 301 (c, b), 328 (tl), 331 (c), 334 (r), 335 (bl), 337 (bl), 338 (c); Jurgen & Christine Sohns: 111 (b); Roger Tidman: 26 (tr), 27 (t), 305 (tr); Stefanie Krause-Wieczorek: 60 (tl), 190 (cr), 249 (cl); Martin B Withers 108 (tl), 112 (c), 195 (cr)

Johan Gallant: 314 (b)

© **John Grogan/Harper Collins**: 47 (tl)

© **Eric Hill**, 1980. Reproduced by kind permissions of Ventura Publishing Ltd (a Penguin Company): 47 (bl)

© **Henry Holt & Company**: 46 (b)

Mary Holt: 339 (b)

iStock: 80 (b), 308 (l), 314 (c)

Carol Ann Johnson: 76 (b), 78 (bc), 85 (bl), 87 (br), 99 (c), 100 (cr), 103 (tl), 104 (br), 119 (tl), 119 (b), 274 (tl, c), 292 (br), 302 (tl, c), 303 (cr, bl), 313 (cr, bl)

Kennel Club Picture Library: 1, 3, 5 (br), 9 (b), 9 (t), 8, 14 (t, c), 16 (t), 18 (b), 19 (t), 20 (bl), 21 (bl), 23 (br), 25 (tl), 26 (bl, br), 28 (tl, cr), 34 (t), 42 (b), 43 (c, bl), 56 (bl, br), 63 (bl), 68 (cl), 74 (bl), 78 (t), 82 (bl), 84 (b), 92 (cr), 104 (tl, bl), 105 (tr), 118 (c), 122 (cl, cr, b), 123 (t, b), 124 (t, cr, bl), 125 (tl, tr, cl), 126 (tl, tr, b), 127 (bl, br), 128 (l, r), 129 (tr), 130, 131 (tr, c), 133 (c), 135 (tr), 136 (tl, tcl), 137 (tr, cl), 139 (tr), 140, 142 (cl), 143 (br), 144 (tl, cl), 145 (tr, bcr), 150, 151 (tr, tcr), 153 (tl), 155 (tl), 157 (tr, ctr, cbr), 158 (tl, cr, br), 159 (tr, cl), 160 (tl, cl, cr), 161, 162, 163 (tr, cl, br), 164, 165 (cr), 166 (tl, cr), 167, 168 (tl, cr), 169, 170 (tl, ctl), 171 (tr, br), 172, 173, 174 (ctl, cbl), 175, 176 (tl, cr), 177 (tr, cl, br), 178 (tl, c), 180, 181 (tr, c), 182 (tl), 183 (tr, cl, cr), 184 (ctl, cbl, br), 185, 186, 187, 188, 189, 190 (tl, cl, br), 191 (tr, b), 192, 193 (bcr, bl), 194 (t), 196, 197 (cl, br), 198, 199, 200 (bcl, br), 201, 202 (ct, cl), 203 (cl, cr, br), 204, 205, 206 (tl, b), 207 (tr, tcr, bcr), 208 (tl, bcl, br), 210, 211 (tr, ct, cbr), 212 (tl, b), 213 (tr), 214, 215 (tr, cl), 216, 218 (tl, cr), 220 (br), 221, 222 (tl, cr), 223, 224 (bcl, br), 225 (cr, b), 226 (cl, bl), 227, 228, 233 (cr, b), 234, 235 (cr, bl), 236 (br), 237, 239 (tr, cl, cr), 240 (tl, cr, br), 241, 242 (tl, b), 243 (cl), 244 (tl, c), 245 (b, cr), 246, 247 (cr, b), 248 (tl, ct), 249 (tr, cr), 250, 251, 253 (tr, c), 254, 255, 256 (cl, br), 257 (tr, cl, cr), 258, 259, 263 (cr), 264 (cl, br), 265 (tr), 266 (c, bl, br), 267 (tr, cl), 268 (t), 269, 271, 272 (tl, cl, cr), 273 (tr, cr, bl), 277 (cl, cr, bl), 278 (tl), 279 (tr, cr), 280 (tl, cl), 282 (cl), 283, 286, 289 (cr, bl), 291 (tr, bl), 293 (cl, b), 294 (cl, b), 295 (tr, c, bl), 297, 298 (cl, cr, br), 299 (cr, bl), 300 (tl), 301 (tr), 303 (tr, cl), 304 (tl, cr), 305 (b), 308 (c, r), 309 (tr, bcr, br), 310 (bcl, br), 311, 312, 313 (cl), 316, 318 (tl, cr), 319, 320 (tl, c), 321 (tr, cl, cr), 322, 323, 324, 326, 327 (cl, cr), 328 (tcl, bcl, br), 329 (tr, c), 330 (cl, br), 331 (tr), 335 (tr, tcr, bcr), 336 (tl, c, br), 337 (tr, c), 343, 345

Martina Krüger: 318 (cl, br)

Mary Evans Picture Library: 13 (t), 30 (t), 36 (b), 37 (b), 115 (b)

Crista Niehus: 262 (cl, br)

Mary Peaslee: 148 (tl, bl, br)

Karyn Pingel: 148 (cl, cr)

Christine Prince: 134 (cl, bl)

Shutterstock: 89 (bl); Jerri Adams: 27 (b); afarland: 97 (t); alexan55: 71 (t), 305 (cr); Utekhina Anna: 58 (bl), 60 (bl), 67 (bl), 143 (bcr); Laura Aqui: 118 (br); Yuri Arcurs: 17 (br), 95 (r); Arvind Balaraman: 87 (t); Stacey Bates: 306 (c); Gualberto Becerra: 109 (tl); Emmanuelle Bonzami: 73 (r), 74 (br), 92 (tl), 92 (cl), 95 (l), 97 (cr), 116 (tl), 118 (bl); Joy Brown: 72, 73 (l), 76 (tl), 78 (bl), 79 (bl); Lori Carpenter: 103 (t); Andraz Cerar: 100 (b); Paul Clarke: 82 (c); Clearviewstock: 120 (b); Stephen Coburn: 75 (t), 121 (t); Neale Cousland: 113 (bl), 334 (l); Waldemar Dabrowski: 17 (bl), 53 (b), 98 (cl); Phil Date: 80 (tl), 81 (t); Sandra A. Dunlap: 110 (br); Anna Dzondzua: 35 (tl); EcoPrint: 111 (tl); Jan Erasmus: 70 (b), 77 (b); Martin Garnham: 78 (br); Jack Gau: 69 (b); Sebastien Gauthier: 108 (c); Joe Gough: 118 (tl), 121 (b); Natalia V Guesva: 106, 121 (c); Julie de Guia: 76 (cl); HANA: 79 (tr); Tomas Hlavacek: 109 (tc); Daniel Hughes: 30 (br); Dee Hunter: 84 (cl); IgorXIII: 59 (t); In-Finity: 80 (l); Iofoto: 107 (l), 116 (b); Eric Isselée: 21 (br), 60 (br), 114 (tl), 117 (tr); Sarah Johnson: 52 (tl); Wendy Kaveney Photography: 76 (cr); Tan Kian Khoon: 23 (bl); Justin Kinney: 87 (bl); Crystal Kirk: 86 (tr); K. Kolygo: 109 (b); Vasiliy Koval: 64 (bl); Emilia Kun: 94 (bl); Morgan Lane Photography: 81 (cl); Philip Lange: 89 (br); Patricia Marroquin: 68 (b), 84 (tl); Pat Masek: 35 (tr); Joy Miller: 53 (cr);

Phil Morley: 43 (br); Niderlander: 89 (tr); Iztok Noc: 25 (c), 296 (cr); Regien Paassen: 12 (tl), 15 (b); Edyta Pawlowska: 88 (cr); Marek Pawluczuk: 91 (t); Denis Pepin: 111 (tr); Maxim Petrichuk: 61 (b); Pieter: 100 (tl); Pixshots: 5 (tr), 82 (tl), 83 (br), 120 (c); Plastique: 108 (l); Tina Rencelj: 18 (tr); Damien Richard: 109 (cr); Rick's Photography: 119 (tr), 120 (l), 341 (tr); Robynrg: 77 (t); SilksAtSunrise: 110 (bl); Ana de Sousa: 58 (br); Dale A Stork: 35 (b); Temelko Temelkov: 73 (c), 98 (t); TheSupe87: 20 (br); Tootles: 81 (b); Nikolai Tsvetkov: 93 (tl); Ursula: 88 (b); Graca Victoria: 63 (cr), 341 (c); Elliot Westacott: 5 (bl), 85 (br); Ivonne Wierink: 28 (bl), 86 (b); Jeffrey Ong Guo Xiong: 66 (t), 314 (tl), 315 (br); Zuzule: 292 (cl)

Vicki Rand, United Kennel Club, Inc.: 142 (tl, cr)

Toolalla Kennels: 339 (tl)

TopFoto: 31 (t), 50 (b), 65 (br), 282 (tl); HIP: 51 (tr, cl), 74 (tl); ImageWorks: 68 (cr); PA: 40 (br); John Powell: 23 (t); Tifas: 33 (b)

Heather Yates: 149 (b)

www.devrolijkeviervoeters.org: 230 (tl), 338 (bl); www.dogbreedinfo.com: 338 (br); www.habland.com: 333 (br); www.hinduonnet.com: 333 (bl); www.pedigreedatabase.com: 135 (cr, b)

Index